SOUTH-WESTERN

Introduction To
COMPUTER SCIENCE
USING C++

Todd Knowlton

Programming and Computer
Education Consultant

JOIN US ON THE INTERNET
WWW: http://www.thomson.com
EMAIL: findit@kiosk.thomson.com

A service of I(T)P®

South-Western Educational Publishing

an International Thomson Publishing company I(T)P®

Cincinnati • Albany, NY • Belmont, CA • Bonn • Boston
Detroit • Johannesburg • London • Madrid • Melbourne
Mexico City • New York • Paris • Singapore • Tokyo
Toronto • Washington

Library of Congress Cataloging-in-Publication Data
Knowlton, Todd, 1966–
    Introduction to computer science using C++ / Todd Knowlton.
        p.   cm.
    Includes index.
    ISBN 0-538-67600-0
    1. C++ (Computer program language)   I. Title.
    QA76.73.C153K64   1998
    005.13'3—dc21   96-37463
                                                                            CIP

Managing Editor:	Janie F. Schwark
Project Manager:	Dave Lafferty
Marketing Manager:	John Wills
Production Services:	Custom Editorial Productions, Inc.

Copyright © 1998
by SOUTH-WESTERN EDUCATIONAL PUBLISHING
Cincinnati, Ohio

ISBN: 0-538-67600-0

4 5 C1 00 99 98

Printed in the United States of America

I(T)P®

International Thomson Publishing

South-Western Educational Publishing is a division of International Thomson Publishing, Inc. The ITP trademark is used under license.

Contents

JOIN US ON THE INTERNET

WWW: **http://www.thomson.com**
E-MAIL: **findit@kiosk.thomson.com**

South-Western Educational Publishing is a partner in *thomson.com*, an on-line portal for the products, services, and resources available from International Thomson Publishing (ITP). Through our site, users can search catalogs, examine subject-specific resource centers, and subscribe to electronic discussion lists.

South-Western Educational Publishing is also a reseller of commercial software products. See our printed catalog or view this page at:

http://www.swpco.com/swpco/comp_ed/com_sft.html

For information on our products, visit our World Wide Web site at:

http://www.swpco.com/swpco.html

To join the South-Western Computer Education discussion list, send an e-mail message to: **majordomo@list.thomson.com**. Leave the subject field blank, and in the body of your message key: SUBSCRIBE SOUTH-WESTERN-COMPUTER-EDUCATION <your e-mail address>.

A service of I(T)P®

Preface

I n writing this book, my goal was to create an easy-to-read, clearly-written, friendly tutorial that covers the fundamentals of computer science and the C++ programming language. Rather than focus solely on C++, the book covers important data structures and algorithms, which better equips students to create more professional software.

Introduction to Computer Science Using C++ includes hands-on exercises integrated into the flow of the chapters. Realistic, yet imaginative, programs, problems, and interdisciplinary projects are presented throughout the book.

This book is based on the belief that students should master the basics of C++ before learning about object-oriented programming. Therefore, the course builds a strong foundation of structured programming before introducing students to the concept of object-oriented programming. After object-oriented programming is introduced, students will use ready-made classes to simplify work with strings, arrays, stacks, and queues.

Introduction to Computer Science Using C++ is designed for use in a variety of courses. The instructor's manual includes course schedules for 6-week, 12-week, one-semester (18-week), and two-semester courses. The order of the material allows optional coverage of the advanced topics.

This book is also well-suited for an Advanced Placement Computer Science course. The classes used in this book are compatible with the classes used on the AP exam.

COMPILERS AND SYSTEMS SUPPORTED

This book was written with a focus on programming fundamentals, rather than specific features of any operating system. C++ is designed to be a portable language. The programs in the exercises of this book will compile successfully under MS-DOS, Windows, and the MacOS. This book has been tested with major compilers and minor inconsistencies are noted in the instructor's manual.

A COMPLETE INSTRUCTIONAL PACKAGE

Introduction to Computer Science Using C++ is a complete instructional package. In addition to this student textbook, there are other components to supplement the text and provide additional reinforcement. These components include:

➤ A consumable student workbook with additional questions, problems, coding and debugging exercises, and vocabulary reinforcement.

➤ A template disk that includes the source code and data files necessary to complete the exercises in the textbook.

➤ A regularly-updated Internet Web site at http://www.ProgramCPP.com devoted entirely to supplementing this book and providing up-to-date information, additional case studies, and links to important resources on the Internet.

> An AP Study Guide for students preparing to take the AP Computer Science examination. The study guide provides summaries of AP topics and questions similar to those on the AP exam.

> An instructor's manual that provides scheduling help, teaching suggestions, chapter tests, and solutions to questions and problems from the student textbook and workbook.

INSTRUCTIONAL ELEMENTS OF THE TEXT

The text incorporates the following instructional elements.

> **Objectives.** Each chapter begins with a list of learning goals.

> **Overview.** Following the objectives, the Overview puts the goals of the chapter into focus.

> **Sections.** Each chapter is divided into sections, which helps break the material into manageable pieces.

> **Exercises.** Hands-on exercises appear at places where reinforcement is needed. Some exercises require students to enter program code, others only require that students load, compile, and run existing programs.

> **End-of-Section Questions.** Review questions appear at the end of each section.

> **End-of-Section Problems.** Most sections include programming problems that challenge students to apply what they just learned. These problems are designed to be completed in 5–30 minutes.

> **Key Terms.** A list of the important terminology is presented in each chapter.

> **Summary.** Each chapter ends with a quick reference of the concepts covered in the chapter.

> **Projects.** The projects at the end of each chapter provide programming practice to challenge students with all levels of experience. These interdisciplinary projects typically require more time than the problems at the end of sections.

> **Case Studies.** Six case studies appear in strategic locations throughout the book. The case studies allow students to see practical programs that make use of the concepts learned in the chapters just prior to the case study. The source code for each case study is already complete, allowing the student to concentrate on analyzing the existing code. Each case study ends with suggestions of possible extensions or modifications to the program.

> **Sidebars.** Sidebars warn students of potential pitfalls and note special features or information that can enrich students' understanding.

A MESSAGE TO STUDENTS

You may be an experienced programmer, you may be new to programming, or you may be somewhere in between. Whatever the case, this book will help you develop your programming skills and understanding of the fundamentals of computer science.

In this book, you will be programming in C++, which is the language used to develop most operating systems and commercial microcomputer software. You won't be programming the next blockbuster computer program overnight, but you will be taking the first steps toward the kind of knowledge required to produce professional computer software.

Programming computers is not difficult, but programming in a professional language like C++ is challenging. The rewards for facing the challenges are many, however. The ability to program computers is undeniably a valuable skill in today's world. But even if you have no plans to make a career of computer programming, you will realize benefits from the time spent studying computer science. Learning to program computers develops your ability to solve problems of all kinds. You will learn to break a problem into manageable parts and think in logical ways. In addition, programming allows you to be creative.

This book is for you and the students who will study programming after you. I want to know what you think of the book and how it can be improved. I can be reached by electronic mail at tknowlton@aol.com. I promise a prompt and personal reply.

Todd Knowlton

ACKNOWLEDGMENTS

This book is the result of a lot of hard work by many people. I want to thank the team of editors, reviewers, instructors, and students who fulfilled distinct roles in the development of this book.

I thank **Dave Lafferty** and **Janie Schwark** of South-Western for their interest in this book and devotion to its success. I also thank those involved in the development and field testing of the original edition: **Brandon Adkins, Angela Askins, William Bakken, John Baldwin, Greg Buxkemper, Bruce Charbonneau, Rebecca Dailey, Brian Davis, Mark Durrett, Mark Gentry, Eric Hosch, Brian Jurries, Heath Keene, Mark Kim, Jonathan Kleid, Michael Landrum, Scott McGrew, Bill Perry, Tan Pham, Joe Sherwood, Macneil Shonle, Mark Tittle, Aliver Villarreal, John Walter, Michael Wester, Jeremy Wilson,** and **Todd Woolery.**

I thank **Bryan Stephens** for his work on this edition, including much of the workbook and the appendix on numerical algorithms, and **Jonathan Kleid** for his work on the analysis of algorithms appendix. I also thank **Michael Landrum** for his review of the book, and **Macneil Shonle** for his technical expertise in the area of object-oriented programming and his work on the error handling appendix.

I especially thank **Greg Buxkemper** for his hard work preparing programs and manuscript for this edition. Greg was instrumental in integrating object-oriented programming into the book.

I also thank the students and teachers who have provided suggestions and uncovered errors that we were able to address in this edition. Keep that e-mail coming.

Finally, I thank my wife **Melissa** and my daughters **Kaley** and **Amy** for making life fun and for allowing me to spend the hours necessary to produce these books.

1

Introduction to Computers

OBJECTIVES

➤ Understand the history of computers and how they evolved into today's powerful desktop computers.

➤ Understand the components that make up a typical desktop computer.

➤ Understand the basics of microcomputer architecture.

Overview

You may be wondering, "When do we get to the programming?" But before you can successfully write a program, you must understand the machine you are programming. A programmer is like a coach of a team, a director of a movie, or a conductor of a symphony. A good coach knows the abilities of the team members, the movie director knows what cameras, lights, and props are available, and the conductor understands the instruments in the orchestra. In the same way, the successful programmer understands the machine being programmed.

This chapter begins with the history of computers and how they evolved into today's powerful desktop computers. Then we will take a look at the components that you see when you look at a typical microcomputer. Next, you will learn how a computer operates internally. You will see how the microprocessor is the center of all activity inside the computer and how the other parts help it do its job.

CHAPTER 1, SECTION 1
The History of Computers

People have almost always looked for tools to aid in calculations. The human hand was probably the first tool used to help people count. And although the fingers are still used as counting tools, devices have been invented to make the job easier and to keep people from taking off their shoes when counting to twenty. Calculating tools evolved from manually-operated devices, to more complex mechanical devices, to electro-mechanical devices, and finally to electronic computers.

MANUALLY-OPERATED DEVICES

The abacus, shown in Figure 1-1, may have existed as early as the third century A.D. However, the Chinese perfected it in the 12th century.

MECHANICAL DEVICES

In 1642, Blaise Pascal designed the first gear-driven counting machine. He was eighteen years old at the time. Blaise designed the machine in an attempt to make his father's work as a tax collector easier. The machine could add and subtract by using a series of interlocking wheels and gears. The wheels were marked with the numbers 0 through 9, and there was a wheel for the ones, tens, hundreds, and so on. Pascal named the machine the Pascaline, and he developed more than 50 versions of it. The principle behind the Pascaline was used in adding machines for the next 300 years.

In the early 1670's, the German mathematician Gottfried Wilhelm Leibniz invented a mechanical calculator that improved greatly on Pascal's design.

FIGURE 1-1
The abacus is a manually-operated device used to aid in counting. The abacus is still in use in some parts of the world.

Leibniz's calculator employed a crank on the side that simplified the repetitive operations necessary to multiply and divide.

Do These Names Sound Familiar?

The names of these inventors may be familiar. Blaise Pascal became a world-renowned mathematician and philosopher. The programming language Pascal, used today, is named in his honor. Gottfried Wilhelm Leibniz invented calculus.

In 1834, an English mathematician named Charles Babbage proposed the construction of an "Analytical Engine." Babbage's design was unique and could be characterized as the first general-purpose programmable computer.

If Babbage's Analytical Engine had been built, it would have included the use of punched cards to feed instructions to the machine. It also would have had the capability to calculate and store numbers. Punched cards and the capability to calculate and store numbers became standard features of many computers to follow.

ELECTRO-MECHANICAL DEVICES

Do you believe that necessity is the mother of invention? Well, if it had not been for a need that the United States Census Bureau had, the world of computing might have developed quite differently.

Tabulating the 1880 census took seven and a half years. The United States Census Bureau became convinced that a better way to tabulate the census had to be found. An employee of the census office in Washington D.C., named Herman Hollerith, spent the 1880's working on a machine that would tabulate census figures using punched cards. Hollerith had perfected his machine by 1890—and just in time. By 1890, the population of the U.S. had grown by 25% since 1880 to over 62 million people. Hollerith's machine performed a simple count of the population in only six weeks, and full statistical analysis in two and a half years.

Hollerith's invention allowed him to start a company called the Tabulating Machine Company, which sold his machines to others. That company eventually became the International Business Machines Corporation (IBM).

Hollerith's machine was an electro-mechanical device that used gears and wheels and other mechanical parts, but was powered by electricity.

In 1944, IBM built the Mark I. The machine used a combination of electrical signals and mechanical gears to quickly add and subtract large numbers. The machine was 51 feet long and 8 feet high, and included almost 500 miles of wires. The Mark I was the most elaborate electro-mechanical computer ever built.

The era of electronic computers was about to dawn.

ELECTRONIC COMPUTERS

In 1946, the Electronic Numerical Integrator and Computer (ENIAC) was developed by John William Mauchly and John Presper Eckert. ENIAC was one of the first computers without mechanical parts.

Instead of mechanical switches and gears, ENIAC used electronic switching devices called vacuum tubes. Figure 1-2 shows a row of vacuum tubes. Vacuum tubes made ENIAC about 1000 times faster than the Mark I.

By the late 1950's, the transistor began to replace the vacuum tube in computers (see Figure 1-3). Transistors accomplish the same work as vacuum tubes, but are smaller and faster. The transistor also proved to be more reliable than vacuum tubes, which had to be replaced often.

In the 1960's the integrated circuit, commonly called a chip, was developed. An *integrated circuit* is a thin slice of photo-sensitive silicon, usually smaller than a dime, upon which microscopic circuits have been inscribed. The first integrated circuits usually performed only one function, such as adding. But in the 1970's, designers began to put multiple functions on a single chip. Soon, nearly all of the main functions of a computer were placed on a single chip. This new invention was called the *microprocessor,* shown in Figure 1-4.

F I G U R E   1 - 2
The vacuum tube began the era of electronic computers.

A revolution began as manufacturers started building complete computer systems that had microprocessors at their core. The first microcomputers became available in the 1970's.

Since the 1970's, microcomputers have evolved more rapidly than ever. Each new model does more and costs less than the one before. The timeline below shows some of the major events in microcomputers from 1975 to the early 1990's. You may not recognize many of the items on the timeline. That is because most of them quickly became history. The timeline is intended to show you how rapidly the industry has evolved since the 1970's. The computers you are using today will probably become obsolete as quickly as the computers in this timeline.

1971 ➤ The first microprocessor (the Intel 4004)

1975 ➤ The first real microcomputer (the Altair 8800)

1976 ➤ Apple I appears and Apple Computer is founded

1977 ➤ Apple II

➤ Radio Shack TRS-80 Model I

1978 ➤ Epson introduces the first affordable dot-matrix printer

1979 ➤ Intel 8088 microprocessor (later used in the first IBM PC)

➤ Motorola 68000 microprocessor (later used in the first Macintosh)

1980 ➤ Commodore VIC-20

➤ Apple III

➤ TRS-80 Color Computer

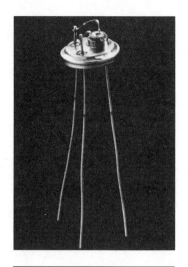

F I G U R E   1 - 3
Transistors were a faster, smaller, and more reliable alternative to the vacuum tube.

F I G U R E   1 - 4
The microprocessor is the device that put computers within reach of small businesses and individuals.

1981	➤ IBM PC (see Figure 1-5)
	➤ Hayes Smartmodem 300
1982	➤ Intel 80286 microprocessor
	➤ Commodore 64
1983	➤ Apple Lisa
	➤ Apple IIe
	➤ IBM PC Jr.
	➤ IBM PC/XT
1984	➤ Macintosh (see Figure 1-6)
	➤ Apple IIc
	➤ IBM AT
	➤ Motorola 68020 microprocessor
1985	➤ Commodore Amiga 1000
	➤ The first hard disk is made available for Macintosh computers
1986	➤ Intel 80386 microprocessor
	➤ Motorola 68030 microprocessor
	➤ Apple IIgs
1987	➤ IBM PS/2
1989	➤ Intel 80486 microprocessor
1990	➤ Motorola 68040 microprocessor
1992	➤ Intel 80486-DX2 microprocessor

F I G U R E   1 - 5
The original IBM PC.

1993   ➤ Intel Pentium microprocessor

➤ PowerPC 601 microprocessor

On the Net

You know that new computers continually replace existing models. But do you know how dramatically the power and capacity of computers has increased while prices have dropped? See the actual numbers for yourself at http://www. ProgramCPP.com. See topic 1.1.1.

SECTION 1.1 QUESTIONS

1. What manually-operated calculating device existed prior to the 12th century A.D.?

2. List two mechanical calculating devices.

3. What is the name of the most elaborate electro-mechanical computer ever built?

4. What type of computers replaced electro-mechanical computers?

5. What device replaced the vacuum tube?

6. What device integrated nearly all of the main functions of a computer on a single chip?

7. During what decade did the first microcomputers become available?

Computers Today

Today computers are everywhere. Both large and small businesses use computers for everything from word processing and bookkeeping to desktop publishing. Computers are used at home for personal finance, correspondence, education, entertainment, and more. Because computers have become inexpensive to make, they have also become a part of many products we buy. Special purpose computers are usually made to carry out a specific task, whereas other computers are made to be programmed for a variety of tasks.

COMPUTERS FOR SPECIFIC PURPOSES

Computers can now be found in our wrist watches, cameras, televisions, and VCRs. In automobiles, computers control fuel injection and the spark plugs. Computers monitor everything from fuel efficiency to the comfort of the passengers. Computers tell automatic transmissions when to shift gears. Computers can also help you quickly change from one radio station to another.

Specific purpose computers can be used for little else other than for what they are designed to accomplish. For example, the computer in a camera calculates the settings and exposure time required for a perfect photograph, but it can't help you with your math homework. The computer in your VCR will remember to record your favorite show Tuesday night at 8 PM, but it can't remind you that you have a project due tomorrow.

GENERAL PURPOSE COMPUTERS

The kind of machine most people think of when they hear the term *computer* looks something like Figure 1-7. What makes this computer system so popular is that it can perform a wide variety of tasks. Computers like the one in Figure 1-7 are general-purpose computers and can be programmed to perform many different tasks. General purpose computers can balance checkbooks, perform calculations, schedule events, help you write letters, store important information, and (of course) play great games. Try to do all that with the computer in your car's transmission.

SYSTEM COMPONENTS

The equipment that makes up a computer is called *hardware.* Each piece of hardware is involved in one of four tasks: input, output, processing, or storage.

INPUT AND OUTPUT

All computers, whether on your wrist or on your desk, *interact* with someone or something. Interaction involves getting information and giving a response. In a computer, this interaction is called *input* and *output.* For example, input could be a user entering customer names and addresses into a database program. An example of output would be the printing of mailing labels from a database.

A desktop computer interacts primarily with people. A typical desktop computer interacts using a keyboard, a mouse, speakers, a monitor, and a printer. Some desktop computers may also have other input and output devices, such as

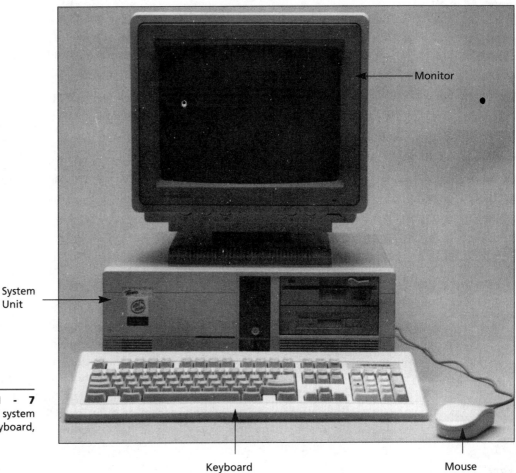

Monitor

System
Unit

Keyboard

Mouse

F I G U R E   1 - 7
A typical microcomputer system includes a monitor, keyboard, mouse, and system unit.

a microphone or modem. A *modem,* which is a device that allows interaction to occur between computers over the telephone, is capable of both input and output.

The keyboard, mouse, and microphone are input devices. The computer uses these devices to get information and instructions from the person using the computer (the user). The computer gives information back to the user via output devices, such as the monitor, printer, and speakers.

You may not have thought about speakers as an output device, but they have become an important way for the computer to give information to the user. Early computers were incapable of sophisticated sound output. They could only beep. Now multimedia computers speak, play music, and have sound cards that add realism to games.

When you think of computer input and output, you may think of data going in and answers coming out. For example, a program might receive the temperature in Fahrenheit as input and then convert it to provide the temperature in Celsius as output. But even a game has input and output. The keys you strike, or the movement of a mouse or joystick is the input. The image on the monitor and sound through the speakers is the output.

PROCESSING AND STORAGE

At the heart of the computer, the inputs are processed and stored, and output is created. This is accomplished using a variety of devices such as a microprocessor, RAM, ROM, a bus, and disk drives. In the next section, you will learn more about these devices and how they work together.

1. Name an item other than one mentioned in this chapter that includes a specific-purpose computer.

2. What are the four tasks in which hardware is involved?

3. List two devices used for input in a general-purpose computer.

4. List three devices involved in output from a general-purpose computer.

5. List two devices involved in either processing or storage in a general-purpose computer.

CHAPTER 1, SECTION 3

Computer Architecture

omputer architecture is a term used to describe the way the many devices that make up a computer are put together. The devices that programmers need to understand the most are the microprocessor, RAM, ROM, and the "bus" that connects them together.

Figure 1-8 shows a diagram of how the RAM, ROM, and microprocessor work together by way of the bus. Let's examine each part of the diagram, beginning with RAM.

RAM

RAM, which is an acronym for Random Access Memory, is your computer's primary storage. RAM is where currently running programs and active data are stored. Some RAM is also used to store items that support your program and its input and output. For example, when you are using your word processor, the word processor program is stored in RAM along with the document upon which you are working. Later in this chapter, you will read about data stored on disk that is waiting to be used.

Think of RAM like the top of your desk. RAM holds the programs and data you are working on, and space is limited. When you buy a computer, one of the important specifications is the amount of RAM installed. You must have enough RAM to hold the items your system requires to operate, along with the program you want to run and its data. Optional features like screen savers also use RAM.

The subject of RAM will come up several times in this book. Because there is so much to understand about your computer's memory, we will cover the information as you need it.

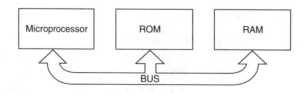

FIGURE 1-8
The microprocessor is connected to the RAM and ROM by a system called the bus.

ROM

ROM is an acronym for Read-Only Memory. Your computer's ROM is a set of memory chips that have data permanently stored upon them. Typically, ROM chips store data and programs necessary to get the computer started.

However, ROM can contain much more than startup procedures. Many of the first personal computers included the BASIC programming language on ROM chips. IBM-compatible computers have a whole set of programs in ROM, called the *BIOS* (Basic Input/Output System), used to interact with the screen, keyboard, and disks. Macintosh computers have an extensive set of programs, called the *Toolbox,* stored on ROM chips.

MICROPROCESSOR

Entire books have been written about microprocessors. But as a programmer, you need only a basic understanding of what goes on inside a microprocessor.

The microprocessor does the computing and controls everything else that is going on in the computer. All of the other parts of the computer support the microprocessor. As soon as you turn on your computer, the microprocessor begins processing millions of commands every second.

THE INSTRUCTION SET

A microprocessor is designed to "understand" a set of commands called an *instruction set.* Although there are similar instructions among different microprocessors, each model (i.e., 80486, Pentium, PowerPC, etc.) has its own instruction set. Microprocessors can accept and carry out operations that are written in the format of their own unique instruction set only. This is one reason that software written for one kind of computer does not automatically work on another kind of computer.

THE PARTS OF A MICROPROCESSOR

There are many kinds of microprocessors and several manufacturers that make them. Most microprocessors, however, contain some of the same basic parts. Figure 1-9 illustrates the most common and important parts of a microprocessor.

On the Net

For more information about microprocessors, including links to web sites of major microprocessor manufacturers, see http://www.ProgramCPP.com. See topic 1.3.1.

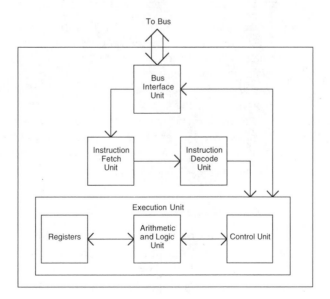

F I G U R E   1 - 9
While microprocessors from different manufacturers vary in their design, most microprocessors contain parts similar to these.

The *bus interface unit* links the microprocessor to the bus. The bus is the system of connections that links the microprocessor to the RAM, ROM, and input and output ports. Anything that goes in or out of the microprocessor passes through the bus interface unit. You will learn more about the bus later in this section.

The instructions that the microprocessor is following are stored in either RAM or ROM. It is the job of the *instruction fetch unit* to get the instructions from RAM or ROM.

Once an instruction is brought into the microprocessor by the instruction fetch unit, the *instruction decode unit* determines what must be done to get the instruction processed. Some instructions need other data pulled out of RAM. Some instructions can be executed as they are. Once the instruction is decoded, the execution unit actually carries out the instruction.

The *execution unit* is made up of three main parts:

1. the control unit

2. the arithmetic and logic unit

3. registers.

The *control unit* coordinates the activity of the execution unit. To successfully execute an instruction, the parts of the execution unit must do their job quickly and precisely. You can think of the control unit as the manager of the execution unit.

The *arithmetic and logic unit (ALU)* is the calculator and decision maker in the microprocessor. The actual data processing takes place in the ALU. Even though the ALU performs only simple math and comparisons, these operations are the building blocks for every other operation—regardless of complexity.

The ALU works closely with the *registers.* A register is a memory circuit that holds data that is being manipulated by the execution unit. There are a number of registers in the execution unit, and each has its own purpose. For example, when the ALU is performing addition, the values to be added are placed in registers and so is the result of the addition.

Other registers keep track of important locations in memory. For example, microprocessors have a register devoted to referencing where the next instruction to be executed is located.

What Is a CPU?

You have probably heard the term CPU used when describing computers. CPU is an acronym for **central processing unit.** The CPU is the part of the computer where the processing takes place. Unfortunately, people have a hard time deciding what to include in the definition of CPU. Some call the entire metal case that holds the disk drives, power supply, and circuitry the CPU. Some say the CPU is the microprocessor chip only.

So who is right? It is a matter of opinion. The important thing is that you are familiar with the term and that you know that it gets used to mean slightly different things. In this book, we will use more specific terms, rather than "CPU," to help avoid confusion.

MICROPROCESSOR SPEED AND CISC VS. RISC

The speed of a microprocessor is controlled by a device called a *clock.* The clock produces a signal that turns on and off millions of times per second. This signal that the clock generates is like a heart beat for the computer. The timing of the computer's operations is controlled by the beat of the clock.

Clock speeds are measured in *megahertz,* abbreviated as MHz, which means millions per second. For example, a microprocessor running at 66 MHz has a clock that sends 66 million signals per second.

There are two categories of microprocessors: CISC and RISC. *CISC* is an acronym for Complex Instruction Set Computer. *RISC* is an acronym for Reduced Instruction Set Computer.

A RISC processor typically accepts fewer commands than a CISC processor, but the RISC's commands are fundamental operations that can be combined to do any complex task that the CISC processor can do.

Computer scientists have discovered that a microprocessor with an instruction set of less complexity (a RISC processor) can generally run programs more quickly than a microprocessor with a complex instruction set (a CISC processor), even though the RISC processor may have to execute more instructions to do the same job.

CISC vs. RISC in the Real World

Until 1994, almost all microcomputers used CISC microprocessors. The Intel 8088, 8086, 80286, 80386, 80486, and Pentium microprocessors are all examples of CISC processors. The Motorola 68000 series of microprocessors used in all of the pre-1994 Macintoshes are also CISC processors. In 1994, the PowerPC microprocessor became the first widely-used RISC processor in microcomputers when Apple released the Power Macintosh.

TAKING THE BUS

As mentioned earlier, the microprocessor is connected to the RAM, ROM, and other devices by a system of wires called a *bus.* In most computers the wires that make up the bus are not actually individual wires, but lines etched on a circuit board.

The bus is composed of four different kinds of lines: power, data, address, and control. Figure 1-10 shows how the data lines, address lines, and control lines connect the microprocessor, ROM, and RAM.

The power lines carry power to the devices connected to the bus. The data lines carry data between input devices, the microprocessor, the storage devices, and the output devices.

The address lines make sure the data goes to or comes from the correct place. Each device in the computer has an address, like every house on a street. The

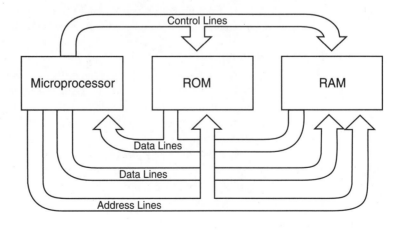

FIGURE 1-10
The bus connects the microprocessor to the RAM, ROM, and other devices.

address lines specify the address where the data is traveling to or from along the data lines. For example, each memory location in the computer has a different address. To store the data that is on the data lines to a specific memory location, the computer places that memory location's address on the address lines.

The control lines send signals from the microprocessor to the various devices. For example, when storing data to a location in memory, the computer places the data to be stored on the data lines and the address of the memory location on the address lines. But the data is stored in the chip only when the control lines activate the RAM chip's circuitry so the data will be stored.

PRIMARY AND SECONDARY STORAGE

RAM is sometimes referred to as *primary storage*. RAM is electronic, and requires a constant supply of electricity to store the data. Because data stored in RAM is lost if power is interrupted, RAM is called *volatile* storage.

So why use RAM if it loses data when the power goes off? The answer is speed. RAM offers a relatively fast way to store and retrieve data. RAM is usually installed near the microprocessor on the computer's main circuit board, called a *motherboard*. The microprocessor constantly stores data to RAM and retrieves data from RAM.

You will recall that earlier in this chapter we compared RAM to the top of your desk. Obviously, the space on the surface of a desk is limited. So is RAM.

Data which is waiting to be used needs to be stored in some type of "filing cabinet." In the computer, this more permanent "filing cabinet" storage is called *secondary storage*. Secondary storage usually comes in the form of disks. Programs and data stored on disks remain stored when power is turned off. The *hard disk* installed in your computer is an example of secondary storage. Figure 1-11 shows a hard disk drive with its top removed. A hard disk is sealed to prevent dust from affecting the sensitive disk.

A *floppy disk* is also an example of secondary storage. A floppy disk uses a thin flexible disk on which to store the data. Both hard disks and floppy disks store data by placing magnetic fields on the surface of the disk—the same principle used by audio and video tapes. The data stored on hard or floppy disks, by means of magnetic fields, remains when the power is turned off.

FIGURE 1-11
A hard disk drive is an example of secondary storage.

Extra for Experts

Comparing Primary and Secondary Storage

Programming computers requires that you understand trade-offs. A trade-off occurs when you must choose between two or more solutions, none of which are perfect solutions. Data storage in a computer involves a trade-off among speed, capacity, volatility, and cost.

The advantage of RAM is its speed. Its disadvantages are its volatility and its cost. Although the price of RAM has come down dramatically over the years, when compared to other types of storage, it is still relatively expensive. Therefore, the capacity of a computer's RAM is almost always less than the capacity of other forms of storage.

Disks offer large capacity and less volatility at low cost. The trade-off is that, in general, the less-expensive the storage, the slower the access speed. It takes longer to get data from a disk than from RAM.

NETWORKS

Individual computers, working alone, can accomplish very sophisticated tasks. However, when groups of computers work together, expanded opportunities present themselves. Connecting computers together is called **networking**. *Networks* are groups of computers that are connected by some communications link that allows them to share data or hardware resources. For example, two or more computers in an office or school can be networked so that hard drive space or printers can be shared. A network can also reach around the world. Every day, computers communicate with each other over phone lines (using modems), over special wires, or even using satellites.

Networks allow computer users to send electronic mail (*e-mail*) to other computer users in the same building or on the other side of the planet. Networks allow programs and data to be shared quickly and efficiently.

The Internet is a network of networks. Because the Internet is world-wide, it allows information, e-mail, messages, and files to be exchanged by anyone in the world whose computer has access to the Internet. Access to the Internet is available to practically anyone with a computer, a modem, and a phone line.

On the Net

More information about the history and development of the Internet is available at http://www.ProgramCPP.com. See topic 1.3.2.

SECTION 1.3 QUESTIONS

1. In a microprocessor, what coordinates the activity of the execution unit?

2. What part of the microprocessor takes the instructions from the instruction fetch unit and determines what must be done to get the instruction processed?

3. The speed of a microprocessor's clock is measured in what units?

4. CISC is an acronym for what phrase?

5. Define instruction set.

6. What is typically stored on ROM chips?

7. What are the four types of lines that make up the computer's bus?

8. What is typically used for a computer's primary storage?

9. What does it mean when we say RAM is volatile?

10. Why does a computer use RAM rather than just using disks for all of its storage?

KEY TERMS

arithmetic and logic unit

basic input/output system (BIOS)

bus

bus interface unit

central processing unit (CPU)

clock

complex instruction set computer (CISC)

computer architecture

control unit

e-mail

execution unit

floppy disk

hard disk

hardware

input

instruction decode unit

instruction fetch unit

instruction set

integrated circuit

interact

Internet

megahertz

microprocessor

modem

motherboard

network

output

primary storage

random-access memory (RAM)

read-only memory (ROM)

reduced instruction set computer (RISC)

registers

secondary storage

Toolbox

volatile

SUMMARY

➤ The history of computers shows that calculating tools evolved from manually-operated devices, to more complex mechanical devices, to electromechanical devices, and finally to electronic computers.

➤ Today computers are everywhere. Some computers are designed to perform specific tasks and some are designed to be programmable general-purpose computers.

➤ The equipment that makes up a computer is called hardware. Each piece of hardware is involved in input, output, processing, or storage.

➤ Computer architecture is a term used to describe the way a computer is put together. RAM is the computer's primary storage for currently running programs and current data. ROM is memory that has data permanently stored on it. ROM is used by the computer to store startup procedures and data that the system needs to operate.

➤ The microprocessor does the computing and controls everything that goes on in the computer. The commands the microprocessor understands are called its instruction set.

- There are two categories of microprocessors: CISC and RISC. Typically CISC processors have a more complex instruction set. RISC processors have fewer instructions than CISC processors. RISC processors are generally faster than CISC processors.

- The bus is the system that connects the components of the computer. The bus is divided into power lines, data lines, address lines, and control lines.

- RAM is the computer's primary storage. Hard disks and floppy disks are usually used as secondary storage.

- Networks are groups of computers that are connected by some communications link that allows them to share data or resources. The Internet is a well-known network.

PROJECTS

PROJECT 1-1

Write a short report on one of the computers developed prior to 1960 or one of the people involved with the early computers.

PROJECT 1-2

Research and write a report about the abacus which includes a brief history and then focuses on how to use an abacus.

PROJECT 1-3

Write a report about one of the computers from the timeline in Section 1.1. Include the specifications of the computer (such as amount of RAM, speed, etc.) if available. Also, include information about the computer's place in history. What computers preceded the one upon which you are writing your report and what computers are descendants of it?

PROJECT 1-4

Answer the following questions about the computer you will be using to program.

1. What microprocessor is in the computer?

2. What is the computer's clock speed?

3. Is the microprocessor a CISC or RISC processor?

4. How much RAM does the computer have?

5. What size is the computer's hard drive?

6. What is the capacity of the floppy disk drive?

PROJECT 1-5

Go to a store which sells computer software or locate a current software catalog. Investigate the hardware requirements for different kinds of software. Document your findings and determine what kinds of programs generally require the most powerful computers and why.

The Internet

By Laura Goldhar

The Internet was begun to help U.S. authorities communicate in the aftermath of a nuclear attack; it has now become a way to let people all over the world share ideas and work. From a very modest beginning in the early 1960s, the Internet has rapidly evolved into a worldwide network with over 1,000 computers being added each month as of 1996. In the past, communications networks were point-to-point, meaning that each computer on the network was dependent on the one before it. This meant that if one point on the network was destroyed, the whole network would be, too. What if the communications network were set up more like a fishnet: no center and not point-to-point? This structure allows information to find a path through the network regardless of whether a section of the network is gone.

Many universities began offering Internet access for scientific collaboration. This quickly spawned a general interest in and awareness of the Internet. A result of this is that there are now many services that allow you to access the Internet to exchange electronic mail, transfer files between computers, and find information. Many schools and businesses offer direct connections to the Internet and dial-in access to allow you to use the Internet from home via a modem. There are also many commercial services. Some of the most popular are America Online and the Microsoft Network.

If you have never used the Internet, you might be wondering what you can actually find on the Internet and if it is worth the trouble to get access. You can find information on almost every topic, from airline fares to quadratic equations. There is even information from the White House about current policies and what is going on in the world. Research from universities is often posted on the Internet, allowing people to keep up with the latest scientific discoveries. If you are looking for information about a company, product, or movie, the Internet should definitely tell you something. The Internet also has the benefit of being a live, interactive system; its information can be updated 24 hours a day.

One of the most phenomenal aspects of the Internet is electronic mail (e-mail). Thanks to e-mail it is possible to communicate with people around the globe, instantly expressing your thoughts to them. Commercial companies, along with many businesses, organizations, and education centers are able to issue e-mail addresses. These usually look like anyuser@somecomputer.place.type. This consists of a username, *anyuser* (a unique name for each person on a system), and the symbol @ which separates the user from the hostname. The hostname is usually in three parts. The first part is a unique host (computer on the Internet), in this case *somecomputer*. The second part of the address is the organization, *place*, and the third part is the type of organization. For colleges and universities this is *edu*. Commercial hosts use *com;* government, *gov;* military, *mil;* organization, *org;* and primary and secondary educational hosts in the United States use *k12.state-name.us.* The three parts of the hostname are separated by periods. The scheme of naming computers is known as the Domain Name System (DNS).

If you want to communicate with a large group of people with common interests, Newsgroups are a great way to learn and express thoughts about almost every subject. You can join a Newsgroup about computer programming, developments on the Internet, or music—there is something on almost every subject. *Usenet* is the electronic news and discussion forum that makes this possible. Newsgroups are easy to join, and often prove very interesting and helpful.

Another primary use of the Internet is the File Transfer Protocol (FTP). FTP allows information to be transferred from host to host on the Internet. You can do this to transfer information between different accounts. FTP can also be used to transfer to your computer (download) files from the many public FTP servers on the Internet. This allows a user to get computer programs,

Internet browsers, and more. Programs, pictures, and text can be downloaded from FTP sites.

The World Wide Web is what many people think of when they hear the Internet mentioned. In the early 1990s, the World Wide Web was conceived as a way to allow words, pictures, and sounds to be combined into a new way to communicate over the Internet. This means that it is easy for a person to look at information with the help of browsers, such as Netscape and the Microsoft Internet Explorer, which navigate World Wide Web (nicknamed Web) pages. The World Wide Web is what has made the Internet so popular. As it has become easier for people to find information, the number of Internet users has grown swiftly.

Though only recently entering the mainstream, the Internet has existed for several decades. As we move into the 21st century, worldwide communication becomes more imperative for the spreading of ideas. The Internet allows people globally to share ideas, learn, and express themselves. It can and will influence and improve almost every aspect of our lives. We are living in a glorious age of information thanks to the Internet.

Laura Goldhar is a Junior at Montgomery Blair High School, Silver Spring, Maryland.

2

How Computers Are Programmed

OBJECTIVES

➤ Understand how data and instructions are represented inside the computer.

➤ Understand the basics of the binary numbering system.

➤ Understand the differences between high- and low-level computer languages and the advantages of each.

➤ Understand the roles of assemblers, interpreters, and compilers.

➤ Understand the role of an operating system.

➤ Understand and be able to describe the steps in the programming process.

Overview

omputers are complex machines. But unless they are given instructions, all that great hardware is wasted. In order to be useful, computers must be programmed.

Compared to the computers of today, the first computers were simple devices. They were programmed by flipping switches or by inserting cards with holes punched in them. Early computers were only used to do simple math or tabulation. Today's computers, however, are used to display pictures, play sounds, and perform very complex tasks. To make programming modern computers possible, more sophisticated languages had to be developed.

In this chapter, you will see how the circuits in a computer are used to represent data and give instructions. Also, you will learn about programming languages that free programmers to concentrate on the function of the program rather than the computer's circuits.

Finally, you will learn about the five-step process that is essential for every programmer to follow in order to produce good computer programs.

CHAPTER 2, SECTION 1

The Computer's Language

s you learned in Chapter 1, computers are complex devices where electrical signals pulse through the system millions of times per second. These electrical signals are what the computer uses to represent data and give instructions to system components.

REPRESENTING DATA

Data is a computer representation of something that exists in the real world. For example, data can be values such as money, measurements, quantities, or a high score. Data can also be alphabetic, such as names and addresses or a business letter.

In a computer, all data is represented by numbers, and the numbers are represented electronically in the computer. To understand how electrical signals become numbers, let's begin by looking at a simple electric circuit that everyone is familiar with: a switch controlling a light bulb.

FROM CIRCUITS TO NUMBERS

When you think of an electric circuit, you probably think of it being either on or off; for example, a light bulb is turned on and off by a switch. The light bulb can exist in two conditions: on or off. In technical terms, the light bulb has two *states*.

Imagine you had two light bulbs on two switches. With two light bulbs there are four possible states, as shown in Figure 2-1. You could assign a number to each of the states and represent the numbers 0 through 3.

F I G U R E   2 - 1
There are four light combinations possible with two light bulbs.

You can't do much using only the numbers 0 through 3, but if more circuits are added, the number of states increases. For example, Figure 2-2 shows how three circuits can represent the numbers 0 through 7 because there are eight possible states.

If you are the mathematical type, you may have noticed that the number of states is determined by the formula 2^n where n is the number of circuits (see Table 2-1).

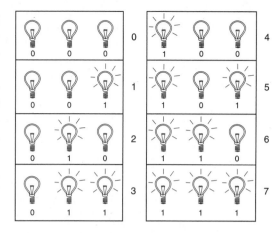

F I G U R E   2 - 2
There are eight light combinations possible with three light bulbs.

NUMBER OF CIRCUITS	NUMBER OF STATES	NUMBERS THAT CAN BE REPRESENTED
1	$2^1=2$	0,1
2	$2^2=4$	0..3
3	$2^3=8$	0..7
4	$2^4=16$	0..15
5	$2^5=32$	0..31
6	$2^6=64$	0..63
7	$2^7=128$	0..127
8	$2^8=256$	0..255

T A B L E   2 - 1

Now instead of lights, think about circuits in the computer. A single circuit in a computer is like a single light; it can be on or off. A special number system, called the ***binary number system***, is used to represent numbers with groups of these circuits. In the binary number system each binary digit, called a ***bit*** for short, is either a 0 or a 1. As shown in Figure 2-3, circuits that are off are defined as 0, and circuits that are on are defined as 1. Binary digits (bits) are combined into groups of eight bits called ***bytes***.

If a byte is made up of eight bits, then there are 256 possible combinations of those eight bits representing the numbers 0 through 255 (see Table 2-1). Even though 255 is not a small number, it is definitely not the largest number you will ever use. So to represent larger numbers, computers group bytes together. You will learn more about how the computer uses bytes to represent numbers in Chapter 4.

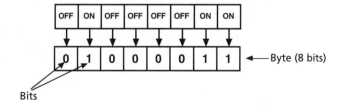

F I G U R E   2 - 3
In the computer, signals that are off are defined as 0 and signals that are on are defined as 1.

The binary number system may seem strange to you because you count using the *decimal number system*, which uses the digits 0 through 9. Counting in the decimal number system comes very naturally to you because you learned it from a very young age. But someone invented the decimal number system just like someone invented the binary number system. The decimal number system is based on tens because you have ten fingers on your hands. The binary number system is based on twos because of the circuits in a computer. *Both systems, however, can be used to represent the same values.*

In the decimal number system, each digit of a number represents a power of 10. That is why the decimal number system is also called the base 10 number system. Consider the number 3208 for example. When you read that number, you automatically understand it to mean three thousands, two hundreds, no tens, and eight ones. Represented mathematically, you could say $(3 \times 1000) + (2 \times 100) + (0 \times 10) + (8 \times 1) = 3208$, as shown in Figure 2-4.

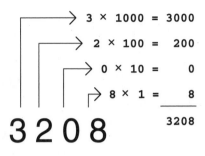

FIGURE 2-4
Each digit of the decimal number 3208 represents a power of 10.

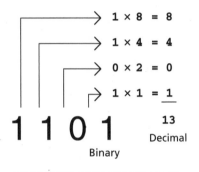

FIGURE 2-5
Each digit of the binary number 1101 represents a power of 2, so conversion to the decimal system is easy.

In the binary number system, each digit represents a power of 2, like you saw in Table 2-1. Working with powers of 2 is not as natural to you as working with powers of 10. But with a little practice you will see that base 2 numbers are not so mysterious. Consider the binary number 1101. Even though the number is four digits long, its value is nowhere near a thousand. The powers of 2 are 1, 2, 4, 8, 16, 32, and so on. So for this number, its decimal equivalent is $(1 \times 8) + (1 \times 4) + (0 \times 2) + (1 \times 1) = 13$, as shown in Figure 2-5. So the binary number 1101 is equivalent to thirteen in the decimal number system.

Extra for Experts

Decimal Points and Binary Points

You have used decimal points for a long time. Did you know there is a binary point? A decimal point divides the ones place and the tenths place, or 10^0 from 10^{-1}. There is an equivalent in the binary number system called the binary point. It divides the 2^0 place from the 2^{-1} place.

With a binary point, it is possible to have binary numbers like 100.1, which in decimal is 4.5. Can you convert the binary number 10.01 to decimal? If you got 2.25 as the answer, you are correct. Try converting the binary number 11.001001 to decimal.

If all data in a computer is represented by numbers, how are letters and symbols stored? Letters and symbols, called *characters,* are assigned a number that the computer uses to represent them. Most computers assign numbers to characters according to the *American Standard Code for Information Interchange (ASCII).* Figure 2-6 shows some of the ASCII (pronounced *ask-e*) codes. For a complete ASCII table, see Appendix A.

ASCII CODES

Character	Decimal Number System	Binary Number System
$	36	010 0100
*	42	010 1010
A	65	100 0001
B	66	100 0010
C	67	100 0011
D	68	100 0100
a	97	110 0001
b	98	110 0010
c	99	110 0011
d	100	110 0100

F I G U R E   2 - 6
In the computer, each character is stored as a number.

The basic ASCII code is based on 7 bits, which gives 128 characters. About 95 of these are upper and lowercase letters, numbers, and symbols. Some of the characters are used as codes for controlling communication hardware and other devices. Others are invisible characters like Tab and Return. Most computers extend the ASCII code to 8 bits (a whole byte) to represent 256 characters. The additional 128 characters are used for graphical characters and characters used with foreign languages.

REPRESENTING INSTRUCTIONS

You have seen how computers use bits to represent data. We use computers to do much more than represent data for storage. Computers are useful because they follow instructions to do work. And just like data, instructions are represented by combinations of bits.

Recall that the microprocessor is the device in which instructions are executed. Each instruction consists of ones and zeros, called *machine language.*

Writing a program in machine language would be very difficult because even a simple program requires hundreds or even thousands of microprocessor instructions. Another problem is that the numbers used to represent microprocessor instructions are difficult for people to understand. Figure 2-7 shows a short machine language program. Each line is one instruction for the microprocessor. To find out what the program does, you would have to look up the machine language instructions in the microprocessor's reference manual.

```
01010101
10001011 11101100
01001100
01001100
01010110
01010111
10111111 00000011 00000000
10111110 00000010 00000000
10001011 11000111
00000011 11000110
10001001 01000110 11111110
01011111
01011110
10001011 11100101
01011110
11000011
```

FIGURE 2 - 7
Machine language is the language of the microprocessor. This machine language program adds 3 + 2 and stores the result.

Analog vs. Digital

The early computers used gears, wheels, or other mechanical devices to represent numbers. These are called analog devices. Something is an **analog** device if it uses quantities that are variable or exist in a range. For example, a second hand on a clock is an analog device because it represents a value with a continuously variable quantity.

Electronics made digital devices the basis for computers. A **digital** device uses switches in combination (or digits) to represent something in the real world. For example, rather than have a second hand rotate at a fixed speed to represent a value, a digital clock counts the seconds electronically.

On the Net

In this section you learned about the base 2 number system called the binary number system. Another number system used frequently in computer programming is a base 16 number system called the hexadecimal number system. To learn how to use the hexadecimal system and to see the machine language program from Figure 2-7 represented in the hexadecimal system, go to http://www.ProgramCPP.com. See topic 2.1.1.

SECTION 2.1 QUESTIONS

1. Define data.

2. How many bits are in a byte?

3. What is the language called that is "understood" by the microprocessor?

4. How many combinations of bits are possible with three bits?

5. Looking at the table in Appendix A, add the decimal values of the ASCII characters that spell your first name. Remember to use a capital letter where necessary. Write each character, its decimal equivalent, and the sum of all the ASCII values.

Programming Languages

Supplying computers with instructions would be extremely difficult if machine language were the only option available to programmers. Fortunately, special languages have been developed that are more easily understood. These special languages, called *programming languages,* provide a way to program computers using instructions that can be understood by computers and people.

Like human languages, programming languages have their own vocabulary and rules of usage. Some programming languages are very technical, and others are made to be as similar to English as possible. The programming languages available today allow programming at many levels of complexity.

ASSEMBLY LANGUAGE

The programming language most like machine language is *assembly language.* Assembly language uses letters and numbers to represent machine language instructions (see Figure 2-8). However, assembly language is still difficult for novices to read.

Assembly language programming is accomplished using an assembler. An *assembler* is a program that reads the codes the programmer has written and assembles a machine language program based on those codes.

LOW-LEVEL VS. HIGH-LEVEL LANGUAGES

Machine language and assembly language are called *low-level languages.* In a low-level language, it is necessary for the programmer to know the instruction set of the microprocessor in order to program the computer. Each instruction in a low-level language corresponds to one or only a few microprocessor instructions. In the program in Figure 2-8 each assembly language instruction corresponds to one machine language instruction.

Most programming is done in *high-level languages.* In a high-level language, instructions do not necessarily correspond one-to-one with the instruction set of the microprocessor. One command in a high-level language may represent many microprocessor instructions. Therefore, high-level languages reduce the number of instructions that must be written. A program that might take hours to write in a low-level language can be done in minutes in a high-level language. Programming in a high-level language also reduces the number of errors because the programmer doesn't have to write as many instructions, and the instructions are easier to read. Figure 2-9 shows a program written in three popular high-level languages. Like the machine language and assembly language programs you saw earlier, these high level programs add the numbers 3 and 2 together.

Another advantage of programs written in a high-level language is that they are easier to move among computers with different microprocessors. For example, the microprocessors in Macintosh computers use a different instruction

Machine Language	Assembly Language
01010101	PUSH BP
10001011 11101100	MOV BP,SP
01001100	DEC SP
01001100	DEC SP
01010110	PUSH SI
01010111	PUSH DI
10111111 00000011 00000000	MOV DI, 0003
10111110 00000010 00000000	MOV SI, 0002
10001011 11000111	MOV AX, DI
00000011 11000110	ADD AX, SI
10001001 01000110 11111110	MOV [BP-02], AX
01011111	POP DI
01011110	POP SI
10001011 11100101	MOV SP, BP
01011110	POP BP
11000011	RET

FIGURE 2 - 8
In assembly language, each micro-processor instruction is assigned a code that makes the program more meaningful to people. It is still difficult, however, for the un-trained person to see what the program will do.

set than the microprocessors in DOS-compatible computers. An assembly language program written for a DOS computer will not work on a Macintosh. However, a simple program written in a high-level language can work on both computers with little or no modification.

So why use a low-level language? It depends on what you need to do. The drawback of high-level languages is that they do not always provide a command for everything the programmer wants a program to do. Using assembly language, the programmer can write instructions that enable the computer to do anything the hardware will allow.

Another advantage of low-level languages is that a program written in a low-level language will generally require less memory and run more quickly than the same program written in a high-level language. This is because high-level languages must be translated into machine language before the micro-processor can execute the instructions. The translation is done by another

BASIC	Pascal	C++
10 I = 3	program AddIt;	main()
20 J = 2		{
30 K = I + J	var	int i,j,k;
	i, j, k : integer;	i = 3;
		j = 2;
	begin	k = i + j;
	i := 3;	return 0;
	j := 2;	}
	k := i + j;	
	end.	

FIGURE 2 - 9
The same program can be written in more than one high-level language.

program, and is usually less efficient than the work of a skilled assembly-language programmer. Table 2-2 summarizes the advantages of low- and high-level languages.

ADVANTAGES OF LOW-LEVEL LANGUAGES	ADVANTAGES OF HIGH-LEVEL LANGUAGES
Better use of hardware's capabilities	Requires less programming
Requires less memory	Fewer programming errors
Runs more quickly	Easier to move among computers with different microprocessors
	More easily read

T A B L E   2 - 2

INTERPRETERS AND COMPILERS

Programmers writing in a high-level language enter the program's instructions into a text editor. A *text editor* is similar to a word processor, except the files are saved in ASCII format without the font and formatting codes word processors use. The files saved by text editors are called *text files.* A program in the form of a high-level language is called *source code.*

Programmers must have their high-level programs translated into the machine language the microprocessor understands. The translation may be done by interpreters or compilers. The resulting machine language code is known as *object code.*

INTERPRETERS

An *interpreter* is a program that translates the source code of a high-level language into machine language. An interpreter translates a computer language in a way similar to the way a person might interpret between languages like English and Spanish. Each instruction is interpreted from the programming language into machine language as the instructions are needed. Interpreters are normally used only with very high-level languages, such as most versions of BASIC.

To run a program written in an interpreted language, you must first load the interpreter into the computer's memory. Then you load the program to be interpreted. The interpreter steps through the program one instruction at a time and translates the instruction into machine language, which is sent to the microprocessor. Every time the program is run, the interpreter must once again translate each instruction.

Because of the need to have the interpreter in memory before the program can be interpreted, interpreted languages are not widely used to write programs that are sold. The buyer of the program would have to have the correct interpreter in order to use the program.

COMPILERS

A *compiler* is another program that translates a high-level language into machine language. A compiler, however, makes the translation once, then saves the machine language so that the instructions do not have to be translated each time

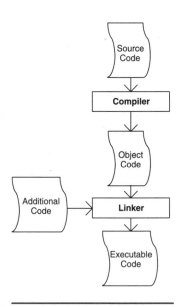

FIGURE 2-10
Compiling a program involves a compiler and a linker.

the program is run. Programming languages such as Pascal and C++ use compilers rather than interpreters.

Figure 2-10 shows the steps involved in using a compiler. First, the source code is translated using the compiler to a file called an *object file.* An object file, however, is incomplete. A program called a *linker* is used to create an executable program. The linker combines the object file with other machine language necessary to create a program that can run without an interpreter. The linker produces an *executable file* which can be run as many times as desired without the need for translating again.

Although using a compiler involves more steps than using an interpreter, most C++ compilers automate the task and make it easy for the programmer to use. For example, most compilers allow you to compile and link in a single operation.

Programs you use regularly, such as word processors and games, are examples of programs written with a compiler. Compiled programs require less memory than interpreted programs because a compiled program does not require that an interpreter be loaded into memory. Compiled programs also run faster than interpreted programs because the translation has already been done. When a compiled program is run, the program is loaded into memory in the machine language the microprocessor needs.

INTRODUCING C++

In this book you will learn to program in a compiled language called *C++*. You may have also heard of a language named C. The C++ language evolved from C. Most people call C++ a "better" C.

Why Is It Called C?

The language C got its name because it is a descendent of a language called B. Both languages were developed at Bell Laboratories. There was no A language. The language B probably got its name because it was based on a language named BCPL.

On the Net

Learn more about the history of programming languages at http://www. ProgramCPP.com. See topic 2.2.1.

Although C and C++ are high-level languages, they provide the programmer with much of the power and flexibility of a low-level language. In fact, C and C++ are widely used by professional programmers to write many of the applications with which you are familiar, such as your word processor and spreadsheet programs.

Categories of Software

There are two basic categories of software: application software and system software. Application software is the software that performs the tasks you want the computer to perform. For example, application software is what you use to produce a document or balance your checkbook. System software coordinates the interaction of the hardware devices, controls the input and output, and loads application software into memory so that you can run the programs you want to run. The system software required to run your computer is most often packaged together and called an operating system.

OPERATING SYSTEMS

Programs you buy or write, in order to operate properly, need additional instructions. They are found in the computer's *operating system.* The operating system is in charge of the fundamental system operations.

The operating system manages the hardware resources. For example, the operating system allocates memory to programs and system operations. It also can allocate processor time in situations where multiple programs are running.

The operating system maintains the system of files on disks and other means of secondary storage. Programs and files are organized into directories by the operating system.

The operating system also controls input and output operations. Keyboard input, mouse movements, displaying to the screen, and printing all involve the operating system.

Finally, the operating system loads programs and supervises their execution. When you issue a command to start a program, the operating system loads the program into memory and allows it to begin executing. The operating system regularly interrupts the program so that housekeeping chores like updating the system date and time can take place.

Some operating systems you may have seen or used are MS-DOS (the operating system written by Microsoft for PCs), OS/2, Windows, and the Macintosh operating system (MacOS).

The DOS prompt, shown in Figure 2-11 is actually a program that is part of the MS-DOS operating system.

Microsoft Windows, OS/2, and the Macintosh use graphical user interfaces as a control center from which programs are loaded. A *graphical user interface* is a system for interacting with the computer user through pictures. Graphical user interface is often abbreviated as GUI, pronounced "gooey."

The Macintosh operating system includes a program called the Finder (Figure 2-12) that organizes and loads programs and documents. The Macintosh

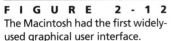

F I G U R E   2 - 1 1
The DOS prompt is part of the MS-DOS operating system.

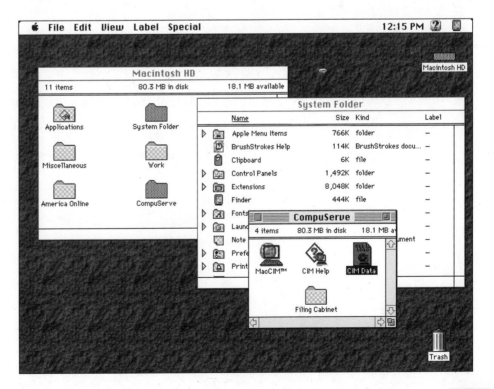

F I G U R E   2 - 1 2
The Macintosh had the first widely-used graphical user interface.

had the first widely-used graphical interface. The Macintosh helped set the standard for other GUI operating systems.

Later, Microsoft and IBM created their own graphical operating systems. Figure 2-13 shows Microsoft's Windows 95 operating system. Windows and IBM's OS/2 do more than put a pretty face on the DOS prompt. They allow multiple programs to be run at the same time and provide resources that programs can share. They also make it easier to learn new programs, because each program has the same look and feel.

FIGURE 2-13
Microsoft Windows 95 is a graphical alternative to the DOS prompt.

SECTION 2.2 QUESTIONS

1. Give an example of a low-level programming language.

2. List three examples of high-level programming languages.

3. Describe the process involved when using a compiler to program a computer.

4. Describe one advantage that compiled programs have over interpreted programs.

5. List three operations managed by operating systems.

The Programming Process

P rogrammers are always tempted to immediately begin writing code to solve a problem. There is a better way. Sure, if you are writing a program to print your name on the screen a million times you might get by with just sitting down and keying in a program. But most programs are more complicated, and therefore a more structured and disciplined approach to programming is necessary.

Although there are different approaches used by different programmers, most good programmers follow five basic steps when developing programs:

1. Define the problem.

2. Develop an algorithm.

3. Code the program.

4. Test and debug the program.

5. Document and maintain the program.

DEFINING THE PROBLEM

Defining the problem to be solved requires an understanding of what the program is to accomplish.

For example, a program that calculates interest on a loan is fairly easy to define. Start by identifying the inputs and outputs. As input, the program needs the loan amount, the interest rate, and the number of months that the money is to be borrowed. A specific known formula can be applied to the data, and the amount of interest is the output.

Many programs are more difficult to define. Suppose you are defining a game program that involves characters in a maze. In your definition, the abilities of each character must be defined. In addition, the maze and how the characters interact with the maze and each other must also be defined. The list goes on and on.

Imagine how much there is to define before writing a program to handle airline reservations for a world-wide airline or the software that controls the launch of the space shuttle. Before any part of the program is written, the programmer must know exactly what the goal is.

Defining the problem does not take into consideration *how* the program will do the job, just *what* the job is. Exactly how a program accomplishes its work is addressed in the second step of the process.

DEVELOPING AN ALGORITHM

The second step in the programming process is to develop an algorithm. An *algorithm* is a set of sequential instructions that are followed to solve a problem. Algorithms have been commonly used for years. A recipe for baking a cake, instructions for assembling a bicycle, and directions to a shopping mall are all examples of algorithms. The directions to a mall, shown in Figure 2-14, are a set of steps that you execute sequentially.

Drive south on University Avenue to 50th Street.
Turn right (west) on 50th.
Drive west on 50th to Slide Road.
Turn left (south) on Slide Road.
Drive south on Slide Road until you see the mall entrance on the right.

Some algorithms involve decisions that change the course of action or cause parts of the algorithm to be repeated. Consider the algorithm for parking the car once you reach the mall. A more complicated algorithm is best illustrated with symbols in a *flowchart* as shown in Figure 2-15.

Programming a computer requires that you create an algorithm. The instructions the program gives the computer must tell the computer exactly what steps to do and in what order to do them. The computer executes each instruction sequentially, except when an instruction causes the flow of logic to jump to another part of the program.

When first developing an algorithm, you should avoid the temptation of initially writing in a programming language. A better method is to use pseudocode. *Pseudocode* expresses an algorithm in everyday English, rather than in a programming language. Pseudocode makes it possible for you to describe the instructions to be executed by the program. The precise choice of words and punctuation, however, is less important. Figure 2-16 is an example of pseudocode for a mathematical program that prompts the user for an integer (a whole number without any decimal places) and squares it.

Depending on the complexity of your program, developing algorithms can be a quick process or the most time consuming part of developing your program.

Flowchart Symbols

Each shape used in a flowchart has a special meaning. The shapes are connected with arrows that show the direction of the flow of the algorithm. The symbols below are the most common flowchart symbols.

Use the rectangle for processing or taking action.

Use the diamond for making decisions. See Figure 2-15 for examples.

Use the parallelogram to show that something is input or output.

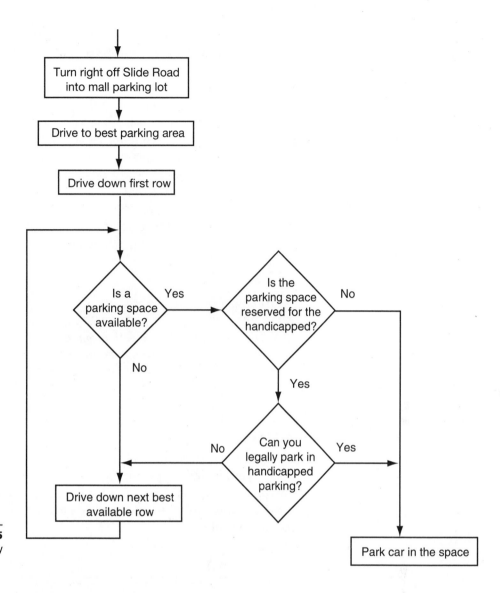

F I G U R E   2 - 1 5
Some steps in an algorithm may
be repeated many times.

Later in the book you will learn methods programmers use to break down complex problems into manageable parts.

F I G U R E   2 - 1 6
Pseudocode allows you to develop
an algorithm without being concerned about the commands and
punctuation of a programming
language.

```
declare i and j as integers

prompt user for i

j = i * i

print j
```

CODING THE PROGRAM

An algorithm's pseudocode is next translated into program code. Most of the rest of this book teaches you the commands and structures you need to translate algorithms into actual programs. In the next chapter you will enter and compile your first program.

Errors can be made during coding that can prevent the program from successfully compiling and linking. So part of the coding step involves resolving errors that prevent the program from running.

A common error is called a *syntax error*. A syntax error occurs when you key a command or some other part of the program incorrectly. Computers must be told exactly what to do. If someone leaves you a note that says "Lock the back *dore* before you leave," you will be able to figure out what the instruction is. When the computer recognizes a syntax error, the programmer is notified immediately. Everything has to be just right or the computer will not accept it.

There are other errors that the computer may detect when compiling. Most of them are easily resolved. When all of those errors are resolved, the program will compile, link, and be ready to run. Even if a program runs, it may still fail to do its job correctly. That is where the next step of the programming process comes in.

On the Net

There are different kinds of programming errors. It is important to understand that a program which runs is not necessarily error-free. Learn more about errors and bugs at http://www.ProgramCPP.com. See topic 2.3.1.

TESTING AND DEBUGGING

Testing and debugging is an important step that is too often ignored. Programs typically fail to operate 100% correctly the first time they are compiled or interpreted. Logic errors and other hidden problems called *bugs* must be located. Software must be tested and "debugged" to make sure the output is correct and reliable.

Why Bugs?

Back when computers used vacuum tubes, the heat and light generated by the tubes sometimes attracted bugs such as moths. The bugs sometimes caused short circuits, resulting in the need to "debug" the computer.

One way to test a program is to provide input for which the results are known. For example, a program that converts meters to feet can be easily tested by giving the program input values for which you know the output. Carefully select a wide variety of inputs. Use values that are larger or smaller than those which are typical. Use zero and negative numbers as inputs when allowable.

You should also test every part of a program. Make sure you provide input that tests every line of your code. Test each part of the program repeatedly to make sure that consistent results are obtained.

A type of error that can cause your program to stop running (or *crash*) is called a *run-time error*. A run-time error occurs when a program gives the computer an instruction that it is incapable of executing. A run-time error may lead to a program "crash." For example, if your program tries to divide a number by zero, a run-time error will occur on most systems. A run-time error could also occur if the system runs out of memory while your program is running.

You will experience lots of bugs and errors as a programmer. They are a part of every programmer's day. Even the best programmers spend lots of time testing and debugging. Throughout this book you will be warned of possible pitfalls and bugs so that you can avoid as many as possible. But the best way to learn how to avoid bugs is to experience them.

DOCUMENTING AND MAINTAINING THE PROGRAM

This fifth step applies mostly to programs used in the real world. But since you may someday write such programs, you should be aware of this step as well. Programmers must document their work so that they and other programmers can make changes or updates later. Documentation may also have to be written for the program's users.

The Importance of Documentation

You should document your programs while you are programming and avoid saving the task for last. The time to write documentation for a program is while you are programming. By the time you finish the programming, you may have already forgotten some of what you did.

You may also be less likely to write proper documentation once a program is complete. You may think your time is better spent on another project. You will be pleased to have the documentation when it is needed.

DOCUMENTATION IN THE PROGRAM

Documentation that is included in the program itself is very important. Virtually all programming languages allow comments to be included in the source code. The comments are ignored by the interpreter or the compiler. Therefore the programmer can include notes and explanations that will make the program easier for people to read. You will learn how to use comments in your source code in the next chapter.

DOCUMENTATION OUTSIDE OF THE PROGRAM

Many times a program is complex enough that documents should be written that explain how the programming problem was solved. This documentation might be diagrams, flowcharts, or descriptions.

DOCUMENTATION FOR THE USER

You have probably already been exposed to user documentation. Programs that are to be used by more than a few people usually include user documentation that explains the functions of the software.

PROGRAM MAINTENANCE

Maintenance is an important part of the programming process. Most programs are written to help with a task. As the task changes, the program must also change. Users are likely to request additions and changes be made to the program. Maintaining a program is an important part of the process because it keeps the programmer's work up-to-date and in use.

During the maintenance phase of the programming process, bugs may be found that were not uncovered during the testing and debugging phase. It is also possible that better ways to accomplish a task in the program may be discovered. It is important to understand that the steps of the programming process may be repeated in order to refine or repair an existing program.

SECTION 2.3 QUESTIONS

1. List the five basic steps in the programming process.

2. Define algorithm.

3. Give an example of an algorithm used in everyday life.

4. Define the term *bug* as it relates to programming.

5. What is the purpose of documentation inside a program?

6. Write an algorithm that gives directions from one location to another. Choose a starting point (your home, for example), and give detailed, step-by-step directions that will lead anyone who might be reading the algorithm to the correct destination.

7. Draw a flowchart that describes the steps you follow when you get up in the morning and get ready for your day. Include as many details as you want, including things such as hitting the snooze button on your alarm clock, brushing your teeth, and eating breakfast.

KEY TERMS

algorithm

American Standard Code for Information Interchange (ASCII)

analog

assembler

assembly language

binary number system

bit

bugs

byte

C++

characters

compiler

crash

data

decimal number system

digital

executable file

flowchart

graphical user interface (GUI)

high-level language

interpreter

linker

low-level language

machine language

object code

object file

operating system

programming language

pseudocode

run-time error

source code

states

syntax error

text editor

text file

SUMMARY

> Inside a computer, signals called bits represent data and give instructions. Bits are commonly arranged in groups of eight, called bytes. At the heart of the work a computer does is a device called a microprocessor. The microprocessor responds to commands called machine language.

> High-level programming languages allow programmers to work in a language that people can more easily read. Machine language and assembly language are low-level languages because each instruction in the language corresponds to one or only a few microprocessor instructions. In high-level languages, instructions may represent many microprocessor instructions.

> High-level languages must be translated into machine language by an interpreter or compiler. An interpreter translates each program step into machine language as the program runs. A compiler translates the program before it is run, and saves the machine language as an object file. A linker then creates an executable file from the object file.

> Input and output operations and loading of executable files are handled by the operating system. The operating system loads a program and turns over control of the system to the program. When the program ends, the operating system takes control again.

> Programming involves five basic steps: defining the problem; developing an algorithm; coding the program; testing and debugging; and documenting and maintaining.

PROJECTS

PROJECT 2-1

Choose some large value, like the salary of your favorite professional athlete, and convert it to the binary number system.

PROJECT 2-2

Make a chart of at least 12 high-level languages. Include a brief description of each language that tells the primary use of the language or its historical significance. If you can find the date the language was created, include that on your chart. Some languages to consider are Ada, ALGOL, BASIC, C, C++, COBOL, FORTRAN, LISP, Logo, Oberon, Pascal, PL/I, and Smalltalk.

PROJECT 2-3

Choose a computer program with which you are familiar. List the inputs and outputs of the program. Draw a basic flowchart for the program. If the program is too large for a simple flowchart, draw a flowchart for one part of the program.

Grace Hopper: Pioneer of the Information Age

By Kristia Cadavero

It's not everyday when someone gets the highest award possible for his or her work. It's especially unusual when that someone is a woman who worked in a field dominated by men. But to Grace Hopper, such distinctions were transparent; nothing could hold her back from anything she wanted to do.

Grace Brewster Murray was born on December 9, 1906. She spent her summers in Wolfeboro, New Hampshire (where she met her future husband), and apparently had a very happy childhood. Compared to today, Grace's schooling was much stricter; she even had to do homework over the summer.

Grace graduated from Vassar College in 1928 with a Phi Beta Kappa membership. She received her M.A. at Yale University in 1930 and married Vincent Foster Hopper that same year.

During the years 1931–1943, Grace taught at Vassar in the Department of Mathematics and

received a Vassar Faculty Fellowship. In 1934 she earned her Ph.D. from Yale in mathematics. But Grace still felt compelled to continue her education, so she studied at New York University during 1941–1942. She became an assistant professor of mathematics at Barnard College in 1943, then enlisted in the U.S. Naval Reserve (USNR) because of the war. Her husband died in World War II in 1945, and Grace, with no children, continued in her career.

When Grace graduated USNR Midshipmen's School-W in Northampton, Massachusetts, she was commissioned Lieutenant. She was ordered to the Bureau of Ordnance Computation Project at Harvard University and worked on Howard Aiken's Mark I, II, and III computers for the Navy. In 1946 she joined Harvard as a researcher in engineering sciences and applied physics. It was there that the term "debug" became en vogue, reportedly when a moth got stuck inside the computer and caused the computer to "crash."

In 1949 Grace worked on programming Univac I, the first large commercial computer, which the U.S. Census Bureau began using in 1951. In 1952 she published a paper on compilers and was appointed systems engineer director of automatic programming in the Univac Division of the Sperry Rand Corporation. Throughout her career she published over fifty papers on software and programming languages.

The Department of Defense, in 1959, sponsored the Conference on Data Systems Languages (CODASYL). The outcome of this conference was the CODASYL committee, of which Grace was an executive member. The committee strove for the development of a programming language convenient for business applications, which consisted of a set of symbols, letters, words, and numbers used for giving instructions to a computer. Grace helped enormously with this development because she believed that programming languages should be more like everyday instructions so many people could use computers. She invented a system of translating common language into instructions computers could process. The CODASYL committee named the language COBOL (Common Business-Oriented Language).

COBOL quickly became a widespread procedure-oriented language. One of the reasons could have been because the government required that all computers bought or leased by the government be able to use a COBOL compiler. Today COBOL is still used in commercial and government computer installations.

In 1966 Grace retired from the Naval Reserve with a rank of Commander in the Retired Reserve. She was recalled to duty in 1967 to help standardize the Navy's computer languages and promoted to the rank of Captain on the retired list of the Naval Reserve in 1973. She retired again in 1986, this time an eighty-year-old Rear Admiral, the nation's oldest active-duty officer.

During the early 1980s, Grace predicted that computers would be used to predict weather patterns, manage energy resources, and increase agricultural output. More than a decade later one can recognize her foresight. Grace acquired many awards and fellowships, and she was even awarded the National Medal of Technology, the nation's highest honor in engineering and technology, by President George Bush in 1991. But Grace felt that her greatest contribution was the youngsters she had trained and taught.

Grace died in Arlington, Virginia, on January 1, 1992. Because of her continued duty, service, and loyalty to her country, she was buried in one of her country's most sacred grounds, Arlington National Cemetery. Her plain white granite headstone can be found in Section 59. Engraved is her name, dates of birth and death, rank in the Navy, and the three wars in which she served: World War II, Korea, and Vietnam. As with all veterans, a presidential wreath adorns her grave every Memorial and Veterans Day.

Kristia Cadavero is a Senior at Eastern Christian High School, North Haledon, New Jersey.

3 Entering, Compiling, and Running a Program

OBJECTIVES

➤ Understand the structure of a C++ program.

➤ Access the text editor and enter C++ source code.

➤ Compile, link, and run C++ programs.

Overview

You learned in the previous chapter that C++ source code has to be entered into a text editor, translated by a compiler, and made into an executable program by a linker.

Your task in this chapter will be to create an actual C++ program on your system. You will first examine the structure of a C++ program. Then you will enter a simple program into the text editor, compile, link, and run the executable file that is created.

CHAPTER 3, SECTION 1

C++ Program Structure

++ programs have the basic structure illustrated in Figure 3-1. They are:

1. *Comments* - Comments are remarks that are ignored by the compiler.

2. *Compiler Directives* - Compiler directives are commands for the compiler, which are needed to effectively compile and run your program.

3. *Main Function* - The main function is where every C++ program begins.

4. *Braces* - Braces are special characters used to mark the beginning and ending of blocks of code.

5. *Statement* - A statement is a line of C++ code. Statements end with a semi-colon.

Let's examine each part of a C++ program in more detail.

> ### Note
>
> *As you will learn later in this course, a C++ program can have other functions in addition to the main function.*

COMMENTS

When writing a program, you may think that you will always remember what you did and why. Most programmers, however, eventually forget. But more importantly, others may need to make changes in a program you wrote. They probably will be unaware of what you did when you wrote the program. That is why comments are important.

Use comments to:

➤ explain the purpose of a program

➤ keep notes regarding changes to the source code

➤ store the names of programmers for future reference

➤ explain the parts of your program.

Figure 3-2 is an example of a program that is well-documented with comments. The comments at the top of the program assign the program a name,

```
              ┌  // Simple C++ Program
              │  //
    Comments  ┤  // Purpose: To demonstrate the parts of a
              └  // simple C++ program.

Compiler Directive { #include <iostream.h>  // necessary for cout command

                  ┌  main()
                  │  {
    Main Function ┤        cout << "This is a simple C++ program.";  ┐ Statements
            Braces└        return 0;                                  ┘
                     }
```

FIGURE   3 - 1
A C++ program has several parts.

```
// Travel Efficiency
// Programmer: Jonathan Kleid
//
// Purpose: Calculates miles per gallon and price per mile when
// given miles traveled, number of gallons used, and gas price.

#include <iostream.h> // necessary for cin and cout commands

main()
{
// Variable declarations
float MilesTraveled;     //   stores number of miles
float GallonsUsed;       //   stores number of total gallons used
float PricePerGallon;    //   stores price per gallon
float PricePerMile;      //   stores the price per mile
float MilesPerGallon;    //   stores the number of miles per gallon

// Ask user for input values.
cout << "How many miles did you travel? ";
cin  >> MilesTraveled;
cout << "How many gallons of gas did you use? ";
cin  >> GallonsUsed;
cout << "How much did one gallon of gas cost? $";
cin  >> PricePerGallon;

// Divide the number of miles by the number of gallons to get MPG.
MilesPerGallon = MilesTraveled / GallonsUsed;

// Divide price per gallon by miles per gallon
// to get price per mile.
PricePerMile = PricePerGallon / MilesPerGallon;

// Output miles per gallon and price per mile.
cout << "You got " << MilesPerGallon << " miles per gallon,\n";
cout << "and each mile cost $" << PricePerMile << '\n';
return 0;
}
```

FIGURE   3 - 2
Comments help make this program understandable.

```
float MilesTraveled;    // stores number of miles
float GallonsUsed;      // stores total number of gallons used
float PricePerGallon;   // stores price per gallon
float PricePerMile;     // stores the price per mile
float MilesPerGallon;   // stores the number of miles per gallon
```

F I G U R E   3 - 3
Comments can follow a statement.

identify its programmer as Jonathan Kleid, and indicate that the purpose of the program is to calculate miles per gallon and price per mile. Within the program, comments help the reader identify what the lines in the program do.

Comments, which are ignored by the compiler, begin with a double slash (//) and may appear anywhere in the program. An entire line can be a comment or may appear to the right of program statements, as shown in Figure 3-3. Everything to the right of the // is ignored. Therefore, do not include any statements to the right of a comment. Be sure to use the forward-leaning slash (/) rather than the backslash (\) or the compiler tries to translate your comments and an error message results.

COMPILER DIRECTIVES

Directives are instructions to the compiler rather than part of the C++ language. The most common compiler directive is the **#include** directive, which instructs the compiler to treat the text file that is enclosed in brackets as if it were keyed into the source code. See Figure 3-4.

So why do you need other code included in your source code? The code you are including makes additional commands available to you. For example, the **#include <iostream.h>** directive that you have seen in programs in this chapter makes a set of input and output commands available. These commands make it easy to get input from the user and print to the screen.

Note

#include is pronounced simply as include. Ignore the # sign when you pronounce the word.

```
#include <iostream.h>
```
Name of File to Be Included

F I G U R E   3 - 4
The **#include** compiler directive inserts other code into your program as if it were actually keyed into your program.

What Is iostream.h?

*Files like **iostream.h** are called **header files**. They may be identified by their file extension ".h". A header file serves as a link between your program code and standard C++ code that is needed to make your program run.*

You will learn more about compiler directives in later chapters.

MAIN FUNCTION

Every C++ program has a main function (see Figure 3-1). The main function is run first. Although simple programs can be written entirely within the main function, C++ programs are typically divided into multiple functions, which are accessed through the main function.

What Is a Function?

*A **function** is a block of code that carries out a specific task. For example, a function could be written to calculate the area of a circle. That function could be used (or "called") wherever the calculation is needed in the program.*

The parentheses that follow the word **main** are required. They tell the compiler that main is a function. All functions have parentheses, although most of them have information inside the parentheses. You will learn how to write your own functions in a later chapter.

The program ends with a **return 0;** statement. This statement ends the main function and returns a value of zero to the operating system. In Chapter 9, you will learn why it is important to include the **return** statement and why a zero is returned to the operating system when your program ends.

BRACES

Braces are used to mark the beginning and end of blocks of code. Every opening brace must have a closing brace. Notice in Figure 3-5 that the main function is enclosed in a set of braces. Providing comments after each closing brace helps to associate it with the appropriate opening brace. Also, aligning the indention of opening and closing braces is a good idea.

STATEMENTS

Functions contain statements that consist of instructions or commands that make the program work. Each statement in C++ ends with a semicolon.

SEMICOLONS

You must have a semicolon after every statement. The semicolon terminates the statement. In other words, it tells the compiler that the statement is complete. Notice, however, that directives such as **#include** and function declarations like **main()** are exempt from being punctuated by semicolons.

```
// COMMENT.CPP
// This program prints the common uses for comments
// to the screen.
// Program written by Greg Buxkemper

#include <iostream.h> // necessary for output statements

main()
{
  cout << "Use comments to:\n";
  cout << " - explain the purpose of a program.\n";
  cout << " - keep notes regarding changes to the program.\n";
  cout << " - store the names of programmers.\n";
  cout << " - explain the parts of a program.\n";
  return 0;
} // end of main function
```

F I G U R E   3 - 5
Comments can help identify braces.

C++ AND BLANK SPACE

C++ allows for great flexibility in the spacing and layout of the code. Use this feature to make it easier to read the code by indenting and grouping statements as shown in the sample program in Figure 3-2.

UPPERCASE OR LOWERCASE

Remember the ASCII codes? In the computer, an *A* is represented by a different number than an *a*. The capital letters are referred to as **uppercase**, and small letters are called **lowercase.**

C++ is known as **case sensitive** because it interprets uppercase and lowercase letters differently. For example, to a C++ compiler, the word *cow* is different than the word *Cow*. Be careful to use the same combination of lettering (either uppercase or lowercase) when you enter source code. Whatever capitalization was used when the command was originally named is what must be used. Most of what you will see in C++ will be in lowercase letters. If you key a command in uppercase that is supposed to be lowercase, you will get an error.

SECTION 3.1 QUESTIONS

1. List four uses for comments.

2. What compiler directive inserts source code from another file into your program?

3. What is a function?

4. What purpose do braces serve?

5. What does the term "case sensitive" mean?

From Source Code to a Finished Product

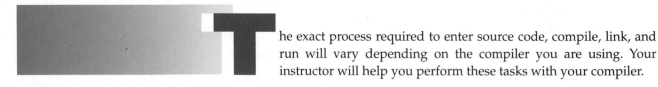

he exact process required to enter source code, compile, link, and run will vary depending on the compiler you are using. Your instructor will help you perform these tasks with your compiler.

ENTERING SOURCE CODE

The first step is to enter your C++ source code into a text file. Most C++ compilers have an integrated programming environment that contains a text editor you can use. An integrated programming environment allows you to enter your source code, compile, link, and run while your text editor is on the screen.

EXERCISE 3-1   ENTERING SOURCE CODE

1. Start your text editor with a new, blank file.

2. Enter the C++ source code *exactly* as it is shown below.

```
// MYPROG
// My first C++ Program

#include <iostream.h>

main()
{
  cout << "My first C++ program.\n";
  return 0;
}
```

Special Note: The "**\n**" causes the compiler to move the cursor to the beginning of the next line after printing the output to the screen.

3. Save the file as *MYPROG.CPP* and leave the program on your screen for the next exercise.

COMPILING, LINKING, AND RUNNING THE PROGRAM

Most compilers allow you to compile, link, and run with a single command from the integrated environment.

EXERCISE 3-2   COMPILING, LINKING, AND RUNNING THE PROGRAM

1. Compile, link, and run the program you entered in Exercise 3-1. If your compiler allows all of these operations to be performed with a single command, use that command. If your program fails to compile or link, check to see if you entered the code exactly as shown in Exercise 3-1 and try again.

2. If your program runs successfully, you should see the text *My first C++ program* on the screen. Otherwise, ask your instructor for help. *Note:* Some compilers may require that you give the integrated programming environment a command to show the program's output. Your instructor will know what command is necessary.

3. Leave the source file open for the next exercise.

MAKING CHANGES AND COMPILING AGAIN

You can add, change, or delete lines from a program's source code and compile it again. The next time the program is run, the changes will be in effect.

EXERCISE 3-3   MAKING CHANGES AND COMPILING AGAIN

1. Add the statement below to the main function, substituting your name in place of Angela Askins.

```
cout << "By Angela Askins\n";
```

Your program should now appear like the one below, except your name should be on the new line.

```
// MYPROG
// My first C++ program.

#include <iostream.h>

main()
{
  cout << "My first C++ program.\n";
  cout << "By Angela Askins\n";
  return 0;
}
```

2. Compile, link, and run the program again to see the change.

3. Save the source code file and leave it open for the next exercise.

CREATING A STANDALONE PROGRAM

Compiling, linking, and running a program, depending upon your specific compiler, may have already created a standalone program on disk. Your instructor will know for sure.

EXERCISE 3-4   CREATING A STANDALONE PROGRAM

If a standalone program was generated as a result of completing Exercise 3-3, quit the integrated programming environment and run the standalone program from the operating system. Otherwise, complete steps 1-3.

1. Select the option that allows you to compile and link to disk so that a standalone executable file is created.

2. Quit the integrated programming environment.

3. Run the executable program from the operating system.

LOADING AND COMPILING AN EXISTING SOURCE FILE

Often you will load an existing source code file and compile it. Most integrated programming environments have an Open command that can be used to open source files.

EXERCISE 3-5   LOADING AND COMPILING AN EXISTING SOURCE FILE

1. Start your integrated programming environment.

2. Open the source file TRAVEL.CPP. Your instructor will either provide you with a work disk or give you instructions for accessing the file from the hard disk or network.

3. Compile, link, and run the program.

4. When the program prompts you for data, enter values that seem realistic to you and see what output the program gives.

5. Run the program several times with different values.

6. Close the source file and quit.

Responsibilities of the Programmer

As you write more advanced computer programs, you should keep certain responsibilities in mind.

1. ***Privacy.*** *Programmers often have access to databases and other information about individuals. Programmers have a responsibility to protect the privacy of this information.*

2. ***Property Rights.*** *Ideas are not protected by copyright law. Actual program code, however, is. Using software that you do not have legal license to use, or using other programmers' source code without proper permissions is illegal and irresponsible.*

3. ***Impact of Software.*** *Software can do physical damage (such as viruses) or have social ramifications. Computers should not be used by programmers to cause harm to users, and the impact of a program on society should be considered before writing a program.*

4. ***Reliability.*** *Individuals, schools, businesses, and the government rely on computers more every year. Programmers have a responsibility to produce software that is as reliable as possible and to report and/or repair problems that may affect the reliability of the system.*

CONGRATULATIONS

Congratulations. You now know the basics of creating and running C++ programs. From here you will simply add to your knowledge to enable you to write more useful programs. If you feel you need more experience with compiling and running C++ programs, repeat the exercises in this chapter or ask your instructor for additional help. Future exercises require that you know how to compile, link, and run.

On the Net

For links to the web pages of major C++ compiler makers, see http://www. ProgramCPP.com. See topic 3.2.1.

SECTION 3.2 QUESTIONS

1. What company developed the compiler you are using?

2. What is the name of the compiler you are using and its version number?

3. What command or commands are used to run a program with your compiler?

4. What command opens a source code file from a disk?

5. What command saves a source code file?

KEY TERMS

braces

case sensitive

comments

compiler directive

function

header file

lowercase

main function

statements

uppercase

SUMMARY

➤ A C++ program has several parts.

➤ Comments are remarks that are ignored by the compiler. They allow you to include notes and other information in the program's source code.

➤ Directives are commands for the compiler, rather than part of the C++ language.

➤ All C++ programs have a main function. The main function is where the program begins running.

➤ Braces mark the beginning and end of blocks of code.

➤ Statements are the lines of code the computer executes. Each statement ends with a semicolon.

➤ C++ allows you to indent and insert space in any way that you want. You should take advantage of this flexibility to format source code in a way that makes programs more readable.

➤ C++ is case sensitive, which means that using the wrong capitalization will result in errors.

PROJECTS

PROJECT 3-1

Enter the program shown below but substitute your name and the appropriate information for your compiler. Compile, link, and run. Save the source code as *COMPINFO.CPP*.

```
// COMPINFO
// By Jeremy Wilson

#include <iostream.h>

main()
{
  cout << "This program was compiled using\n";
  cout << "Colossal C++ version 2.5.\n";
  return 0;
}
```

PROJECT 3-2

Open the source file *BRACES.CPP*, compile it, link, and run. After you have run the program, close the source file and quit.

PROJECT 3-3

Write a program that prints the message of your choice to the screen. Make the message at least four lines long. Save the source code file as *MY_MSG.CPP*.

4

Variables and Constants

OBJECTIVES

➤ Understand the different variable types used in C++ and how they differ from constants.

➤ Declare, name, and initialize variables.

➤ Use constants.

Overview

Computer programs process data to provide information. The job of the programmer is to properly organize data for storage and use. Most data used by programs is stored in either variables or constants. A *variable* holds data that can change while the program is running. A *constant* is used to store data that remains the same throughout the program's execution.

Variable Types

There are more than a dozen types of variables in C++ that can store numbers and characters. Some variables are for storing integers (whole numbers). Other variables are for floating-point numbers (real numbers).

You may recall from math courses that an integer is a positive or negative whole number, such as -2, 4, and 5133. Real numbers can be whole numbers or decimals and can be either positive or negative, such as 1.99, -2.5, 3.14159, and 4.

Data types are of little concern in the real world. When programming in C++, however, you must select a type of variable, called a **data type**, that best fits the nature of the data itself. Let's now examine the data types that are available for C++ variables.

INTEGER TYPES

When you are working with either positive or negative whole numbers, you should use integer data types for your variables. There are several integer data types available in C++. Selecting which integer data type to use is the next step.

Table 4-1 lists the variable data types that are for storing integers. Notice the range of values that each type can hold. For example, any value from -32,768 to 32,767 can be stored in a variable if the *int* data type is chosen. If you need to store a value outside of that specific range, you must choose a different data type.

INTEGER DATA TYPES	MINIMUM RANGE OF VALUES	MINIMUM NUMBER OF BYTES OCCUPIED
char	–128 to 127	1
unsigned char	0 to 255	1
int	–32,768 to 32,767	2
short	–32,768 to 32,767	2
unsigned int	0 to 65,535	2
long	–2,147,483,648 to 2,147,483,647	4
unsigned long	0 to 4,294,967,295	4

T A B L E   4 - 1

Notice the range of values for *unsigned* data types in Table 4-1. An unsigned variable can store only positive numbers. For example, if you were to be storing the weights of trucks in variables, an unsigned data type might be a good choice. A truck can't weigh less than zero.

Why would you want to use the int type when the long type has a bigger range? The answer is that you *can* use the long type when an int would do, but there is more to consider. Notice the third column of Table 4-1. The variables with the larger ranges require more of the computer's memory. In addition, it often takes the computer longer to access the data types that require more memory. Having all of these data types gives the programmer the ability to use only what is necessary for each variable, decrease memory usage, and increase speed.

CHARACTERS

Recall from Chapter 2 that in the computer, characters are stored as numbers, and that the ASCII codes are what the computer uses to assign numbers to the characters. Because the computer considers characters to be numbers, they are stored in an integer data type named *char*.

Each variable of the char data type can hold only one character. In order to store words or sentences, you must *string* characters together. A group of characters put together to make a word or more is called a *string*. Sometimes you will hear a string referred to as an array of characters. You will learn more about characters and strings in a later chapter.

FLOATING-POINT TYPES

Integer variables are inappropriate for certain types of data. For example, tasks as common as working with money call for using floating-point numbers. Just as there is more than one type of integer, there is more than one type of floating-point variable.

Extra for Experts

Making Floating-Point More Efficient

*Earlier you read that floating-point numbers are not as efficient as integers. This is true. But many computer manufacturers include a floating-point unit (FPU) to help with the problem. A **floating-point unit** is a processor that works with floating-point numbers. FPUs are often called **math coprocessors.** Microprocessors with an FPU can perform calculations with floating-point numbers much more quickly than a microprocessor without an FPU. Some FPUs are on a chip separate from the microprocessor and some are built into the microprocessor chip.*

On the Net

To learn more about math coprocessors in modern microprocessors and how dramatically floating-point operations are increased by an FPU, see http://www.ProgramCPP.com. See topic 4.1.2.

Table 4-2 lists the three floating-point data types and their range of values. The range of floating-point data types are more complicated than the range of integers. Selecting an appropriate floating-point type is based upon both the range of values and the required decimal precision.

FLOATING POINT DATA TYPES	APPROXIMATE RANGE OF VALUES	DIGITS OF PRECISION	NUMBER OF BYTES OCCUPIED
float	3.4×10^{-38} to 3.4×10^{38}	7	4
double	1.7×10^{-308} to 1.7×10^{308}	15	8
long double	3.4×10^{-4932} to 1.1×10^{4932}	19	10

T A B L E   4 - 2

Note

The information in Table 4-2 may vary among compilers. Check your compiler's manual for exact data type ranges and bytes occupied for both integers and floating-point numbers.

When you are choosing a floating-point data type, first look to see how many digits of precision are necessary to store the value you need to store. For example, if you need to store π as 3.1415926535897, 14 digits of precision are required. Therefore you should use the double type. You should also verify that your value will fit within the range of values the type supports. But unless you are dealing with very large or very small numbers, the range is not usually as important an issue as the precision.

Let's look at some examples of values and what data types would be appropriate for the values.

Dollar amounts in the range $-99,999.99 to $99,999.99 can be handled with a variable of type *float*. A variable of type *double* can store dollar amounts in the range $-9,999,999,999,999.99 to $9,999,999,999,999.99.

The number 5.98×10^{24} kg, which happens to be the mass of the Earth, can be stored in a variable of type float because the number is within the range of values and requires only three digits of precision.

On the Net

To learn more about how floating-point numbers are stored in RAM, see http://www.ProgramCPP.com. See topic 4.1.3.

BOOLEAN VARIABLES

A *Boolean variable* is a variable which can have only two possible values. One of the values represents true (or some other form of the affirmative) and the other value represents false (or some other form of the negative). Boolean variables are very useful in programming to store information such as whether an answer is yes or no, whether a report has been printed or not, or whether a device is currently on or off.

On the Net

Boolean variables are named in honor of George Boole, an English mathematician who lived in the 1800s. Boole created a system called **Boolean algebra,** which is a study of operations that take place using variables with the values true and false. For more information about George Boole and Boolean algebra see http://www.ProgramCPP.com. See topic 4.1.4.

Some C++ compilers do not support a Boolean variable. Others have a data type **bool** which can be used to declare Boolean variables. If your compiler does not support the **bool** data type, you can use the **bool.h** header file on your work disk to make the feature available in your programs. Your instructor can help you access this header file. Later in this course, you will use the **bool** data type and examine the header file which makes it work.

SECTION 4.1 QUESTIONS

1. What integer data type is necessary to store the value 4,199,999,999?

2. Why is it important to use data types that store your data efficiently?

3. What range of values can be stored in an unsigned int variable?

4. What is a string?

5. What floating-point data type provides the most digits of precision?

Using Variables

You are now going to have an opportunity to put your knowledge to work and select the right variable for the job. You must first indicate to the compiler what kind of variable you want and what you want to name it. Then it is ready to use.

DECLARING AND NAMING VARIABLES

Indicating to the compiler what type of variable you want and what you want to call it is called *declaring* the variable.

DECLARING VARIABLES

You must declare a variable before you can use it. The C++ statement declaring a variable must include the data type followed by the name you wish to call the variable, and a semicolon. An integer variable named **i** is declared in Figure 4-1.

```
#include <iostream.h> // necessary for cout command

main()
{
  int i;     // declare i as an integer

  i = 2;
  cout << i << '\n';
  return 0;
}
```

F I G U R E   4 - 1
This program declares *i* as an integer.

Table 4-3 shows that declaring variables for other data types is just as easy as the example in Figure 4-1.

DATA TYPE	EXAMPLE C++ DECLARATION STATEMENT
char	`char Grade;`
unsigned char	`unsigned char T5;`
int	`int DaysInMonth;`
short	`short temperature;`
unsigned int	`unsigned int Age_in_dog_years;`
long	`long PopulationChange;`
unsigned long	`unsigned long j;`
float	`float CostPerUnit;`
double	`double Distance;`
long double	`long double x;`

T A B L E   4 - 3

C++ will allow you to declare a variable anywhere in the program as long as the variable is declared before you use it. However, you should get into the habit of declaring all variables at the top of the function. Declaring variables at the top of the function makes for better organized code, makes the variables easy to locate, and helps you plan for the variables you will need.

NAMING VARIABLES

The names of variables in C++ are typically referred to as *identifiers*. Notice how the variable names in Table 4-3 are very descriptive and consider how they might help the programmer recall the variable's purpose. You are encouraged to use the same technique. For example, a variable that holds a bank balance could be called **balance**, or the circumference of a circle could be stored in a variable named **circumference**. The following are rules for creating identifiers.

➤ Identifiers must start with a letter or an underscore (_). You should, however, avoid using identifiers that begin with underscores because the language's internal identifiers often begin with underscores. By avoiding the use of underscores as the first character, you will ensure that your identifier remains out of conflict with C++'s internal identifiers.

➤ As long as the first character is a letter, you can use letters or numerals in the rest of the identifier.

➤ Use a name that makes the purpose of the variable clear, but avoid making it unnecessarily long. Most C++ compilers will recognize only the first 31 or 32 characters.

➤ There can be no spaces in identifiers. A good way to create a multi-word identifier is to use an underscore between the words, for example **last_name**.

➤ The following words, called *keywords,* must NOT be used as identifiers because they are part of the C++ language. Your compiler may have additional keywords not listed here.

asm	delete	if	return	try
auto	do	inline	short	typedef
break	double	int	signed	union
case	else	long	sizeof	unsigned
catch	enum	new	static	virtual
char	extern	operator	struct	void
class	float	private	switch	volatile
const	for	protected	template	while
continue	friend	public	this	
default	goto	register	throw	

Recall from the previous chapter that C++ is case sensitive. The capitalization you use when the variable is declared must be used each time the variable is accessed. For example, **total** is not the same identifier as **Total**.

Table 4-4 gives some examples of illegal identifiers.

IMPROPER C++ VARIABLE NAMES	WHY ILLEGAL
Miles per gallon	Spaces are not allowed
register	register is a keyword
4Sale	Identifiers cannot begin with numerals

T A B L E   4 - 4

You can declare more than one variable in a single statement as long as all of the variables are of the same type. For example, if your program requires three variables of type float, all three variables could be declared by placing commas between the variables like this:

```
float x, y, z;
```

INITIALIZING VARIABLES

The compiler assigns a location in memory to a variable when it is declared. However, a value already exists in the space reserved for your variable. A random value could have been stored when the computer was turned on, or the location could retain data from a program that ran earlier. Regardless, the memory location now belongs to your program and you must specify the initial value to be stored in the location. This process is known as initializing.

Extra for Experts

Each byte of memory is filled with a value upon turning on your computer. The compiler sets up memory locations for your variables, and you initialize them. When your program is through with a variable, that memory location is once again made available to be used by a different variable or for another purpose. The value you last stored in the variable will remain in that memory location until it is assigned another value.

To *initialize* a variable, you simply assign it a value. In C++, the equal sign (=) is used to assign a value to a variable. In Figure 4-2, the variables **i** and **j** are initialized to the values of 3 and 2 respectively. Notice that the variable **k** has yet to be initialized because it is to be assigned the sum of **i** and **j**.

```
main()
{
  int i,j,k;      // declare i, j, and k as integers

  // initialize i, j, and k
  i = 3;
  j = 2;
  k = i + j;
  return 0;
}
```

F I G U R E   4 - 2
This program declares three integers and assigns values to them.

EXERCISE 4-1   DECLARING VARIABLES

1. Enter the following program into a blank editor screen:

```
// IDECLARE.CPP
// Example of variable declaration.

#include <iostream.h>

main()
{
  int i;              // declare i as an integer
  i = 0;              // initialize i to 0
  cout << i << '\n';
  return 0;
}
```

2. Save the source code file as *IDECLARE.CPP*.

3. Compile and run the program. The program should print the number 0 on your screen. If no errors are encountered, leave the program on your screen. If errors are found, check the source code for keyboarding errors and compile again.

4. Change the initialization statement to initialize the value of **i** to -40 and run again. The number -40 is shown on your screen. Save the source code again and leave the source code file open for the next exercise.

Assigning a floating-point value to a variable works the way you probably expect, except when you need to use *exponential notation.* You may have used exponential notation and called it scientific notation. In exponential notation, very large or very small numbers are represented with a fractional part (called the mantissa) and an exponent. Use an *e* to signify exponential notation. Just place an *e* in the number to separate the mantissa from the exponent. Below are some examples of statements that initialize floating-point variables.

```
x = 2.5;
ElectronGFactor = 1.0011596567;
Radius_of_Earth = 6.378164e6;    // radius of Earth at equator
Mass_of_Electron = 9.109e-31;    // 9.109 x 10^-31 kilograms
```

EXERCISE 4-2   DECLARING AND INITIALIZING FLOATING-POINT VARIABLES

1. Modify the program on your screen to match the program below.

```
// IDECLARE.CPP
// Example of variable declaration.

#include <iostream.h>

main()
{
```

```
float x, Radius_of_Earth, Mass_of_Electron;
int i;                  // declare i as an integer
i = 0;                  // initialize i to 0
x = 2.5;
Radius_of_Earth = 6.378164e6;
Mass_of_Electron = 9.109e-31;
cout << i << '\n';
cout << x << '\n';
cout << Radius_of_Earth << '\n';
cout << Mass_of_Electron << '\n';
return 0;
}
```

2. Compile and run the program. The integer and three floating-point values should print to the screen.

3. When the program runs successfully, close the source code file.

SECTION 4.2 QUESTIONS

1. Write a statement to declare an integer named **age** as an unsigned char.

2. What are the words called that cannot be used as identifiers because they are part of the C++ language?

3. Why can't "first name" be used as an identifier?

4. Write a statement that declares four int data type variables **i, j, k,** and **l** in a single statement.

5. What character is used to assign a value to a variable?

CHAPTER 4, SECTION 3

Constants

n C++, a constant holds data that remains the same as the program runs. Constants allow you to give a name to a value that is used several times in a program so that the value can be more easily used. For example, if you use the value of π (3.14159) several times in your program, you can assign the value 3.14159 to the name **PI**. Then, each time you need the value 3.14159, you need only use the name **PI**.

Constants are defined in a manner that is similar to the way you define a variable. You still must select a data type and give the constant a name. The difference is you tell the compiler that the data is a constant using the *const* keyword and assign a value all in the same statement.

The statement below declares **PI** as a constant.

```
const float PI = 3.14159;
```

Any valid identifier name can be used to name a constant. The same rules apply as with variables. Traditionally, uppercase letters have been used when naming constants. Lowercase letters are generally used with variable names. Therefore, uppercase letters help distinguish constants from variables. Some C++ programmers think lowercase letters should be used for constants as well as variables. In this book, we will use uppercase letters for constants because it will help you quickly identify constants in programs. Just be aware that you may see programs elsewhere that use lowercase letters for constants.

EXERCISE 4-3   USING CONSTANTS

1. Enter the following program. Save the source code as *CIRCLE.CPP.*

```cpp
// CIRCLE.CPP
// Example of using a constant.

#include <iostream.h>

main()
{
  const float PI = 3.14159;    // declare PI as a constant
  float circumference, radius;

  // Ask user for the radius of a circle
  cout << "What is the radius of the circle? ";
  cin  >> radius;

  circumference = 2 * PI * radius;   // calculate circumference

  // Output the circle's circumference
  cout << "The circle's circumference is ";
  cout << circumference << '\n';
  return 0;
}
```

2. Compile and run the program. Enter 4 as the radius of the circle. The program will return 25.132721 as the circumference.

3. An error message is generated if you add the following line at the end of the program. Add the line before the closing brace (}).

```cpp
PI = 2.5;
```

Remember that the value of a constant remains the same while the program is running.

4. Compile the program again to see the error generated.

5. Delete the line causing the error and compile the program again.

The compiler prohibits the assignment of another value to a constant after the declaration statement. If you fail to initialize the constant in the declaration statement, however, whatever value is in the memory location remains assigned to the constant throughout the execution of the program.

A good reason to use constants in a large program is that it gives you the ability to easily change the value of the constant in one place in the program. For example, suppose you have a program that needs the sales tax rate in several places. If you declare a constant named **TAX_RATE**, when the tax rate changes you have to change the constant only where it is declared. Every place in the program that uses the **TAX_RATE** constant is now going to use the new value.

SECTION 4.3 QUESTIONS

1. What is a constant?

2. What keyword is used to declare a constant in C++?

3. Write a declaration statement to create a constant named **PI** with 16 digit precision and use 3.141592653589793 for π. *Hint:* Choose your data type carefully.

4. Write a constant declaration statement to create a constant for the number of feet in a mile (5,280).

5. When is it appropriate to use constants?

KEY TERMS

Boolean variable	initialize
constant	keyword
data type	math coprocessor
declaring	string
exponential notation	unsigned
floating-point unit	variable
identifier	

SUMMARY

➤ Most data is stored in either variables or constants.

➤ There are several types of variables. Some are for integer data and some are for floating-point data.

➤ Integer data types are selected based on the range of values you need to store. Some integer data types are unsigned, meaning they can store only positive numbers.

➤ Characters are stored in the computer as numbers. The char data type can store one character of data.

➤ Floating-point data types are selected based on the range of values and the required precision.

➤ Boolean variables are variables which can have only two possible values: true or false.

➤ Variables must be declared before they are used. Variables should also be initialized to clear any random values that may be in the memory location. When a variable is declared, it must be given a legal name called an identifier.

▶ Constants are declared in a way similar to variables. The const keyword tells the compiler that the data is a constant. The constant must be assigned a value in the declaration statement.

PROJECTS

PROJECT 4-1

1. Enter, compile, and run the following program. Save the source code file as *DATATYPE.CPP*.

```
// DATATYPE.CPP
// Examples of variable declaration and
// initialization.

#include <iostream.h>

main()
{
  // declare a constant for the square root of two
  const double SQUARE_ROOT_OF_TWO = 1.414214;

  int i;              // declare i as an integer
  long j;             // j as a long integer
  unsigned long k;    // k as an unsigned long integer
  float n;            // n as a floating point number

  i = 3;              // initialize i to 3
  j = -2048111;       // j to -2,048,111
  k = 4000000001;     // k to 4,000,000,001
  n = 1.887;          // n to 1.887

  // output constant and variables to screen
  cout << SQUARE_ROOT_OF_TWO << '\n';
  cout << i << '\n';
  cout << j << '\n';
  cout << k << '\n';
  cout << n << '\n';
  return 0;
}
```

2. Add declarations using appropriate identifiers for the values below. Declare *e*, the speed of light, and the speed of sound as constants. Initialize the variables. Use any identifier you want for those values that give you no indication as to their purpose.

100	*e* (2.7182818)
−1000	Speed of light (3.00×10^8 m/s)
−40,000	Speed of sound (340.292 m/s)
40,000	

3. Print the new values to the screen.

4. Save, compile, and run. Correct any errors you have made.

5. Close the source code file.

PROJECT 4-2

Write a program that declares two constants (A and B). Initialize A = 1 an B = 2.2. Next, declare an int named C and a float named D. Initialize C = A and D = B. Write statements to print C and D to the screen.

PROJECT 4-3

Use your compiler's manuals or on-line help to determine the ranges and sizes of the data types available in your compiler. Compare your findings to Tables 4-1 and 4-2. If your compiler differs from the tables, record those differences. Also record any additional data types not listed in the tables.

Math Operations

➤ Use the arithmetic operators.

➤ Increment and decrement variables.

➤ Understand the order of operations.

➤ Use mixed data types.

➤ Avoid overflow, underflow, and floating-point errors.

Overview

n this chapter, you will learn about C++ math operations and demonstrate each concept by compiling and running programs.

First you will learn about C++ operators, some of which have already been mentioned. Next, you will learn how to build expressions using the operators. You will also learn shortcuts and how to avoid pitfalls.

CHAPTER 5, SECTION 1

The Fundamental Operators

here are several types of operators. In this chapter you will be concerned only with the assignment operator, arithmetic operators, and some special operators.

ASSIGNMENT OPERATOR

You have already used the assignment operator (=) to initialize variables. So you already know most of what there is to know about the assignment operator. The *assignment operator* changes the value of the variable to the left of the operator. Consider the statement below:

```
i = 25;
```

The statement **i = 25;** changes the value of variable **i** to 25, regardless of what it was before the statement.

EXERCISE 5-1   THE ASSIGNMENT OPERATOR

1. Turn on your computer and access the C++ compiler's text editor. Enter the following program onto a blank editor screen and save your source code file as *IASSIGN.CPP*.

```cpp
#include <iostream.h> // necessary for cout command

main()
{
  int i;     // declare i as an integer
  i = 10000;   // assign the value 10000 to i
  cout << i << '\n';
  i = 25;      // assign the value 25 to i
  cout << i << '\n';
  return 0;
}
```

2. Compile and run the program. Notice the difference between the value of **i** when it is displayed after the first **cout << i** and after the second.

3. Leave the source code file open for the next exercise.

Recall from Chapter 4 that you can declare more than one variable in a single statement. For example, instead of:

```
int i;
int j;
int k;
```

you can use:

```
int i,j,k;
```

You can use a similar shortcut when initializing multiple variables. If you have more than one variable that you want to initialize to the same value, you can use a statement like:

```
i = j = k = 25;
```

EXERCISE 5-2   MULTIPLE ASSIGNMENTS

1. Modify the program on your screen to read as follows:

```
#include <iostream.h> // necessary for cout command

main()
{
  int i,j,k;          // declare i,j, and k as integers

  i = j = k = 10;     // initialize all of the variables to 10
  cout << i << '\n';
  cout << j << '\n';
  cout << k << '\n';
  return 0;
}
```

2. Compile and run the program. The program's output is:

```
10
10
10
```

3. Close the source code file without saving.

Variables may also be declared and initialized in a single statement. For example, both of the following are valid C++ statements.

```
int i = 2;
float n = 4.5;
```

ARITHMETIC OPERATORS

A specific set of *arithmetic operators* is used to perform calculations in C++. These arithmetic operators, shown in Table 5-1, may be somewhat familiar to you. Addition and subtraction are performed with the familiar + and - operators. Multiplication uses an asterisk (*), and division uses a forward slash (/). C++ also uses what is known as a modulus operator (%) to determine the integer remainder of division. A more detailed discussion of the modulus operator is presented later in this section.

SYMBOL	OPERATION	EXAMPLE	READ AS...
+	Addition	3 + 8	three plus eight
-	Subtraction	7 - 2	seven minus two
*	Multiplication	4 * 9	four times nine
/	Division	6 / 2	six divided by two
%	Modulus	7 % 3	seven modulo three

T A B L E   5 - 1

USING ARITHMETIC OPERATORS

The arithmetic operators are used with two operands, as in the examples in Table 5-1. The exception to this is the minus symbol which can be used to change the sign of an operand. Arithmetic operators are most often used on the right side of an assignment operator, like the examples in Table 5-2. The portion of the statement on the right side of the assignment operator is called an *expression*.

STATEMENT	RESULT
`cost = price + tax;`	*cost* is assigned the value of *price* plus *tax*.
`owed = total - discount;`	*owed* is assigned the value of *total* minus *discount*.
`area = 1 * w;`	*area* is assigned the value of *l* times *w*.
`one_eighth = 1 / 8;`	*one_eighth* is assigned the value of 1 divided by 8.
`r = 5 % 2;`	*r* is assigned the remainder of 5 divided by 2 by using the modulus operator.
`x = -y;`	*x* is assigned the value of *-y*.

T A B L E   5 - 2

The assignment operator (=) functions differently in C++ than the equal sign functions in algebra. Consider the following statement:

```
x = x + 10;
```

The statement above is invalid for use in algebra because the equal sign is the symbol around which both sides of an equation are balanced. The left side equals the right side. But your C++ compiler looks at the statement differently. The expression on the right side of the equal sign is evaluated, and the result is *stored* in the variable to the left of the equal sign. In the statement above, the value of **x** is increased by 10.

EXERCISE 5-3

USING ARITHMETIC OPERATORS

1. Retrieve the file named *ASSIGN.CPP*.

2. Look at the source code and try to predict the program's output.

3. Run the program and see if you were correct in your prediction.

4. Close the source code file.

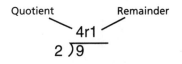

Quotient   Remainder

FIGURE 5-1
The division operator and modulus operator return the quotient and the remainder.

MORE ABOUT MODULUS

The *modulus operator*, which may be used only for integer division, returns the remainder rather than the result of the division. As shown in Figure 5-1, integer division is similar to the way you divide manually.

When integer division is performed, any fractional part that may be in the answer is lost when the result is stored into the integer variable. The modulus operator allows you to obtain the fractional part of the result as an integer remainder.

Consider the program in Figure 5-2. The user is prompted for two integers. Notice the program calculates the quotient using the division operator (/) and the remainder using the modulus operator (%).

```
// REMAIN.CPP
#include <iostream.h> // necessary for cin and cout commands

main()
{
  int dividend, divisor, quotient, remainder;

  // Get the dividend and divisor from the user.
  cout << "Enter the dividend ";
  cin >> dividend;
  cout << "Enter the divisor ";
  cin >> divisor;

  // Calculate the quotient and remainder
  quotient = dividend / divisor;
  remainder = dividend % divisor;

  // Output the quotient and remainder
  cout << "The quotient is " << quotient;
  cout << " with a remainder of " << remainder << '\n';
  return 0;
}
```

FIGURE 5-2
This program uses the modulus operator.

EXERCISE 5-4

THE MODULUS OPERATOR

1. Enter, compile, and run the program from Figure 5-2. Save the source file as *REMAIN.CPP*.

2. Run the program several times using values that will produce different remainders.

3. Leave the source file open for the next exercise.

USING OPERATORS IN OUTPUT STATEMENTS

The program in Figure 5-2 required four variables and nine program statements. The program in Figure 5-3 accomplishes the same output with only two variables and seven statements. Notice in Figure 5-3 that the calculations are performed in the output statements. Rather than storing the results of the expressions in variables, the program sends the results to the screen as part of the output.

```
// REMAIN.CPP
#include <iostream.h> // necessary for cin and cout commands

main()
{
  int dividend, divisor;

  // Get the dividend and divisor from the user.
  cout << "Enter the dividend ";
  cin >> dividend;
  cout << "Enter the divisor ";
  cin >> divisor;

  // Output the quotient and remainder
  cout << "The quotient is " << dividend/divisor;
  cout << " with a remainder of " << dividend % divisor << '\n';
  return 0;
}
```

FIGURE 5-3
Operators can be used in an output statement.

Avoid including the calculations in the output statements if you need to store the quotient or remainder and use them again in the program. But in situations like this, it is perfectly fine to use operators in the output statement.

EXERCISE 5-5

OPERATORS IN OUTPUT STATEMENTS

1. Modify the program on your screen to match Figure 5-3. Save the source file as *REMAIN2.CPP*. Compile it and run it.

2. Test the program to make sure you are still getting the same results.

3. Leave the source file open for the next exercise.

DIVIDING BY ZERO

Dividing by zero in math is without a practical purpose. The same is true with computers. In fact, division by zero always generates some type of error message.

EXERCISE 5-6

DIVISION BY ZERO

1. Run the program on your screen again. Enter zero for the divisor and see what error message is generated.

2. Close the source code file.

SPACES AROUND OPERATORS

Your C++ compiler ignores blank spaces. Both of the statements shown below are valid.

```
x=y+z;
x = y + z;
```

The only time you must be careful with spacing is when using the minus sign to change the sign of a variable or number. For example, **x = y - -z;** is perfectly fine. The sign of the value in the variable **z** is changed and then it is subtracted from **y**. If you failed to include the space before the **-z**, you would have created a problem because two minus signs together (--) has another meaning, which is examined later in this chapter.

COMPOUND OPERATORS

Often you will write statements which have the same variable on both sides of the assignment operator. For example, you may write a statement like **x = x + 2;** which adds 2 to the variable **x**. In cases like this, you may wish to use special operators, called *compound operators,* available in C++ that provide a shorthand notation for writing such statements.

Table 5-3 lists the compound operators, gives an example of each, and shows the longhand equivalent.

COMPOUND OPERATOR	EXAMPLE	LONGHAND EQUIVALENT
+=	i += 1;	i = i + 1;
-=	j -= 12;	j = j - 12;
*=	z *= 5.25;	z = z * 5.25;
/=	w /= 2;	w = w / 2;
%=	d %= 3;	d = d % 3;

T A B L E   5 - 3

If you want to use a compound operator on a statement such as the one below, be careful.

```
price = price - discount + tax + shipping;
```

Because the compound operators have a lower precedence in the order of operations (see Appendix B), you may get unexpected results. For example, simplifying the statement as shown below results in the wrong value because **discount + tax + shipping** is calculated and the sum of those are subtracted from **price**.

```
price -= discount + tax + shipping;   // this gives the incorrect result!
```

In this case, you can work around the problem by using parentheses and changing the compound operator to +=. To properly calculate the discount, the unary operator (-) is used to subtract the discount by adding it as a negative value.

```
price += (-discount + tax + shipping);
```

The complexity of dealing with the order of operations on statements with more than one value on the right side of the operator sometimes makes the short-hand notation more trouble than it's worth. Until you are comfortable with the problems presented by the order of operators, you may want to use compound operators with simple statements only.

On the Net

To learn more about the use of compound operators, and to see other related operators, see http://www.ProgramCPP.com. See topic 5.1.2.

SECTION 5.1 QUESTIONS

1. What is the assignment operator?

2. What does the modulus operator do?

3. Write a statement that stores the remainder of dividing the variable **i** by **j** in a variable named **k**.

4. Write a statement that calculates the volume of a box (V = abc) given the dimensions of the box. Use appropriate identifiers for the variables. You do not have to declare types.

5. Write a statement that calculates the sales tax (use 7%) for an item given the cost of the item and the tax rate. Store the value in a variable named **tax_due**. Use appropriate identifiers for the other variables. You do not have to declare types.

PROBLEM 5.1.1

Write a program that uses the statement you wrote in question 4 above in a complete program that calculates the volume of a box. Save the source code file as *VOLBOX.CPP*.

PROBLEM 5.1.2

Write a program that uses the statement you wrote in question 5 above in a complete program that calculates the sales tax for an item given the cost of the item and the tax rate. Save the source code file as *SALESTAX.CPP*.

Counting by One and the Order of Operations

n this section, you will learn two operators that allow you to increase or decrease the value stored in an integer variable by one. You will also learn the order that the computer applies operators in an expression.

INCREMENTING AND DECREMENTING

Adding or subtracting 1 from a variable is very common in programs. Adding 1 to a variable is called *incrementing* and subtracting 1 from a variable is called *decrementing*. You will have the need to increment or decrement a variable when a program must execute a section of code a specified number of times or when you need to count the number of times a process has been repeated.

THE ++ AND -- OPERATORS

C++ provides operators for incrementing and decrementing. In C++, you can increment an integer variable using the **++** *operator,* and decrement using the **--** *operator,* as shown in Table 5-4.

STATEMENT	EQUIVALENT TO...
counter++;	counter = counter + 1;
counter--;	counter = counter - 1;

T A B L E   5 - 4

> **Note**
>
> The ++ and -- operators can be used with any arithmetic data type, which includes all of the integer and floating-point types.

C = C + 1 or C++

The ++ operator is also part of the C programming language which was invented before C++. The ++ operator was made part of the new language's name because it was the next step after the C language.

You can increment or decrement a variable without the ++ or -- operators. For example, instead of **j++** you can use **j = j + 1**. With today's compilers, either way will produce efficient machine code. Some of the early C and C++ compilers translated the ++ and -- operators into more efficient machine language than would be generated by the addition or subtraction operator. Now, however, compilers optimize the machine code and will recognize that **j = j + 1** is the equivalent of **j++**.

EXERCISE 5-7

USING ++ AND --

1. Retrieve the file *INC_DEC.CPP*.
2. Compile and run the program.
3. Examine the output and leave the source code file open for the next exercise.

On the Net

Computers can increment and decrement numbers more quickly than they can add to or subtract from numbers. To learn why, go to http://www.ProgramCPP. com. See topic 5.2.1.

VARIATIONS OF INCREMENT AND DECREMENT

At first glance, the ++ and -- operators seem very simple. But there are two ways each of these operators can be used. The operators can be placed either before or after the variable. The way you use the operators changes the way they work.

Used in a statement by themselves, the ++ and -- operators can be placed before or after the variable. For example, the two statements shown below both increment whatever value is in **j**.

```
j++;
++j;
```

The difference in where you place the operator becomes important if you use the ++ or -- operator in a more complex expression, or if you use the operators in an output statement. First let's look at how the placement of the operators affects the following statement. Assume that **j** holds a value of 10.

```
k = j++;
```

In the case of the statement above, **k** is assigned the value of the variable **j** *before* **j** is incremented. Therefore, the value of 10 is assigned to **k** rather than the new value of **j**, which is 11. If the placement of the ++ operator is changed to precede the variable **j** (for example **k = ++j;**), then **k** is assigned the value of **j** *after* **j** is incremented to 11.

EXERCISE 5-8   OPERATOR PLACEMENT

1. Add a statement to the file named *INC_DEC.CPP* that declares **k** as a variable of type int.

2. Add the following lines to the program on your screen before the closing brace.

```
k = j++;
cout << "k = " << k << '\n';
cout << "j = " << j << '\n';
k = ++j;
cout << "k = " << k << '\n';
cout << "j = " << j << '\n';
```

3. Save the new source code file as *INC_DEC2.CPP*.

4. Compile and run the program to see the new output.

5. Close the source code file.

The increment and decrement operators can be used to reduce the number of statements necessary in a program. Consider the two statements below.

```
attempts = attempts + 1;
cout << "This is attempt number " << attempts << '\n';
```

Using the increment operator, one statement can do the job of two.

```
cout << "This is attempt number " << ++attempts << '\n';
```

In both cases, the variable named **attempts** is incremented and its value is printed to the screen. In the second example, the variable is incremented within the cout statement. The ++ operator must come before the variable named **attempts**. Otherwise, the value of the variable will be printed before it is incremented.

Note

Remember, the ++ operator actually changes the variable. If you replaced ++attempts with attempts + 1 in the cout statement, the value of the variable would remain the same. The screen, however, would print the result of attempts + 1.

ORDER OF OPERATIONS

You may recall the rules related to the order in which operations are performed from your math classes. These rules are called the *order of operations.* The C++ compiler uses a similar set of rules for its calculations.

1. Minus sign used to change sign (-)

2. Multiplication and division (* / %)

3. Addition and subtraction (+ -)

C++ lets you use parentheses to override the order of operations. For example, consider the two statements in Figure 5-4.

There are additional operators you will learn about later. To see how they fit into the order of operations, see Appendix B for a complete table of the order of operators.

FIGURE 5 - 4
Parentheses can be used to change the order of operations.

```
x = 1 + 2 * 3

x = 1 +    6

    x = 7


x = (1 + 2) * 3

x = 3    * 3

    x = 9
```

EXERCISE 5-9   ORDER OF OPERATIONS

1. Load the program ORDER.CPP.

2. Look at the source code and try to predict the program's output.

3. Run the program and see if your prediction is correct.

4. Close the source code file.

SECTION 5.2 QUESTIONS

1. Write a statement that increments a variable **m** using the increment operator.

2. If the value of **i** is 10 before the statement below is executed, what is the value of **j** after the statement?

   ```
   j = i++;
   ```

3. If the value of **i** is 4 before the statement below is executed, what is the value of **j** after the statement?

   ```
   j = --i;
   ```

4. What will the value of **j** be after the following statement is executed?

   ```
   j = 3 + 4 / 2 + 5 * 2 - 3;
   ```

5. What will the value of **j** be after the following statement is executed?

   ```
   j = (3 + 4) / (2 + 5) * 2 - 3;
   ```

PROBLEM 5.2.1

1. Write a program that declares an integer named **up_down** and initializes it to 3.

2. Have the program print the value of **up_down** to the screen.

3. Have the program increment the variable and print the value to the screen.

4. Add statements to the program to decrement the variable and print the value to the screen again.

5. Save the source code as *UPDOWN.CPP*, compile it, and run it.

PROBLEM 5.2.2

Write a program that evaluates the following expressions and prints the different values that result from the varied placement of the parentheses. Store the result in a float variable to allow for fractional values. Save the source code file as *PAREN.CPP*.

2 + 6 / 3 + 1 * 6 - 7

(2 + 6) / (3 + 1) * 6 - 7

(2 + 6) / (3 + 1) * (6 - 7)

How Data Types Affect Calculations

C++ allows you to mix data types in calculations (such as dividing a float value of 125.25 by an integer like 5). Although you should avoid it whenever possible, this section will show you the way to do it should you need to.

You learned in Chapter 4 that each data type is able to hold a specific range of values. When performing calculations, the capacity of your variables must be kept in mind. It is possible for the result of an expression to be too large or too small for a given data type.

MIXING DATA TYPES

Sometimes you may need to perform operations that mix data types but doing so is less than desirable. In fact, many programming languages do not allow it. But if you have to mix data types, it is important that you understand how to do it properly.

C++ can automatically handle the mixing of data types (called promotion), or you can direct the compiler on how to handle the data (called typecasting).

PROMOTION

Consider the program in Figure 5-5. The variable **number_of_people** is an integer. The other variables involved in the calculation are floating-point numbers. Before you mix data types, you should understand the way the compiler is going to process the variables.

```cpp
// SHARE.CPP
#include <iostream.h>

main()
{
   int number_of_people;   // declare number_of_people as an integer
   float money;            // declare money as a float
   float share;            // declare share as a float

   cout << "How many people need a share of the money? ";
   cin >> number_of_people;
   cout << "How much money is available to divide among the people? ";
   cin >> money;

   share = money / number_of_people;

   cout << "Give each person $" << share << '\n';
   return 0;
}
```

F I G U R E   5 - 5
This program uses mixed data types in its calculation.

In cases of mixed data types, the compiler makes adjustments so as to produce the most accurate answer. In the program in Figure 5-5, for example, the integer value is temporarily converted to a float so that the fractional part of the variable **money** can be used in the calculation. This is called *promotion.* The variable called **number_of_people** is not actually changed. Internally, the computer treats the data as if it were stored in a float. But after the calculation, the variable is still an integer.

MIXING DATA TYPES

1. Retrieve the file named *SHARE.CPP*. The program from Figure 5-5 appears in your editor.

2. Compile and run the program and observe how the mixed data types function.

3. Leave the source code file open for the next exercise.

Promotion of the data type can occur only while an expression is being evaluated. Consider the program in Figure 5-6.

The variable **i** is promoted to a float when the expression is calculated, which gives the result 1.5. But then the result is stored in the integer variable **answer**. You are unable to store a floating-point number in space reserved for an integer variable. The floating-point number is *truncated*, which means the digits after the decimal point are dropped. The number in **answer** is 1, which is not correct.

TYPECASTING

Even though C++ handles the mixing of data types fairly well, unexpected results can occur. C++ allows you to explicitly change one data type to another using operators called *typecast operators.* Using a typecast operator is usually referred to as *typecasting.*

Consider the program on your screen (*SHARE.CPP*). The calculated value in the variable **share** is of type float. If you are interested only in even dollar amounts, you can force the compiler to interpret the variable **money** as an integer data type by typecasting.

Note

Truncation is the equivalent of chopping off everything to the right of the decimal point. When a number is truncated, 1.00001 becomes 1 and 1.999999 also becomes 1.

```
#include <iostream.h>

main()
{
   int answer, i;
   float x;

   i = 3;
   x = 0.5;
   answer = x * i;

   cout << answer << '\n';
   return 0;
}
```

F I G U R E   5 - 6
Mixing data types can cause incorrect results.

To typecast a variable, simply supply the name of the data type you want to use to interpret the variable, followed by the variable placed in parentheses. The statement below, for example, typecasts the variable **diameter** to a float.

```
C = PI * float(diameter);
```

In cases where the data type to which you want to typecast is more than one word (for example long double), place both the data type and the variable in parentheses as shown in the example below.

```
C = PI * (long double)(diameter);
```

On the Net

There is more than one way to typecast variables in C++: an older style, which was used in C; the style you are using in this chapter; and a new style that is not yet supported by all C++ compilers. To learn more about typecasting and to see examples of all three styles, see http: //www.ProgramCPP.com. See topic 5.3.1.

EXERCISE 5-11   TYPECASTING

1. Change the type of **share** to int.
2. Change the calculation statement to read as follows.

```
share = int (money) / number_of_people;
```

3. Compile and run the program again.
4. Save the source code file and close it.

There are a number of ways to accomplish what was done in Exercise 5-11. The purpose of the exercise is to show you how to use the typecast operator in case you ever need it.

OVERFLOW

Overflow is the condition where an integer becomes too large for its data type. The program in Figure 5-7 shows a simple example of overflow. The expression **j = i + 2000;** results in a value of 34000, which is too large for the short data type.

An overflow condition may be difficult to identify. Figure 5-8 shows a program very similar to the one in Figure 5-7. In Figure 5-8, 34000 is divided by 2 before it is stored in the short data type. The result of 34000/2 is 17000, which is within the range of a short type. Although everything appears to be fine, a problem exists.

Because the short type is used in the calculation, even an intermediate result that exceeds the range of the short type (-32768 to 32767) will cause an overflow that results in an incorrect answer.

```
#include <iostream.h> // necessary for cout command

main()
{
  short i,j;

  i = 32000;
  j = i + 2000;   // The result (34000) overflows the short int type
  cout << j << '\n';
  return 0;
}
```

FIGURE 5-7
The result of the expression will not fit in the variable j.

```
#include <iostream.h> // necessary for cout command

main()
{
  short i,j;

  i = 32000;
  j = (i + 2000) / 2;
  cout << j << '\n';
  return 0;
}
```

FIGURE 5-8
What is wrong with this program?

EXERCISE 5-12   OVERFLOW

1. Enter, compile, and run the program in Figure 5-7. Notice that the calculation resulted in an overflow and an incorrect result.

2. Change the calculation statement to match Figure 5-8. Compile and run to see the result of the intermediate overflow.

3. Change the data type from short to long. Compile and run again. This time the result should not overflow.

4. Close the source file. There is no need to save.

UNDERFLOW

Underflow is similar to overflow. *Underflow* occurs with floating-point numbers when a number is too small for the data type. For example, the number 1.5×10^{-44} is too small to fit in a standard float variable. A variable of type double, however, can hold the value.

FLOATING-POINT ROUNDING ERRORS

Using floating-point numbers can produce incorrect results if you fail to take the precision of floating-point data types into account.

When working with very large or very small floating-point numbers, you can use a form of exponential notation, called **"E" notation**, in your programs. For example, the number 3.5×10^{20} can be represented as 3.5e20 in your program.

You must keep the precision of your data type in mind when working with numbers in "E" notation. Look at the program in Figure 5-9.

At first glance, the two calculation statements appear simple enough. The first statement adds 3.9×10^{10} and 500. The second one subtracts the 3.9×10^{10} which should leave the 500. The result assigned to **y**, however, is not 500. Actual values vary depending on the compiler, but the result is incorrect whatever the case.

The reason is that the float type is not precise enough for the addition of the number 500 to be included in its digits of precision. So when the larger value is subtracted, the result is not 500 because the 500 was never properly added.

```cpp
// FLOATERR.CPP
#include <iostream.h> // necessary for cout command

main()
{
  float x,y;

  x = 3.9e10 + 500.0;
  y = x - 3.9e10;

  cout << y << '\n';
  return 0;
}
```

F I G U R E   5 - 9
The precision of floating-point data types must be considered to avoid rounding errors.

EXERCISE 5-13   FLOATING-POINT PRECISION

1. Enter, compile, and run the program in Figure 5-9. See that the result in the variable **y** is not 500.

2. Change the data type of **x** and **y** to double and run again. The increased precision of the double data type should result in the correct value in **y**.

3. Save the source code file as *FLOATERR.CPP* and close the source code file.

SECTION 5.3 QUESTIONS

1. What is the term that means the numbers to the right of the decimal point are removed?

2. What is the typecast operator that changes a variable to an int?

3. Define overflow.

4. What is "E" notation?

5. How would you write 6.9×10^8 in "E" notation?

KEY TERMS

++ operator	modulus operator
-- operator	order of operations
arithmetic operators	overflow
assignment operator	promotion
compound operators	truncate
decrementing	typecast operators
"E" notation	typecasting
expression	underflow
incrementing	

SUMMARY

➤ The assignment operator (=) changes the value of the variable to the left of the operator to the result of the expression to the right of the operator.

➤ You can initialize multiple variables to the same value in a single statement.

➤ The arithmetic operators are used to create expressions.

➤ The modulus operator (%) returns the remainder of integer division.

➤ Expressions can be placed in output statements.

➤ Dividing by zero generates an error in C++.

➤ Spaces can be placed around all operators, but are not required in most cases.

➤ The ++ and -- operators increment and decrement arithmetic variables respectively.

➤ The placement of the ++ and -- operators becomes important when the operators are used as part of a larger expression or in an output statement.

➤ C++ calculations follow an order of operations.

➤ C++ allows data types to be mixed in calculations, but it should be avoided. When C++ is allowed to handle mixed data types automatically, variables are promoted to other types. You can explicitly change data types using typecasting.

➤ Overflow, underflow, and floating-point rounding errors can occur if you are not aware of the data types used in calculations.

PROJECT 5-1 • TRANSPORTATION

Suppose you have a group of people who need to be transported on buses and vans. You can charter a bus only if you can fill it. Each bus holds 50 people. You must provide vans for the 49 or fewer people who will be left over after you charter buses. Write a program that accepts a number of people and determines how many buses must be chartered and reports the number of people left over that must be placed on vans. *Hint:* Use the modulus operator to determine the number of people left over.

PROJECT 5-2 • MATHEMATICS

Write a program that calculates the area of an ellipse. Locate the formula for the calculation, prompt the user for the required inputs, and output the area.

PROJECT 5-3 • MATHEMATICS

Write a program that converts degrees to radians using the formula below.

radians = degrees / 57.3

PROJECT 5-4 • SPEED

Write a program that converts miles per hour to feet per second.

PROJECT 5-5 • FINANCE

Write a program that calculates simple interest (I = PRT) given the principal, the interest rate, and a period in years.

PROJECT 5-6 • ELECTRICITY

Write a program that calculates the current through a resistor given the voltage drop across the resistor and the resistance in ohms. Use the formula I = V/R, where V is voltage, R is resistance in ohms, and I is current in amps.

PROJECT 5-7 • PHYSICS

Write a program that calculates force (F=ma), where F = force in Newtons, m = mass in kilograms, and a = acceleration in meters/second.

PROJECT 5-8 • PHYSICS

Write a program that uses Einstein's $e=mc^2$ equation to find the amount of energy for a given mass.

PROJECT 5-9 • LAW ENFORCEMENT

Write a program that calculates the fine for a speeding ticket. Choose a base fine for violating the speed limit and an additional fine for each mile per hour over the speed limit.

PROJECT 5-10 • SURVEYING

Steel measuring tapes vary in length slightly depending on the temperature. When they are manufactured, they are standardized for 20 degrees Celsius (68 degrees Fahrenheit). As the temperature varies above or below 20 degrees C, the tape becomes slightly inaccurate, which must be taken into consideration. The formula below will produce a length correction given the length measured by the tape and the temperature in Celsius. (T = temperature, L = measured length)

$$C = 0.0000116 * (T - 20) * L$$

The adjusted length can be calculated using the following formula.

$$\text{new length} = L + C$$

Write a program that asks the user for a measured length and temperature in Celsius, and outputs an adjusted length using the formulas above.

Source of formulas: Elementary Surveying, Seventh Edition, Brinker & Wolf, Harper & Row, 1984.

Computer Graphics

By Steve Ferrera

In recent years, computers have changed the lives of many people through their capabilities of generating graphics. Although most people have seen and interacted with computer graphics, most have little or no understanding of the technology behind the pictures. It is helpful, however, to have some knowledge of computer graphics and to be familiar with the methods and terms used when dealing with them.

Computer graphics are pictorial representations of information. Their application can range from a graph of a company's earnings to a maze for a video game. Computers can store many graphic images which can later be used and manipulated by the user. In order to produce these graphics, a user needs a computer, a graphics software program, and the appropriate input and output devices. A common personal computer system, with a keyboard and a color monitor, can run fairly sophisticated graphics programs. Other input and output devices, including electronic sketchpads, video digitizers, video cameras, printers, and color plotters, can increase a computer's graphics capabilities.

Computer graphics utilize particular hardware and software technologies. On the hardware side, a great deal of time has been devoted to improving video displays. Most computer graphics are presented on a monitor, or Video Display Terminal, in the form of a cathode-ray tube, or CRT for short. The display method most commonly used is called raster-scan.

In a raster-scan CRT, an electron beam passes across the screen horizontally many times per second, generating an image that consists of a two-dimensional grid of dots. All of these dots together are known as a bit map and are closely spaced and arranged in rows and columns to produce an image. Each of these dots, called pixels, may be manipulated in color and intensity. As the number of pixels produced increases, the image resolution becomes finer and more distinct. However, the higher this resolution becomes, the greater is the amount of memory required to store the image.

On the software side, graphics programs apply special display algorithms, or internal data processing procedures, to form realistic images. For example, fractal algorithms create computer-generated geometric images. They are suitable for producing and analyzing irregular patterns and shapes in nature, such as clouds, mountains, and coastlines. Algorithms based on statistical probabilities, called fuzzy sets, are helpful in generating images of natural phenomena. An iterative algorithm can duplicate the same image many times, only making small changes in each successive image. Hidden-surface removal algorithms can delete lines and surfaces from unseen parts of an image. Colorizing can give a colorless image a wide range of colors.

Using computer-aided design (CAD) systems, images can be elaborately detailed and easily changed and manipulated, allowing them to be observed from any angle. Researchers use computer graphics for such purposes as producing three-dimensional perspectives of the human brain or studying how pollutants interact with certain meteorological phenomena. Besides the exploration of 3-D possibilities in a virtual reality, there is also an increasing application for education. For example, flight simulators help pilots and astronauts in training, and visualizations of complex mathematical equations have assisted students in learning.

Few industries, however, have taken advantage of the computer's ability to create and manipulate graphic images the way the entertainment industry has. Video games offer increasingly realistic play, and computers create special effects for movies.

Improved capabilities of personal computers and their programs have allowed consumers access to powerful graphics tools. Paint programs enable users to make a drawing and then apply color to it. Draw programs allow the creation of two- and three-dimensional images. Animation tools let users make action sequences automatically. Photographs, drawings, and video clips can be digitized and introduced into many graphics programs. Often computer users have collections of stored images called clip art, which can be used in the documents and images created by the user.

As users become familiar with computer graphics, their uses and applications will grow. For ex-ample, the charting abilities of spreadsheet software allow a person using a personal computer to create sophisticated charts and graphs. Other software helps computer users produce complicated graphics such as three-dimensional animation. With a good understanding of computer graphics and the methods and terms involved in creating graphics, users have an almost infinite range of possibilities.

Steve Ferrera is a Junior at Fenwick High School, Oak Park, Illinois.

6

Strings and Screen I/O

OBJECTIVES

➤ *Understand C++ strings.*

➤ *Use character arrays.*

➤ *Use console I/O for input and output.*

Overview

You learned about the character data type in Chapter 4 and that a group of characters put together to create text is called a string. Two types of strings are discussed in this chapter: string literals and strings stored in character arrays. You will learn how each type of string is stored and how they can be used in your programs.

You will also learn more about cin and cout as well as how to make the best use of them, including formatting your output.

Strings

Strings are one of the most useful kinds of data in a program. Strings help programs communicate with the user and allow computers to process data other than numbers. For example, when you prompt the user with a statement like "Enter the cow's weight:" you are using a string. Or when you ask the user to enter the cow's name, the name is a kind of string.

You must thoroughly understand how strings are stored and used in C++ so that you can avoid any difficulty or frustration. C++, in reality, provides the programmer with a flexibility in working with strings that you may come to appreciate.

WHAT IS A STRING AND HOW IS IT STORED?

A string is a group of characters that are put together to create text. In C++, you will be concerned with two ways of storing strings: string literals and character arrays.

UNDERSTANDING STRING LITERALS

The text "Hello" in the statement below is a string, specifically, a *string literal.* You used string literals with cout statements in earlier chapters.

```
cout << "Hello";
```

Notice that a string literal is "hard coded" into your program and is enclosed in quotation marks. A string literal is similar to a constant because it is part of the program's source code and remains the same while the program runs.

A lone character that appears in single quotes (') is a *character literal.* Single quotes are used only when a single character is between the quotes. String literals must be in double quotes. Figure 6-1 shows an example of a character literal and a string literal.

String literals end with an invisible character called a *null terminator.* The null terminator is the character represented by the ASCII value zero. For example, Figure 6-2 shows how the string literal in Figure 6-1 is stored in memory.

```
        initial = 'T';              // 'T' is a character literal

        cout << "Mark Gentry";      // "Mark Gentry" is a string literal
```

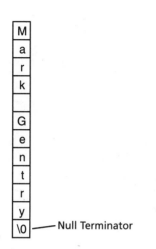

FIGURE 6 - 1
Character literals are enclosed in single quotes. String literals are enclosed in double quotes.

Each character in the string literal, including the null terminator, appears sequentially in memory. The null character tells the compiler the string has ended.

Note

In C++, \0 represents the null terminator. Together, the \ and 0 represent one character: the ASCII value zero.

String literals are different from an array of characters. An array of characters is used to store strings that change as the program runs. A string literal remains the same throughout the program's execution.

UNDERSTANDING ARRAYS OF CHARACTERS

String literals are very useful. But just like you need variables for numbers, you often need the equivalent of a variable for strings. However, C++ lacks a dedicated string data type, at least in the same way as there is an int or float type for numbers. Arrays of characters are used to store strings in C++.

An *array* is a group of variables of the same data type that appear together in the computer's memory. Later in this book, you will learn how to use all kinds of arrays. For now we will be concerned only with arrays of characters.

FIGURE 6 - 2
Strings end with a character called the null terminator.

An array of characters is a group of variables of the type char. When used together, each variable holds a character and the last variable in the string holds the null terminator. Remember, each char variable holds an ASCII value for the character, and the null terminator is the ASCII value zero. Figure 6-3 shows how the name Kaley would be stored as a character array.

USING C++ STRINGS

Because C++ strings are stored in character arrays, programmers have a great deal of flexibility when using strings. You can devote exactly the amount of memory you need to strings and easily manipulate individual characters in strings. But like other data types, using character arrays requires that you know how to properly declare and initialize them for use.

DECLARING CHARACTER ARRAYS

Declaring a character array is easy. The statement below declares a character array.

```
        char student_name[21];
```

FIGURE 6 - 3
An array of characters holds the ASCII value of each character in the string. The null terminator has the ASCII value of zero.

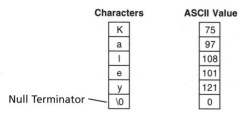

The name of the character array is **student_name**. Twenty-one char variables are set aside for the array. The character array **student_name** can hold a string of up to 20 printable characters plus the null terminator. You must always save room for the null terminator when declaring character arrays for strings.

Extra for Experts

A character array and a string are different. In C++, you declare a character array rather than a string. A string may then be stored in a character array.

INITIALIZING CHARACTER ARRAYS WITH STRINGS

A character array can be initialized when the array is declared. In fact, C++ makes the job easy. Consider the statement below.

```
char student_name[21] = "Aliver Villarreal";
```

The character array is declared and initialized with a string in a single statement. The null terminator is automatically entered by the compiler.

You may even use an initialization string to set the length of your character array if you are using fixed data as shown below:

```
char phone_number[] = "(806) 555-3210";
```

Because all of the phone numbers use the same format, the character array may be declared without specifying the exact number of characters. When you leave out the length of the array, the compiler creates an array just large enough for your string and the null terminator.

Note

Character arrays are the best data type to use with ZIP codes and phone numbers because ZIP codes and phone numbers are, in essence, characters. Phone numbers stored in character arrays, for example, can include parentheses and hyphens which are not allowed in numeric data types.

WARNING

Do not leave the brackets empty when declaring a character array if you have no initialization string. A statement like `char phone_number[];`*, by itself, will fail to allocate storage space for the array and on some compilers will cause an error.*

Also realize that once an initialization string is used to declare a character array its size is fixed. Attempting to store larger strings can cause problems in your program's execution and the output.

EXERCISE 6-1   DECLARING AND INITIALIZING CHARACTER ARRAYS

1.   Enter the following program and save the source code as *CHARRAY.CPP*.

```
// CHARRAY.CPP
#include <iostream.h>

main()
{
  char student_name[21] = "Aliver Villarreal";
  char phone_number[] = "(806) 555-3210";
```

```
  cout << student_name << '\n';
  cout << phone_number << '\n';
  return 0;
}
```

2. Compile and run the program to see if the character arrays are correctly initialized.

3. Leave the source code file open for the next exercise.

THE strcpy FUNCTION

If you try to assign a string to a variable as shown below you will get an error message. You can use an assignment operator only to store a string in a variable in the declaration statement.

```
student_name = "Aliver Villarreal";    // NOT LEGAL!!!
```

To get a string into an existing character array, you must use a special function: the **strcpy** function.

The **strcpy** function (pronounced "string copy") is very convenient when working with strings in C++. With the **strcpy** function, a string literal can be stored in a character array, or one character array can be copied to another. However, you must be sure the character array receiving the new data is long enough to accommodate it. The statement below shows how **strcpy** could be used to store a name in the **student_name** character array.

```
strcpy(student_name,"Aliver Villarreal");
```

The **strcpy** function can also be used to initialize a character array or to make a character array empty. The statement below initializes the **student_name** character array.

```
strcpy(student_name, "");
```

Shown below is the format of a statement that copies the contents of one character array to another.

```
strcpy(destination_array, source_array);
```

In order for the **strcpy** function to work, the compiler directive **#include <string.h>** must appear at the top of the program.

EXERCISE 6-2   USING strcpy

1. Add the following compiler directive at the top of the program you prepared in Exercise 6-1.

```
#include <string.h>
```

2. Add the following lines at the end of the program, before the closing brace.

```
strcpy(student_name, "Tan Pham");
cout << student_name << '\n';
```

3. Compile and run the program to see that the string "Aliver Villarreal" was replaced with "Tan Pham" in the character array.

4. Save the source code and close.

GETTING INTO TROUBLE

The flexibility of C++ strings can sometimes get you into trouble. The reason is that C++ does not prevent you from storing a string that is too long for the character array. What happens to the part of the string that extends beyond your array? It spills over into other storage spaces in memory and writes over them. This can cause real problems. In most cases, other variables or character arrays are overwritten. The result can be unpredictable at best. At worst, the computer can crash.

EXERCISE 6-3   STRING ERROR

1. Enter the following program and save the source code file as *STRERROR.CPP*.

```
// STRERROR.CPP
// Program that demonstrates string pitfalls.

#include <iostream.h>
#include <string.h>

main()
{
  char student_name[21] = "Brandon Adkins";  // declare four
  char city[] = "Lubbock";                    // character strings
  char state[3] = "TX";
  char ZIP_code[11] = "79413-3640";

  cout << student_name << '\n'; // display the strings
  cout << city << '\n';
  cout << state << '\n';
  cout << ZIP_code << '\n';

  strcpy(state,"California");    // copy a string that is too long
                                 // into the state character array

  cout << student_name << '\n'; // display the strings again
  cout << city << '\n';         // showing the overwritten array
  cout << state << '\n';
  cout << ZIP_code << '\n';
  return 0;
}
```

2. Compile and run the program. The results will vary depending on how your compiler orders the data in memory. But when the word *California* is copied into an array that is intended to hold only a two-character abbreviation, part of the word *California* will probably end up in another character array. Check the output from the second set of output statements to see if you can find the array that was overwritten.

3. Close the source code file.

1. What signifies the end of a C++ string?

2. Write a statement that prints the string literal "ABC" to the screen.

3. Write a statement that declares a character array of length 10 named ZIP.

4. Write a statement that declares a character array and initializes it to "555-55-5555". Let the compiler determine the length of the array.

5. Write a statement that copies the string in **new_string** to the character array **my_string**.

6. Write a statement that stores the string literal "New York" into the character array **state**.

PROBLEM 6.1.1

Write a program that declares a character array of length 20 and initializes it with your name. Next, have the program replace your name with the name Betsy Little. Have the program print the contents of the character array to the screen before and after replacing your name with Betsy Little's name. Save the source code file as *BETSY.CPP*.

PROBLEM 6.1.2

Write a program that declares two character arrays named A and B, and make each of length 10. Initialize B with the string "Hello", then copy the contents of B to A. Finally, copy the string "World" into B and print the contents of both strings to the screen. Save the source code file as *HELLO.CPP*.

CHAPTER 6, SECTION 2

Screen Input/Output

 ou have used simple input and output statements like the ones below without knowing all of the details.

```
cout << i << '\n';
cin >> j;
```

In this section, you will learn how to get the most out of input and output statements by learning about the missing details.

USING cin AND cout

We have treated cin and cout (pronounced *see-in* and *see-out*) as commands up to this point. You may be surprised, however, to learn that the << and >> symbols actually represent the action. Consider the simple statements below.

```
cout << j;
cin >> i;
```

The << and >> symbols are actually operators, like + and * are operators. The << symbol is the output operator, and >> is the input operator. As you know, the variable to the right of the << or >> operator is what is being input or output. So what are cout and cin? Well, cout is the *destination* of the output, and cin is the source of the input. The words "cin" and "cout" represent sources and destinations for data.

Some beginning programmers find it difficult to remember when to use << and when to use >>. There is a method you can use to help you remember. The symbols in the input and output operators point in the direction that the data is flowing. For example, in the statement **cout << j;**, the data is flowing from the variable **j** to the destination of the output (cout). When you use the input operator (as in **cin >> i;**), the data flows from the source of the input (cin) to the variable **i**.

STREAMS

When you think of a stream, you probably think of water flowing from one place to another. In C++, a *stream* is data flowing from one place to another. You should think of C++ streams as channels that exist to provide an easy way to get data to and from devices. The stream that brings data from your keyboard is cin, and the stream that takes data to your screen is cout.

For example, your monitor (screen) is a device. You don't have to understand exactly how output gets to the screen. You just have to know that cout is the stream that leads to your screen. When you use the output operator to place something in the cout stream, your screen is the destination.

There is almost always an exception to the rule, right? You should know that cin and cout may represent devices other than the keyboard and screen. The cin stream reads from what is called the *standard input device,* and the cout stream leads to the *standard output device.* By default, the standard input device is the keyboard and the standard output device is the screen. There are other streams that you will learn about in later chapters.

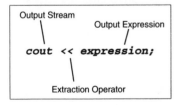

F I G U R E   6 - 4
The << operator is used for output.

USING CONSOLE I/O

The term *console I/O* refers to using the screen and keyboard for input and output (I/O is an abbreviation of input/output). In other words, the standard use of cin and cout is console I/O. Let's look at some examples of console I/O to make sure you understand the role of each part of the statements.

Figure 6-4 illustrates the general form of the << operator. The << operator indicates to the compiler that the statement is producing output. The destination of the output is the standard output device (the screen). The output can be any valid C++ expression.

The examples in Figure 6-5 show how the output can be a string literal, a variable, or a mathematical expression. The figure also shows that more than one item can be output in a single statement by using multiple output operators.

```
cout << "This string literal will appear on the screen. \n";
cout << distance;
cout << length_of_room * width_of_room;
cout << "The room is " << area << " square feet.\n";
```

FIGURE 6-5
The output operator can be used in a variety of ways.

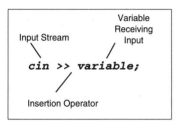

FIGURE 6-6
The >> operator is used for input.

Note

Remember, << is an operator. Therefore you can use it many times in the same output expression, just like you can use a mathematical operator multiple times in the same expression. For example, the statement n = 2 + 4 + 5, uses the addition operator twice. In the same way, the output operator can appear more than once in a statement.

Figure 6-6 illustrates the general form of the >> operator. The >> operator tells the compiler that the statement is requesting input. The source of the input is the standard input device (the keyboard). The destination of the input must be a variable or variables.

EXERCISE 6-4

BASIC CONSOLE I/O

1. Load, compile, and run *BASICIO.CPP* to review the basic use of input and output operators.

2. Close the source code file.

You will learn more about using the input operator later. For now, let's consider the options associated with the output operator.

FORMATTING OUTPUT

On the Net

The end-of-line character can mean different things on different operating systems. To learn more about how computers handle the end-of-line character, see http://www.ProgramCPP.com. See topic 6.2.1.

The appearance of the text on the screen can be controlled by formatting the output of your program. Usually, the output operator does a good job of formatting whatever data you output. There are times, however, when you need more control over the appearance of the output. C++ provides some options to help you get the output you want.

WHAT IS '\n'?

You have been including **'\n'** in output statements without a good explanation of what **'\n'** does. It is an important part of formatting output because it causes the cursor to return to the next line of the screen. The **\n** character is called the new line character or the end-of-line character. Use it in any output statement that completes a line. The new line character has the same effect in an output statement as pressing the Return or Enter key in a word processor.

The `\n` character must appear in double quotes if it is used in conjunction with other characters or may be used with single quotes if it appears alone. See the examples below.

```
cout << i << '\n';    // single quotes because it is a single character
cout << "String\n";   // double quotes because it is part of a string
```

The `\n` character can be enclosed in double quotes, even when it appears alone. The compiler will treat the character as a string because it is in double quotes. The statement will, however, produce the same result.

There is an alternative to `\n` that you may find easier to enter and more readable. You can enter **endl** in the place of `'\n'`. For example, the two statements below are functionally identical.

```
cout << i << '\n';
cout << i << endl;
```

You can use **endl** in place of the character `'\n'`, but do not use **endl** as part of a larger string. Think of **endl** as a constant that holds the value `'\n'`. If used in a statement like **cout << "String endl";**, the **endl** will be considered as part of the string and no end-of-line character will be included.

Other Special Characters

In addition to \n, there are other special characters (sometimes called escape sequences) you can use in output statements. The first one generates a tab character. The others allow you to print characters to the screen which would otherwise be unprintable because of the way they would be interpreted by the compiler.

The table below lists the important escape sequences.

Character Sequence	Result
\t	*Generates a tab character to move the cursor to the next tab stop.*
\\	*Prints a backslash (\).*
\'	*Prints a single quote mark (').*
\"	*Prints a double quote mark (").*

USING setf AND unsetf

Each stream has format options that can be changed. Table 6-1 lists the options that can be used.

OPTION	DESCRIPTION
left	Left-justifies the output
right	Right-justifies the output
showpoint	Displays decimal point and trailing zeros for all floating-point numbers, even if the decimal places are not needed
uppercase	Displays the "e" in E-notation as "E" rather than "e"
showpos	Displays a leading plus sign before positive values
scientific	Displays floating-point numbers in scientific ("E") notation
fixed	Displays floating-point numbers in normal notation

T A B L E   6 - 1

Now, examine how the format option *right* (indicating that the output is to be right justified) is used in the expanded format statement below.

```
cout.setf(ios::right);
```

You will learn more about how to use statements like the one above later. What is important now is that you understand that the word *right* is the format option.

Extra for Experts

If neither the scientific nor fixed option is set, the compiler decides the method to display floating-point numbers based on whether the number can be displayed more efficiently in scientific or fixed notation.

You can remove the options by replacing **setf** with **unsetf**, as in the example below.

```
cout.unsetf(ios::scientific);
```

EXERCISE 6-5   USING setf AND unsetf

1. Enter the following program and save the source code file as *COUTSETF.CPP*.

```
// COUTSETF.CPP
#include <iostream.h>

main()
{
  float x = 24.0;

  cout << x << '\n';            // displays 24

  cout.setf(ios::showpoint);
  cout << x << '\n';            // displays 24.000000

  cout.setf(ios::showpos);
  cout << x << '\n';            // displays +24.000000

  cout.setf(ios::scientific);
  cout << x << '\n';            // displays +2.400000e+01

  cout.setf(ios::uppercase);
  cout << x << '\n';            // displays +2.400000E+01

  cout.unsetf(ios::showpoint);
  cout << x << '\n';            // displays +2.4E+01

  cout.unsetf(ios::showpos);
  cout << x << '\n';            // displays 2.4E+01

  cout.unsetf(ios::uppercase);
  cout << x << '\n';            // displays 2.4e+01

  cout.unsetf(ios::scientific);
  cout << x << '\n';            // displays 24
  return 0;
}
```

2. Compile and run the program to see the effects of the format options.

3. Close the source code file.

Another set of format options are available in C++: the *I/O manipulators.* They may be placed directly in the output statement. Look at the example below which uses the **setprecision** I/O manipulator.

```
cout << setprecision(2) << price << '\n';
```

The **setprecision** manipulator sets the number of digits displayed to the number provided in the parentheses. The **setprecision** manipulator affects all floating-point numbers that follow it in the statement. It also affects any floating-point numbers output to the cout stream until **setprecision** is called again to set another precision. Table 6-2 shows two of the manipulators available.

Note

In order to use I/O manipulators, you must use the directive #include `<iomanip.h>` to include the necessary code to make the manipulators available.

WARNING

The setprecision manipulator may have a different effect depending on your compiler. Most compilers use setprecision to set the total number of digits displayed. For example, the value 5.2 will display as 5.20 if the precision is set to 3. Some compilers (particularly older compilers) use setprecision to set the number of digits to the right of the decimal place. For example, the value 5.2 will display as 5.200 if the precision is set to 3.

The **setw** manipulator can be used to change default field widths. You can use **setw** to set a minimum field width or use it to format numbers.

MANIPULATOR	DESCRIPTION
setprecision(*digits*)	Set the number of digits to be displayed
setw(*width*)	Set the width of the field allocated for the output

T A B L E   6 - 2

For example, if i = 254, j = 44, and k = 6, the statement **cout << i << j << k << '\n';** produces the output **254446** because only the space necessary to output the numbers is used. The statement below, however, adds spaces to the left of each number to give formatted output.

```
cout << setw(10) << i << setw(10) << j << setw(10) << k << endl;
```

The output of the statement above appears as shown below.

```
254        44        6
```

The best way to see the difference is to try it yourself in the next exercise.

EXERCISE 6-6   I/O MANIPULATORS

1. Enter the following program and save the source code as *IOMANIP.CPP*.

```
// IOMANIP.CPP
#include <iostream.h>
#include <iomanip.h>

main()
```

```
{
  int i = 1499;
  int j = 618;
  int k = 2;
  float a = 34.87432;

  cout << setw(10) << i << setw(10) << j << setw(10) << k << endl;
  cout << setw(10) << k << setw(10) << i << setw(10) << j << endl;

  cout << setprecision(3) << setw(10) << a << endl;
  return 0;
}
```

2. Compile and run the program to see how the **setw** manipulators affect the output of the integers. Notice how the last statement combines the **setprecision** and **setw** manipulators to properly align columns and decimal places.

3. Close the source code file.

GETTING INPUT WITH >>

You have learned most of what there is to know about using the >> operator. However, you must still learn how to input more than one variable in a single statement and understand the limitations of the >> operator.

GETTING MORE THAN ONE VALUE

More than one value can be input from the keyboard using a statement like the one below.

```
cin >> i >> j >> k;
```

When the statement above is executed, the program will pause and wait for three inputs. The three inputs could be entered all on the same line with spaces or tabs between them. Or the user can press Enter between the entries. A space, tab, or Enter is considered whitespace, and therefore is a delimiter or separator between the data. The use of a comma to separate data is prohibited in C++.

Note

*A **delimiter** is a character that signals the computer that one piece of data is ending and another one is beginning. In C++, spaces, tabs, and the Enter key create what is called **whitespace**.*

EXERCISE 6-7   MULTIPLE INPUTS IN A STATEMENT

1. Open *MULTI_IN.CPP*.

2. Compile and run the program. Enter **23 4 786** as input.

3. Run again and this time delimit the data by pressing Enter between the numbers.

4. Close the source file.

The >> operator can be used to input characters. If the user enters more than one character, only the first character will be stored in the variable.

EXERCISE 6-8   INPUTTING CHARACTERS

1. Enter the following program. Save the source code file as *INCHAR.CPP*.

```
// INCHAR.CPP
#include <iostream.h>

main()
{
  char c;

  cout << "Enter a single character: ";
  cin >> c;
  cout << "You entered " << c << '\n';
  return 0;
}
```

2. Compile and run the program. Provide different input (both single characters and complete words) and observe how they are processed similarly.

3. Close the source file.

INPUTTING STRINGS

The >> operator can be used to input strings, but there is a problem. As soon as a space or tab is reached (delimiters), the rest of the string is ignored. If you want to input a single word, you can use the same kinds of statements you use for numeric or character input. If you need to input strings with whitespace in them, you will have to use a function called **get**, which you will learn about after the next exercise.

EXERCISE 6-9   INPUTTING WORDS

1. Open *INWORD.CPP.*

2. Compile and run the program. Enter *Heath Keene* at the prompt. Notice that only the first name *Heath* is stored in the string. The space between *Heath* and *Keene* caused the rest of the string to be ignored.

3. Close the source code file.

USING get

The **get** function allows a string containing spaces and almost any other character to be entered into a character array. Therefore, using the **get** function is a better way to get a string from the user. The string input ends when you press Enter. You get to specify the maximum number of characters in your statement. Consider the example below.

```
cin.get(student_name, 20);
```

The identifier **student_name** is the character array and 20 is the maximum allowed length. The maximum allowed length includes one character for the null terminator, which the **get** function adds to the end of the string. So if you need a string of 20 printable characters, you should declare your character array for 21 characters and set the maximum length in the **get** function call to 21.

FLUSHING THE INPUT STREAM

Statements like **cin >> first_name;** and **cin.get(name, 21);** pull characters out of the standard input stream and place them in a character array. In both cases, it is possible for characters to be left over in the input stream after the statement is complete.

For example, in the statement **cin >> first_name;**, if the user enters *Becky Dailey*, only the first name will be placed in the character array because the space between *Becky* and *Dailey* terminates the operation. The last name and carriage return remain in the input stream.

A similar problem occurs with the **get** function. If the user enters a string that is longer than the length specified in the call to the **get** function, the remaining characters are left in the input stream. Furthermore, the **get** function always leaves the new line character in the input stream.

The problem with leaving characters in the input stream is that the next statement that asks for input will receive the characters left over from the previous input statement. To avoid this, you can use the **ignore** function to flush the contents of the input stream (also called the buffer). Consider the statement below.

```
cin.ignore(80, '\n');
```

The 80 tells the program to ignore the next 80 characters in the stream. The **'\n'** tells the function to stop ignoring characters when it gets to a carriage return. You could use a number smaller than 80 in most cases. The function will usually stop ignoring after only a few characters, because it will find a carriage return.

Flush the contents of the buffer after a call to the **get** function because the **get** function always leaves a new line character in the stream.

EXERCISE 6-10   USING THE get FUNCTION

1.   Enter the following program. Save the source code file as *INLINE.CPP*.

```
// INLINE.CPP
#include <iostream.h>

main()
{
  char name[21];

  cout << "Enter a name: ";
  cin.get(name, 21);
  cin.ignore(80, '\n');
  cout << "You entered " << name << '\n';
  return 0;
}
```

2. Compile and run the program. Enter *Heath Keene* at the prompt. Notice that the entire string is stored in the character array.

3. Close the source code file.

USING DESCRIPTIVE PROMPTS

When writing programs that interact with the user, be sure to output prompts that clearly explain the input the program is requesting. For example, if prompting the user for their name, use a descriptive prompt like the one below.

`Please enter your last name:`

If prompting for a telephone number or some other formatted data, you may want to use the prompt to give an example.

`Please enter your phone number using the format (555) 555-5555:`

The more descriptive and clear your prompts, the more likely the user is to enter the information in the form your program is expecting.

CLEARING THE SCREEN AND PRINTING A HARDCOPY

The techniques required to clear the screen and print to a printer vary, depending on the compiler and operating system you are using. Your compiler may have a function available for clearing the screen, or you may have to use another technique. Modern operating systems sometimes require special programming in order to send output to a printer. You may wish to send output to a text file on disk and then use a text editor to print the contents of the file.

On the Net

For more information about clearing the screen and printing, including sample code specific to your compiler, see http: //www.ProgramCPP.com. See topic 6.2.1.

SECTION 6.2 QUESTIONS

1. What is the purpose of **cout**?

2. What is another name for the input operator (>>)?

3. What is another name for the output operator (<<)?

4. What format option displays floating-point numbers in E-notation?

5. What I/O manipulator sets the number of digits to be displayed after the decimal point?

6. Write a statement that gets a number from the keyboard and stores it in a variable **i**.

7. Write a statement that outputs the result of the expression *PI * diameter*.

8. Write a statement that uses **setf** to display a leading plus sign before positive values.

9. Write a statement that outputs the variable **cost** with two decimal places.

10. Write a statement that inputs a line of text of maximum length 25 and stores it to a character array named **address**.

Write a program that asks the user for the diameter of a circle and returns the circumference of the circle. First, store the user's input (diameter) in a floating point variable. Next, the program should calculate PI * diameter using a declared constant for PI of 3.14159. Output the result of PI * diameter in normal notation with a precision of four digits to the right of the decimal point. Save the source code file as *CIRCUMFR.CPP*.

KEY TERMS

array	null terminator
character literal	standard input device
console I/O	standard output device
delimiter	stream
extraction operator	string literal
I/O manipulators	whitespace
insertion operator	

SUMMARY

➤ A string is a group of characters put together to make words or other text. A string in C++ can be any length and ends with a character called the null terminator.

➤ A string literal is any string of characters in a C++ program that appears between two quotation marks.

➤ Character arrays are used to store strings.

➤ Character arrays are declared by providing a name for the array and its length given in spaces.

➤ Character arrays can be initialized with a string when declared or a string can be copied to a character array after the declaration using **strcpy**.

➤ Because C++ allows you to store a string that is too long for an array, you must be careful when using strings.

➤ Streams as well as the << and >> operators are used for input and output in C++.

➤ Output can be formatted using **setf** and I/O manipulators.

➤ The input operator (>>) can be used to get more than one value in a statement and to input numbers or characters.

➤ If you need to input strings, you should use **get** rather than the >> operator.

PROJECT 6-1

Write a program that asks the user for a name, address, city, state, ZIP code, and phone number and stores each in appropriate character arrays. Use the ignore function to flush the input stream between inputs. After the strings are stored in the arrays, print the information back to the screen in the following format:

Name

Address

City, State, ZIP Code

Phone Number

PROJECT 6-2

Write a program that asks the user for three floating-point numbers in a single statement. Print the numbers back to the screen with a precision of one decimal point. Use a field width for the output that places the three numbers across the screen as in the example below.

Input: **123.443   33.22   1.9**

Output: **123.4   33.2   1.9**

PROJECT 6-3

Write a program that asks the user for two floating-point numbers. The program should multiply the numbers together and print the product to the screen. Next, ask the user how many digits to display to the right of the decimal point and print the product again with the new precision.

PROJECT 6-4 • THE STOCK MARKET

Write a program takes in the name, opening value, closing value, and number of shares owned for a stock. Have the program print the stock name, opening value, closing value, and amount of value the stock gained or lost in a formatted line.

PROJECT 6-5 • CALCULATING COSTS

A photoshop frames pictures as part of its business. All frames are one inch wide. The shop charges 25 cents for each inch of frame and 10 cents for each square inch of matting material. Write a program that takes the length and width of the picture as input and calculates the cost of framing the picture.

PROJECT 6-6 • CALCULATING COSTS

Write a program that calculates the cost of painting a room. Ask the user for the number of square feet of surface to be painted, the number of square feet per gallon intended (typically varies between 200 and 400 square feet, depending on thickness of the coat), and the cost per gallon of paint. Calculate the number of gallons required and the cost, assuming that the paint must be purchased in even gallons.

Overview

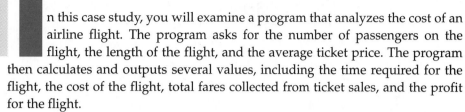

n this case study, you will examine a program that analyzes the cost of an airline flight. The program asks for the number of passengers on the flight, the length of the flight, and the average ticket price. The program then calculates and outputs several values, including the time required for the flight, the cost of the flight, total fares collected from ticket sales, and the profit for the flight.

Obviously, there is much more to take into consideration when calculating the profit an airline makes on a specific flight. The program, however, demonstrates many of the topics covered in the previous chapters.

Let's begin by loading, compiling, and running the program. Then we'll analyze the source code.

EXERCISE

1.   Retrieve the source code file *AIRLINE.CPP*.

2.   Compile and run the program. The program is configured for the Boeing 747-400 jet.

3.   Enter 300 for the number of passengers, 2500 for the length of the flight, and 349.25 as the average ticket price.

4.   The program provides the following as output:

```
Analysis for Boeing 747-400

The flight will take approximately 4.69 hours.
The cost of the flight will be $32546.90, with a
cost per passenger of $108.49.
The total fares collected from ticket sales is $104775.00,
resulting in a profit of $72228.09.
```

5.   Leave the source code file open.

Analyzing the Program

he complete source code for the program appears below. Spend a few minutes looking over the complete source code before reading the analysis that follows.

```
// Airline Flight Cost Analysis
// By Brian Davis and Todd Woolery

#include<iostream.h>   // necessary for input/output
#include<iomanip.h>    // necessary for setprecision manipulator
```

```
// main function
main ()
{
// constants to set specifications for a Boeing 747-400
// Source: The World Almanac and Book of Facts 1995
char const plane_name[] = "Boeing 747-400";
int const plane_speed = 533;
int const number_of_seats = 398;
int const max_flight_length = 4331;
int const cost_per_hour = 6939;

int num_pass;            // number of passengers on the plane
float num_miles;         // flight distance
float avg_ticket_price;  // average ticket price for flight
float flight_cost;       // cost for the flight
float cost_per_pass;     // cost per passenger
float total_fares;       // total fares collected for the flight
float profit;            // profit for the flight
float hours;             // length of flight in hours

cout << "\nAIRLINE FLIGHT ANALYSIS\n";
cout << "Airplane name: " << plane_name << endl;
cout << "Enter the number of passengers on the flight (maximum "
    << number_of_seats << "): ";
cin >> num_pass;
cout << "Enter the distance (in miles) of the flight (maximum "
    << max_flight_length << "): ";
cin >> num_miles;
cout << "Enter the average ticket price: ";
cin >> avg_ticket_price;

hours = num_miles / plane_speed;  // calculate time required for flight
flight_cost = hours * cost_per_hour; // calculate cost of flight
cost_per_pass = flight_cost / num_pass; // calculate cost per passenger
total_fares = num_pass * avg_ticket_price; // calculate total fares
profit = total_fares - flight_cost; // calculate flight profit

cout.setf(ios::showpoint);  // force decimal point to be displayed
cout.setf(ios::fixed);      // prevent scientific notation
cout << "\nAnalysis for " << plane_name << endl;
cout << "\nThe flight will take approximately " << setprecision(2)
    << hours << " hours.\n";
cout << "The cost of the flight will be $" << flight_cost
    << ", with a \n";
cout << "cost per passenger of $" << cost_per_pass << ".\n";
cout << "The total fares collected from ticket sales is $"
    << total_fares << ",\n";
cout << "resulting in a profit of $" << profit << ".\n";
return 0;
}
```

The program begins with two compiler directives that include **iostream.h**
and **iomanip.h**. They are both necessary to make the input and output functions
available.

Next, the main function begins. The remainder of the program is contained in the main function. Notice that the **#include** directives must appear before the main function.

The first set of statements in the main function (shown again below) define constants for a particular aircraft. Currently, the constants are based on a particular model of the Boeing 747. The plane name is stored in a constant character array. The brackets are left empty, which causes the compiler to allocate the appropriate array length based on the string being stored in the array. The other constants are integer values. These values will be used in calculations later in the program.

```
// constants to set specifications for a Boeing 747-400
// Source: The World Almanac and Book of Facts 1995
char const plane_name[] = "Boeing 747-400";
int const plane_speed = 533;
int const number_of_seats = 398;
int const max_flight_length = 4331;
int const cost_per_hour = 6939;
```

The next step is to declare variables. The variable that holds the number of passengers on the flight is declared as an integer; the others are floating-point variables. All of the constants and variables could have been declared as floating-point types to avoid the mixing of data types. Here, we will use integers where appropriate and allow the integer data types to be promoted during calculation.

```
int num_pass;            // number of passengers on the plane
float num_miles;         // flight distance
float avg_ticket_price;  // average ticket price for flight
float flight_cost;       // cost for the flight
float cost_per_pass;     // cost per passenger
float total_fares;       // total fares collected for the flight
float profit;            // profit for the flight
float hours;             // length of flight in hours
```

You should always clarify the use for each variable using comments, as was done in the declarations above.

The next group of statements (shown below) gets the required input from the user. Remember, **\n** or **endl** can be used to force the cursor to the next line of the screen. To give the user more information about the range of possible input, the number of seats and maximum flight length for the particular aircraft are part of the prompt for the input.

```
cout << "\nAIRLINE FLIGHT ANALYSIS\n";
cout << "Airplane name: " << plane_name << endl;
cout << "Enter the number of passengers on the flight (maximum "
    << number_of_seats << "): ";
cin >> num_pass;
cout << "Enter the distance (in miles) of the flight (maximum "
    << max_flight_length << "): ";
cin >> num_miles;
cout << "Enter the average ticket price: ";
cin >> avg_ticket_price;
```

After the input is gathered, the calculations must be performed. First, the time required for the flight is calculated using the statement below.

```
hours = num_miles / plane_speed;  // calculate time required for flight
```

The constant **plane_speed** is an integer, but **num_miles** and **hours** are both floating-point variables. Therefore, **plane_speed** is promoted to a floating-point type for the calculation, and the result, also a floating-point value, is stored in **hours**.

A similar promotion of an integer type occurs in the other calculations that follow. In each case, the result is a floating-point value. As shown in the statements below, the cost of the flight is calculated by multiplying the time required by the cost of operating the aircraft for an hour. That flight cost is divided by the number of passengers to get a cost per passenger. The total number of dollars collected from ticket sales is estimated by multiplying the average ticket price by the number of passengers. Finally, the projected profit for the flight is calculated by subtracting the cost of the flight from the dollars collected from ticket sales.

```
flight_cost = hours * cost_per_hour; // calculate cost of flight
cost_per_pass = flight_cost / num_pass; // calculate cost per passenger
total_fares = num_pass * avg_ticket_price; // calculate total fares
profit = total_fares - flight_cost; // calculate flight profit
```

The only task remaining is printing the output to the screen. The statements below format the output in paragraph form. The first two statements below are necessary to have the numbers appear in the desired format. The **showpoint** format option causes the decimal point to be displayed, even if a non-fractional value is being printed. The **fixed** option prevents numbers from appearing in scientific or "E" notation. In the fourth statement, the **setprecision** manipulator is used to specify that only two digits should be displayed to the right of the decimal point.

```
cout.setf(ios::showpoint);  // force decimal point to be displayed
cout.setf(ios::fixed);      // prevent scientific notation
cout << "\nAnalysis for " << plane_name << endl;
cout << "\nThe flight will take approximately " << setprecision(2)
    << hours << " hours.\n";
cout << "The cost of the flight will be $" << flight_cost
    << ", with a \n";
cout << "cost per passenger of $" << cost_per_pass << ".\n";
cout << "The total fares collected from ticket sales is $"
    << total_fares << ",\n";
cout << "resulting in a profit of $" << profit << ".\n";
```

Modifying the Program

As an additional exercise, modify the program to analyze another aircraft. Choose one of the four airplanes in the following table. *Hint:* Only the constants need to be modified to change the aircraft for the analysis.

AIRCRAFT	SEATS	SPEED	FLIGHT LENGTH	COST PER HOUR
L-1011	288	496	1498	4564
DC-10-10	281	492	1493	4261
B737-500	113	408	532	1594
F-100	97	366	409	1681

Source: The World Almanac and Book of Facts 1995.

When you run the program with specifications from an airplane other than the 747-400, notice how the input prompts change to provide you with the allowable range of values.

Decision Making in Programs

Overview

When you worked with algorithms in Chapter 2 you saw a flowchart that involved branching into different directions based on the answer to a question. In this chapter you will learn how branching is accomplished in C++ programs. You will learn the building blocks of computer decision making, and programming structures that cause different parts of a program to be executed based on a decision.

The Building Blocks of Decision Making

When you make a decision, your brain goes through a process of comparisons. For example, when you shop for clothes you compare the prices with those you previously paid. You compare the quality to other clothes you have seen or owned. You probably compare the clothes to what other people are wearing or what is in style. You might even compare the purchase of clothes to other possible uses for your available money.

Although your brain's method of decision making is much more complex than what a computer is capable of, decision making in computers is also based on comparing data. In this section, you will learn to use the basic tools of computer decision making.

DECISION MAKING IN PROGRAMS

Almost every program that is useful or user-friendly involves decision making. Although some algorithms progress sequentially from the first to the last instruction, most algorithms branch out into more than one path. At the point where the branching out takes place, a decision must be made as to which path to take.

The flowchart in Figure 7-1 is part of an algorithm in which the program is preparing to output a document to the printer. The user enters the number of copies he or she wants to print. To make sure the number is valid, the program verifies that the number of copies is not less than zero. If the user enters a negative number, a message is printed and the user is asked to reenter the value. If the user's input passes the test, the program simply goes on to whatever is next.

Decisions may also have to be made based on the wishes of the user. The flowchart in Figure 7-2 shows how the response to a question changes the path the program takes. If the user wants instructions printed on the screen, the program displays the instructions. Otherwise, that part of the program is bypassed.

The examples in Figures 7-1 and 7-2 are two common needs for decisions in programs. There are many other instances in which decisions must be made. As you do more and more programming, you will use decision making in countless situations.

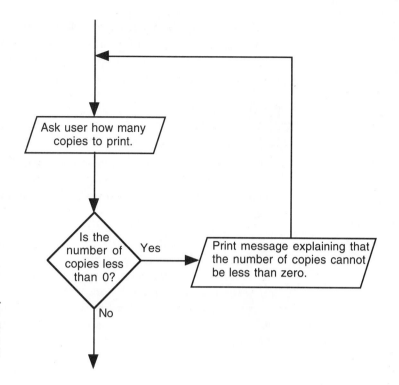

REPRESENTING TRUE AND FALSE IN C++

True and false are represented in C++ as numbers just like everything else. You may be surprised, however, to learn how important the concept of true and false is to programming.

The way computers make decisions is very primitive. Even though computers make decisions in a way similar to the way the human brain does, computers don't have intuition or "gut" feelings. Decision making in a computer is based on doing simple comparisons. The microprocessor compares two values and "decides" if they are equivalent. Clever programming and the fact that computers can do millions of comparisons per second sometimes make computers appear to be "smart."

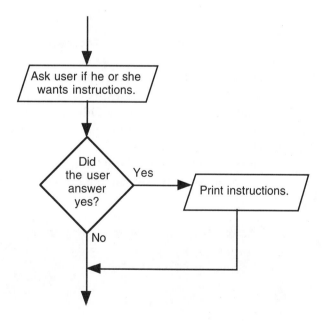

FIGURE 7-2
The path a program takes may be dictated by the user.

When the computer makes a comparison, the comparison results in a value of zero or one. If the resulting value is zero, it means the comparison proved false. If the result is one, the comparison proved true. So in C++, false is represented by the integer 0 and true is represented by the integer 1.

Extra for Experts

Fuzzy Logic

Fuzzy logic is a system that allows more than simply true or false. Fuzzy logic allows for some gray area. For example, instead of simply having a 0 for false and a 1 for true, fuzzy logic might allow a 0.9 as a way of saying "it's probably true."

Practical applications of fuzzy logic include things like the thermostat on your home's air conditioner. A standard thermostat turns the air conditioner on when the temperature goes above the desired comfort level. This causes the temperature in the house to rise and fall above and below the thermostat setting. A fuzzy logic thermostat could sense that the temperature is rising, and turn on the air conditioner before the temperature rises above the desired level. The result is a more stable room temperature and conservation of energy.

On the Net

For more information about fuzzy logic, see http://www.ProgramCPP.com. See topic 7.1.1.

RELATIONAL OPERATORS

To make comparisons, C++ provides a set of *relational operators,* shown in Table 7-1. They are similar to the symbols you have used in math when working with equations and inequalities.

RELATIONAL OPERATOR	MEANING	EXAMPLE
==	equal to	i == 1
>	greater than	i > 2
<	less than	i < 0
>=	greater than or equal to	i >= 6
<=	less than or equal to	i <= 10
!=	not equal to	i != 12

T A B L E   7 - 1

The relational operators are used to create expressions like the examples in Table 7-1. The result of the expression is one (true) if the data meets the requirements of the comparison. Otherwise, the result of the expression is zero (false). For example, the result of 2 > 1 is one (true), and the result of 2 < 1 is zero (false).

The program in Figure 7-3 demonstrates how expressions are made from relational operators. The result of the expressions is to be displayed as either a one or zero.

Note

Be careful when using the >= and <= operators. The order of the symbols is critical. Switching the symbols will result in an error.

WARNING

Do not confuse the relational operator (==) with the assignment operator (=). Use == for comparisons and = for assignments.

```
#include<iostream.h>

main()
{
 int i = 2;
 int j = 3;
 int true_false;

 cout << (i == 2) << '\n'; // displays a 1 (true)
 cout << (i == 1) << '\n'; // displays a 0 (false)
 cout << (j > i) << '\n';
 cout << (j < i) << '\n';  // Can you predict the
 cout << (j <= 3) << '\n'; // output of the rest of
 cout << (j >= i) << '\n'; // these statements?
 cout << (j != i) << '\n';

 true_false = (j < 4); // The result can be stored to an integer
 cout << true_false << '\n';
 return 0;
}
```

F I G U R E   7 - 3
Expressions created using relational operators return either a 1 or a 0.

EXERCISE 7-1

RELATIONAL OPERATORS

1. Load the program *RELATE.CPP*. The program from Figure 7-3 will appear. Can you predict its output?

2. Compile, link, and run the program.

3. After you have analyzed the output, close the source code file.

LOGICAL OPERATORS

Note

The key used to enter the or operator (||) is usually located near the Enter or Return key. It is usually on the same key with the backslash (\).

Sometimes it takes more than two comparisons to obtain the desired result. For example, if you want to test to see if an integer is in the range 1 to 10, you must do two comparisons. In order for the integer to fall within the range, it must be greater than 0 *and* less than 11.

C++ provides three *logical operators* for multiple comparisons. Table 7-2 shows the three logical operators and their meaning.

Figure 7-4 shows three diagrams called *truth tables*. They will help you understand the result of comparisons with the logical operators *and, or,* and *not*.

LOGICAL OPERATOR	MEANING	EXAMPLE
&&	and	(j == 1 && k == 2)
||	or	(j == 1 || k == 2)
!	not	result = !(j == 1 && k == 2)

T A B L E   7 - 2

AND			OR			NOT	
A	B	A && B	A	B	A || B	A	!A
false (0)	false (0)	false (0)	false (0)	false (0)	false (0)	false (0)	true (1)
false (0)	true (1)	false (0)	false (0)	true (1)	true (1)	true (1)	false (0)
true (1)	false (0)	false (0)	true (1)	false (0)	true (1)		
true (1)	true (1)	true (1)	true (1)	true (1)	true (1)		

F I G U R E   7 - 4
Truth tables illustrate the results of logical operators.

Consider the following C++ statement.

```
in_range = (i > 0 && i < 11);
```

The variable **in_range** is assigned the value 1 if the value of **i** falls into the defined range, and 0 if the value of **i** does not fall into the defined range.

The not operator (!) turns true to false and false to true. For example, suppose you have a program that catalogs old movies. Your program uses an integer variable named **InColor** that has the value zero if the movie was filmed in black and white and the value one if the movie was filmed in color. In the statement below, the variable **Black_and_White** is set to one (true) if the movie is *not* in color. Therefore, if the movie is in color, **Black_and_White** is set to zero (false).

```
Black_and_White = !InColor;
```

EXERCISE 7-2   LOGICAL OPERATORS

1. Enter the following program into a blank editor screen. Save the source code as *LOGICAL.CPP*.

```cpp
#include<iostream.h>

main()
{
  int i = 2;
  int j = 3;
  int true_false;

  true_false = (i < 3 && j > 3);
  cout << "The result of (i < 3 && j > 3) is " << true_false << '\n';

  true_false = (i < 3 && j >= 3);
  cout << "The result of (i < 3 && j >= 3) is " << true_false << '\n';

  cout << "The result of (i == 1 || i == 2) is "
      << (i == 1 || i == 2) << '\n';

  true_false = (j < 4);
  cout << "The result of (j < 4) is " << true_false << '\n';

  true_false = !true_false;
  cout << "The result of !true_false is " << !true_false << '\n';
  return 0;
}
```

2. Compile and run the program to see the output.

3. After you have analyzed the output, close the source code file.

COMBINING MORE THAN TWO COMPARISONS

You can use logical operators to combine more than two comparisons. Consider the statement below that decides whether it is okay for a person to ride a roller coaster.

```
ok_to_ride = (height_in_inches > 45 && !back_trouble
              && !heart_trouble);
```

In the statement above, **back_trouble** and **heart_trouble** hold the value 0 or 1 depending on whether the person being considered has the problem. For example, if the person has back trouble, the value of **back_trouble** is set to 1. The not operator (!) is used because it is okay to ride if the person does *not* have back trouble and does *not* have heart trouble. The entire statement says that it is okay to ride if the person's height is greater than 45 inches *and* the person has no back trouble *and* no heart trouble.

ORDER OF LOGICAL OPERATIONS

You can mix logical operators in statements as long as you understand the order in which the logical operators will be applied. The *not* operator (!) is applied first, then the *and* operator (&&), and finally the *or* operator (||). Consider the statement below.

```
dog_acceptable = (white || black && friendly);
```

The example above illustrates why it is important to know the order in which logical operators are applied. At first glance it may appear that the statement above would consider a dog to be acceptable if the dog is either white or black and also friendly. But in reality, the statement above considers a white dog that wants to chew your leg off to be an acceptable dog. Why? Because the *and* operator is evaluated first and then the result of the *and* operation is used for the *or* operation. The statement can be corrected with some additional parentheses, as shown below.

```
dog_acceptable = ((white || black) && friendly);
```

C++ evaluates operations in parentheses first just like in arithmetic statements.

EXERCISE 7-3   MIXING LOGICAL OPERATORS

1. Open *LOGICAL2.CPP*.

2. Compile, link, and run the program to see the effect of the parentheses.

3. Close the source code file.

SHORT-CIRCUIT EVALUATION

Suppose you have decided you want to go to a particular concert. You can only go, however, if you can get tickets and if you can get off work. Before you check whether you can get off work, you find out that the concert is sold out and you cannot get a ticket. There is no longer a need to check whether you can get off work because you don't have a ticket anyway.

C++ has a feature called *short-circuit evaluation* that allows the same kind of determinations in your program. For example, in an expression like **in_range = (i > 0 && i < 11);**, the program first checks to see if **i** is greater than 0. If it is not, there is no need to check any further because regardless of whether **i** is less than 11, **in_range** will be false. So the program sets **in_range** to false and goes to the next statement without evaluating the right side of the &&.

Short-circuiting also occurs with the or (||) operator. In the case of the or operator, the expression is short-circuited if the left side of the || is true because the expression will be true regardless of the right side of the ||.

On the Net

C++ has another set of operators, called **bitwise operators,** which allow you to work with the actual bits within a number or character. The bitwise operators allow you to apply operations such as AND and OR to the bits which make up a number or character. Although many programmers never use the bitwise operators, there are some interesting uses for them. To learn more about the bitwise operators and to see some programs which use bitwise operations, see http://www.ProgramCPP.com. See topic 7.1.2.

SECTION 7.1 QUESTIONS

1. In C++, what value represents false?

2. List two relational operators.

3. Write an expression that returns the numeric equivalent of true if the value in the variable **k** is 100 or more.

4. Write any valid expression that uses a logical operator.

5. Write an expression that returns the numeric equivalent of false if the value in the variable **m** is equal to 5.

6. What is the value returned by the following expression?

```
(((2 > 3) || (5 > 4)) && !(3 <= 5))
```

PROBLEM 7.1.1

In the blanks beside the statements in the program below, write a T or F to indicate the result of the expression. Fill in the answers beginning with the first statement and follow the program in the order the statements would be executed in a running program.

```
main()
{
 int i = 4;
 int j = 3;
```

```
    int true_false;

    true_false = (j < 4);                                    _____

    true_false = (j < 3);                                    _____

    true_false = (j < i);                                    _____

    true_false = (i < 4);                                    _____

    true_false = (j <= 4);                                   _____

    true_false = (4 > 4);                                    _____

    true_false = (i != j);                                   _____

    true_false = (i == j || i < 100);                        _____

    true_false = (i == j && i < 100);                        _____

    true_false = (i < j || true_false && j >= 3);            _____

    true_false = (!(i > 2 && j == 4));                       _____

    true_false = !1;                                         _____

    return 0;
}
```

CHAPTER 7, SECTION 2
Selection Structures

Programs consist of statements that solve a problem or perform a task. Up to this point, you have been creating programs with *sequence structures*. Sequence structures execute statements one after another without changing the flow of the program. Other structures, such as the ones that make decisions, do change the flow of the program. The structures that make decisions in C++ programs are called *selection structures*. When a decision is made in a program, a selection structure controls the flow of the program based on the decision. In this section, you will learn how to use selection structures to make decisions in your programs. The three selection structures available in C++ are the if structure, the if/else structure, and the switch structure.

USING if

Many programming languages include an *if structure*. Although the syntax varies among programming languages, the *if* keyword is usually part of every language. If you have used *if* in other programming languages, you should have little difficulty using *if* in C++. The if structure is one of the easiest and most useful parts of C++.

The expression that makes the decision is called the ***control expression.*** Look at the code segment below. First the control expression (i == 3) is evaluated. If the result is true, the code in the braces that follow the *if* is executed. If the result is false, the code in the braces is skipped.

```
if (i == 3)
    { cout << "The value of i is 3\n"; }
```

You can place more than one line between the braces, as in the code segment below.

```
if (YesNo == 'Y')
    {
    cout << "Press Enter when your printer is ready.\n";
    cin >> TempIn;
    }
```

Figure 7-5 shows the flowchart for an if structure. The if structure is sometimes called a ***one-way selection structure*** because the decision is whether to go "one way" or just bypass the code in the if structure.

Analyze the program in Figure 7-6. The program declares a character array of length 25 and an unsigned long integer. The user is asked for the name of their city or town, and for the population of the city or town. The if structure compares the population to a value that would indicate whether the city is among the 100 largest U.S. cities. If the city is one of the 100 largest U.S. cities, the program prints a message saying so.

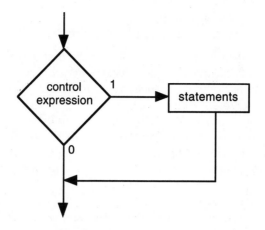

FIGURE 7-5
The if structure is sometimes called a one-way selection structure.

```cpp
#include <iostream.h>

main()
{
  char city_name[25];
  unsigned long population;

  cout << "What is the name of your city or town? ";
  cin.get(city_name, 25);
  cin.ignore(80,'\n');

  cout << "What is the population of the city or town? ";
  cin >> population;

  if (population >= 171439)
    {
      cout << "According to the 1990 census, " << city_name
           << " is one of\nthe 100 largest U.S. cities.\n";
    }
  return 0;
}
```

FIGURE 7-6
This program uses a one-way selection structure.

EXERCISE 7-4

USING if

1. Open *CITY.CPP*. The program from Figure 7-6 appears without the if structure.

2. Add the if structure shown in Figure 7-6 to the program. Enter the code carefully.

3. Compile, link, and run the program. Enter your city or town to test the program.

4. If your city or town is not one of the 100 largest cities, enter Newport News, a city in Virginia with a population of 171,439.

5. Leave the source code file open for the next exercise.

Earlier in this chapter you learned that 0 represents false and 1 represents true. But when it comes to making decisions based on a control expression, C++ considers anything other than 0 to be true. Therefore, any non-zero integer can represent true.

Why is this useful? Suppose you are using an integer to hold a value that represents an error condition. Zero (0) represents an error-free condition. When a value other than zero is present, however, an error exists and a message like the one below can be printed regardless of what error has occurred.

```
if (ErrorCode)
  { cout << "An error has occurred.\n"; }
```

USING if/else

The *if/else structure* is sometimes called a *two-way selection structure*. Using if/else, one block of code is executed if the control expression is true and another block is executed if the control expression is false. Consider the code fragment below.

```
if (i < 0)
   {cout << "The number is negative.\n"; }
else
   {cout << "The number is zero or positive.\n";}
```

The *else* portion of the structure is executed if the control expression is false. Figure 7-7 shows a flowchart for a two-way selection structure.

The code shown in Figure 7-8 adds an else clause to the if structure in the program in Exercise 7-4. Output is improved by providing information on whether the city's population qualifies it as one of the 100 largest U.S. cities. If

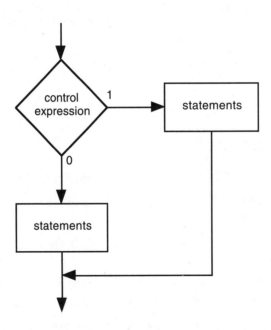

F I G U R E   7 - 7
The if/else structure is a two-way selection structure.

```
if (population >= 171439)
  {
    cout << "According to the 1990 census, " << city_name
         << " is one of\nthe 100 largest U.S. cities.\n";
  }
else
  {
    cout << "According to the 1990 census, " << city_name
         << " is not one of\nthe 100 largest U.S. cities.\n";
  }
```

F I G U R E   7 - 8
With an if/else structure, one of the two blocks of code will *always* be executed.

the population is 171,439 or more, the first output statement is executed; otherwise the second output statement is executed. In every case, either one or the other output statement is executed.

PITFALLS

Many programmers make the mistake of using > or < when they really need >= or <=. In the code segment in Figure 7-8, using > rather than >= would cause Newport News, the 100th largest city, to be excluded because its population is 171,439, not greater than 171,439.

EXERCISE 7-5   USING if/else

1. Add the else clause shown in Figure 7-8 to the if structure in the program on your screen. Save the new program as *CITYELSE.CPP*.

2. Compile, link, and run the program.

3. Enter the city of Gary, Indiana (population 116,646).

4. Run the program again using Raleigh, North Carolina (population 212,050).

5. Close the source code file.

NESTED if STRUCTURES

You can place if structures within other if structures. When an if or if/else structure is placed within another if or if/else structure, the structures are said to be *nested*. The flowchart in Figure 7-9 decides whether a student is exempt from a final exam based on grade average and days absent.

To be exempt from the final, a student must have a 90 average or better and cannot have missed more than three days of class. The algorithm first determines if the student's average is greater than or equal to 90. If the result is false, the student must take the final exam. If the result is true, the number of days absent is checked to determine if the other exemption requirement is met. Figure 7-10 shows the algorithm as a C++ code segment.

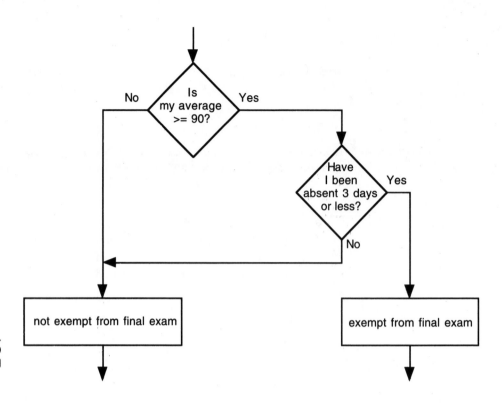

F I G U R E   7 - 9
This flowchart can be programmed using nested if structures.

```
exempt_from_final = FALSE;
if (my_average >= 90)
  {
    if (my_days_absent <= 3)
       { exempt_from_final = TRUE; }
  }
```

F I G U R E   7 - 1 0
Nested if structures can be used to check two requirements before making a final decision.

Algorithms involving nested if structures can get more complicated than the one in Figure 7-9. Figure 7-11 shows the flowchart from Figure 7-9 expanded to include another way to be exempted from the final exam. In this expanded algorithm, students can also be exempted if they have an 80 or higher average, as long as they have been present every day or missed only once.

Note

In the code segment in Figure 7-10, TRUE and FALSE have been declared as constants with the values 1 and 0 respectively. The variable that tells whether the person is exempt from the final is set to false. The program assumes that the student fails to meet the exemption qualification and tests to determine otherwise.

As you can probably imagine, programming the algorithm in Figure 7-11 will require careful construction and nesting of if and if/else structures. Figure 7-12 shows you how it is done.

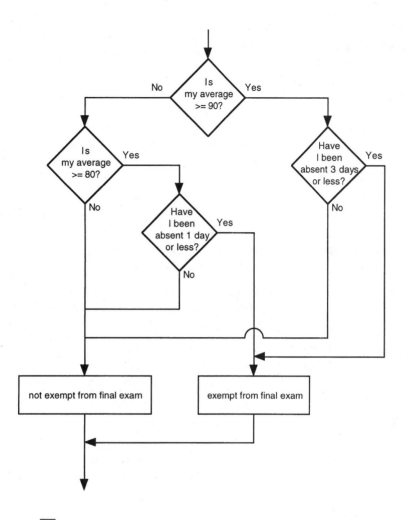

FIGURE 7-11
This algorithm provides two paths to exemption from the final.

Note

Earlier you learned that it is a good idea to always use braces with if structures. Figure 7-12 illustrates another reason why you should do so. Without the braces, the compiler may assume that the else clause goes with the nested if structure rather than the first if.

```
if (my_average >= 90)
  {                               // if your average is 90 or better
   if (my_days_absent <= 3)       // and you have missed three days
     { exempt_from_final = TRUE; } // or less, you are exempt.
  }
else  // if you don't have a 90+ average, you still have a chance
  { if (my_average >= 80)
     {                            // if your average is 80 or
      if (my_days_absent <= 1)    // better and you have missed
        { exempt_from_final = TRUE; } // one day or less, you are
     }                            // exempt.
  }
```

FIGURE 7-12
Nested if structures can require careful construction.

NESTED if STRUCTURES

1. Open *FINAL.CPP.*

2. Compile, link, and run the program. Run the program several times, testing different combinations of values.

3. When you have verified that the output is correct, close the source code file.

Extra for Experts

The nested if structure in Figure 7-12 is used to set the `exempt_from_final` *variable to true or false. Any type of statements could appear in the nested if statement. However, because the code in this case simply sets the value of the* `exempt_from_final` *variable, the entire nested if structure can be replaced with the statement below.*

```
exempt_from_final = (((my_average >= 90) && (my_days_absent <= 3)) ||
                      ((my_average >= 80) && (my_days_absent <= 1)));
```

Using logical operators, the statement above combines the expressions used in the nested if structure. The result is the value desired for `exempt_from_final`*. To prove it, replace the nested if structure in FINAL.CPP with the statement above and run the program again.*

Do not be fooled, however, into thinking that statements like the one above make if structures unnecessary. Ordinarily, a selection structure cannot be replaced with a sequence structure and achieve the same result.

Figure 7-13 shows a simple program that includes a nested if structure. The program asks the user to input the amount of money he or she wishes to deposit in order to open a new checking account. Based on the value provided by the user, the program recommends a type of account.

```cpp
#include <iostream.h>

main()
{
  float amount_to_deposit;

  cout << "How much do you want to deposit to open the account? ";
  cin  >> amount_to_deposit;

  if(amount_to_deposit < 1000.00 )
   {
     if(amount_to_deposit < 100.00 )
      { cout << "You should consider the EconoCheck account.\n"; }
     else
      { cout << "You should consider the FreeCheck account.\n"; }
   }
  else
   { cout << "You should consider an interest-bearing account.\n"; }
  return 0;
}
```

FIGURE 7-13
The nested if structure is used to make a recommendation.

MORE NESTED if

1. Open *DEPOSIT.CPP.* The program in Figure 7-13 appears.

2. Compile, link, and run the program. Run the program several times using values which are less than $100, between $100 and $1000, and greater than $1000.

3. Close the source code file.

THE switch STRUCTURE

Note

A **menu** *is a set of options presented to the user of a program.*

You have studied one-way (if) and two-way (if-else) selection structures. C++ has another method of handling multiple options known as the ***switch structure***. The switch structure has many uses, but may be most often used when working with menus. Figure 7-14 is a code segment that displays a menu of choices and asks the user to enter a number that corresponds to one of the choices. Then a case statement is used to handle each of the options.

Let's analyze the switch structure in Figure 7-14. It begins with the keyword *switch*, followed by the control expression (the variable **shipping_method**) to be compared in the structure. Within the braces of the structure are a series of *case* keywords. Each one provides the code that is to be executed in the event that **shipping_method** matches the value that follows case. The *default* keyword tells the compiler that if nothing else matches, execute the statements that follow.

The *break* keyword, which appears at the end of each case segment, causes the flow of logic to jump to the first executable statement after the switch structure.

```cpp
cout << "How do you want the order shipped?\n";
cout << "1 - Ground\n";
cout << "2 - 2-day air\n";
cout << "3 - Overnight air\n";
cout << "Enter the number of the shipping method you want: ";
cin >> shipping_method;

switch(shipping_method)
  {
    case 1:
     shipping_cost = 5.00;
     break;
    case 2:
     shipping_cost = 7.50;
     break;
    case 3:
     shipping_cost = 10.00;
     break;
    default:
     shipping_cost = 0.00;
     break;
  }
```

F I G U R E 7 - 1 4
The switch structure takes action based on the user's input.

EXERCISE 7-8   USING switch

1. Open *SHIPPING.CPP*. The program includes the segment from Figure 7-14.

2. Compile, link, and run the program. Choose shipping method 2.

3. Add a fourth shipping option called *Carrier Pigeon* to the menu and add the necessary code to the switch structure. You decide how much it should cost to ship by carrier pigeon.

4. Compile, link, and run to test your addition to the options.

5. Save the source code as *PIGEON.CPP* and close.

Nested if/else structures could be used in the place of the switch structure. But the switch structure is easier to use and a programmer is less prone to making errors that are related to braces and indentions. Remember, however, that an integer or character data type is required in the control expression of a switch structure. Nested if's must be used if you are comparing floats.

When using character types in a switch structure, enclose the characters in single quotes like any other character literal. The following code segment is an example of using character literals in a switch structure.

```cpp
switch(character_entered)
{
  case 'A':
    cout << "The character entered was A, as in albatross.\n";
    break;
  case 'B':
    cout << "The character entered was B, as in butterfly.\n";
    break;
  default:
    cout << "Illegal entry\n";
    break;
}
```

Extra for Experts

C++ allows you to place your case statements in any order. You can, however, increase the speed of your program by placing the more common choices at the top of the switch structure and less common ones toward the bottom. The reason is that the computer makes the comparisons in the order they appear in the switch structure. The sooner a match is found, the sooner the computer can move on to other processing.

SECTION 7.2 QUESTIONS

1. What is the purpose of the *break* keyword?

2. Write an if structure that prints the word *help* to the screen if the variable **need_help** is equal to 1.

3. Write an if/else structure that prints the word *Full* to the screen if the float variable **fuel_level** is equal to 1 and prints the value of **fuel_level** if it is not equal to 1.

4. What is wrong with the if structure below?

    ```
    if (x > y);
       { cout << "x is greater than y\n"; }
    ```

5. What is wrong with the if structure below?

    ```
    if (x = y)
       { cout << "x is equal to y\n"; }
    ```

PROBLEM 7.2.1

Write a program that asks for an integer and displays for the user whether the number is even or odd. *Hint:* Use if/else and the modulus operator. Save the source code file as *EVENODD.CPP*.

PROBLEM 7.2.2

Rewrite *FINAL.CPP* so that it begins with the assumption that the student is exempt and makes comparisons to see if the student must take the test. Save the revised source code as *FINAL2.CPP*.

KEY TERMS

bitwise operators	one-way selection structure
control expression	relational operators
fuzzy logic	selection structures
if structure	sequence structures
if/else structure	short-circuit evaluation
logical operators	switch structure
menu	truth tables
nested	two-way selection structure

SUMMARY

➤ Computers make decisions by comparing data.

➤ In C++, true is represented by 1 and false is represented by 0.

➤ Relational operators are used to create expressions that result in a value of 1 or 0.

➤ Logical operators can combine relational expressions.

➤ Selection structures are how C++ programs make decisions.

➤ The if structure is a one-way selection structure. When a control expression in an if statement is evaluated to be true, the statements associated with the structure are executed.

➤ The if/else structure is a two-way selection structure. If the control expression in the if statement evaluates to true, one block of statements is executed; otherwise another block is executed.

➤ The switch structure is a multi-way selection structure that executes one of many sets of statements depending on the value of the control expression. The control expression must evaluate to an integer or character value.

PROJECTS

PROJECT 7-1 • LENGTH CONVERSION

1. Open *LENGTHS.CPP* and analyze the source code.

2. Run it several times and try different conversions and values.

3. Add a conversion for miles to the program. Use 0.00018939 for the conversion factor.

4. Test the program.

PROJECT 7-2 • FINANCE

Obtain the exchange rates for at least three foreign currencies. Write a program similar in form to *LENGTHS.CPP* that asks for an amount of money in American dollars and then prompts the user to select the currency into which the dollars are to be converted.

PROJECT 7-3 • COMPUTERIZED TESTING

Write a program that asks the user a multiple-choice question on a topic of your choice. Test the user's answer to see if the correct response was entered. When the program works for one question, add two or three more.

PROJECT 7-4 • ASTRONOMY

Write a program that determines your weight on another planet. The program should ask for the user's weight on Earth, then present a menu of the other planets in our solar system. The user should choose one of the planets from the menu, and use a switch statement to calculate the weight on the chosen planet. Use the following conversion factors for the other planets.

Planet	Multiply by	Planet	Multiply by
Mercury	0.37	Saturn	1.15
Venus	0.88	Uranus	1.15
Mars	0.38	Neptune	1.12
Jupiter	2.64	Pluto	0.04

PROJECT 7-5 • CONSTRUCTION

Write a program that calculates the number of fence posts and amount of barbed wire necessary to build a barbed-wire fence. Ask the user how long the fence is to be, the distance between the posts, and how many strands of wire are to be placed on the fence.

Loops

OBJECTIVES

➤ *Explain the importance of loops in programs.*

➤ *Use for loops.*

➤ *Use while loops.*

➤ *Use do while loops.*

➤ *Use the break and continue statements.*

➤ *Nest loops.*

Overview

You have probably noticed that much of the work a computer does is repeated many times. For example, a computer can print a personalized letter to each person in a database. The basic operation of printing the letter repeats for each person in the database. When a program repeats a group of statements a given number of times, the repetition is accomplished using a *loop*.

In Chapter 7 you learned about sequence structures and selection structures. The final category of structures is *iteration structures*. Loops are iteration structures. Each "loop" or pass through a group of statements is called an *iteration*. A condition specified in the program controls the number of iterations performed. For example, a loop may iterate until a specific variable reaches the value 100.

In this chapter you will learn about the three iteration structures available in C++: the *for loop*, the *while loop*, and the *do while loop*.

CHAPTER 8, SECTION 1

The for Loop

The *for loop* repeats one or more statements a specified number of times. A for loop is difficult to read the first time you see one. Like an if statement, the for loop uses parentheses. In the parentheses are three items called *parameters*, which are needed to make a for loop work. Each parameter in a for loop is an expression. Figure 8-1 shows the format of a for loop.

```
for (initializing expression; control expression; step expression)
    {statement or statement block}
```

F I G U R E   8 - 1
A for loop repeats one or more statements a specified number of times.

Look at the program in Figure 8-2. The variable **i** is used as a counter. The counter variable is used in all three of the for loop's expressions. The first parameter, called the *initializing expression*, initializes the counter variable. The second parameter is the expression that will end the loop, called the *control expression*. As long as the control expression is true, the loop continues to iterate. The third parameter is the *step expression*. It changes the counter variable, usually by adding to it.

In Figure 8-2, the statements in the for loop will repeat three times. The variable **i** is declared as an integer. In the for statement, **i** is initialized to 1. The control expression tests to see if the value of **i** is still less than or equal to 3. When **i** exceeds 3, the loop will end. The step expression increments **i** by one each time the loop iterates.

─PITFALLS─

Placing a semicolon after the closing parenthesis of a for loop will prevent any lines from being iterated.

```
#include <iostream.h>

main()
{
 int i;
 for(i = 1; i <= 3; i++)
   cout << i << '\n';
 return 0;
}
```

F I G U R E   8 - 2
A for loop uses a counter variable
to test the control expression.

EXERCISE 8-1

USING A for LOOP

1. Key the program from Figure 8-2 into a blank editor screen.

2. Save the source code file as *FORLOOP.CPP*.

3. Compile and run the program.

4. Close the source file.

COUNTING BACKWARD AND OTHER TRICKS

A counter variable can also count backward by having the step expression decrement the value rather than increment it.

EXERCISE 8-2

USING A DECREMENTING COUNTER VARIABLE

1. Key the following program into a blank editor screen:

```
#include <iostream.h>

main()
{
  int i;
  for(i = 10; i >= 0; i--)
    cout << i << '\n';
  cout << "End of loop.\n";
  return 0;
}
```

2. Save the source file as *BACKWARD.CPP*.

3. Compile and run the program. Figure 8-3 shows the output you should see.

4. Close the source code file.

The output prints numbers from 10 to 0 because **i** is being decremented in the step expression. The phrase "End of loop." is printed only once because the loop ends with the semicolon that follows the first cout statement.

```
10
9
8
7
6
5
4
3
2
1
0
End of loop.
```

A for loop can decrement the counter variable.

The counter variable can do more than step by one. In the program in Figure 8-4, the counter variable is doubled each time the loop iterates. In the next exercise, you will see the effect of this for loop.

```cpp
#include <iostream.h>

main()
{
  int i;    // counter variable
  for(i = 1; i <= 100; i = i + i)
     cout << i << '\n';
  return 0;
}
```

F I G U R E   8 - 4
The counter variable in a for loop can be changed by any valid expression.

EXERCISE 8-3

INCREMENTING BY A STEP OTHER THAN ONE

1. Key the program from Figure 8-4 into a blank editor screen.

2. Save the source file as *DBLSTEP.CPP*. Can you predict the program's output?

3. Compile and run the program to see if your prediction was right.

4. Close the source file.

The for statement gives you a lot of flexibility. As you have already seen, the step expression can increment, decrement, or count in other ways. Some more examples of for statements are shown in Table 8-1.

for STATEMENT	COUNT PROGRESSION
for (i = 2; i <= 10; i = i + 2)	2, 4, 6, 8, 10
for (i = 1; i < 10; i = i + 2)	1, 3, 5, 7, 9
for (i = 10; i <= 50; i = i + 10)	10, 20, 30, 40, 50

T A B L E   8 - 1

USING A STATEMENT BLOCK IN A for LOOP

If you need to include more than one statement in the loop, use braces to make a statement block below the for statement. If the first character following a for statement is an open brace ({), all of the statements between the braces are repeated. The same rule applies as with if structures.

EXERCISE 8-4   USING A STATEMENT BLOCK IN A for LOOP

1. Open *BACKWARD.CPP* and edit the source code to match the following:

```
#include <iostream.h>

main()
{
  int i;
  for(i = 10; i >= 0; i--)
    {
      cout << i << '\n';
      cout << "This is in the loop.\n";
    }
  return 0;
}
```

2. Compile and run the program to see that the phrase *This is in the loop* prints on every line. The second cout statement is now part of the loop because it is within the braces.

3. Close the source file without saving changes.

Extra for Experts

Earlier in this chapter, you learned that placing a semicolon at the end of the parentheses in a for statement will cause the loop to do nothing. While it is true that the statements that follow will not be iterated, there are cases where you might actually want to do just that.

Suppose you are given an integer and asked to calculate the largest three-digit number that can be produced by repeatedly doubling the given integer. For example, if the given integer is 12, repeatedly doubling the integer would produce the sequence 12, 24, 48, 96, 192, 384, 768, 1536. Therefore 768 is the largest three-digit number produced by repeatedly doubling the number 12.

The program below uses an empty loop to achieve the result outlined above.

```
#include <iostream.h>
main()
 {
   long i;
   cin >> i;
   for ( ; i <= 1000; i = i * 2);
   cout << i/2 << '\n';
   return 0;
 }
```

The first parameter of the for statement is left blank because i is initialized by the user in the cin statement. Even though the loop is empty, the stepping of the counter variable continues and the value is available after the loop terminates. The value of i is 1000 or more when the loop ends. The cout statement then divides the counter by two to return it to the highest three-digit number.

On the Net

In some for loops, the variable referenced in the parameters is only needed inside the for loop. To accommodate this problem, C++ allows you to declare and initialize variables in the initializing expression of a for loop. For example, in Exercise 8-2 the variable i is used within the loop only. The program in Exercise 8-2 could be replaced with the source code below.

```
#include <iostream.h>

main ()
{
  for(int i = 10; i >= 0; i--)
    cout << i << endl;
  cout << "End of the loop.\n";
  return 0;
}
```

To learn more about advanced features of for loops see http://www.Program CPP.com. See Topic 8.1.1.

SECTION 8.1 QUESTIONS

1. What category of structures includes loops?

2. What is the name of the for loop parameter that ends the loop?

3. What for loop parameter changes the counter variable?

4. What happens if you key a semicolon after the parentheses of a for statement?

5. How many statements can be included in a loop?

6. Write a for statement that will print the numerals 3, 6, 12, 24.

7. Write a for statement that will print the numerals 24, 12, 6, 3.

PROBLEM 8.1.1

Write a program that uses a for loop to print the odd numbers from 1 to 21. Save the source file as *ODDLOOP.CPP*.

while Loops

A while loop is similar to a for loop. Actually, while loops are sometimes easier to use than for loops and are better suited for many loops. With a for loop, the parameters in the parentheses control the number of times the loop iterates and the statements in the loop structure are just along for the ride. In a while loop, something inside the loop triggers the loop to stop.

For example, a while loop may be written to ask a user to input a series of numbers until the number 0 is entered. The loop would repeat until the number 0 is entered.

There are two kinds of while loops: the standard while loop and the do while loop. The difference between the two is where the control expression is tested. Let's begin with the standard while loop.

THE WHILE LOOP

The *while loop* repeats a statement or group of statements as long as a control expression is true. Unlike a for loop, a while loop does not use a counter variable. The control expression in a while loop can be any valid expression. The program in Figure 8-5 uses a while loop to repeatedly divide a number by 2 until the number is less than or equal to 1.

In a while loop, the control expression is tested before the statements in the loop begin. Figure 8-6 shows a flow chart of the program in Figure 8-5. If the number provided by the user is less than or equal to 1, the statements in the loop are never executed.

PITFALLS

As with the for loop, placing a semicolon after the closing parenthesis of a while loop will prevent any lines from being iterated.

```
#include<iostream.h>

main()
{
 float num;
 cout << "Please enter the number to divide:";
 cin >> num;
 while (num > 1.0)
   {
    cout << num << '\n';
    num = num / 2;
   }
 return 0;
}
```

F I G U R E   8 - 5
A while loop does not use a counter variable.

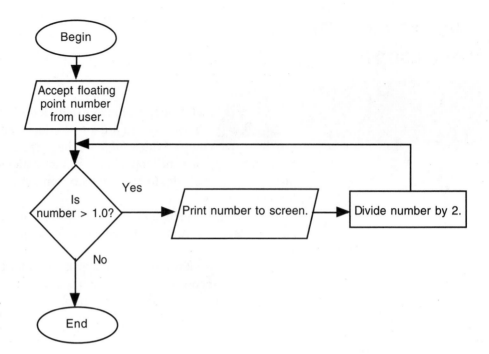

F I G U R E   8 - 6
A while loop tests the control expression before the loop begins.

EXERCISE 8-5

USING A while LOOP

1. Enter the program shown in Figure 8-5 into a blank editor screen.

2. Save the source file as *WHILE1.CPP*.

3. Compile and run the program. Run the program several times. Try the following numbers as input: 8, 21, 8650, 1, 2.1, 0.5.

4. Close the source file.

In order for a while loop to come to an end, the statements in the loop must change a variable used in the control expression. The result of the control expression must be false for a loop to stop. Otherwise, iterations continue indefinitely in what is called an *infinite loop*. In the program you compiled in Exercise 8-5, the statement **num = num / 2;** divides the number by two each time the loop repeats. Even if the user enters a large value, the loop will eventually end when the number becomes less than 1.

A while loop can be used to replace any for loop. So why have a for loop in the language? Because sometimes a for loop offers a better solution. Figure 8-7 shows two programs that produce the same output. The program using the for loop is better in this case because the counter variable is initialized, tested, and incremented in the same statement. In a while loop, a counter variable must be initialized and incremented in separate statements.

THE do while LOOP

The last iteration structure in C++ is the do while loop. A *do while loop* repeats a statement or group of statements as long as a control expression is true at the end of the loop. Because the control expression is tested at the end of the

```
#include <iostream.h>                    #include <iostream.h>

main()                                   main()
{                                        {
 int i;                                   int i;
 for(i = 1; i <= 3; i++)                  i = 1;
   cout << i << '\n';                     while(i <= 3)
 return 0;                                  {
}                                             cout << i << '\n';
                                             i++;
                                           }
                                          return 0;
                                         }
```

F I G U R E   8 - 7
Although both of these programs produce the same output, the for loop gives a more efficient solution.

loop, a do while loop is executed at least one time. Figure 8-8 shows an example of a do while loop.

To help illustrate the difference between a while and a do while loop, compare the two flow charts in Figure 8-9. Use a while loop when you need to test the control expression before the loop is executed the first time. Use a do while loop when the statements in the loop need to be executed at least once.

EXERCISE 8-6   USING A do while LOOP

1. Enter the program from Figure 8-8 into a blank editor screen.

2. Save the source file as *DOWHILE.CPP*.

3. Compile and run the program. Enter several numbers greater than 0 to cause the loop to repeat. Enter 0 to end the program.

4. Close the source file.

```
#include <iostream.h>

main()
{
 float num, squared;
 do
   {
    cout << "Enter a number (Enter 0 to quit): ";
    cin >> num;
    squared = num * num;
    cout << num << " squared is " << squared << '\n';
   }
 while (num != 0);
 return 0;
}
```

F I G U R E   8 - 8
In a do while loop, the control expression is tested at the end of the loop.

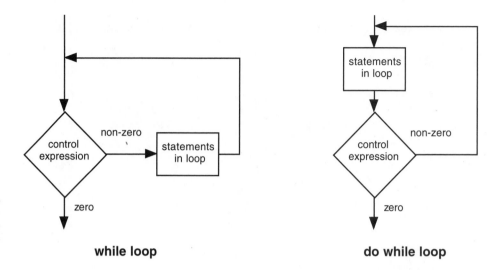

while loop   **do while loop**

F I G U R E   8 - 9
The difference between a while
loop and a do while loop is where
the control expression is tested.

On the Net

*Modern operating systems often require that programs be **event driven**, meaning that events such as the click of a mouse or a menu selection drives the flow of the program. At the heart of an event-driven program is a loop called an **event loop** which constantly iterates waiting for an event to occur. The program then takes action based on the event which has occurred. This differs from programs which pause at a prompt and wait for a command to be entered. To learn more about event-driven programming and event loops, see http://www.ProgramCPP.com. See topic 8.2.1.*

STOPPING IN THE MIDDLE OF A LOOP

The keyword *break*, also utilized with switch statements, can be used to end a loop before the conditions of the control expression are met. Once a break terminates a loop, the execution begins with the first statement following the loop. In the program you ran in Exercise 8-6, entering zero caused the program to end. But the program squares zero before it ends, even though the step is unnecessary. The program in Figure 8-10 uses a break statement to correct the problem.

In the program in Figure 8-10, the value entered by the user is tested with an if statement as soon as it is input. If the value is zero, the break statement is executed to end the loop. If the value is any number other than zero, the loop continues. The control expression can remain **num != 0** without affecting the function of the program. In this case, however, the break statement will stop the loop before the control expression is reached. Therefore, the control expression can be changed to 1 to create an infinite loop. The 1 creates an infinite loop because the loop continues to iterate as long as the control expression is true, which is represented by the value 1. The loop will repeat until the break statement is executed.

Note

You should allow the control expression to end an iteration structure whenever practical. Whenever you are tempted to use a break statement to exit a loop, make sure that using the break statement is the best way to end the loop.

```
#include <iostream.h>

main()
{
 float num, squared;
 do
   {
     cout << "Enter a number (Enter 0 to quit): ";
     cin >> num;
     if (num == 0)
        { break; }
     squared = num * num;
     cout << num << " squared is " << squared << '\n';
   }
 while (1);
 return 0;
}
```

FIGURE 8-10
The break statement ends the loop as soon as the value of zero is input.

The continue statement is another way to stop a loop from completing each statement. But instead of continuing with the first statement after the loop, the continue statement skips the remainder of a loop and starts the next iteration of the loop. Figure 8-11 shows an example of how the continue statement can be used to cause a for loop to skip an iteration.

The continue statement in Figure 8-11 causes the statements in the for loop to be skipped when the counter variable is 5. The continue statement also can be used in while and do while statements.

```
#include <iostream.h>

main()
{
 int i;
 for(i = 1; i <= 10; i++)
   {
     if (i == 5)
       continue;
     cout << i << '\n';
   }
 return 0;
}
```

FIGURE 8-11
The continue statement causes the number 5 to be skipped.

EXERCISE 8-7   USING THE continue STATEMENT

1. Open CONTINUE.CPP.

2. Compile and run the program. Notice that the number 5 does not appear in the output because of the continue statement.

3. Close the source file.

NESTING LOOPS

In Chapter 7 you learned how to nest if structures. Loops can also be nested. In fact, loops within loops are very common. You must trace the steps of the program carefully to understand how *nested loops* behave. The program in Figure 8-12 provides output that will give you insight into the behavior of nested loops.

```cpp
#include <iostream.h>

main()
{
  int i,j;
  cout << "BEGIN\n";
  for(i = 1; i <= 3; i++)
    {
      cout << " Outer loop: i = " << i << '\n';
      for(j = 1; j <= 4; j++)
        cout << "      Inner loop: j = " << j << '\n';
    }
  cout << "END\n";
  return 0;
}
```

F I G U R E   8 - 1 2
Even though this program has little practical use, it illustrates what happens when loops are nested.

The important thing to realize is that the inner for loop (the one that uses **j**) will complete its count from 1 to 4 every time the outer for loop (the one that uses **i**) iterates. That is why in the output, for every loop the outer loop makes, the inner loop starts over (see Figure 8-13).

```
BEGIN
 Outer loop: i = 1
      Inner loop: j = 1
      Inner loop: j = 2
      Inner loop: j = 3
      Inner loop: j = 4
 Outer loop: i = 2
      Inner loop: j = 1
      Inner loop: j = 2
      Inner loop: j = 3
      Inner loop: j = 4
 Outer loop: i = 3
      Inner loop: j = 1
      Inner loop: j = 2
      Inner loop: j = 3
      Inner loop: j = 4
END
```

F I G U R E   8 - 1 3
The output of the program in Figure 8-12 illustrates the effect of the nested loops.

EXERCISE 8-8   NESTED LOOPS

1. Open *NESTLOOP.CPP.*

2. Compile and run the program. *Note:* If you know how to use your compiler's debugger, step through the program to trace the flow of logic. (See Appendix F for more information on debugging.)

3. Close the source file.

```cpp
#include <iostream.h>

const char ERROR = '\0';

main()
{
 int num_reps;
 int i;              // counter used by for loop
 int democrats = 0, republicans = 0, independents = 0;
 char party;

 cout << "\nHow many U.S. representatives does your state have? ";
 cin  >> num_reps;  // ask user for number of representatives

 cout << "Enter the party affiliation for each representative.\n";
 cout << "Enter D for Democrat, R for Republican,\n";
 cout << "and I for independents or other parties.\n";
 for (i = 1; i <= num_reps; i++)
   {
    do
     {
      cout << "Party of representative #" << i << ": ";
      cin  >> party;
      switch(party)
        {
         case 'D':
         case 'd':          // if democrat,
          democrats++;      // increment democrats counter
          break;
         case 'R':
         case 'r':          // if republican,
          republicans++;    // increment republicans counter
          break;
         case 'I':
         case 'i':          // if independent or other,
          independents++;   // increment independents counter
          break;
         default:
          cout << "Invalid entry. Enter D, R, or I.\n";
          party = ERROR;
          break;
        } // end of switch structure
     } while (party == ERROR); // loop again if invalid choice is made
   } // end of for loop
 cout << "\nYour state is represented by " << democrats << " Democrats, "
      << republicans << " Republicans,\nand " << independents
      << " independents and members of other parties.\n\n";
 return 0;
} // end of program
```

F I G U R E   8 - 1 4
This program has a do while loop
nested within a for loop.

Nesting may also be used with while loops and do while loops, or in combinations of loops. The program in Figure 8-14 nests a do while loop in a for loop.

The program in Figure 8-14 asks the user for the number of U.S. Representatives in his or her state. A for loop is used to ask the user to identify the party of each representative. The do while loop is used to repeat the prompt if the user enters an invalid party choice.

EXERCISE 8-9 MORE NESTED LOOPS

1. Open *REPS.CPP.*

2. Study the program carefully before you run it.

3. Compile and run the program. Enter some invalid data to cause the nested loop to iterate. If you have trouble understanding the program, study the source code and run it again.

4. Close the source code file.

SECTION 8.2 QUESTIONS

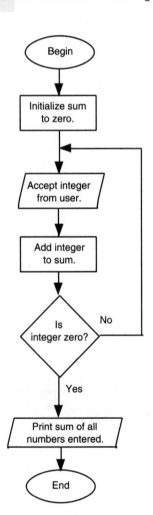

1. Where does a do while loop test the control expression?

2. What is the term for a loop without a way to end?

3. What is the loop control expression in the code segment below?

```
while (!done)
  {
   if (i < 1)
     { done = TRUE; }
   i--;
  }
```

4. What is the error in the code segment below?

```
do;
  {
   if (i < 1)
      { done = TRUE; }
   i--;
  }
while (!done);
```

5. Write a loop that prints your name to the screen once, and then asks you to enter 0 (zero) to stop the program or any other number to print the name again.

6. Write a for loop to print the odd numbers from 1 to 999.

PROBLEM 8.2.1

Write a program that implements the flow chart in Figure 8-15. Save the source file as *SUMITUP.CPP.*

FIGURE 8-15

PROBLEM 8.2.2

Write a program that prints the numbers 1 to 20, but skips the numbers 15, 16, and 17. Save the source code file as *SKIPTHEM.CPP*.

PROBLEM 8.2.3

Modify the program from Exercise 8-9 (*REPS.CPP*) so that it calculates the percentage of your state's representatives that belong to each party. Save the modified source code as *REPS2.CPP*.

PROBLEM 8.2.4

1. Write a program that asks the user for a series of integers one at a time. When the user enters the integer 0, the program displays the following information:

   ➤ the number of integers in the series (not including zero)

   ➤ the average of the integers

   ➤ the largest integer in the series

   ➤ the smallest integer in the series

   ➤ the difference between the largest and smallest integer in the series

2. Save the source file as *INTS.CPP*.

KEY TERMS

control expression	iteration
do while loop	iteration structures
event driven	loop
event loop	nested loop
for loop	parameter
infinite loop	step expression
initializing expression	while loop

SUMMARY

➤ A loop is a group of statements that is repeated a number of times. A loop is an iteration structure.

➤ A for loop causes one or more statements to be repeated a specified number of times. The three parameters of a for loop are the initializing expression, the control expression, and the step expression.

➤ A while loop executes one or more statements as long as the control expression is true. The control expression is tested before the statements in the loop begin. A do while loop works like a while loop except the control expression is tested at the end of the loop.

➤ A break statement can be used to exit a loop before the control expression ends the loop. The continue statement causes the loop to skip to the next iteration of the loop.

➤ A loop within a loop is called a nested loop. The more deeply nested the loop, the more times the loop will be executed.

PROJECTS

PROJECT 8-1

1. Draw a flow chart for a simple program of your own design that uses a while loop.

2. Write the C++ source code for the program.

3. Enter the source code into a blank editor screen and give it an appropriate filename.

4. Compile and run the program. Close.

PROJECT 8-2

Write a program that uses nested loops to produce the following output.

A1B1B2B3A2B1B2B3

PROJECT 8-3 • FINANCIAL PLANNING

Write a program that calculates the amount of time necessary to reach a certain financial goal by consistently depositing the same amount of money into an interest-bearing account each month. The account is compounded monthly.

PROJECT 8-4 • GAME PROGRAMMING

Write a program that asks the user to think of a number between 1 and 100, then attempts to guess the number. The program should make an initial guess of 50. The program should then ask the user if 50 is the number the user has in mind, or if 50 is too high or too low. Based on the response given by the user, the program should make another guess. Your program must continue to guess until the correct number is reached. Save the source file as *HI-LO.CPP*.

PROJECT 8-5 • NUMBER SYSTEMS

1. Open *BINARY.CPP*. The program uses four nested loops to print the binary equivalent of 0 to 15 to the screen. Study the source code and run the program to see its output.

2. Modify the program to generate an additional column of digits. The resulting output should be the binary equivalent of 0-31. Save the modified source file as *BINARY31.CPP*.

3. Close the source code file.

PROJECT 8-6 • NUMBER SYSTEMS

Write a program that converts a binary number (up to seven digits) to a decimal value.

PROJECT 8-7 • NUMBER SYSTEMS

Write a program that converts standard Arabic numbers to Roman numerals.

PROJECT 8-8 • NUMBER SYSTEMS

Extend the program from Project 8-7 to convert from Roman numerals to standard Arabic numbers.

PROJECT 8-9 • MAKING CHANGE

Write a program that calculates the number of quarters, dimes, nickels, and pennies necessary to generate the number of cents entered as input. For example, if 93 cents is entered as input, the program should indicate that three quarters, one dime, one nickel, and three pennies are necessary to add up to 93 cents.

PROJECT 8-10 • MATHEMATICS

Write a program that finds the integer from 1 to 1000 with the most divisors that produce no remainder. For example, the integer 60 has 12 divisors that produce no remainder. They are 1, 2, 3, 4, 5, 6, 10, 12, 15, 20, 30, 60.

PROJECT 8-11 • MATHEMATICS

Write a program that will reduce fractions. Ask the user for the numerator and the denominator. Output a new, reduced fraction, and the greatest common factor.

Computer Ethics
By Chuck McKiel

Programmers and developers have certain responsibilities when creating material that will be released to the public. They must always consider the rights and feelings of other people who may be involved. It is also their duty to be able to judge, to some degree, right from wrong and appropriate from inappropriate.

In addition, developers should carefully cover and research all legal areas concerning property rights. Credit for contributions should be properly distributed among those who helped create the software. Programmers should never use programming code that they have not written, unless permission is obtained. In addition, programmers should not use development tools such as compilers that they do not have a legal license for.

Another area in which programmers have tremendous responsibilities is judging what material is appropriate for their audience. For example, it would be wrong to create a children's game containing violence and profanity. All software should be clearly labeled to show to whom it is intended.

One issue that is sure to arise when dealing with any kind of public exchange of information or storage of data is reliability. It is the programmer's responsibility to create reliable systems.

Computer programmers and systems analysts may also have access to a company or individual's private information. It is the duty of such professionals to keep confidential any information learned through access to such private material.

Everyone who works on a project should be held accountable for the impact the product has on society. While most of the advances in computer technology have had a positive impact on society, some applications of technology have been controversial.

An area of computers today that is becoming more important is the Internet. The Internet can be very useful for anyone who wants to use it, but one problem with the Internet is that it is easy to create material on-line and make it available to anyone who has access to a computer with a modem. It is virtually impossible to close off certain sites to, for example, children under the age of eighteen. This is because it is so difficult to verify any information given.

Some material available on the Internet is of a controversial nature, and much of it is inaccurate. Others use the Internet to defraud computer users. Before making information accessible on the Internet, computer users should consider the impact the information will have. There is also a responsibility to provide accurate information and not to use the Internet as a means to commit crime.

In conclusion, there must be boundaries and guidelines to follow when creating software, talking in a chat room, creating a home page, or posting information on-line. Programmers, developers, and all other computer users have a duty to know and judge what is appropriate and what is not.

Chuck McKiel is a Sophomore at Fenwick High School, Oak Park, Illinois.

9

Functions

➤ Learn how to build structured programs that are divided into functions.

➤ Understand what is meant by the phrase "scope of variables."

➤ Understand how data is passed to functions.

➤ Learn how to use the library functions that are included with the compiler.

Overview

p to now you have written programs with only a main function. In Chapter 3 you learned that programs are often divided into more than one function. Programs are divided up so that the functions perform a specific task or *function*. You will learn how to create functions in this chapter as well as how to use the pre-written functions that are included with your compiler.

How to Build Programs with Functions

xamine the source code in Figure 9-1. The program consists of one function, **main()**. You may have difficulty, however, quickly determining what the program accomplishes.

When the program is run, the user is prompted from a menu to choose to view a series of numbers. Depending upon the user's choice, the program displays a series of odd numbers, even numbers, or all integers from 1 to 30.

Let's run the program to see its output.

EXERCISE 9-1   SINGLE-FUNCTION PROGRAM

1. Retrieve the source file *SERIES.CPP*.

2. Compile and run the program to see the program's output.

3. Close the source code file.

The program you just executed could have been better built using more than one function. The diagram in Figure 9-2, known as a **Visual Table of Contents (VTOC)**, illustrates the point. The lines represent connections between functions. Each function can be accessed by the function above it as long as they are connected by a line.

In this case, the main function "calls" the **get_choice** function to ask the user to choose the series to display. Next, the **handle_choice** function is called to direct the program flow to one of the three functions under it—one for each series. The source code for Figure 9-2 is presented later in this chapter.

GUIDELINES FOR BUILDING A PROGRAM WITH FUNCTIONS

You may recall from Chapter 2 that good programmers follow the five basic steps shown below when developing programs.

1. Define the problem.

2. Develop an algorithm.   *Set of instructions for solving a problem*

3. Code the program.

```
#include<iostream.h>

main()
{
 int choice;   // variable for user input
 int i;        // variable for loops and output

 do  // loop until a valid choice is entered
   {
    cout << "Which series do you wish to display?\n";
    cout << "1 - Odd numbers from 1 to 30\n";
    cout << "2 - Even numbers from 1 to 30\n";
    cout << "3 - All numbers from 1 to 30\n";
    cin >> choice;  // get choice from user
    if ((choice < 1) || (choice > 3))  // if invalid entry, give message
      {
       cout << "Choice must be 1, 2, or 3\n";
      }
   } while ((choice < 1) || (choice > 3));

 switch (choice)
    {
     case 1:
        for (i = 1; i <= 30; i = i + 2)
        cout << i << ' ';
        cout << endl;
        break;
     case 2:
        for (i = 2; i <= 30; i = i + 2)
        cout << i << ' ';
        cout << endl;
        break;
     case 3:
        for (i = 1; i <= 30; i++)
        cout << i << ' ';
        cout << endl;
        break;
    }
   return 0;
}
```

FIGURE 9-1
This entire program is in the main function.

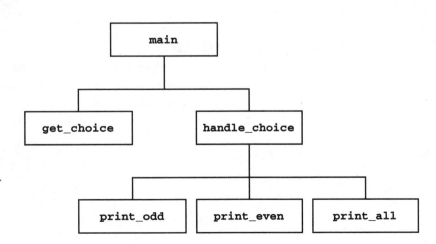

FIGURE 9-2
A diagram that shows the functions of a program is sometimes called a Visual Table of Contents.

4. Test and debug the program.

5. Document and maintain the program.

Using functions helps the programmer develop programs that can be easily coded, debugged, and maintained. Keep the following guidelines in mind when building programs of more than one function.

1. **Organization.** A large program is easier to read and modify if it is logically organized into functions. It is easier to work with a program in parts, rather than one large chunk. A well-organized program, consisting of multiple functions, is easier to read and debug. Once a single function is tested and performs properly, you can set it aside and concentrate on problem areas.

2. **Autonomy.** Programs should be designed so that they consist mainly of stand-alone functions or modules. Each function is autonomous, meaning the function does not depend on data or code outside the function any more than necessary.

3. **Encapsulation**. The term *encapsulation* refers to enclosing the details of a function within the function itself, so that those details do not have to be known in order to use the function.

4. **Reusability**. Because functions typically perform a single and well-defined task, they may be reused in the same program or even in other programs.

Functions may be written for any purpose. For example, you could create a function that converts Fahrenheit temperatures to Celsius or a function that gets input from the user. A function can also be a go-between for other parts of the program, as illustrated in the **handle_choice** function of Figure 9-2.

On the Net

For more information about program design and coding standards, see http://www.ProgramCPP.com. See topic 9.1.1.

Program Design

*There are two popular methods of designing programs. The first method, called **top-down design**, begins with the functions at the top of the VTOC and works toward the functions at the bottom of the VTOC. In other words, the general organization and flow of the program is decided before the details are coded.*

*   **Bottom-up design** involves beginning with the bottom of the VTOC and working your way up. Some programmers prefer to work out the details of how the program will perform specific tasks and then bring the details together to create the overall organization and flow.*

*   Whether you use top-down or bottom-up design, it is important to take an organized approach to writing a multi-function program.*

THE SYNTAX OF FUNCTIONS

With each program you have written, you have created a main function. You can use a similar syntax to create other functions. But before we look at other functions, let's take another look at the main function. Up to this point, the main functions shown in this book have looked like the one below.

```
main()
{
  // body of program
  return 0;
}
```

When the program reaches the **return 0;** statement, the value zero is returned to the operating system. This value tells the operating system that the program ended normally. The value returned is a standard integer because we did not specify otherwise. The **int** type is assumed because we did not specify another type. To be more explicit, programs are often written using a main function like the one below.

```
int main()
{
// body of program
return 0;
}
```

To prevent a value from being returned, the **void** keyword is used in place of a data type. You may have seen programs with a main function like the one below.

```
void main()
{
// body of program
}
```

In a **void** function, no value is returned, therefore no **return** statement is included. Newer operating systems are more likely to take advantage of the value returned by the main function. Therefore, you should get into the habit of creating main functions which return a zero when they terminate normally. The **void** main functions are used less frequently now than in the past.

As mentioned earlier, creating other functions in C++ programs is similar to creating the main function. Let's begin by looking at a simple function that prints a message to the screen.

```
void print_title()
{
  cout << "Tennis Tournament Scheduler Program\n";
  cout << "By Jennifer Baker\n";
}
```

The name of the function is **print_title**. The **void** keyword indicates that no value is returned. The parentheses after the name let the compiler know that **print_title** is a function. The statements between the braces are executed when the function **print_title** is "called." The main function below includes an example of a call to the **print_title** function.

```
int main()
{
  print_title(); // call to print_title

  // insert the rest of the program here

  return 0;
}
```

FUNCTIONS AND PROGRAM FLOW

In the example above, the main function, called the **print_title** function is executed, then the remainder of the program is executed. When a function is called, the computer executes the statements in the function beginning with the first statement. When the end of the function is reached, program execution resumes with the statement that follows the call to the function. Figure 9-3 shows the sequence of execution in a simple three-function example.

The program begins with the first statement of the main function (1), which is a call to the **print_title** function. The flow of logic goes to the **print_title** function which includes two statements (2 and 3) and they are executed next. When the last statement (3) in the **print_title** function is executed, the flow of logic returns to the statement (4) that follows the previous function call in **main()**. The statement in the **print_goodbye** function (5) is then executed. The flow of logic then returns to **main()** where the program ends (6).

FUNCTION PROTOTYPES

There is one more thing you have to do to make your own functions work. At the top of your program, you must tell the compiler that your function exists. You do this by creating a *prototype*. Basically, a prototype defines the function for the compiler. Figure 9-4 shows the functions from Figure 9-3 assembled into a working program.

```
                int main()
Program         {
Begins      ①   print_title();      // call to print_title

                // insert the rest of the program here

            ④   print_goodbye();

                return 0;
Program     ⑥   } // end of main function
Ends

                // Function to print program title to screen.
                void print_title()
                {
            ②   cout << "Tennis Tournament Scheduler Program\n";
            ③   cout << "By Jennifer Baker\n";
                }

                // Function to print closing message to screen.
                void print_goodbye()
                {
            ⑤   cout << "Thank you for using the Tennis Tournament Scheduler.\n";
                }
```

FIGURE   9 - 3
The numbers next to the statements show the order of execution.

```
#include<iostream.h>

void print_title();      // prototype for print_title function
void print_goodbye();    // prototype for print_goodbye function


int main()
 {
  print_title();         // call to print_title

  // insert the rest of the program here

  print_goodbye();
  return 0;

 } // end of main function


// Function to print program title to screen.
void print_title()
 {
  cout << "Tennis Tournament Scheduler Program\n";
  cout << "By Jennifer Baker\n";
 }

// Function to print closing message to screen.
void print_goodbye()
 {
  cout << "Thank you for using the Tennis Tournament Scheduler.\n";
 }
```

F I G U R E   9 - 4
Functions you create must be prototyped at the beginning of the program.

PITFALLS

Notice that a function's prototype is just like the first line of the function, except for the semicolon. An error will result if you forget to include the semicolon at the end of a prototype.

On the Net

C++ programs begin with a main function. The order that other functions are placed in the program is not important because the function prototype has defined the function for the compiler. Therefore, when a call is made to one of your functions, the compiler knows that the function being called exists, even if it exists below the place where it is called.

Some languages (such as Pascal) end with the main part of the program and place the other functions above the main function (called a procedure in Pascal). In Pascal, you must include a special declaration called a forward declaration if you plan to call a function from code which is above the function. The concept is similar to the function prototypes used in C++.

For more information about the order of functions and the effects of the order of functions, see http://www.ProgramCPP.com. See topic 9.1.2.

EXERCISE 9-2   MAKING A FUNCTION

1. Open *1STFUNCT.CPP*. The program from Figure 9-4 appears.

2. Compile, link, and run the program.

3. When you have run the program successfully, close the source code file.

SECTION 9.1 QUESTIONS

1. Describe an advantage of dividing a program into multiple functions.

2. What is the name of the diagram that shows the functions that make up a program?

3. List two guidelines that you can use to decide what code is a good candidate for being made into a function.

4. Briefly describe top-down and bottom-up design.

5. Write the prototype for the function below.

```
void print_warning()
{
  cout << "WARNING: Calculations indicate that you will run\n";
  cout << "out of fuel before the next available gas station.\n";
}
```

6. Write an if structure to be added to the main function below that calls the **print_warning** function above if **fuel_miles < miles_remaining**.

```
int main()
{
  float miles_remaining, fuel_remaining, mpg, fuel_miles;

  cout << "How many miles are you from the next gas station? ";
  cin >> miles_remaining;
  cout << "How much fuel do you have left (in gallons)? ";
  cin >> fuel_remaining;
  cout << "What is your average miles to the gallon? ";
  cin >> mpg;

  fuel_miles = fuel_remaining * mpg;




  return 0;
} // end of main function
```

PROBLEM 9.1.1

Write a complete program based on the functions in questions 5 and 6 above. Add another function called **print_okay** that tells the user that he or she will make it to the next gas station. Convert the if structure to an if/else and include the call to the **print_okay** function in the else clause. Save the source code as *GASCHECK.CPP*.

PROBLEM 9.1.2

Write a program that asks the user for an integer. The program should call one of three functions, based on the value entered. If the value is negative, call a function that prints a message indicating that the value is negative. Create similar functions to call when the value is zero and positive. Save the source code as *VALTEST.CPP*.

Data and Functions

When building a program that consists of functions, you must be concerned with how data is made available to the functions. In this section, you will learn about the accessibility of variables in functions and how to get data to and from functions.

SCOPE OF VARIABLES

Note

Local variables are sometimes called **automatic variables** *and global variables are sometimes called* **external variables.**

You have been working mostly with programs that have one function: **main()**. Within **main()**, you declared variables. These variables, however, would be inaccessible outside of **main()**. The "availability" of a variable is known as its *scope*. While this may sound difficult, in C++ the scope of variables is easy to understand.

Variables in C++ can either be local or global. A *local variable* is a variable declared within a function and is accessible only within that function. A *global variable* is a variable declared before the main function. Global variables are accessible by any function.

Consider the program in Figure 9-5. One variable (**i**) is declared before the main function, making it a global variable. Because **j** and **k** are declared in the main function, they are local to the main function. Therefore, **j** and **k** cannot be used outside of the main function. Within the function named **myfunction**, the variable **l** is declared. It too is local, and accessible only within **myfunction**. After the last statement in **myfunction** is executed, the variable **l** is gone from memory.

If a statement were added to **myfunction** that attempted to access the variable **k**, located in main, an error would result. The variable **k** is accessible only from within the main function. In a similar manner, the variable **l** is inaccessible outside of **myfunction** because it is local to **myfunction**.

EXERCISE 9-3   SCOPE OF VARIABLES

1. Open *SCOPE.CPP*. The program from Figure 9-5 appears on your screen.

2. Compile and run the program as it appears. Study the source code to get clear in your mind where each variable is available.

3. Enter the following statement at the end of **myfunction**.

```
k = i + j;
```

4. Compile the program to see the errors the new statement generates. Your compiler will probably generate an error telling you that the variable **j** and **k** are not defined. The error is generated because **j** and **k** are available only in the main function.

5. Delete the erring statement and close the source code file.

Why have local variables if they are inaccessible to other parts of the program? One reason is that they exist only while the function is executing and

```
#include<iostream.h>

int i = 3;        // global variable

void myfunction();

int main()
 {
  int j,k;        // variables local to the main function
                  // j and k are not accessible outside of main
  j = 2;
  k = i + j;
  cout << "j = " << j << " and k = " << k << '\n';
  cout << "i = " << i << " before the call to myfunction.\n";
  myfunction(); // call to myfunction
  cout << "i = " << i << " after the call to myfunction.\n";
  return 0;
 }

void myfunction()
 {
  int l;          // local variable
  l = ++i;        // the variable i is accessible because i is global
                  // the variable i is changed globally
  cout << "l = " << l << '\n';
  cout << "The variable l is lost as soon as myfunction exits.\n";
 }
```

FIGURE 9-5
This simple program illustrates the difference between local and global variables.

memory is released when the function terminates. If a variable is needed only within a particular function, you save memory by creating and disposing of the variable within the function.

Using local variables could limit the number of errors that occur in a program. If all variables were global, an error made in a variable and used by various functions could cause multiple errors. However, if you use local variables, any errors are limited to the function in which the variable is declared.

Use local variables whenever possible. Even a large program should have very few global variables. Using local variables keeps a tighter control over your program's data, resulting in fewer bugs and programs which are easier to maintain.

You may be wondering how data can get to other functions if everything is local. As you will learn next, when a function is created, you can choose what data you want to send to the function.

GETTING DATA TO AND FROM FUNCTIONS

You have learned that the parentheses following a function's name lets the compiler know that it is a function. The parentheses can serve another purpose as well. That is, parentheses can be used to pass data to a function and in some cases to return data from a function.

When a function is called, the data in the parentheses (called the *argument*) is *passed* into the receiving function. There are three ways to pass data to functions: passing by value, passing by reference, and passing by address.

When you pass a variable to a function by value, a copy of the value in the variable is given to the function for it to use. If the variable is changed within the function, the original copy of the variable in the calling function remains the same. Shown below is an example of a function that passes data to a function using the *passing by value* technique.

```
void print_true_or_false(int True_False)
 {
  if True_False          // If True_False is not equal to zero,
   {                     // display the word TRUE.
    cout << "TRUE\n";
   }
  else                   // If the True_False is equal to zero,
   {                     // display the word FALSE.
    cout << "FALSE\n";
   }
 }
```

A value comes into the function through the parentheses and the copy of the value will be placed in the variable **True_False**. The variable **True_False** is called a *parameter*.

Arguments and Parameters

Many people use the terms argument *and* parameter *interchangeably, but there is a difference. An argument is a value or expression passed to a function through the parentheses when a function is called. A parameter is the variable that receives the value or any other identifier in the parentheses of the function declaration. In other words, an argument is passed to a function, but once in the function, the argument is a parameter.*

When you write a call to a function, you can put any variable or literal in the parentheses to be passed to the function as long as the data types do not conflict. For example, the statements below are all legal calls to the **print_true_or_false** function.

```
print_true_or_false(complete);       // passes a variable
print_true_or_false(1);              // passes a literal
print_true_or_false(j == 3 && k == 2); // passes the result of an
                                     // expression
```

The program in Figure 9-6 illustrates how a value passed to the function named **print_value** does not pass back to the main function. Notice that the **print_value** function uses a variable named **j**, even though the main function passes a variable named **i**. The data types must match, but the names are often different.

```
#include<iostream.h>

void print_value(int j);  // function prototype

int main()
 {
   int i = 2;
   cout << "The value before the function is " << i << endl;
   print_value(i);
   cout << "The value after the function exits is " << i << endl;
   return 0;
 }

void print_value(int j)
 {
   cout << "The value passed to the function is " << j << endl;
   j = j * 2; // the value in the variable i is doubled
   cout << "The value at the end of the function is " << j << endl;
 }
```

F I G U R E   9 - 6
This program uses passing by value to pass an integer to the **print_value** function. The argument **i** which appears in the parentheses in the function call is passed to a parameter named **j** in the receiving function.

EXERCISE 9-4

PASSING BY VALUE

1. Enter the program shown in Figure 9-6. Save the source code as *PASSVAL.CPP*.

2. Compile and run the program to see that the value passed to the **print_value** function is not passed back to the main function.

3. Leave the source code file open for the next exercise.

PASSING BY REFERENCE

Functions that pass variables by reference will pass any changes you make to the variables back to the calling function. For example, suppose you need a function that gets input from the user. The function below uses *passing by reference* to get two values from the user and pass them back through parentheses.

```
void get_values(float &income, float &expense)
 {
   cout << "Enter this month's income amount: $";
   cin >> income;
   cout << "Enter this month's expense amount: $";
   cin >> expense;
 }
```

To pass a variable by reference, simply precede the variable name with an ampersand (&) in the function definition. But even though it is easy to pass by reference, you should do so sparingly. You should write functions that pass variables by value whenever possible. The reason is because passing variables by value is safer. When you pass a variable by value, you know it cannot be changed by the function you call. When you pass a variable by reference, a programming error in the function could cause a problem throughout the program.

As a general rule, you should use passing by reference only when data needs to be passed back to the calling function. In the preceding example, the data entered by the user must be passed back to the calling function.

The program you ran in the last exercise passed a variable by value. Let's modify the program to make it pass the variable by reference.

EXERCISE 9-5

PASSING BY REFERENCE

1. Add an ampersand (&) before the identifier **j** in both the prototype and the function declaration. Save the source code as *PASSREF.CPP*.

2. Compile and run the program again to see the difference passing by reference makes.

3. Close the source code file.

PASSING BY ADDRESS

When you pass an array (such as a character array), the syntax looks just like passing by value. However, what C++ passes to the function is the address of the location in memory where the first element of the array resides. So even though it may seem like you are passing by value, you are actually using a technique called *passing by address*. Because of the way arrays are passed, any changes made to an array in a function remain when the function is complete.

EXERCISE 9-6

PASSING ARRAYS

1. Open *PASSARRY.CPP*.

2. Study the source code to see how the array is passed.

3. Compile, link, and run the program.

4. Close the source code file.

RETURNING VALUES USING RETURN

As you learned earlier in this chapter, unless a function is declared with the keyword **void**, the function will return a value. In the case of the main function, it returns a value to the operating system. Other functions, however, return a value to the calling function. The value to be returned is specified using the **return** statement.

The function below is an example of a function that returns a value of type **float**. The temperature in Celsius is passed into the function by value and the temperature in Fahrenheit is returned using the **return** statement.

```
float celsius_to_fahrenheit(float celsius)
{
  float fahr;  // local variable for calculation
  fahr = celsius * (9.0/5.0) + 32.0;
  return(fahr);
}
```

Any function which is not declared as void should include a **return** statement. The value or expression in the return statement is that which is returned to the calling function. In the **celsius_to_fahrenheit** function, the value stored in **fahr** is returned to the calling function.

The program below shows how you can use this function.

```
#include<iostream.h>
int main()
 {
  float fahrenheit;
  float celsius = 22.5;

  fahrenheit = celsius_to_fahrenheit(celsius);

  cout << celsius << " C = " << fahrenheit << " F\n";
  return 0;
 }
```

The statement **fahrenheit = celsius_to_fahrenheit(celsius);** calls the **celsius_to_fahrenheit** function and passes the value in the variable **celsius** to the function. The function returns the temperature in Fahrenheit degrees and the calling statement assigns the Fahrenheit temperature to the variable **fahrenheit**.

The **celsius_to_fahrenheit** function could be rewritten to include only one statement and return the same result. Any valid expression can appear in the parentheses of the return statement. In this case, the local variable **fahr** is eliminated by performing the calculation in the return statement.

```
float celsius_to_fahrenheit(float celsius)
 {
  return(celsius * (9.0/5.0) + 32.0);
 }
```

On the Net

Important Points Regarding Return

1. *The return statement does not require that the value being returned be placed in parentheses. You may, however, want to get into the habit of placing variables and expressions in parentheses to make the code more readable.*
2. *A function can return only one value using return. Use passing by reference to return multiple values from a function.*
3. *When a return statement is encountered, the function will exit and return the value specified, even if other program lines exist below the return.*
4. *A function can have more than one return statement to help simplify an algorithm.*
5. *The calling function is not required to use or even to capture the value returned from a function it calls.*

To learn more about the ways return can be used, and to see examples of the points listed above, see http://www.ProgramCPP.com. See topic 9.2.1.

When the last line of a function is reached, or when a **return()** *statement is executed, the function ends and the program returns to the calling function and begins executing statements from where it left. Do not end functions with a call back to the original function or the function will not terminate properly. Continually calling functions without returning from them will eventually cause the program to crash.*

If you call the main function at the end of a function you wrote, the main function will begin with the first statement, rather than beginning with the statement following the call to your function.

EXERCISE 9-7   USING RETURN

1. Open *CTOF.CPP*. The complete Celsius to Fahrenheit program appears.

2. Compile, link, and run the program. After you have seen it work, close the source code file.

DIVIDING THE SERIES PROGRAM INTO FUNCTIONS

Now that you have practiced creating functions and moving data to and from them, let's take another look at the program from Exercise 9-1. Earlier in this chapter, you studied a VTOC of the program divided into functions. Refer back to the first few pages of this chapter if you need to review the program or VTOC.

EXERCISE 9-8   MULTI-FUNCTION PROGRAM

1. Retrieve the source code file *SERIES2.CPP*. Analyze the source code to see that the program is divided into functions.

2. Compile and run the program to see that it has the same result as the single-function version you ran in Exercise 9-1.

3. Close the source code file.

More About Function Prototypes

A function prototype consists of the function's return type, name and argument list. In this chapter, the function prototypes specified the parameter names in the argument list. However, this is not necessary as long as the type is specified. For example, the prototype for the **celsius_to_fahrenheit** *function could be written as:*

```
float celsius_to_fahrenheit(float);
```

The prototype for the **get_values** *function could be written as:*

```
void get_values(float &, float &);
```

1. What is meant by the scope of a variable?

2. Describe one advantage to using local variables.

3. Where must a variable be declared in order for it to be local?

4. Where must a variable be declared in order for it to be global?

5. Describe what happens when a variable is passed by value?

6. When should you pass variables by reference?

7. What method is used to pass character arrays to functions?

PROBLEM 9.2.1

Modify *SERIES2.CPP* so that the calls to **get_choice** and **handle_choice** are in a do while loop. Add an item to the menu numbered 0 (zero) that exits the program. Have the loop continually redisplay the menu until zero is chosen. *Note:* Make sure you change the do while loop in the **get_choice** function so that zero is a valid input. Save the source code as *SERIES3.CPP*.

PROBLEM 9.2.2

Add a function to the *CTOF.CPP* program that asks the user for the temperature in Celsius and uses passing by reference to return the temperature to the main function. Save the source code as *CTOF2.CPP*.

CHAPTER 9, SECTION 3

Library Functions

++ compilers include pre-written, ready-to-use functions to make programming easier. The number and type of functions available to you will vary depending on your compiler. The functions that come with your compiler are called *library functions.* This section shows you how to use some of the more common library functions.

USING LIBRARY FUNCTIONS

Library functions are just like functions you create and may be used in the same way. The difference is that the source code for library functions does not appear in your program. The prototypes for library functions are provided to your program using the **#include** compiler directive.

Let's examine a common C++ library function, **pow()**, which is used to raise a value (x) by the power (y). The **pow()** function prototype is shown below.

```
double pow(double x, double y);
```

The function pow receives two values or expressions of type double and returns the result as a double. Below is an example of a call to the pow function.

```
x_to_the_y = pow(x, y);
```

In order to use the pow function, you must include the **math.h** header file using the compiler directive below. A *header file* is a text file that provides the prototypes of a group of library functions. The linker uses the information in the header file to properly link your program with the function you want to use.

```
#include<math.h>
```

EXERCISE 9-9   USING LIBRARY FUNCTIONS

1. Write a program that prompts the user for two values of type double and uses the **pow** function to calculate x^y. Be sure to include the header files for **iostream.h** and **math.h**.

2. Add appropriate comments to your program to describe the parts of your program.

3. Save the program as *POWER.CPP*, compile, run, and test your program.

4. When you have completed the program and verified that it is working properly, close the source code file.

POPULAR MATH FUNCTIONS

Many C++ compilers provide basic math functions, such as the one you used to calculate x^y. Table 9-1 describes some basic math functions, and shows their prototypes and their purpose.

Note

All of the functions in Table 9-1 require that **math.h** be included in the calling program.

FUNCTION	PROTOTYPE	DESCRIPTION
abs	int abs(int x);	Returns the absolute value of an integer
labs	long int labs(long int x);	Returns the absolute value of a long integer
fabs	double fabs(double x);	Returns the absolute value of a floating-point number
ceil	double ceil(double x);	Rounds up to a whole number
floor	double floor(double x);	Rounds down to a whole number
hypot	double hypot(double a, double b);	Calculates the hypotenuse (c) of a right triangle where $c^2 = a^2 + b^2$
pow	double pow(double x, double y);	Calculates x to the power of y
pow10	double pow10(int x);	Calculates 10 to the power of x
sqrt	double sqrt(double x);	Calculates the positive square root of x

T A B L E   9 - 1

EXERCISE 9-10   USING sqrt

1. Write a program that uses the **sqrt** function to calculate the circumference of a circle, given its area. Use the formula $2\sqrt{\pi * area}$.

2. Save the program as *CIRC.CPP* and close the source code when you have completed the exercise.

TRIGONOMETRIC AND LOGARITHMIC FUNCTIONS

Included with many C++ compilers are also trigonometric and logarithmic library functions. These functions, shown in Table 9-2, also require that **math.h** be included in the calling program.

FUNCTION	PROTOTYPE	DESCRIPTION
cos	double cos(double x);	Calculates the cosine of x
sin	double sin(double x);	Calculates the sine of x
tan	double tan(double x);	Calculates the tangent of x
acos	double acos(double x);	Calculates the arc cosine of x
asin	double asin(double x);	Calculates the arc sine of x
atan	double atan(double x);	Calculates the arc tangent of x
atan2	double atan2(double y, double x);	Calculates the arc tangent of y/x
cosh	double cosh(double x);	Calculates the hyperbolic cosine of x
sinh	double sinh(double x);	Calculates the hyperbolic sine of x
tanh	double tanh(double x);	Calculates the hyperbolic tangent of x
exp	double exp(double x);	Calculates the exponential function e^x
log	double log(double x);	Calculates the natural logarithm of x
log10	double log10(double x);	Calculates the base 10 logarithm of x

T A B L E   9 - 2

EXERCISE 9-11   TRIG AND LOG FUNCTIONS

1. Write a program that prompts the user for a variable of type double and returns the cosine, sine, tangent, and natural logarithm of the value entered.

2. Save the source code as *TRIGLOG.CPP* and close.

FUNCTIONS FOR WORKING WITH CHARACTERS

C++ compilers also include many functions for analyzing and changing characters. The header file **ctype.h** must be included for a calling program to use the functions listed in Table 9-3. The conditional functions in the table return a non-zero integer if the condition is true and zero if the condition is false.

FUNCTION	PROTOTYPE	DESCRIPTION
isupper	int isupper(int c);	Determines if a character is upper case
islower	int islower(int c);	Determines if a character is lower case
isalpha	int isalpha(int c);	Determines if a character is a letter (a–z, A–Z)
isdigit	int isdigit(int c);	Determines if a character is a digit (0 – 9)
toupper	int toupper(int c);	Convert a character to uppercase
tolower	int tolower(int c);	Convert a character to lowercase

T A B L E   9 - 3

EXERCISE 9-12   CHARACTER FUNCTIONS

1. Write a program that accepts a single character as input and uses the character functions to report back to the user the following information:
   a. Whether the character is a letter, a digit, or some other type of character.
   b. If the character is a letter, tell the user whether the letter is uppercase or lowercase.

2. Save the source code as *CHARFUN.CPP* and close.

SECTION 9.3 QUESTIONS

1. What is the term for functions that come with your compiler?

2. What do you do to provide prototypes for functions that come with your compiler?

3. What does the **pow10** function do?

4. What type of variable is passed to the **sqrt** function?

5. Write a function call that returns the tangent of 1.0.

6. What library function can be used to convert a character to uppercase?

KEY TERMS

argument	parameter
automatic variable	pass
bottom-up design	passing by address
encapsulation	passing by reference
external variable	passing by value
global variable	prototype
header file	scope
library functions	top-down design
local variable	Visual Table of Contents (VTOC)

SUMMARY

➤ Designing a program that consists of functions results in code that is better organized, reusable, and easier to debug.

➤ The syntax of functions you create is very similar to that of the main function. The parentheses after the function name tell the compiler that you are defining a function.

➤ You must create a prototype for your functions to let the compiler know your function exists. Prototypes are placed at the top of the program.

- A local variable is created within a function and is accessible only from within that function. A global variable is declared outside of all functions and is accessible from any function.

- Data can be passed to functions by value, by reference, or by address. When possible, you should pass by value. Passing by value passes a copy of the data, and the original data cannot be changed from within the function. Data passed by reference brings back changes made to it within a function. Arrays are always passed by address, which means the memory address of the array is passed to the function. Any changes to an array made in a function affect the array throughout the program.

- Functions that come with your compiler are called library functions.

PROJECTS

PROJECT 9-1 • SOFTWARE DEVELOPMENT

Write a program source code template that you can use as a starting point for programs you create in the future. Include comments at the top that give your name and provide places for you to fill in the date and description of the program. Set aside a place for **#include** directives, prototypes, constants, and global variables. Create an empty main function. Save the source code file as *NEWPROG.CPP* and close the file.

PROJECT 9-2 • MATHEMATICS

Write a program that returns the square root of a number as a multiplier and a square root. For example, given the value 45, the program should output that the square root of 45 is equal to 3 times the square root of 5.

PROJECT 9-3 • POINT-OF-SALE SYSTEM

Use the template you created in Project 9-1 as a starting point to write a program that will function as a point-of-sale system at a rodeo snack bar. The snack bar sells only six different items: a sandwich, chips, pickle, brownie, regular drink, and a large drink. All items are subject to sales tax. Set prices for the products.

The program should repeatedly display the menu below until the sale is totaled. The program should keep a running total of the amount of the sale based on costs that you place in constants for each of the food items. The running total should be displayed somewhere on the screen each time the menu is displayed again.

S - Sandwich

C - Chips

B - Brownie

R - Regular Drink

L - Large Drink

X - Cancel sale and start over

T - Total the sale

If the sale is canceled, clear your running total and display the menu again. When the sale is totaled, calculate the sales tax based on your local tax rate (use 6% if you have no sales tax in your area). Print the final total due on the screen.

You can use your own functions to design a solution to the problem. You are required to use a function to calculate the sales tax. Other use of functions is up to you.

PROJECT 9-4 • TRAFFIC CONTROL

Write a program that simulates the operation of traffic lights at an intersection. Use a *for loop* to create a delay or refer to your compiler's manual for a function such as **sleep()** to create a delay. The program should display information about the traffic lights of all four directions. Include a left-turn arrow, and don't forget the yellow lights.

PROJECT 9-5 • PHYSICS

Einstein predicted that the length of an object gets smaller as the object moves more quickly. Use the formula **length = (length_at_zero * sqrt(1 - ((velocity * velocity)/(C * C))))**, where C equals the speed of light $(3.00 \times 10^8 \text{ m/sec})$, to calculate the new length when given the velocity and length at zero speed. Declare C as a constant. Lengths should be entered in meters.

Overview

n this case study, you will follow the steps of the programming process to develop a program that calculates the growth of money using compound interest. When money is placed in an interest-bearing account, the bank adds the interest earned at a regular interval, often monthly. Each month, you earn interest on a larger amount of money because you are also earning interest on the interest you earned in previous months.

Defining the Problem

e'll begin by defining the problem. As input, the program will ask for several pieces of data.

1. The amount of money placed in the savings account.

2. The interest rate the money will earn in the account.

3. The year that the money is placed in the account.

4. The month that the money is placed in the account.

5. The number of months the money is to remain in the account.

The output will be a table that shows the month and year and the amount of money to which the account has grown by that month.

Developing an Algorithm

he flow of the program is fairly simple. First, it must ask the user for the needed values. Then the program will use a loop as it calculates the new principal amount for each month. The flowchart in Figure II-1 illustrates the flow of logic necessary for the program.

The next step would be to develop a Visual Table of Contents (VTOC) to decide what functions must be written. Functions would need to be written that get the input from the user, that

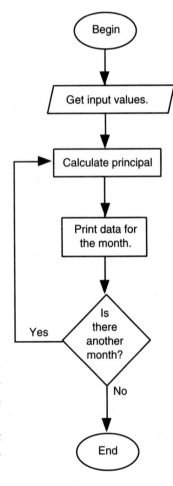

F I G U R E   I I - 1
A flowchart helps a programmer visualize the flow of logic in a program.

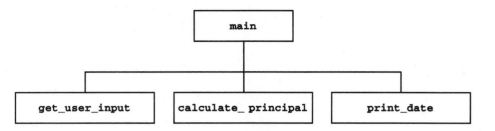

F I G U R E   I I - 2
A visual table of contents shows
the functions of the program.

calculate the new account balance, and that print a line of the table, as shown in
the VTOC in Figure II-2.

Coding the Program

A top-down approach to coding the program is followed. We begin
by writing the main function, and then write the functions on
which the main function depends. As our flowchart showed, the
program must first ask the user to input values. But before we ask the user for
those values, there must be variables in which to store the data. The code below
shows the main function.

```cpp
// main function
int main()
{
  float principal, interest_rate;
  int first_year, first_month,
      total_months, month_count,
      current_year, current_month;
  char WaitTemp[2];

  get_user_input(principal, interest_rate, first_year,
                 first_month, total_months);

  current_year = first_year;
  current_month = first_month;

  cout.setf(ios::fixed);      // prevent exponential notation
  cout.setf(ios::showpoint); // always show decimal point
  for (month_count = 0; month_count < total_months; month_count++)
   {
     calculate_principal(principal, interest_rate);
     print_date(current_year, current_month);
     cout << "$" << setprecision(2) << principal << '\n';
     if (current_month < 12)
      {                       // If not yet December, increment month
       current_month++;
      }
     else            // else stop output until Enter is pressed,
      {              // set month back to January, and increment year
       cout << "\nPress Enter to Continue...\n";
       cin.get(WaitTemp,0);
       cin.ignore(80,'\n');
```

```
        current_month = 1;
        current_year++;
      }
    }
  return 0;
}
```

After the variables are declared, the main function calls **get_user_input** to get the necessary values from the user. Once those values are returned to the main function, **current_year** and **current_month** are initialized to the initial values entered by the user.

Next, two format options are set to ensure that the output does not appear in exponential notation, and that the decimal point always appears. Now we're ready for the loop that prints the output.

We'll use a for loop to print the table because we know the number of times we need to iterate. A loop counter variable named **month_count** is used by the for loop.

The first statement in the loop calls a function named **calculate_principal** that takes the principal and interest rate and returns a new principal amount. The principal will grow with each iteration of the loop.

Next, the current year and current month are passed to a function called **print_date**, which prints the name of the month followed by the year. The principal is then printed on the same line of the screen.

The remainder of the loop is an if structure used to increment the month and, when necessary, the year. Each time the year is incremented, the output pauses to allow the user time to read the output.

EXERCISE II-1   CREATING THE main FUNCTION

1. Enter the following lines into a blank editor screen.

```
// COMPOUND.CPP
// By Jonathan Kleid
// Calculates future value of an amount of money placed in an interest
// bearing account over time.

#include <iostream.h>
#include <iomanip.h>

// function prototypes
void get_user_input(float &principal, float &interest_rate,
                int &first_year, int &first_month, int &total_months);
void calculate_principal(float &principal, float interest_rate);
void print_date(int year, int month);
```

2. Add the main function at the bottom of the source code file.

3. Save the source code file as *COMPOUND.CPP* and leave it open for the next exercise.

Now that we have analyzed the main function, let's look at the functions required to finish the program.

The **get_user_input** function (shown below) receives variables by reference, prompts the user for values for the variables, and returns the values to the main function. The function uses do while loops to repeat prompts until valid values are input.

```cpp
// Function that gets the input values from the user.
void get_user_input(float &principal, float &interest_rate,
                    int &first_year, int &first_month, int &total_months)
{
  cout << "Enter the starting principal: ";
  cin  >> principal;
  cout << "Enter the current interest rate (Ex. 0.09 for 9%): ";
  cin  >> interest_rate;
  do
   {
     cout << "Enter the first year: ";
     cin  >> first_year;
     if ((first_year < 1900) || (first_year > 2050))
      {
       cout << "Invalid year.\n";
      }
   } while((first_year < 1900) || (first_year > 2050));

  do
   {
     cout << "Enter the first month (1 for Jan., 2 for Feb., etc...): ";
     cin  >> first_month;
     if ((first_month < 1) || (first_month > 12))
      {
       cout << "Invalid month.\n";
      }
   } while((first_month < 1) || (first_month > 12));

  cout << "Enter the total number of months: ";
  cin  >> total_months;
  cin.ignore(80,'\n');
}
```

EXERCISE II-2   ADDING THE USER INPUT FUNCTION

1. Add the **get_user_input** function to the source code on your screen.

2. Leave the source code file open for the next exercise.

The **print_date** function (shown below) is primarily a switch structure that prints the name of the month based on the month number that is passed to the function. The year and month are passed by value because there is no need to return the values to the main function. After the switch structure prints the month, a statement prints the year.

```cpp
// Function that prints the month and year to the screen.
void print_date(int year, int month)
{
  switch(month)
```

```
  {
    case 1:
      cout << "Jan";
      break;
    case 2:
      cout << "Feb";
      break;
    case 3:
      cout << "Mar";
      break;
    case 4:
      cout << "Apr";
      break;
    case 5:
      cout << "May";
      break;
    case 6:
      cout << "Jun";
      break;
    case 7:
      cout << "Jul";
      break;
    case 8:
      cout << "Aug";
      break;
    case 9:
      cout << "Sep";
      break;
    case 10:
      cout << "Oct";
      break;
    case 11:
      cout << "Nov";
      break;
    case 12:
      cout << "Dec";
      break;
  }
  cout << " " << year << ": ";
}
```

The final function required for the program is a simple function (shown below) that calculates the new principal amount. The variable **principal** is passed by reference because the new principal amount must be passed back to the main function. The interest rate is passed by value because there is no need to pass it back to the main function.

```
// Function that adds the interest earned and calculates the
// new principal amount.
void calculate_principal(float &principal, float interest_rate)
{
  principal = principal + (principal * (interest_rate / 12));
}
```

EXERCISE II-3   FINISHING THE CODING

1. Enter the **print_date** and **calculate_ principal** functions.

2. Save the source code file and leave the source code file for the next exercise.

Testing and Debugging

nce the code for a program has been entered, the program must be tested and debugged before it can be used and distributed as a reliable program.

EXERCISE II-4   COMPILING THE PROGRAM

1. Issue the command to compile the program. If errors occur during the compilation, check your source code for syntax errors or other typographical errors.

2. When the program compiles and runs successfully, test it with the following input.
   Starting Principal: 1000.00
   Interest Rate: 0.08
   Year: 1996
   Month: 4 (April)
   Number of months: 12

3. Calculating by hand, we have determined that the input above should produce the output below. Compare the program's output to the values below to see if the program is working correctly. When the program is run, the values do not match the expected output below. Can you determine what is going wrong?

```
Apr 1996: $1000.00
May 1996: $1006.67
Jun 1996: $1013.38
Jul 1996: $1020.13
Aug 1996: $1026.93
Sep 1996: $1033.70
Oct 1996: $1040.67
Nov 1996: $1047.61
Dec 1996: $1054.59
Jan 1997: $1061.63
Feb 1997: $1068.70
Mar 1997: $1075.83
```

4. Your testing should have revealed that the output of the program is paying interest on the principal before a month has passed. The program should print the first month with the initial principal amount and add interest to the months that follow. The problem can be fixed by moving one line of the program to a different location in the program. Do you know what line to move and where to move it?

5. Study the source code to find the line that is out of place. Your instructor can help you locate the necessary fix.

6. After you make the correction, run the program again to see if the output is correct.

7. When the program functions properly, save the source code and close.

Documenting and Maintaining

The final step is to write documentation and maintain the program. Some of the lines in the program already contain comments. The analysis in this case study is similar to the external documentation written for some programs.

The user documentation for a program such as this should explain how the program expects the input to be entered. For example, the user should be shown the proper format for entering each of the required inputs.

EXERCISE II-5   DOCUMENTING THE PROGRAM

1. Write user documentation for the program. Begin with a paragraph describing the purpose of the program.

2. Next, describe the necessary inputs, and explain the formats required for each.

3. If you entered the documentation in a text editor or word processor, print it.

Modifying the Program

As an additional exercise, modify the program to display the interest earned each month, in addition to the new principal. You may also want to change the program so that a yearly total of interest earned is printed.

10

Pointers, enum, and Structures

OBJECTIVES

➤ *Understand the basics of pointers.*

➤ *Declare pointers.*

➤ *Use the address-of and dereferencing operators.*

➤ *Use pointers with character arrays.*

➤ *Use subscript notation.*

➤ *Use enum.*

➤ *Understand what structures are and how to use them.*

Overview

A pointer is a variable or constant that holds a memory address. Pointers may be a new term to you, or you may have heard that they are difficult to understand. As with any new concept, however, once you become familiar with the principles and how to apply them you will see that pointers are not difficult. This chapter will cover the basics of pointers and give you a firm foundation that you will use in chapters to come.

You will also take another look at character arrays. You will learn how to access individual characters using a method called subscript notation and using pointers. Finally, you will use a feature of C++ that lets you create your own data types.

CHAPTER 10, SECTION 1

Pointer Basics

C++'s extensive support of pointers is one of the things that makes it such a powerful language. In this chapter, you will not see all of the power that pointers bring to the language. You will, however, learn the basics of pointers that you need to unleash that power in later chapters.

REFRESH YOUR MEMORY ABOUT MEMORY

Each byte of a microcomputer's memory has a unique address. The address is just a number. Memory addresses start at zero and count up from there. Actually, the way memory is organized and the way addresses are assigned varies among computers. The important thing to know is that each byte is numbered in order. For example, memory location 221345 is next to memory location 221346.

Programming would be more difficult if you had to remember the addresses where you stored your data. Instead, the compiler lets you assign names to memory locations when you declare variables.

WHAT IS A POINTER?

A *pointer* is a variable or constant that holds a memory address. In fact, you have been using pointers already. For example, when you declare a character array like the one shown below, **state_code** is a pointer to the first character in the character array.

```
char state_code[3];
```

Figure 10-1 shows how the character array looks in memory.

The pointer occupies four bytes of RAM. The pointer stores the value 140003, which is the memory location where the character array begins.

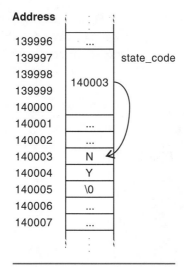

Address

139996	...
139997	state_code
139998	140003
139999	
140000	
140001	...
140002	...
140003	N
140004	Y
140005	\0
140006	...
140007	...

FIGURE 10-1
Declaring a character array creates a pointer to the first character contained in the array.

Note

Pointer size varies among computers and operating systems. For our purposes, the size of pointers is unimportant.

Pointers can point to more than arrays. You can create a pointer that points to any data type. For example, suppose you want a pointer that points to an integer. Figure 10-2 shows how the actual integer is stored, and how the pointer variable points to the integer.

In this example, the integer **i** (with value 3) is stored in two bytes of memory at address 216801. The pointer **iptr** points to the variable **i**.

You may be wondering why anyone would want a pointer to an integer. At this level, pointers may seem "pointless." In later chapters, however, you will learn how to put the power of pointers to work for you when more advanced methods of handling data are discussed.

DECLARING POINTERS

The code below shows how an integer and pointer like the one in Figure 10-2 is declared.

```
int main()
{
   int i;        // declare an integer i
   int *iptr;    // declare a pointer to an integer

   iptr = &i;           // initialize the pointer to the address of i
   i = 3;               // initialize i to 3;
   return 0;
}
```

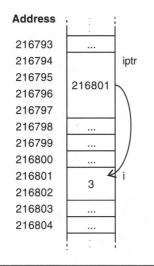

Address

216793	...
216794	iptr
216795	216801
216796	
216797	
216798	...
216799	...
216800	...
216801	3 i
216802	
216803	...
216804	...

FIGURE 10-2
A pointer can point to an integer or other data type.

Working with pointers requires the use of two new operators: the *dereferencing operator* (*) and the *address-of operator* (&). Let's examine what is accomplished by the code above.

The statement **int *iptr;** declares a pointer by preceding the variable name with a dereferencing operator (*). Notice this is the same symbol used to indicate multiplication; however, your compiler can tell the difference by the way it is used.

Notice that pointers have types just like other variables. The pointer type must match the type of data you intend to point to. In the example above, an int pointer is declared to point to an int variable. The * before the variable name tells the compiler that we want to declare a pointer, rather than a regular variable. The variable **iptr** cannot hold just any value. It must hold the memory address of an integer. If you try to make a pointer point to a variable of a type other than the type of the pointer, you will get an error when you try to compile the program.

Like any other variable, a pointer begins with a random value and must be initialized to "point" to something. The statement **iptr = &i;** is what makes **iptr** point to **i**. Reading the statement as "**iptr** is assigned the address of **i**" helps the statement make sense. The address-of operator (&) returns the "address of" the variable rather than the variable's contents.

Just because you use pointers does not mean you have to concern yourself with exact memory locations. When you use pointers, you will assign an address to a pointer using the address-of operator (&). The exact address returned by the operator is of importance only to the computer.

EXERCISE 10-1 DECLARING POINTERS

1. Enter the program below. Save the source code as *POINTER.CPP*.

```
#include <iostream.h> // necessary for cout command

int main()
{
  int i, j, k;     // declare three integers
  int *int_ptr;    // declare a pointer to an integer

  i = 1;
  j = 2;
  k = 3;
  int_ptr = &i;    // initialize the pointer to point to i

  cout << "i = " << i << '\n';
  cout << "j = " << j << '\n';
  cout << "k = " << k << '\n';
  cout << "int_ptr = " << int_ptr << '\n';
  return 0;
}
```

2. Compile and run the program to see that **i, j,** and **k** hold the values you expect. The variable **int_ptr** outputs a memory address to your screen when you print it. The address will probably print in a form called hexadecimal, which is a combination of numbers and letters. Learning the exact meaning of the address is of little importance: just realize that it is the address where the variable **i** is stored.

3. Leave the source code file on the screen for the next exercise.

The Hexadecimal Number System

Hexadecimal numbers (often called just "hex") are ideal for representing memory locations. The hexadecimal number system is a base 16 number system. Because base 16 is a multiple of base 2 (binary), the hexadecimal number system is compatible with the computer's internal representations. Hexadecimal numbers can display large values in a form that is easier to read than binary numbers.

In Exercise 10-1, you declared the pointer (**int *int_ptr;**) and initialized it in a different statement (**int_ptr = &i;**). Like other variables, you can initialize a pointer when you declare it. For example, the statement below could have been used in the program in Exercise 10-1 to declare the pointer and initialize it in one statement.

```
int *int_ptr = &i;
```

Note

A pointer can be named using any legal variable name. Some programmers use names that make it clear the variable is a pointer, such as ending the name with ptr *or beginning the name with* p_, *but it is not necessary.*

USING THE * AND & OPERATORS

The dereferencing operator (*) is used for more than declaring pointers. In the statement below, the dereferencing operator tells the compiler to return the value in the variable being pointed to, rather than the address of the variable.

```
result = *int_ptr;
```

The variable **result** is assigned the value of the integer pointed to by **int_ptr**.

EXERCISE 10-2   THE * AND & OPERATORS

1. Enter the following lines of code to the program you saved named *POINTER.CPP*:

```
cout << "&i = " << &i << '\n';
cout << "*int_ptr = " << *int_ptr << '\n';
```

The output statement with the **&i** does the same thing as outputting **int_ptr**, since **int_ptr** holds the address of **i.** Sending ***int_ptr** to the output stream prints the contents of the variable pointed to by **int_ptr**, rather than printing the pointer itself.

2. Compile and run to see the output of the new statements.

3. Enter the following statements at the end of the program:

```
int_ptr = &j; // store the address of j to int_ptr
cout << "int_ptr = " << int_ptr << '\n';
cout << "*int_ptr = " << *int_ptr << '\n';
```

4. Compile and run again. Because **int_ptr** now points to the integer **j** rather than **i**, the output statement prints the value of **j**, even though the exact statement (**cout << "*int_ptr = " << *int_ptr << '\n';**) printed the value of **i** just two statements back.

5. Enter the following statements at the end of the program:

```
int_ptr = &k; // store the address of k to int_ptr
cout << "int_ptr = " << int_ptr << '\n';
cout << "*int_ptr = " << *int_ptr << '\n';
```

6. Compile and run again. The pointer now points to the variable **k**, so ***int_ptr** returns the value of **k**, which is 3.

7. Save and close the source code file.

CHANGING VALUES WITH *

The dereferencing operator allows you to do more than get the value in the variable the pointer is pointing to. You can change the value of the variable the pointer points to. For example, the statement below assigns the value 5 to the integer to which **int_ptr** points.

```
*int_ptr = 5;
```

You are probably now beginning to see why C++ is so powerful—and so dangerous. A statement like the one above should be avoided because it fails to indicate the specific variable that is being changed. Although C++ programmers are given the freedom to work with memory in a rich variety of ways, pointers should be used only when they improve the program.

Consider the program in Figure 10-3. The program declares and initializes two floating-point numbers. Using a do while loop, the program repeatedly picks the larger of the two numbers and divides it by 2. The loop ends when one of the variables becomes less than 1.

The program uses a pointer to provide an efficient solution. By setting a pointer to point to the larger of the two values, the larger value can be printed and divided by 2 by use of the pointer, rather than the variable itself. By using a pointer, the same code can be used no matter which variable is the larger.

```cpp
#include <iostream.h> // necessary for cout command

int main()
{
  float a, b;          // declare two floating-point numbers
  float *float_ptr;    // declare a pointer to a float

  a = 169.8;
  b = 237.5;

  do
    {
      cout << "The two numbers are " << a << " and " << b << endl;

      if (a >= b)
        {
          float_ptr = &a;
        }
      else
        {
          float_ptr = &b;
        }

      cout << "The largest of the two numbers is "
           << *float_ptr << endl;
      cout << *float_ptr;
      *float_ptr = *float_ptr / 2;
      cout << " divided by 2 is " << *float_ptr << endl;
    } while((a > 1.0) && (b > 1.0));
  return 0;
}
```

FIGURE 10-3
This program accesses variables by use of a pointer.

EXERCISE 10-3 USING POINTERS

1. Enter the program shown in Figure 10-3. Save the source code file as *THEPOINT.CPP*.

2. Study the source code closely before you run the program. Compile and run the program to see its output. The program divides the larger of the 2 values by 2 until one of the values becomes less than 1.

3. Close the source code file.

On the Net

Learn more about pointers and see more examples at http://www. ProgramCPP.com. See topic 10.1.1.

SECTION 10.1 QUESTIONS

1. What is stored in a pointer?

2. What symbol is used for the address-of operator?

3. Write a statement that declares a pointer to a variable of type double.

4. Write a statement that assigns the pointer you declared in question 3 to the address of a variable named x.

5. Now change the value of the variable x to 9.9 using the pointer you declared and the dereferencing operator.

PROBLEM 10.1.1

Write a program that declares two variables of type float and a single pointer of type float. First initialize the pointer to point to the first float variable. Use the dereferencing operator to initialize the variable to 1.25. Next point the pointer to the second float variable and use the pointer to initialize the variable to 2.5. Print the value of the first variable to the screen by accessing the variable directly. Print the second variable using the dereferencing operator. Save the source code file as *POINTER2.CPP*.

CHAPTER 10, SECTION 2
More About Character Arrays

ow that you have been exposed to the basics of pointers, some matters relating to character arrays may make more sense. In this section, you will strengthen your knowledge about character arrays.

ALL CHARACTER ARRAYS USE A POINTER

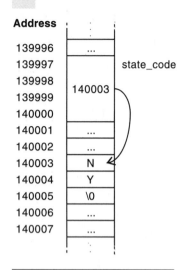

Address	
139996	...
139997	state_code
139998	140003
139999	
140000	
140001	...
140002	...
140003	N
140004	Y
140005	\0
140006	...
140007	...

FIGURE 10-4
The name of a character array is actually a pointer constant.

The first example of a pointer in this chapter was a pointer to a character array. Let's look at that figure again (see Figure 10-4).

When you declare a character array, the name you give the array is actually a *pointer constant.* A pointer constant is like a *pointer variable,* except you cannot change what it points to. In Figure 10-4, the **state_code** pointer constant is initialized by the compiler to point to whatever location is assigned to the first character of the character array.

Note

If you were wondering why C++ requires you to use the **strcpy** *function to assign a string to a character array, here is why. A statement like the one below would try to assign a string of characters to a pointer constant.*

```
state_code = "NY"; // CAN'T DO THIS!
```

USING SUBSCRIPT NOTATION

C++ allows you to access any character in a character array individually using a method called *subscript notation.* Subscript notation looks like the syntax you use when declaring a character array. Consider the program in Figure 10-5. The character array **my_word** is declared to be five characters long and assigned the word *book.*

```
#include <iostream.h> // necessary for cout command

int main()
{
  char my_word[5] = "book";
  cout << my_word << '\n';
  return 0;
}
```

FIGURE 10-5
In this program, the character array **my_word** is initialized with the word *book.*

Recall from Chapter 6 that the characters of a character array are stored together in memory. What you may not know, however, is that the characters of the array are numbered, beginning with zero (see Figure 10-6). So a five-character array is numbered 0 through 4.

Using subscript notation, you can change the first character in the array using a statement like the one below.

```
my_word[0] = 't';
```

The first character is changed to a 't' because the first character is at position 0. You may wonder why the people who created C++ made the subscript of the

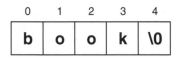

0	1	2	3	4
b	o	o	k	\0

FIGURE 10-6
The characters of an array are numbered, beginning with zero.

first character 0 rather than 1. You might find it helpful to think of the number in the brackets as the number of places you must move over from the first character in the array.

The first character in the array is where the pointer points. To access the fourth character, however, you must move three times. An exercise will give you a little practice with subscript notation.

EXERCISE 10-4   SUBSCRIPT NOTATION

1. Enter the program below. Save the source code as *WORDPLAY.CPP.*

```
#include <iostream.h> // necessary for cout command

int main()
{
  char my_word[5] = "book";

  cout << my_word << '\n';

  my_word[3] = 't';
  cout << my_word << '\n';
  return 0;
}
```

2. Compile and run the program to see how subscript notation changed one character in the word.

3. Add the following statements to the bottom of the program.

```
my_word[0] = 's';
cout << my_word << '\n';
```

4. Run the program again to see the effect of the statements you added.

5. Save the source code and leave it open for the next exercise.

PITFALLS

Be careful when accessing characters in an array individually. The compiler will not prevent you from going beyond the length of your array. You could end up changing other data in memory instead of your array. If the null terminator of your string is changed to another character, the compiler will allow it and errors will result.

Subscript notation can be used without knowledge of pointers. However, since you are becoming familiar with pointers, you would probably be interested in seeing how to change a character in the array without subscript notation.

USING THE * OPERATOR IN CHARACTER ARRAYS

You already know that **my_word** is a pointer to the first character in the array. Because characters occupy one byte of memory, it makes sense that the second character of the array is stored at **my_word + 1**. Using the dereferencing operator and this knowledge of how the array is stored, you can change the fourth character in the array using a statement like the one below.

```
*(my_word + 3) = 'n';  // has the same result as my_word[3] = 'n';
```

You can see that subscript notation makes for more readable code than the dereferencing operator. But as statements like the one above begin to make sense to you, you will begin to unlock the real power of C++. Let's add the statement to the program you entered in Exercise 10-4.

EXERCISE 10-5   CHANGING ARRAY CHARACTERS

1. Add the following lines to the bottom of the program on your screen.

```
*(my_word + 3) = 'n';  // has the same result as my_word[3] = 'n';
cout << my_word << '\n';
```

2. Run the program to see the effect of the new statements.

3. Add a statement that uses subscript notation to change the word to *sown*. Add an output statement to output the new word.

4. Run, save, and close.

SECTION 10.2 QUESTIONS

1. The name of a character array is what kind of pointer?

2. Why can't you assign a string to a character array using the assignment operator?

3. What is the name of the method that allows you to access individual characters of a character array using brackets ([])?

4. Given the character array declared as **char A[8] = "ABCDEFG";**, what character is returned by **A[2]**?

5. Using the same character array you used for question 4, what would be the resulting string if the following statement were executed?

```
A[1] = 'X';
```

PROBLEM 10.2.1

Write a program that declares a character array named **alphabet** and initializes the array to "ABCDEFGHIJKLMNOPQRSTUVWXYZ." In your program, include a loop that replaces one character of the array at a time with the lowercase letters a–z. Print the character array to the screen during each iteration of the loop. *Hint:* Remember that a character array is an array of integer values. Use ASCII values to make the changes. Save the source code file as *ALPHABET.CPP*.

Using enum

The *enum* keyword (short for enumerated) is a C++ feature that is often overlooked. It allows you to create your own simple data types for special purposes in your program. For example, you could create a data type called colors that allows only the values *red*, *green*, *blue*, and *yellow* as data. In this section, you will learn how enum works and how you can use it in your programs.

HOW TO USE enum

The enum keyword is easy to use. You simply create a type, give it a name, and tell the compiler what values your new data type will accept. Consider the statement below.

```
enum sizes {small, medium, large, jumbo};
```

The data type called **sizes** can have one of four values: *small*, *medium*, *large*, or *jumbo*. The next step is to declare a variable that uses **sizes** as a type. Let's declare two variables of the type **sizes**.

```
enum sizes drink_size, popcorn_size;
```

The variable **drink_size** and **popcorn_size** are of type **sizes** and can be assigned one of the four sizes defined in the **sizes** type.

EXERCISE 10-6   USING enum

1. Enter the program below. Save the source code as *ENUMTEST.CPP*.

```
#include <iostream.h> // necessary for cout command

int main()
{
  enum sizes {small, medium, large, jumbo};
  sizes drink_size, popcorn_size;

  drink_size = large;
  popcorn_size = jumbo;

  if (drink_size == large)
   { cout << "You could have a jumbo for another quarter.\n"; }

  if ((popcorn_size == jumbo) && (drink_size != jumbo))
   { cout << "You need more drink to wash down a jumbo popcorn.\n"; }
  return 0;
}
```

2. Run the program to see the output. Close the source code file.

HOW enum WORKS

Internally, the compiler assigns an integer to each of the items in an enum list. For example, the statement below does not print small, medium, large, or jumbo to the screen. It prints either 0, 1, 2, or 3.

```
cout << drink_size << '\n';
```

WARNING

Attempting to print the value of an enumerated type results in an error on some compilers. Enumerated types are best used in expressions and switch structures, rather than directly for output.

By default, the compiler begins assigning integers with zero. For example, in the sizes type, small = 0, medium = 1, large = 2, and jumbo = 3. You can, however, choose your own values. For example, suppose you wanted to use an enumerated type to assign quantities. You could use a statement like the one below to declare an enumerated type with the values 1, 2, 12, 48, and 144.

```
enum quantity {Single=1, Dozen=12, Full_Case=48, Gross=144};
```

As another example, suppose you want to create a type called month that is made up of the months of the year. Because the months are commonly numbered 1 through 12, you decide to have the compiler assign those numbers to your list. The assignment in the first value of the list sets the beginning value for the items in the list, as in the statement below. January will be assigned the value 1, February the value 2, etc.

```
enum month {January=1, February, March, April, May, June, July,
        August, September, October, November, December};
```

You can use the fact that enum uses integers to your advantage. For example, a statement like the one below can be used with the sizes type.

```
if (drink_size > medium)
   { cout << "This drink will not fit in your cup holder.\n"; }
```

USING typedef

Another C++ feature which is related to enum is typedef. You can use typedef to give a new name to an existing data type. For example, if you prefer to use the term *real* to declare variable of type **float**, you can give the data type an *alias* of real with typedef.

```
typedef float real;
```

You should, of course, use typedef sparingly because you may confuse the reader of your code.

You can use typedef for more than just changing the names of data types to fit your liking. For example, recall from Chapter 4 that some C++ compilers include a boolean data type and some compilers do not. You can use typedef and a couple of constants to create your own boolean data type.

```
typedef int bool;
const int TRUE = 1;
const int FALSE = 0;
```

The three statements above make it possible to declare variables of type **bool** and assign values to the variables using **TRUE** and **FALSE**.

```
bool acceptable;
acceptable = TRUE;
```

On the Net

For more information about typedef, including how typedef can be used to make code easier to move among compilers, see http://www.ProgramCPP.com. See topic 10.3.1.

SECTION 10.3 QUESTIONS

1. Write a statement that declares an enum type called speed that allows the values *stopped*, *slow*, and *fast*.

2. Write a statement that declares a variable named rabbit of the type you declared in question 1.

3. Write a statement that assigns the value fast to the *rabbit* variable you declared above.

4. What does the compiler use internally to represent the values of an enum type?

5. Write a statement that declares an enum type called temperature that allows the values *frigid*, *cold*, *cool*, *mild*, *warm*, *hot*, and *sizzling*. Have the list begin with the value 1.

6. What can be used to give a new name to an existing data type?

PROBLEM 10.3.1

Make a list of several different enumerated data types that could be useful in programs. For example, **enum TrueFalse { FALSE, TRUE}** or **enum Position {open, closed}**.

CHAPTER 10, SECTION 4

Structures

C++ *structures* allow variables to be grouped to form a new data type. The data elements in a structure are arranged in a manner that is similar to the way database programs arrange data.

Item ID: ELC224-019

Description: Jet-O-Matic Leaf Blower

Qua

Cos

Item ID: SFW784-455

Description: 9-piece Stainless Steel Cookware Set

Qua

Cos

Item ID: RGG456-299

Description: Remote Control Monster Truck

Quantity On Hand: 9   Reorder Point: 3

Cost: 47.80   Retail Price: 98.99

Records

Field

F I G U R E   1 0 - 7
A record in a database is one completed set of fields.

Note

*All data in a C++ program is stored in a **data structure**. Any organized way of storing data in a computer is a data structure. The basic variable types such as* `int` *and* `float` *are called **primitive data structures**. A character array is an example of a category of data structures called **simple data structures**. The term structure used in this section refers to a specific data structure made by grouping other data structures. Do not confuse the term structure used in this section with the more generic term data structure.*

In a database program, data is stored in *records.* For example, suppose you have a database of items sold by a mail-order company. Each item that the company sells is stored as a record in the database. Each record is made up of data called *fields.* Figure 10-7 shows a series of three records contained in a database. Notice that each record has identical field names (i.e., Item ID).

C++ allows you to create a record by grouping the variables and arrays necessary for the fields into a single structure. The variables in the structure can be of mixed types. For example, in Figure 10-7, character arrays must be used for the item ID and the description, an integer type can be used to store the quantity on hand and reorder point, and a floating-point type is necessary for cost and retail price.

DECLARING AND USING STRUCTURES

A structure must be declared. Because a structure is made up of more than one variable, a special syntax is used to access the individual variables of a structure.

DECLARING A STRUCTURE

Shown below is the declaration for the structure in our example.

```
struct inventory_item
  {
    char item_ID[11];
    char description[31];
    int quantity_on_hand;
    int reorder_point;
    float cost;
```

```
        float retail_price;
    };
```

The **struct** keyword identifies the declaration as a structure. The identifier associated with the structure is **inventory_item**. The variables in the structure are called *members*. The members of the structure are placed within braces. Within the braces, however, the variables and arrays are declared using the syntax to which you are accustomed.

Once you have declared a structure, you must declare a variable that is of the structure's type. This may seem confusing, but what the struct key word does is define a new data type. You can then create as many variables as you want of the new type. The statement below creates a variable named **todays_special** that is of type **inventory_item**.

```
inventory_item todays_special;
```

ACCESSING MEMBERS OF A STRUCTURE

Accessing data in a structure is surprisingly simple. To access a member of the structure, use the name of the variable, a period (.), then the name of the member you need to access, as shown in Figure 10-8. The period is actually an operator called the *dot operator*.

FIGURE 10-8
To access a member of a structure, use the name of the variable, a period, and the name of the member you need to access.

Member

```
todays_special.cost = 47.80;
```

Structure Identifier   Dot Operator

The code segment below declares a variable named **todays_special** of the type **inventory_item** and initializes each member of the structure.

```
inventory_item todays_special;

strcpy(todays_special.item_ID, "RGG456-299");
strcpy(todays_special.description, "Remote Control Monster Truck");
todays_special.quantity_on_hand = 19;
todays_special.reorder_point = 3;
todays_special.cost = 47.80;
todays_special.retail_price = 98.99;
```

EXERCISE 10-7   STRUCTURES

1. Retrieve the source code file *STRUCT.CPP*. A program appears that includes the declaration and initialization of the **todays_special** structure variable.

2. Enter the following code at the bottom of the program (before the closing brace, of course).

```
cout << "Today's Special\n";
cout << "     Item ID: " << todays_special.item_ID << endl;
```

```
cout << "   Description: " << todays_special.description << endl;
cout << "       Quantity: " << todays_special.quantity_on_hand << endl;
cout << "Regular Price: " << setprecision(2)
     << todays_special.retail_price << endl;
cout << "    Sale Price: " << todays_special.retail_price * 0.8
     << endl;
```

3. Compile and run the program to see the output from the structure.

4. Save the source code file and close.

NESTED STRUCTURES

A structure can include enumerated data types and even other structures as members. Consider the program in Figure 10-9. The program sets up a structure to be used to store vital data about blood donors. The structure named **donor_info** includes two enumerated data types (**blood_type** and **rh_factor**) and a structure (**blood_pressure**) among its members.

```
enum blood_type { unknown, A, B, AB, O };
enum rh_factor { negative, positive };

struct blood_pressure
  {
   int systolic;
   int diastolic;
  };

struct donor_info
  {
   blood_type type;
   rh_factor rh;
   blood_pressure bp;
   int heart_rate;
  };

int main()
{
  donor_info current_donor;

  current_donor.type = A;
  current_donor.rh = positive;
  current_donor.bp.systolic = 130;
  current_donor.bp.diastolic = 74;
  current_donor.heart_rate = 69;
  return 0;
}
```

FIGURE 10-9
This program uses nested structures to store blood pressure values.

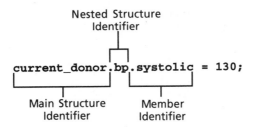

Nested Structure
Identifier

current_donor.bp.systolic = 130;

Main Structure
Identifier

Member
Identifier

FIGURE 10-10
This assignment stores the value 130 in the systolic variable which is in the **bp** structure which is in the **current_donor** structure.

The **blood_type** and **rh_factor** data are good candidates for an enumerated data type because only a few values are possible. Because blood pressure is actually two values, a structure is used to group the two values into one variable. When a structure appears within a structure the resulting data structure is called a *nested structure.*

Accessing the nested structure requires that two periods be used. As the statement in Figure 10-10 illustrates, initializing the blood pressure values requires that the first structure be accessed by name, then the structure variable within the first structure, and finally, the variable within the nested structure.

EXERCISE 10-8   NESTED STRUCTURES

1. Enter the program shown in Figure 10-9. Save the source code as *DONORS.CPP*.

2. Add the following statement to the main function.

```
cout << "The donor's blood pressure is "
     << current_donor.bp.diastolic << " over "
     << current_donor.bp.systolic << ".\n";
```

3. Add the appropriate directive to include the code necessary for the cout statements.

4. Compile and run the progra1m. Save and close the source code.

It is easy to get locked into thinking about structures in terms of database applications. Structures, however, have many other applications. For example, some mathematical or graphical applications use coordinates such as (x,y) in calculations. You can use a structure like the one below to group the x and y into a structure that represents a graphical point.

```
struct point
  {
   float x;
   float y;
  };
```

You might then want to use nested structures to create a data type that defines two points, that when connected, form a line, as shown below.

```
struct line
  {
   point p1;
   point p2;
  };
```

Chapter Ten – Pointers, enum, and Structures **199**

Structures can be passed as parameters, which can reduce the number of parameters that must be passed. For example, passing a variable of the line structure type can take the place of passing four coordinates (two x and two y values). In the exercise that follows, you will run a program that passes a structure variable to calculate the slope of a line.

EXERCISE 10-9   SLOPE OF A LINE

1. Open *LNSLOPE.CPP*. A program appears that uses the structures above to calculate the slope of a line.

2. Compile and run the program. Provide the points (1,2) and (2,5) as input.

3. Add the following statements after the declaration of the variable **m.**

```
line horizontal_line;

horizontal_line.p1.x = 1;
horizontal_line.p1.y = 2;
horizontal_line.p2.x = 5;
horizontal_line.p2.y = 2;
m = slope(horizontal_line);
cout << "The slope of every horizontal line is " << m << endl;
```

4. Compile and run the program again to see the result of the new lines.

5. Save the source code and close.

SECTION 10.4 QUESTIONS

1. What is the purpose of a structure?

2. What is the term for the variables in a structure?

3. Write a declaration for a structure named **house** that is to be used to store records in a database of house descriptions for a real estate agent. The fields in the record should include address, square footage of the house, number of bedrooms, number of bathrooms, number of cars that can fit in the garage, and the listed price of the house.

4. Write a statement that declares a structure variable named **featured_home** using the structure declared in question 3.

5. Write a series of statements that initialize the structure variable declared in question 4. Do your best to initialize the structure variable with realistic values.

6. Write a statement that prints the information in the **featured_home** structure variable in the format of the example below, where 3-2-2 is the number of bedrooms, baths, and garage stalls respectively, and 1800 is the square footage.

3918 Shonle Road   3-2-2   1800 $64,000

PROBLEM 10.4.1

1. Open *STRUCT.CPP* (the program you saved in Exercise 10-7).

2. Add code to the end of the program that asks the user for the anticipated number of sales during the day the item is on special and the anticipated sales for the product if it were not on special.

3. Check the value entered against the quantity on hand to make sure that the anticipated orders can be filled. Warn the user if the quantity on hand is less than the anticipated sales.

4. Calculate the amount of income the product is anticipated to generate if the product is put on special and the amount of income the product is anticipated to generate if the product is not put on special.

5. Save the new source code as *STRUCT2.CPP*. Compile and run the program. After testing the program, close the source code file.

PROBLEM 10.4.2

Write a program that uses the point and line structures from Exercise 10-9 to calculate the midpoint of a given line. Have the program ask the user for the points that define the line, then use the formula below to calculate the midpoint of the line and output the coordinates of the midpoint. Save the program as *MIDPOINT.CPP*.

$$\left(\frac{x_1 + x_2}{2}, \frac{y_1 + y_2}{2} \right)$$

KEY TERMS

address-of operator	pointer
data structure	pointer constant
dereferencing operator	pointer variable
dot operator	primitive data structure
enum	simple data structure
fields	records
members	structures
nested structure	subscript notation

SUMMARY

➤ Pointers are variables and constants that hold memory addresses.

➤ The dereferencing operator (*) is used to declare pointers and to access the value in the variable to which the pointer points.

- The address-of operator (&) returns the address of a variable, rather than the value in the variable.

- The name you give a character array is actually a pointer constant that points to the first character in the array.

- Subscript notation is a method of accessing individual characters in a character array. You can also access individual characters in an array using the dereferencing operator and adding the correct number to the pointer.

- The enum keyword allows you to create custom data types. Internally, the values you include in your enum data types are stored as integers.

- Structures are very useful data structures that allow variables to be grouped to form a new data type.

- The variables within a structure are called members.

PROJECTS

PROJECT 10-1 • REVERSING A STRING

Write a function named **reverse_string** that reverses a string. For example, the function would change the string "ABCDEF" to "FEDCBA." The function should not reverse the position of the null terminator. Write a main function to test the **reverse_string** function.

PROJECT 10-2 • CRYPTOGRAPHY

Write a program that uses a loop to encrypt a string by adding 1 to the ASCII value of each character in the string. The string "ABCDEF" would become "BCDEFG." The string "apple" would become "bqqmf."

PROJECT 10-3 • CRYPTOGRAPHY

Modify the program from Project 10-2 to decrypt a string that has been encrypted using the method of Project 10-2.

PROJECT 10-4 • GEOMETRY

On a coordinate plane, the length of a line connecting two points can be found using the formula below.

$$\sqrt{(x_2 - x_1)^2 + (y_2 - y_1)^2}$$

Extend the *LNSLOPE.CPP* program you saved in Exercise 10-9 to calculate the length of the line using the formula above.

PROJECT 10-5 • GEOMETRY

Write a program that accepts two points as input. Have the program calculate a third point that, with the other two points in a plane, form a right triangle.

Software Piracy
By Jeff Snyder

The software industry is one of the fastest-growing industries in the United States. Billions of dollars are made from the sale of software at home and abroad. However, profits are falling due to illegal use and duplication of software. Illegal use of software, also know as software piracy, is rising at an astounding rate. One study showed that in some cases three illegal copies exist for every legal copy of software. Some countries, such as China, are mass-producing software and other copyrighted materials illegally. To counter this problem, the U.S. government is taking steps to crack down on offenders.

One of the most convenient aspects of computer software is its ease of duplication. This trait is among the most useful applications of computers. Although users like the ease of copying, software manufacturers find it to be a problem. Just like any publication, producers of software rely on sales to make money and continue their development efforts. If someone buys a program and makes five copies for friends, the company loses money.

In 1993, worldwide software pirating accounted for 7.4 billion dollars of lost revenues. Not only do people trade copied floppies, but they also transfer data over phone lines. As modems get faster, the time required to transfer large quantities of data decreases. Illegal computer bulletin boards are growing in popularity and membership. One bulletin board, which was recently busted by officials, distributed copied software to members who paid the $99 membership fee.

Not only do companies lose money from petty private pirating, they are also affected by illegal mass production. China is an enormous haven for software pirates. For the last few years, hundreds of Chinese factories have been mass-producing American software illegally. The U.S. has insisted the Chinese government crack down on pirating.

Although production of illegal software has been curbed, it is by no means eradicated. Many other countries are avid users of illegal software. Almost all software used in Thailand (about 99% according to one study) is pirated. Although it is substantially higher in Asia, pirated software also comprises about 78 percent of French and 69 percent of German software. The widespread abuse of American software in other countries contributes a great deal to our nation's growing trade deficit.

Various groups are working overtime to prevent piracy. The B.S.A. (Business Software Alliance) and the S.P.A. (Software Publishers Association) enforce copyright infringement laws. In 1994, the S.P.A sued 447 organizations and collected 2.5 million in fines. Recently, these and many other groups lobbied successfully to get Congress to join the fight against piracy. Infringements that previously were considered misdemeanors are now classified as felonies. Some software companies have hotlines where disgruntled employees can call to report copying in their places of employment. Companies are looking for inexpensive ways to make duplication difficult for would-be pirates. More research is going into copyright protection and it will hopefully come up with an effective, yet not too obstructive, means of protection.

The illegal duplication of software is a growing problem in the American software industry. Profits are being purged by unknowing citizens and greedy entrepreneurs. While software piracy is rampant, prices of titles will remain high and may even rise in order to alleviate losses. Software piracy affects computer users and the entire software industry.

Jeff Snyder is a Senior at Oak Forest High School, Oak Forest, Illinois.

Data File Basics

➤ *Understand the uses for data files.*

➤ *Understand the difference between sequential-access and random-access data files.*

➤ *Open and close data files.*

➤ *Write to data files.*

➤ *Read from data files.*

➤ *Add to the end of a data file.*

➤ *Detect the end of a file.*

➤ *Use multiple data files at the same time.*

➤ *Prompt the user for file names.*

Overview

Many useful programs collect all input from the keyboard and print all output to the screen. However, the ability to input data from a disk file and send output to a disk file opens the door to many more possibilities. A program that organizes names and addresses, for example, must store the data somewhere other than RAM. Otherwise, the data is lost when the program ends.

In this chapter, you will learn about sequential-access and random-access data files. You will learn how to open and close a sequential-access file, how to write data to a file, how to read data from a file, and how to add data to the end of an existing file. You will also learn how to detect the end of a file, use multiple files at the same time, and prompt the user for file names.

File Concepts

Data files are not difficult to understand. Storing data in a file simply involves taking data from your computer's RAM and copying it to a disk. Retrieving data from a file is just the opposite. Data stored on disk is copied into variables or other data structures in RAM.

WHY USE DATA FILES?

Recall that your computer's memory (RAM) holds data only as long as the computer is on. Furthermore, data in RAM is lost as soon as your program ends. Disks and other forms of secondary storage hold data even after the computer is turned off. Therefore, any data that your program needs again should be stored on disk so that it can be reloaded into your program.

For example, suppose you have a program that prints mailing addresses on labels and envelopes. Unless a data file is used to store the addresses, the user has to enter the data from the keyboard every time the program runs.

Another reason to use data files is the amount of space available on a disk as compared to RAM. In the example of the program that prints addresses, a data file could store hundreds or even thousands of addresses—many times the number that could fit in RAM.

SEQUENTIAL-ACCESS VS. RANDOM-ACCESS FILES

There are two types of data files: sequential access and random access. The difference between the two is in how they access the data that is stored in them.

SEQUENTIAL-ACCESS DATA FILES

A *sequential-access file* works like an audio cassette tape. When you put a cassette tape in a stereo, you must fast forward or rewind to get to a specific song. You must move through the songs *sequentially* until you reach the one you want to hear. Data stored in a sequential-access data file is placed one after the other like songs on a cassette tape. To retrieve specific data from a sequential-access data file, you must start at the beginning of the file and search for the data or records you want while moving through the file.

Sequential-access files are the most widely used data files. Word processors save documents in sequential-access files. Spreadsheets, graphic files, and some databases are stored as sequential-access files.

A sequential-access file can contain data of mixed types and sizes. For example, a word processor file may begin with general information about the document, followed by the text of the document itself. There may even be codes that control formatting mixed in with the document's text. The programmers that developed the word processor program place data in the file using their own rules. When the program loads the document from disk, those same rules are followed in order to correctly interpret the data file.

Figure 11-1 represents a sequential-access file storing a list of names. Notice that the names vary in length. To find the fourth name in the list (Beau Chenoweth), the three names that precede it must be read first.

FIGURE 11-1
A sequential-access file requires that data be read from the beginning of the file each time it is accessed.

Shelley Neff	James MacCloskey	Kim Fan	Beau Chenoweth	Sarah Boyd	Britney Sooter

RANDOM-ACCESS DATA FILES

A *random-access file* works like an audio compact disc (CD). With the touch of a button, you can immediately access any song on the CD. You can play the songs on a CD in any order, regardless of the order they appear on the CD. A random-access data file allows to you move directly to any data in the file.

Random-access files are most often used to store databases. A database with a large number of records is more efficiently managed with a random-access file because you can move quickly to any desired record in the database.

The secret to a random-access file is that data is written to the file in blocks (records) of equal size. In reality, the file appears on the disk as a sequential-access file. Because the file is made up of equally-sized blocks, a program can predict how far to move forward from the beginning of the file in order to get to the desired data.

Figure 11-2 represents a random-access file. Regardless of the length of the name, the same amount of disk space is occupied by the data. While the random-access file allows almost instant access to any data in the file, the disadvantage is that random-access files often occupy more disk space than sequential-access files.

In this book, you will write programs that use only sequential-access data files. However, the concept of a random-access file is important.

FIGURE 11-2
A random-access file allows any data to be accessed directly.

Shelley Neff	James MacCloskey	Kim Fan	Beau Chenowe{

On the Net

Many modern operating systems include a file manager or their own set of file handling functions that programmers use to create consistency among programs. For more information on the resources operating systems provide for handling files, see http://www.ProgramCPP.com. See topic 11.1.1.

1. List three reasons to use data files.

2. What are the two types of data files?

3. List some types of files stored as sequential-access files.

4. Describe an advantage of using random-access data files.

5. Describe a drawback of using random-access data files rather than sequential-access files?

CHAPTER 11, SECTION 2

Using Sequential-Access Files

sing a sequential-access file requires that you complete a few simple (but important) steps. First, the file must be opened. Data can then be stored or retrieved from the file. Finally, the file must be closed.

OPENING AND CLOSING FILES

A file is a container for data. Whether you think of a file as a drawer, a folder, or a box, the concept of opening and closing the file makes sense. Before you can put something in a file or take something out, the file must be opened. When you have finished accessing the file, it must be closed.

WARNING

In a paper filing system, a folder or drawer left open may result in important information getting misplaced or lost. Closing a computer file may be even more important. A data file left open by a program can be destroyed if a power failure occurs or if a program crash occurs. A closed data file is almost always protected from such occurrences.

Note

If you have the need to work with more than one file at a time, you can declare more than one file pointer and assign each file pointer to a different file on the disk.

DECLARING A FILE POINTER

C++ uses a special type of pointer called a ***file pointer*** to work with files. Recall that a pointer is a constant or variable that points to a location in memory. A file pointer is a variable that points to a position in a data file. You will assign an actual disk file to the file pointer, and then use the file pointer to access the file.

How you declare a file pointer varies depending on how you intend to use the file. If you will be storing data to the file (called *writing*), you will declare a file pointer of type **ofstream** as shown below.

```
ofstream outfile;   // declares a file pointer for writing to file
```

If you will be getting data from a file (called *reading*), you will declare a file pointer of type **ifstream** as shown below.

```
ifstream infile;   // declares a file pointer for reading a file
```

To help you remember the file pointer types, understand that **ofstream** is short for *output file stream* and **ifstream** is short for *input file stream*. Recall from Chapter 6 that a stream is data flowing from one place to another. Storing and retrieving data from files also involves input and output streams.

You can use any valid identifier for file pointer variables. The examples above used the names **outfile** and **infile** because they describe the purpose of the file pointer. In some situations, you may want to use a name that describes the data in the file, such as **customers_in** or **high_scores**.

Like any other variable, a file pointer must be declared outside the main function if it is to be accessed globally. There is nothing wrong with declaring file pointers globally. Some programmers prefer to have all their file pointers declared as global variables. In this book, we will declare file pointers globally when more than one function needs access to the file pointer.

After you have declared a file pointer, the next step is to open the file.

OPENING A FILE

When you *open* a file, a physical disk file is associated with the file pointer you declared. You must provide the name of the file you want to open and you must specify whether you want to put data in the file (write) or get data from the file (read). Consider the statements below.

```
ofstream high_scores;   // declares a file pointer for writing to file
high_scores.open("SCORES.DAT", ios::out); // create the output file
```

The statements above declare a file pointer named **high_scores** and opens a file on disk with the filename *SCORES.DAT*. After the filename, you must specify the way you want to access the file, called *stream operation modes*. There are several modes available, most of which you will learn about as you need them. For now, you need to know only two: **ios::out** and **ios::in**. Use **ios::out** when creating an output file and **ios::in** when opening a file for input. Your compiler may not require that you specify the stream operation mode when using these basic modes. It is a good idea, however, to specify the mode in all cases.

If a file named *SCORES.DAT* already exists in the same location, the existing file will be replaced with the new one. If no such file exists, one is created and made ready for data.

On the Net

See http://www.ProgramCPP.com topic 11.2.1 for information about slight differences in the way some compilers implement the opening of a file.

Let's look at another example. The statements below will open a file named *MYDATA.DAT* for input using a file pointer named **infile**.

```
ifstream infile;   // declares a file pointer for reading a file
infile.open("MYDATA.DAT", ios::in); // open the file for input
```

After a file has been opened, you can begin writing to it or reading from it (depending on the stream operation mode). When you complete your work with the file, you must *close* it. The statement below closes the file pointed to by the file pointer named **infile**.

```
infile.close(); // close the input file
```

The statement format is the same whether you are closing an input or output file.

WRITING DATA TO FILES

Writing data to a sequential-access data file employs the extraction operator (<<) that you use when printing data to the screen. Instead of using the output operator to direct data to the standard output device (**cout**), you direct the data to the file using the file pointer. For example, the program listed in Figure 11-3 prompts the user for his or her name and age, opens a file for output, and writes the data to the output file.

PITFALLS

By this time you are sending output to **cout** *by habit. When outputting to a file, make sure you use the file pointer name in place of* **cout***.*

Notice the user is prompted to provide input in a manner similar to previous programs with which you have worked. Next, the statement **if (outfile)** appears. This code is the functional equivalent of **if (outfile != 0)**. Thus, if an error results in the attempt to open the file, the file pointer (**outfile**) is assigned the value of zero.

There are a number of conditions that can cause an error to occur when opening a file. The disk could be protected from new data being written to it. If you are attempting to open a file on a floppy disk, there is always the possibility that the disk is in the wrong drive. Because a disk drive is a hardware device, there may also be mechanical problems. Whatever the case, you must check to be sure that the file was opened successfully before sending data to the file.

Note

In most compilers, the **#include<fstream.h>** *directive makes the use of* **iostream.h** *unnecessary because* **fstream.h** *contains everything* **iostream.h** *has and more. In this chapter we include both for compatibility.*

```
#include<iostream.h>
#include<fstream.h>  // necessary for file I/O

int main()
{
 char user_name[25];
 int age;
 ofstream outfile; // declares file pointer named outfile

 cout << "Enter your name: "; // get name from user
 cin.get(user_name, 25);
 cout << "Enter your age: ";  // get age from user
 cin >> age;

 outfile.open("NAME_AGE.DAT",ios::out);  // open file for output

 if (outfile)  // If no error occurs while opening file
  {           // write the data to the file.
   outfile << user_name << endl;  // write the name to the file
   outfile << age << endl;        // write the age to the file
   outfile.close();  // close the output file
  }
 else          // If error occurred, display message.
  {
   cout << "An error occurred while opening the file.\n";
  }
 return 0;
}
```

F I G U R E   1 1 - 3
This program stores the user's name and age to a sequential-access data file.

EXERCISE 11-1   WRITING SEQUENTIAL FILES

1. Enter the program shown in Figure 11-3. Save the source code as *FILEWRIT.CPP*.

2. Compile and run the program. Enter your name and age at the prompts.

3. When the program ends, open *NAME_AGE.DAT* using your compiler's text editor. The data you entered is in readable form in the file.

4. Close *NAME_AGE.DAT* and *FILEWRIT.CPP*.

When writing to files using the technique of Exercise 11-1, the output file receives data in text form in the same way output sent to **cout** appears on the screen. The output must be separated with spaces or end-of-line characters or the data will run together in the file. The reason you write data to a file is so that it can be read in again later. Therefore, you must separate data with spaces or end-of-line characters when you write it to a text file.

The program in Figure 11-4 uses a loop to ask the user for a series of numbers. Each number the user enters is stored in a file named *OUTFILE.DAT*. When the user enters a zero, the program ends.

```
#include<iostream.h>
#include<fstream.h>  // necessary for file I/O

int main()
{
 float x;            // variable for user input
 ofstream outfile;   // declares file pointer named outfile

 outfile.open("FLOATS.DAT",ios::out);  // open file for output

 if (outfile)
  {
    cout << "Enter a series of floating-point numbers.\n"
         << "Enter a zero to end the series.\n";
    do   // repeat the loop until user enters zero
     {
       cin >> x;                 // get number from user
       outfile << x << endl;   // write the number to the file
      } while (x != 0.0);
  }
 else
  {
    cout << "Error opening file.\n";
  }
 outfile.close();  // close the output file
 return 0;
}
```

F I G U R E   1 1 - 4
This program stores numbers entered by the user until a zero is entered.

EXERCISE 11-2   MORE WRITING SEQUENTIAL FILES

1. Enter the program shown in Figure 11-4. Save the source code as *LOOPWRIT.CPP*.

2. Compile and run the program. Enter at least five or six floating point numbers and then be sure to end by entering a zero.

3. When the program ends, open *FLOATS.DAT* using your compiler's text editor. The numbers you entered are in readable form in the file.

4. Close *FLOATS.DAT* and *LOOPWRIT.CPP*.

READING DATA FROM FILES

The main reason data is written to a file is so that it can be later read and used again. In other cases, your program may read a data file created by another program.

As you learned earlier in this chapter, before you can read data from a file you must open the file for input using a file pointer. The statements below are an example of declaring an input file pointer and opening a file named *MYDATA.DAT* for input.

```
ifstream infile;  // declares a file pointer for reading a file
infile.open("MYDATA.DAT", ios::in); // open the file for input
```

WARNING

When you open a file using `ios::in`*, the file must already exist. Some compilers will create an empty file and give unpredictable results. Other compilers may give an error message.*

Once the file is open, you can read the data using methods familiar to you. However, reading from a data file can be a little more complicated than getting input from the keyboard. In this chapter you will learn two methods of reading from data files. Other methods can be used, but these methods should give the desired results without too much complication.

First you will learn a method that can be used when the file contains only numeric data. Then you will learn how to read data that includes strings or a combination of strings and data.

READING NUMERIC DATA

When reading strictly numeric data, you can use the insertion operator (>>) as if you were getting input from the keyboard. Instead of using **cin** as the input stream, use your file pointer name. The program in Figure 11-5 reads the numbers you wrote to disk in Exercise 11-2, prints the numbers to the screen, and calculates the sum and average of the numbers.

EXERCISE 11-3   READING NUMERIC DATA

1. Retrieve the file *NUMREAD.CPP*. The program shown in Figure 11-5 appears.

2. Compile and run the program. The numbers you entered in Exercise 11-2 should appear, along with the sum of the values, and the average.

3. Close the source code file.

READING STRING DATA AND MIXED STRING AND NUMERIC DATA

When reading string data, use the **get** function as you do to read strings from the keyboard. Like using **get** with the keyboard, using **get** to read from files requires that you flush the stream to remove the end-of-line character.

When you have a file that includes both string data and numeric data (such as the name and age saved in Exercise 11-1), you should read all of the data as string data and convert the strings that contain numbers to numeric variables. This is done using a function called **atoi** or other related functions. The **atoi** function converts a number which is represented in a string to an actual integer value which can be stored in an integer variable. You will learn more about the functions which convert strings to numeric values in Chapter 13.

```
#include<fstream.h>   // necessary for file I/O
#include<iostream.h>
#include<iomanip.h>

int main()
{
 float x, sum, average;
 int count;
 ifstream infile;     // declares file pointer named infile

 infile.open("FLOATS.DAT",ios::in);  // open file for input

 sum = 0.0;  // initialize sum
 count = 0;  // initialize count
 if (infile)  // If no error occurred while opening file
  {           // input the data from the file.
   cout << "The numbers in the data file are as follows:\n"
        << setprecision(1); // set display to one decimal point
   cout.setf(ios::fixed);  // prevent E-notation

   do  // read numbers until 0.0 is encountered
    {
      infile >> x;         // get number from file
      cout << x << endl;   // print number to screen
      sum = sum + x;       // add number to sum
      count++;             // increment count of how many numbers read
    } while(x != 0.0);
   // Output sum and average.
   cout << "The sum of the numbers is " << sum << endl;
   cout << "The average of the numbers (excluding zero) is "
        << sum / (count - 1) << endl;
  }
 else          // If error occurred, display message.
  {
   cout << "An error occurred while opening the file.\n";
  }
 infile.close();  // close the input file
 return 0;
}
```

F I G U R E   1 1 - 5
This program reads numbers from a data file until zero is encountered. Then the program reports the sum and average of the numbers.

The program completed in Exercise 11-1 stores the variable name as a string and age as an integer. However, the program in Figure 11-6 illustrates how both values can be read as strings and the age can be converted to an integer prior to printing the values to the screen.

EXERCISE 11-4   READING STRING DATA

1. Retrieve *STRREAD.CPP*. The program in Figure 11-6 appears on your screen.

2. Before running the program, analyze the source code to see the purpose of each statement.

3. Compile and run the program. Your name and age saved in Exercise 11-1 should appear in the output.

4. Close the source code file.

```
#include<fstream.h>    // necessary for file I/O
#include<iostream.h>
#include<stdlib.h>     // necessary for atoi function

int main()
{
 char user_name[25];
 char user_age[4];
 int age;
 ifstream infile;      // declares file pointer named infile

 infile.open("NAME_AGE.DAT",ios::in);  // open file for input

 if (infile)  // If no error occurred while opening file
   {          // input the data from the file.
     infile.get(user_name,25); // read the name from the file
     infile.ignore(80,'\n');
     infile.get(user_age,4); // read the age from the file as a string
     infile.ignore(80,'\n');
     age = atoi(user_age);
     cout << "The name read from the file is " << user_name << ".\n";
     cout << "The age read from the file is " << age << ".\n";
   }
 else         // If error occurred, display message.
   {
     cout << "An error occurred while opening the file.\n";
   }
 infile.close();  // close the input file
 return 0;
}
```

FIGURE 11-6
This program reads both the name and age from the file as strings and converts the age to an integer.

SECTION 11.2 QUESTIONS

1. What is the danger of leaving a file open?

2. What happens if you open a file for output that already exists?

3. Describe a condition that may cause an error when opening a file.

4. How can you test to see if an error occurred while opening a file?

5. How should you read numbers from a file when the file also contains string data?

PROBLEM 11.2.1

Write a program that asks the user's name, address, city, state, and ZIP code. The program should then save the data to a data file. Save the source code as *ADDRFILE.CPP*.

Modify *HIGHTEMP.CPP* or *HTEMP2.CPP* so that it gets its temperatures from a data file, rather than from the keyboard. Create a text file with sample temperatures in order to test the program. Save the new source code as *HTEMP3.CPP*.

CHAPTER 11, SECTION 3

Sequential File Techniques

Y ou now know how to write and read sequential-access data files. In this section you will learn techniques that will help you work more efficiently with files. You will learn how to add data to the end of a file, detect the end of a file, how to use multiple data files at the same time, and how to prompt the user for the name of a data file.

ADDING DATA TO THE END OF A FILE

One of the limitations of sequential-access files is that most changes require that you rewrite the file. For example, to insert data somewhere in a file, the file must be rewritten. You can, however, add data to the end of a file without rewriting the file. Adding data to the end of an existing file is called *appending*. To append data to an existing file, open the file using the **ios::app** stream operation mode, as shown in the statement below.

```
outfile.open("MYDATA.DAT",ios::app);  // open file for appending
```

Note

*If the file you open for appending does not exist, the operating system creates one just as if you had opened it using **ios::out** mode.*

The program in Figure 11-7 opens the *NAME_AGE.DAT* data file and allows you to add more names and ages to the file. The only difference between the program in Figure 11-7 and the program you ran in Exercise 11-1 is the stream operation mode in the line that opens the file.

EXERCISE 11-5   APPENDING DATA TO A FILE

1. Open the program *FILEWRIT.CPP* that you saved in Exercise 11-1.

2. Run the program without any modification. Enter your name and age as input.

3. Open the output file (*NAME_AGE.DAT*) to see that the file's only contents are what you just entered. Close *NAME_AGE.DAT*.

4. Run the program again. This time enter *Scott McGrew* for the name and *18* for the age.

```
#include<fstream.h>   // necessary for file I/O
#include<iostream.h>

int main()
{
 char user_name[25];
 int age;
 ofstream outfile; // declares file pointer named outfile

 cout << "Enter your name: "; // get name from user
 cin.get(user_name, 25);
 cout << "Enter your age: ";  // get age from user
 cin >> age;

 outfile.open("NAME_AGE.DAT",ios::app);  // open file for appending

 if (outfile)  // If no error occurred while opening file
  {             // output the data to the file.
   outfile << user_name << endl;   // write the name to the file
   outfile << age << endl;         // write the age to the file
  }
 else           // If error occurred, display message.
  {
   cout << "An error occurred while opening the file.\n";
  }

 outfile.close();  // close the output file
 return 0;
}
```

F I G U R E   1 1 - 7

This program adds data to the end of the data file, rather than replacing whatever data was in the file.

5. Open *NAME_AGE.DAT* again to see that Scott McGrew's name and age have replaced yours in the file. Close *NAME_AGE.DAT*.

6. Change the statement that opens the file for output:

```
outfile.open("NAME_AGE.DAT",ios::out);  // open file for output
```

to

```
outfile.open("NAME_AGE.DAT",ios::app);  // open file for appending
```

7. Run the program again. This time enter your name and age again.

8. Open *NAME_AGE.DAT* again to see that Scott McGrew's name and age have not been replaced by yours. Because the file was opened for appending, your name and age were added to the end of the file.

9. Close *NAME_AGE.DAT*.

10. Save the source code as *FILEAPP.CPP* and close the source code file.

DETECTING THE END OF A FILE

Often the length of a file is unknown to the programmer. In Exercise 11-3, the series of numbers you read into your program ended with a zero. Because you knew the data ended with a zero, you knew when to stop reading. In other cases, however, you may not have a value in the file that signals the end of the file. In those cases, there is a technique for detecting the end of the file.

When an attempt is made to read past the end of a file, the results vary depending on the data you are reading. If you try to read a number once the end of the file is reached, the last number in the file will probably be read again. In the case of string data, an empty string is returned. To know for sure whether the end of the file has been reached, use the **eof** function.

The **eof** function returns 1 (true) if an attempt has been made to read past the end of the file. To use the **eof** function, use the name of the file pointer, a period, and **eof()**, as shown in the code segment below.

```
infile >> x;          // Get number from file.
if (!infile.eof())
 {                    // If not the end of file,
  cout << x << endl;  // print the number to the screen.
 }
```

In the example above, the not operator (!) is used so that the statement in the if structure will be executed if the end of the file has *not* been reached. Figure 11-8 shows a program that uses the code segment above.

Note

You can use the eof function whether working with string or numeric data.

EXERCISE 11-6   DETECTING THE END OF A FILE

1. Retrieve the source code file *READEOF.CPP*. The program shown in Figure 11-8 appears.

2. Compile and run the program. If the program reports that an error occurred while opening the file, make sure that the *PRICES.DAT* data file is in the default directory, or provide the path to the correct directory in the statement that opens the file. Your instructor can assist you if necessary.

3. When the program runs correctly, close the source code file.

```
#include<fstream.h>   // necessary for file I/O
#include<iostream.h>
#include<iomanip.h>   // necessary for setprecision manipulator

int main()
{
 float x;             // Declare variable used for input.
 ifstream infile;     // Declare file pointer named infile.

 infile.open("PRICES.DAT",ios::in);  // Open file for input.

 if (infile)  // If no error occurred while opening file,
   {              // input the data from the file.
  cout << "The prices in the file are: \n" << setprecision(2);
  do  // Loop while not the end of the file.
    {
      infile >> x;            // Get number from file.
      if (!infile.eof())
        {                     // If not the end of file,
          cout << x << endl;  // print the number to the screen.
        }
    } while (!infile.eof());
   }
 else           // If error occurred, display message.
   {
     cout << "An error occurred while opening the file.\n";
   }
 infile.close();  // Close the input file.
 return 0;
}
```

FIGURE 11-8
This program continues to read floating point numbers from a file until the end of the file is reached.

On the Net

Some compilers require slightly different syntax to detect the end of a file. For more information, see http://www.ProgramCPP.com topic 11.3.2.

USING MULTIPLE FILES

As mentioned earlier, you can have more than one file open at a time. Just declare and use a separate file pointer for each file. Why would you want more than one file open at a time? There are many reasons. Let's look at a few of them.

Suppose you need to add some data to the middle of a file. Since you cannot insert data in a file, you must read the data from the original file and write it to a new file. At the position where the new data is to be inserted, you write the data to the new file and then continue writing the rest of the data from the original file.

Large database programs, called *relational database systems,* use multiple database files. For example, a program for an animal clinic might use one database file to store the information about the owners of pets and another file for the information about the pets themselves. The database of pets would include a field that linked the pet to its owner in the other database file. The term *relational*

```
#include<fstream.h>   // necessary for file I/O
#include<iostream.h>

int main()
{
  char ch;            // Declare character variable used for input.
  ifstream infile;    // Declare file pointer for input file.
  ofstream outfile;   // Declare file pointer for output file.

  infile.open("LOWER.TXT",ios::in);    // Open file for input.
  outfile.open("UPPER.TXT",ios::out); // Open file for output.

  if ((!infile) || (!outfile))  // If file error on either file,
   {                             // print message and stop program.
     cout << "Error opening file.\n";
     return 0;
   }

  infile.unsetf(ios::skipws); // prevents spaces from being skipped

  while (!infile.eof())  // Loop while not the end of the file.
   {
     infile >> ch;         // Get character from file.
     if (!infile.eof())
      {
        if ((ch > 96) && (ch < 123))  // if character is lowercase a-z,
         {                            // subtract 32 to make uppercase.
          ch = ch - 32;
         }
        outfile << ch;      // Write character to output file.
      }
   } // end of while loop

  infile.close();  // Close the input file.
  outfile.close(); // Close the output file.
  return 0;
}
```

F I G U R E   1 1 - 9
This program converts all lower-case characters in a file to upper-case.

database comes from the fact that multiple database files are related or linked by certain fields.

Another example of when more than one file may be necessary is when performing a conversion process on a file. Suppose you need to convert all of the lowercase alphabetic characters in a file to uppercase letters. The program in Figure 11-9 reads the text in one file one character at a time, converts where necessary, and writes the converted characters to another file.

To convert the lowercase characters to uppercase, the ASCII value of the character is tested to see if it falls within the range of 97 to 122, which are the ASCII values of the lowercase letters. If the character falls within that range, the value in the character variable is reduced by 32 which converts it to the uppercase equivalent of the letter. This works because the uppercase letters have ASCII values from 65 to 90, which is 32 less than 97 to 122. To see the ASCII values in a table, refer to Appendix A.

The code segment

```
if ((ch > 96) && (ch < 123))   // if character is lowercase a-z,
  {                            // subtract 32 to make uppercase.
   ch = ch - 32;
  }
```

could be rewritten as

```
if ((ch >= 'a') && (ch <= 'z'))   // if character is lowercase a-z,
  {                               // subtract 32 to make uppercase.
   ch = ch - 32;
  }
```

The statement **infile.unsetf(ios::skipws);** is probably new to you. Without this statement, the **infile >> ch;** statement will not read the spaces, tabs, or end-of-line characters. By default, white space (spaces, tabs, and end-of-line characters) are ignored when reading from a file. The **skipws** (which is short for *skip white space*) setting allows you to override the default.

The statement **infile.unsetf(ios::skipws);** is necessary in this program because the spaces, tabs, and end-of-file characters that are in the input file must be included in the output file. If the white space is skipped when the input file is read, the white space will not appear in the converted file.

EXERCISE 11-7   USING MULTIPLE FILES

1. Open *CONVERT.CPP*. The program in Figure 11-9 appears.

2. Create a text file that includes a variety of characters, both uppercase and lowercase. Save the file as ASCII text and name it *LOWER.TXT*. Make sure the file is in the current directory or supply the path in the statement that opens the file.

3. Compile and run the program. The program produces no output on the screen.

4. Open *UPPER.TXT* to see that all of the lowercase letters have been converted to uppercase.

5. Close *UPPER.TXT* and *LOWER.TXT*. Leave *CONVERT.CPP* open for the next exercise.

WARNING

Open files only as you need them and close them as soon as possible to avoid data loss in the event of power failure or program crash.

PROMPTING FOR FILE NAMES

Up to now we have used filenames that are **hard coded** into the program, meaning the names cannot be changed when the program runs. In programs with hard-coded filenames, the filenames appear in the source code as string literals. To make a program such as the one in Exercise 11-7 more flexible, you can prompt the user for the filenames. The code segment in Figure 11-10 prompts the user for two filenames and opens the files.

EXERCISE 11-8   PROMPTING FOR FILENAMES

1. Replace the two statements that open the files with the code from Figure 11-10. Save the modified source code as *CONVERT2.CPP*.

2. Run the program. Enter *LOWER.TXT* as the input file and *UPPER2.TXT* as the output file.

3. Check the output file (*UPPER2.TXT*) to make sure the conversion took place.

4. Close the source code file and the output file.

```
char inputfile[13];
char outputfile[13];

cout << "Enter the name of the input file: ";
cin.get(inputfile,13);
cin.ignore(80, '\n'};
cout << "Enter the name of the output file: ";
cin.get(outfile,13);
cin.ignore(80,'\n');

infile.open(inputfile, ios::in);     // Open file for input.
outfile.open(outputfile, ios::out),  // Open file for output.
```

FIGURE 11-10
The filename can be provided by the user.

SECTION 11.3 QUESTIONS

1. What stream operation mode is used when adding data to the end of an existing file?

2. Write a code segment that prints the message END OF FILE REACHED if the file pointer named **infile** has reached the end of the file.

3. Give an example of a situation that may require that more than one file be opened at a time.

4. What statement prevents spaces in a file from being skipped?

5. What is the term used to describe a filename that is part of the program and cannot be changed by the user when the program runs?

PROBLEM 11.3.1

Modify the program written in Problem 11.2.1 so that it appends a name and address to the data file every time the program is run, rather than rewriting the output file. Run the program several times to append several names and addresses to the output file. Save the source code as *NAMEFILE.CPP*.

PROBLEM 11.3.2

Write a program that reads the data saved in Problem 11.3.1 and prints the data to the screen. Save the source code as *NAMEPRNT.CPP*.

PROBLEM 11.3.3

Modify the program you saved in Exercise 11-8 to convert uppercase letters to lowercase, rather than lowercase to uppercase. Save the modified source code as *UPPERLOW.CPP*.

KEY TERMS

appending	reading
close	relational database systems
file pointer	sequential-access file
hard coded	stream operation modes
open	writing
random-access file	

SUMMARY

➤ Data files allow for the storage of data prior to a program's ending and the computer being turned off. Data files also allow for more data storage than can fit in RAM.

➤ A sequential-access file is like an audio cassette tape. Data must be written to and read from the file sequentially.

➤ A random-access file is like a compact disc. Any record can be accessed directly.

➤ The first step to using a file is declaring a file pointer. Some file pointers are for writing data and some are for reading data.

➤ After a file pointer has been declared, the next step is to open the file. Opening a file associates the file pointer with a physical data file.

➤ After data is written or read, the file must be closed.

➤ The extraction operator (<<) is used to write to a data file.

> When reading numeric data, use the insertion operator. When reading string data or when reading from a file with both string and numeric data, read the data as strings and convert the numbers to numeric variables.

> Adding data to the end of an existing file is called appending.

> The **eof** function detects the end of a file.

> You can use more than one file at a time by declaring multiple file pointers.

> You can prompt the user for input and output filenames.

PROJECTS

PROJECT 11-1 • FILE PROCESSING

Write a program that copies a text file. The program should remove any blank lines and spaces between words as it writes the new file.

PROJECT 11-2 • FILE PROCESSING

Write a program that prompts the user for the name of a text file and reports the number of characters in the text file, and the number of end-of-line characters in the text file.

PROJECT 11-3 • STRING CONVERSION

Write a program that prompts the user for his or her full name. The program should check the first character of each name to make sure it appears in upper-case, making conversion where necessary. For example, if the user enters *jessica hope baldwin*, the program should output *Jessica Hope Baldwin*.

PROJECT 11-4 • STRING MANIPULATION

Extend the program from Project 11-3 to output the name last name first in the format below.

Baldwin, Jessica Hope

12

Object-Oriented Programming

OBJECTIVES

➤ Understand the difference between procedural programming and object-oriented programming.

➤ Understand the principles of object-oriented programming.

➤ Learn how to read classes and use objects in C++.

➤ Understand how objects help programmers reuse code.

➤ Understand containment and inheritance in C++ object-oriented programming.

Overview

As the field of computer science has grown over the years, several different methods have been developed for programming computers. The first programming was done by flipping switches on a control panel or feeding machine language instructions into a computer. Recall from Chapter 2 that the development of assembly language was followed by the development of high-level languages which made programming easier.

One of the more recent developments in programming is known as object-oriented programming (OOP). Object-oriented programming in some ways continues the trend toward higher-level programming languages. OOP, however, does more than that. Object-oriented programming changes the way a programmer uses data and functions.

Object-oriented programming is not unique to C++. Many languages support object-oriented programming. In this chapter you will learn about the object-oriented method of programming, its benefits, and how to read and use the C++ implementation of object-oriented programming.

CHAPTER 12, SECTION 1

Procedural Programming vs. Object-Oriented Programming

The different methods used for writing programs are known as paradigms. A *paradigm* is a model or a set of rules that define a way of programming. There are two primary paradigms used to program computers today: the procedural paradigm and the object-oriented paradigm.

PROCEDURAL PARADIGM

The procedural paradigm is the paradigm you have used in this book up to this point. The *procedural paradigm* focuses on the idea that all algorithms in a program are performed with functions and data that a programmer can see, understand, and change. In a program written procedurally, the focus is on the functions that will process the data. The programmer then devises ways to pass the required data to and from the functions which do the processing. To be successful writing procedural programs, the programmer must understand how all data is stored and how the algorithms of the program work.

Consider, for example, what you learned in Chapter 6 about strings. After you learned what strings are, you then had to learn how strings are stored in memory using character arrays and how strings end with a null terminator. Without the knowledge of how strings are implemented in C++, you could not successfully store strings in your programs. Procedural programming typically requires this kind of knowledge about the way data is stored.

Procedural programming also requires that you know how data is stored in order to write the functions that will process the data. For example, recall the exercise from Chapter 6 in which you copied a string into a character array which was not large enough to hold the string. The result was a loss of data in the surrounding bytes of memory. In procedural programming, the programmer must be concerned with many similar technical details.

Procedural programming is not all bad. In fact, procedural programming has served many programmers well for many years and will continue to do so for some time. But computer scientists are always searching for a better way to develop software. By taking a look at the world around them, computer scientists discovered that the world consists of objects that perform work and interact with each other. When applied to programming computers, the result is a different paradigm: object-oriented programming.

Extra for Experts

There are many different programming paradigms in computer science. Some of the paradigms are procedural, functional, object-oriented, and logic. Most common languages such as C, FORTRAN, and standard Pascal are procedural. C++, Smalltalk, and Java are well known object-oriented languages. The functional paradigm includes languages like LISP and Scheme. Finally, Prolog is a language in the logic paradigm.

OBJECT-ORIENTED PARADIGM

The *object-oriented paradigm* centers on the idea that all programs can be made up of separate entities called *objects*. A program built from these objects is called an *object-oriented program*. Each of the objects used to build the program has a specific responsibility or purpose. For example, an object in an object-oriented program might store a string of characters. The string itself, and all of the operations that can be performed with the string are part of the object. The string object can initialize itself, store a string provided to it, and perform other functions such as reporting the length of the string the object holds. In other words, instead of an object being directly manipulated by other parts of the program, an object manipulates itself. Building programs using the object-oriented paradigm is called *object-oriented programming* or *OOP*.

On the Net

For a history of the object-oriented paradigm, see topic 12.1.1 at http://www. ProgramCPP.com.

Communication among objects is similar to communication among people. You cannot look inside of someone's head to see what they know. You must ask questions and allow the person to provide a response. In *OOP*, data is transferred through *messages* which are exchanged among objects. The data in an object is not intended to be accessed directly by code which is outside of the object (see Figure 12-1). For example, the string object mentioned above can be initialized by sending a message to the object. You could also send a message to the object asking for the length of the string currently stored in the object. The string object would then respond with the requested information. Inside the object is the code (called *methods*) necessary to perform the operations on the object.

Note

Messages can do more than simply initialize an object or return a length of a string. A message can perform a high-level task such as sort information in the object. A string object could even include a method to check the spelling of the text in the string.

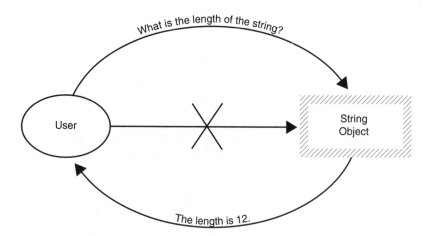

FIGURE 12-1
To get data, objects must pass messages back and forth. Objects cannot simply take the data they need.

Communication among objects takes the form of messages because objects hide all of their data and internal operations. This "hiding" of data and code is known as *encapsulation*. By using encapsulation, objects can protect and guarantee the integrity of their data. In procedural programming, poorly written functions can often change important data, causing problems throughout the program. The threat of a poorly written function changing data is reduced when using the object-oriented paradigm.

Believe it or not, you have already started to use some of the object-oriented features of the C++ language. The first program you compiled and ran contained the statement below.

```
cout << "My first C++ program.\n";
```

Note

When you change format options with **setf** *and* **unsetf**, *you are actually sending a message to the* **cout** *object.*

The streams **cin** and **cout** are actually objects which represent console input (usually the keyboard) and console output (usually the monitor), respectively. Now that you know something about the object-oriented paradigm, you can understand that the statement is actually a message to the **cout** object directing the object to display the indicated text.

There is more to object-oriented programming than what has been mentioned in this section. The first step, however, is to visualize how a program can be implemented using objects, learn what is in an object, and understand how objects communicate with other parts of the program. Object-oriented programming in C++ does not take the place of what you have already learned. Instead, it extends the features of the language and gives you a new way to organize programs. The structures and data types you have been using are also used in object-oriented programs. In fact, what you have learned in previous chapters will provide the foundation you need to be successful as an object-oriented programmer.

On the Net

In some programming languages, such as Smalltalk and Java, practically everything is object-oriented. These languages are sometimes referred to as pure OOP languages. C++, however, is more of a hybrid language. You can make use of OOP, but you can also program without using OOP. For more information about OOP purity and other OOP languages, see http://www.ProgramCPP.com. See topic 12.1.2.

1. What programming paradigm has been used in the previous chapters of this book?

2. How do objects communicate with other objects?

3. Where is the data that an object manipulates stored?

4. What is encapsulation?

5. Identify a C++ object that you have already used.

PROBLEM 12.1.1

Select one of the programs you have written previously in this course and propose a way that the program could be implemented using objects.

PROBLEM 12.1.2

Use a Web search engine to locate information on the WWW about object-oriented programming (OOP). Also search for OOA (object-oriented analysis) and OOD (object-oriented design). After you see what your search finds, go to http://www.ProgramCPP.com and check out the links to object-oriented programming resources found in topic 12.1.3.

CHAPTER 12, SECTION 2

Object-Oriented Programming in C++

Now that you understand some of the concepts of the object-oriented paradigm, you can begin to create programs which use objects. Several different programming languages incorporate the object-oriented paradigm. Each language which supports OOP implements the paradigm in a slightly different way. In this book, you will learn the C++ implementation.

In this section, you will run a program that uses a circle object. You will see how encapsulation and messages make it possible for you to use the object without knowing how the data is stored in the object or how the algorithms are implemented.

CLASSES

Before an object can be created in C++, the compiler must have a definition to know how to create that type of object. The definition for an object is known as a *class*. Using a class is similar to using the basic data types in C++. For example, suppose that a class is created that supports objects which represent circles. This class is named **circle**. The class **circle** is what tells the compiler how to create each object of type **circle**. You can declare a **circle** object like you declare the other data types in C++.

For example, the statement below declares an integer named **my_int**. The statement instructs the compiler to reserve memory for the data.

```
int my_int;
```

In the same way, to declare an object of the type **circle**, the code below would be used.

```
circle my_circle;
```

When the compiler encounters this declaration, it refers to the **circle** definition to find out how much memory to reserve for a **circle** object. The object is then created in memory and given the name **my_circle**. In the same way that many different variables of the same data type can be created, many different objects of the type **circle** can be created. Each different object of the type **circle** is independent of the other **circle** objects in the program.

Because objects are more complex than the simple data types, a different term is used to describe the declaration of an object. When you declare an object, you say that you have *instanciated* the object. In other words, you have created an *instance* of a class. An instance is the data for one object that has the behaviors as defined by the class. If you were to instanciate two **circle** objects, you would have two independent objects which could be used to represent two distinct circles.

Note

When multiple objects are instanciated from the same class, the code required to perform the operations (methods) is not duplicated in memory for each object. The data for each object is stored separately in memory, but all objects defined by the same class share the same code.

EXERCISE 12-1   UNDERSTANDING OBJECTS

1. Load the program *OOP.CPP*.

2. Look at the program and see how the objects are instanciated and how messages are passed between the objects. Notice that there is no way of knowing how the **circle** objects store the radius or how they calculate area.

3. Run the program.

4. Leave the source code file open while you analyze the program in the paragraphs which follow.

On the Net

Another way to look at the relationship between a class and an object is to consider examples in the real world. If the definition of a human being were a class, then you and I are instances of that class. We are not the same person, but we both have the characteristics of the human class. An automobile can be thought of as an instance of a class. Any pickup truck you see on the road is an instance of the pickup truck class of vehicles. For more examples of classes and objects, see http://www.ProgramCPP.com. See topic 12.2.1.

Let's analyze the source code you ran in the previous exercise. After the beginning comments, there are two compiler directives.

```
#include "circle.h"                    // contains the circle class
#include <iostream.h>
```

The first compiler directive includes the header file **circle.h**. The **circle.h** header file contains the definition for the **circle** class. Without the class definition, the compiler would not know how to create a **circle** object nor would it know what properties a **circle** object has. The next compiler directive includes the **iostream.h** header file so that the program can get input from the user and output data to the screen.

___

Note

You may have noticed that the #include directives in this example use different characters around the header file name. Use quotation marks ("") when the header file is a source file in the same location as your program source code. Use the less than and greater than symbols (<>), sometimes called angle brackets, when the header file is one of the compiler's pre-compiled library functions.

In the main function, the program instantiates two copies of the **circle** class, **Circle_One** and **Circle_Two**. A variable to hold a radius and an area of a circle are also declared. The variables **User_Radius** and **Area** are used in your program and are not part of either object.

```
int main()
{
  circle Circle_One;                   // instanciate objects
  circle Circle_Two;                   // of type circle
  float User_Radius;
  double Area;
```

The program then prompts the user for the radius of the first circle. After the program receives the user's response, it sends a message to **Circle_One** requesting that it set its radius to **User_Radius**.

```
cout << "\nWhat is the radius of the first circle? ";
cin  >> User_Radius;

Circle_One.SetRadius(User_Radius); // Send a message to Circle_One telling
                                   // it to set its radius to User_Radius
```

After the radius of **Circle_One** has been set to **User_Radius**, the program prompts the user for the radius of the second circle and sets the radius of **Circle_Two** using the same function that was used to set the radius of **Circle_One**. You can see that messages are sent to the **circle** objects by using the object's name, a period, and the message. The period used between the identifier and the message is called the *class-member operator* or *member selection operator*.

```
cout << "\nWhat is the radius of the second circle? ";
cin  >> User_Radius;

Circle_Two.SetRadius(User_Radius);  // Send a message to Circle_Two telling
                                    // it to set its radius to User_Radius
```

Finally, the program sends a message to each of the **circle** objects and requests their area. The area of **Circle_One** is assigned to **Area** then output to the screen. Then the area of the second circle is also retrieved and output to the screen.

```
Area = Circle_One.Area();          // Send a message to Circle_One asking
                                   // for its area
cout.setf(ios::fixed);
cout << "\nThe area of the first circle is " << Area << ".\n";

Area = Circle_Two.Area();          // Send a message to Circle_Two asking
                                   // for its area
cout << "\nThe area of the second circle is " << Area << ".\n";
cout.unsetf(ios::fixed);
return 0;
}
```

There are many different ways the radius could be stored in the object as well as different ways the area could be calculated. Is the size of the circle stored in the form of the radius or the diameter? How is the area calculated? Neither of these things are known. To use the object, however, you do not need this information.

Also notice that you can only change the properties of the **circle** objects by using messages. To set the radius, you have to send a message to the **circle** object stating the new radius. What would happen if you sent the object a negative radius? The object could check the new radius to make sure it was positive, and not set the new value if it was incorrect. This principle of data protection and encapsulation is fundamental to the object-oriented paradigm.

SECTION 12.2 QUESTIONS

1. What is a class?

2. Suppose you have access to a class named **string**. Write a declaration for an object named **lastname** of type **string**.

3. When you declare an object, you have created an _____ of a class.

4. What is the term that describes the period used to separate an object's identifier from the message to the object?

5. What must you know about the **circle** class in order to use it?

PROBLEM 12.2.1

Write a program similar to *OOP.CPP* that instanciates a circle object, sets the radius of the circle to 1.5, then obtains the area of the circle from the object. The program should then set the radius of the circle to the value provided by the **Area** method. As output, the program should provide the area of the circle with a radius of 1.5 and the area of the circle at the end of the program.

PROBLEM 12.2.2

Write a program that instanciates a bucket object based on the class definition in *BUCKET.H* on your work disk. See if you can write the program without looking at the definition in *BUCKET.H*. The program should perform the following operations:

1. Instanciate an object of type **bucket**.

2. Use the **SetGallonSize()** method to set the bucket size to 5.0 gallons.

3. Use the **FillBucket()** method to fill the bucket with 3.2 gallons of water.

4. Use the **GetWeight()** method to output the weight of the 3.2 gallons of water.

CHAPTER 12, SECTION 3

Designing and Implementing a Class

As you saw in the previous section, using a class can be easy and uses syntax which is similar to what you have used before. At some point, however, you will need to design a class or modify an existing class. To do so, you will have to understand how a class is implemented in C++. Implementing a class is not difficult, but it does involve some new syntax that you may have not seen before. In this section, you will be introduced to class design and the implementation of classes by analyzing the **circle** class you used in the previous section.

DESIGNING A CLASS

Designing a class requires you think in an object-oriented way. For example, consider a typical telephone answering machine. It encapsulates the functions of an answering machine as well as the data (your incoming and outgoing messages). The buttons on the answering machine are the equivalent of messages. Pushing the Play button sends a message to the answering machine to play the stored messages. It is not hard to understand how an answering machine is an object that contains all of the storage and functions it needs within itself.

On the Net

Can you implement a simulated answering machine using object-oriented programming? Design a class that could implement an answering machine. You can see one implementation at http://www.ProgramCPP.com. See topic 12.3.1.

To design a class, you must think of computer programs in the same way you think of an answering machine or other objects around you. If you were to design the **circle** class you used in the previous section, you should first take into account what needs to be stored and what functions are necesssary. In other words, you define the purpose of the object. The purpose will determine how an object is coded, what data it will hold, and how its operations will be implemented.

In the case of the circle, all that is required to define a circle is a radius. You then decide what functions the object needs to perform. For example, you may want the circle to report its area and circumference. The circle also needs to be able to set its radius.

A class should be designed with enough functions and data to perform its responsibilities—no more and no less. You've never seen an answering machine that can function as a stapler. Likewise, a class should not perform an unrelated task. You also do not need to store more data than is necessary. For example, since the radius is all that is necessary to define a circle, you shouldn't store both a radius and a diameter.

Object-oriented design (often abbreviated OOD) involves much more than the guidelines outlined here. In Case Study VI you will learn more about object-oriented design.

IMPLEMENTING A CLASS

The best way to learn how to implement a class is to study the code of an implemented class. Figure 12-2 is the header file **circle.h** which was used in Exercise 12-1. You have used header files such as **iostream.h** and **math.h** before. However, you may not have ever opened one to see what's inside. A header file is a source code file that typically includes code or declarations of code that you intend to include in more than one program. Classes are normally defined in header files so that they may be reused.

Note

Header files normally contain declarations of variables, functions, and classes, but not the implementation of the functions and classes. This is the case with almost all header files that come with a C++ compiler. However, in some situations, the functions and classes may also be implemented in the same header file. In the next chapter, you will see an example of a class that has the implementation in a file separate from the declarations.

Before continuing, familiarize yourself with the code in Figure 12-2. In the paragraphs which follow, the implementation of the **circle** class will be broken down and examined.

COMPILER DIRECTIVES

At the beginning of the file are the compiler directives **#ifndef** and **#define**. These are used to prevent the class from being defined twice, which can create problems. The **#define** directive instructs the compiler to define a symbol and to remember that the symbol exists. The **#ifndef** directive checks the compiler's symbol table for a specified entry.

```
#ifndef _CIRCLE_H
#define _CIRCLE_H
```

```cpp
#ifndef _CIRCLE_H
#define _CIRCLE_H

const float PI = 3.14159;

class circle
{
  public:
        // constructors
        circle();                    // default constructor
        circle(const circle &);      // copy constructor

        // member functions
        void   SetRadius(float);
        double Area();

  private:
        // data
        float radius;
};

// default constructor
circle::circle()
{
  radius = 0;
}

// copy constructor
circle::circle(const circle & Object)
{
  radius = Object.radius;
}

// Method to set the radius of the circle
void circle::SetRadius(float IncomingRadius)
{
  radius = IncomingRadius;
}

// Method to find the area of the circle
double circle::Area()
{
  return(PI*radius*radius);
}

#endif
```

FIGURE 12-2
The definition and implementation of the circle object. This is the circle.h header filer used by the OOP.CPP program.

In this case, these compiler directives are used together to make sure that the circle class has not already been defined. The **#ifndef** directive checks for the existence of a symbol named **_CIRCLE_H**. If the entry is not found, the **#define** directive defines the symbol and the source code that follows defines the **circle** class. If the **_CIRCLE_H** symbol is already defined, it means that this header file has been compiled already and the definition of the **circle** class is skipped.

At the end of Figure 12-2 is the compiler directive **#endif** which ends the original **#ifndef** directive. The **#ifndef** compiler directive works with the **#endif** directive to form an if structure similar to what you have worked with in previous chapters. The **#ifndef** directive instructs the compiler to compile everything between the **#ifndef** and the **#endif** if the symbol is not defined.

CLASS DEFINITION

A class definition is made up of several different parts. The definition begins with the keyword **class**, followed by the class name, and an opening brace. The definition ends with a closing brace and a semicolon. Functions and variables that are prototyped and declared in a class definition are called *members*. The syntax is similar to what you have used with structures.

```
class circle
{
  public:
        // constructors
        circle();                       // default constructor
        circle(const circle &);         // copy constructor

        // member functions
        void    SetRadius(float);
        double Area();

  private:
        // data
        float radius;
};
```

PITFALLS

If the semicolon after a class definition is omitted, the compiler will report several errors. Therefore, if multiple errors are encountered when compiling a class, check for the presence of the semicolon at the end of the class definition.

After the opening brace is the keyword **public** followed by a colon. The **public** keyword tells the compiler to let the programmer using the class have access to all the variables and functions between the **public** and **private** keywords. Any variables and functions after the **private** keyword cannot be accessed from outside the object. The **private** keyword is what allows a **circle** object to protect its data. This data protection is known as *information hiding*, which is an important benefit provided by encapsulation. By using information hiding, objects can protect the integrity of their data.

The constructor prototypes follow the **public** keyword. *Constructors* tell the compiler how to create the object in memory and what the initial values of its data will be. Constructors are given the same name as the class.

```
// constructors
circle();                       // default constructor
circle(const circle &);         // copy constructor
```

For the **circle** class there are two constructors. The first constructor is known as the *default constructor*. The default constructor is used when the object is instanciated with no arguments. The second constructor is known as the *copy constructor*. A copy constructor receives a reference to another object as an argument, and is used when objects are passed to functions by value. You will learn more about copy constructors in the next chapter.

Extra for Experts

If no default constructor is defined, the compiler will actually create a default one for you. A class can have several different constructors that accept different arguments. Though not required, most every class should at least have a default constructor. For example, in addition to the default constructor the **circle** *class could include a constructor that allows you to pass the radius of the circle when the object is instanciated.*

After the constructors are the *member function* prototypes. Member functions allow programmers using an object to send information to it and receive information from it. Member functions are the messages used for communication in object-oriented programming.

```
// member functions
void    SetRadius(float);
double Area();
```

For the **circle** object, two member functions are needed, one to set the radius, and one to retrieve the area. Member function prototypes are written just like normal function prototypes with a return type, a name, and an argument list. Recall from Chapter 9 that it is not necessary for a prototype to include the names of the parameters, just the type. The implementation of the member functions follow the definition of the class.

The **private** keyword comes after the member function prototypes. The only data required for the **circle** object is the radius, so it is declared as a float with the identifier **radius**.

```
private:
        // data
        float radius;
```

Because **radius** is after the **private** keyword, a programmer using a **circle** object cannot access the radius directly, so member functions must be used. After the **radius** variable, the definition of the **circle** class is closed with the closing brace and a semicolon.

IMPLEMENTING MEMBER FUNCTIONS

To implement a member function, a special syntax must be used. The function is implemented like a normal C++ function except that the class name and the *scope-resolution operator* (::) precede the function name. Constructors are slightly different from other member functions because they do not have any return type—not even void.

Constructor implementation in the `circle` class is very simple. The default constructor sets the radius equal to zero. The copy constructor sets the radius equal to the passed object's radius.

```
// default constructor
circle::circle()
{
   radius = 0;
}

// copy constructor
circle::circle(const circle & Object)
{
   radius = Object.radius;
}
```

By initializing all data in an object, errors can be avoided later in the program. For example, if the integer data type were implemented as a class, the constructors could set its value to zero.

Note

The basic C++ data types (such as `int`) are not classes. Because `int` is a primitive data type, it does not have constructors, destructors, or any other properties of a class.

The implementation of the other member functions is also simple. Figure 12-3 shows a template for implementing a member function.

```
return_type class_name::function_name(parameters)
{
   // necessary code
}
```

F I G U R E   1 2 - 3
The proper way to implement a member function.

The `SetRadius` function sets the radius equal to the value it is passed.

```
// Method to set the radius of the circle
void circle::SetRadius(float IncomingRadius)
{
   radius = IncomingRadius;
}
```

The `Area` function returns the area of the circle using the standard formula, Area $= \pi r^2$.

```
// Method to find the area of the circle
double circle::Area()
{
   return(PI*radius*radius);
}
```

EXERCISE 12-2   MODIFYING A CLASS

1. Load the *CIRCLE.H* header file.

2. Add a member function to the **circle** class which will return the radius. Remember to add the prototype to the definition and to implement the function at the end of the header file.

3. Add the necessary code to the *OOP.CPP* program to get the radius from **Circle_One**, then print it to the screen.

4. Save and close the *CIRCLE.H* and *OOP.CPP* files.

On the Net

Through this chapter, classes have been implemented completely in header files. Classes can also be defined in header files and actually implemented in cpp *files. This is done by including the header file at the top of the implementation source file with the* **#include** *directive. To learn more about dividing the source code for a class, see http://www.ProgramCPP.com. See topic 12.3.2.*

SECTION 12.3 QUESTIONS

1. Describe one guideline to follow when designing a class.

2. Why are classes normally defined in header files?

3. What is the purpose of a constructor?

4. What is the purpose of a member function?

5. What are members?

6. What are methods?

PROBLEM 12.3.1

Using the **circle** class definition as a model, create a file called *SQUARE.H* and implement a class which models a square and includes an Area method.

PROBLEM 12.3.2

Modify the class you implemented in Problem 12.3.1 to create a rectangle class which models a rectangle and includes an Area method.

CHAPTER 12, SECTION 4

Reusability, Containment, and Inheritance

 ou have seen some of the advantages of using object-oriented programming. Three more advantages of the paradigm are reusability, containment, and inheritance.

REUSABILITY

Among the greatest advantages that object-oriented programming offers is *reusability.* After an object is designed and coded into a class, that class can be reused in any program. This means that productivity may be increased because less code has to be written. In addition, because less code is written, fewer errors can occur. Although procedural code can be reused, object-oriented code is often easier to use, especially when using more advanced techniques of data handling. In a later chapter, you will see how the same class can be reused to handle different kinds of data without the need to change code in the class.

For example, a class which holds names and addresses could be used in a multitude of programs. An address-book program, a mail-list program, and a point-of-sale program could all use the class to keep track of people. After the class is designed and coded, the coding required for the application programs will be reduced greatly.

CONTAINMENT

One of the features of objects that make them so reusable is that objects can contain other objects and use them to implement another object. For example, suppose you want to create a class that defines a car. If you already have a wheel object that defines the properties of a wheel, your car object can use the wheel class to instanciate four wheel objects. This type of relationship among objects is called *containment* because the car object *contains* four wheel objects. The relationship is also referred to as a *has-a relationship* because a car *has a* wheel (four wheels in this case).

Note

Containment is also sometimes called **composition**. The example of the car and the wheels would be called a compositional relationship.

INHERITANCE

Note

Note that the relationship goes in only one direction. A house is a building, but a building is not necessarily a house. The building might be a skyscraper instead.

Inheritance is the ability of one object to inherit the properties of another object. For example, you might have a building class that defines the properties of a building. The building class could define attributes such as the dimensions of the building, the number of floors, and the type of materials used to construct the building. Suppose you have debugged and perfected your building class, but what you need is a house object. A house has all of the attributes of a building as well as additional attributes such as number of bedrooms, number of bathrooms, and size of garage.

Rather than write a new class from scratch or modify the building class, we can create a house class that inherits the properties of the building and then extends those properties with properties which describe the house. The house object and the building object have what is called an *is-a relationship*, meaning the house *is a* building.

When one class inherits the properties of another, the class from which the properties are inherited is known as the *parent class*. The class which inherits the properties of another is the *child class* or *derived class*. In the example above, the

The is-a/has-a Rule

How do you know when to use containment or inheritance? Apply the is-a/has-a rule. If the object is a type or kind of another object, use inheritance. For example, a house is a building, so inheritance is used. If the object has another object as part of the object, use containment. For example, a house has a kitchen, so containment is used.

building class is the parent class and the **house** class is the child class. The **building** class can also be described as a *base class* upon which other classes are built.

An object created from the derived class can call a parent class's member functions as if they were members of the derived class. Users of the class do not need to know what members are implemented in each class. In fact, the users of the class do not need to know that the class is derived, as long as they know what members are available to them.

Extras for Experts

*Recall from Section 3 that a class definition has **public** and **private** sections. All members in the **public** section of a class can be accessed by any function outside or inside the class. Members in the **private** section of the class can only be accessed by member functions in the class. There is an additional section called **protected** that can be part of the definition. Members in the **protected** section can only be accessed by member functions in the class and member functions of derived classes.*

MULTILEVEL INHERITANCE

Inheritance can be multilevel. For example, a class called **garden_home** could inherit properties of the **house** class which inherits properties of the **building** class (see Figure 12-4). *Multilevel inheritance* is one of the features that makes the work done in an object-oriented program more reusable.

On the Net

Many modern user interfaces are implemented with objects which use multilevel inheritance. For example, a dialog box object might inherit properties from a window object which in turn inherits properties from a primitive frame or rectangle object. To learn more about how programs are developed using object-oriented user interfaces, see http://www.ProgramCPP.com. See topic 12.4.1.

MULTIPLE INHERITANCE

In C++, objects can also inherit properties from multiple objects. With *multiple inheritance*, the object has two parent objects and inherits properties from both (see Figure 12-5). Multiple inheritance is rarely necessary and is not allowed in some pure OOP languages.

FIGURE 12-4
Inheritance can continue for multiple levels.

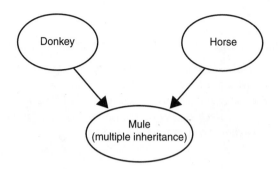

FIGURE 12-5
Multiple inheritance is allowed in C++, but should be used sparingly.

Note

Multiple inheritance is not the same thing as containment. Multiple inheritance involves inheriting the properties of more than one object. It is perfectly acceptable to create a class which includes several other objects as members.

SECTION 12.4 QUESTIONS

1. How does reusability improve productivity and reduce errors?

2. Give an example of an is-a relationship.

3. Give an example of a has-a relationship.

4. What is a class from which properties are inherited called?

5. Give an example of multilevel inheritance.

PROBLEM 12.4.1

List three reusable classes and explain why the classes would be reusable.

PROBLEM 12.4.2

List five everyday objects that contain is-a relationships and five objects that contain has-a relationships.

KEY TERMS

base class	constructor
child class	containment
class	copy constructor
class-member operator	default constructor
composition	derived class

encapsulation	multilevel inheritance
has-a relationship	multiple inheritance
information hiding	object
inheritance	object-oriented paradigm
instance	object-oriented program
instanciated	object-oriented programming (OOP)
is-a relationship	paradigm
member	parent class
member function	procedural paradigm
member selection operator	reusability
message	scope-resolution operator
method	

SUMMARY

➤ In the procedural paradigm, the functions and algorithms are the focus, with data viewed as something for the functions to manipulate.

➤ The object-oriented paradigm dictates that data should be placed inside of objects and that these objects should communicate with each other in the form of messages.

➤ Object-oriented programming (OOP) is the process of developing programs using the object-oriented paradigm.

➤ The design of a class is as important as its implementation.

➤ Constructors allow all data encapsulated within an object to be initialized to preset values so that errors can be avoided.

➤ Member functions provide a way for a programmer to pass data to and get data from an object.

➤ Reusability is a major benefit of object-oriented programming.

➤ Containment is the term used to describe an object that contains one or more other objects as members.

➤ Inheritance is the term used to describe an object that inherits properties from another object.

➤ The class from which an object inherits properties is called a parent class or base class. The class that inherits the properties is called a child class or derived class.

➤ Inheritance can be multilevel.

➤ Objects can inherit properties from multiple objects. Multiple inheritance, however, should be used sparingly.

PROJECT 12-1

You know about the procedural and object-oriented paradigms; research the functional and logic paradigms. Write a report describing the uses for these paradigms.

PROJECT 12-2

Select an object-oriented programming language other than C++ (such as Smalltalk or Java) and compare the way that language uses the object-oriented paradigm to C++.

PROJECT 12-3

Add a method to the circle class that returns the circumference of the circle. Modify *OOP.CPP* to report the circumference.

PROJECT 12-4

Create a class of your own design which has at least two private variables and two member functions. Explain why your class is well designed and has only the required functions.

PROJECT 12-5

Give the source code file for the class you created in Project 12-4 to another student as if he or she is a programmer who wants to use the class. Give the programmer a list of your public member functions and see if your class can be successfully used without opening your source code file to see how it works.

String Functions and Using a String Class

➤ *Understand various string functions and how to use them.*

➤ *Learn how to use a basic string class.*

➤ *Learn how to modify the string class to convert strings to numbers.*

➤ *Understand advanced object-oriented concepts used in the string class.*

Overview

In this chapter, you will learn more about working with strings and their most commonly used functions. You will also learn how to use a basic string class, and modify the basic string class to convert strings to numeric data types. Finally, you will study some object-oriented programming concepts and features that are used in the string class.

CHAPTER 13, SECTION 1

String Functions

Since you first learned about C++ strings, you have been using them in many of your programs. In this section, you will learn how to find the length of a string, how to compare strings, and how to add one string onto the end of another.

FINDING THE LENGTH OF A STRING

Note

Because the character array is accessed beginning with the subscript zero, the position of the null terminator is equivalent to the length of the string. For example, a five-character string would be stored in subscripts 0 through 4 with the null terminator at subscript 5, which is the length of the string.

A string may occupy all or part of the space allocated for it. For example, suppose the name *Brian Jurries* is stored in a character array declared as **char name[25];**. There are actually 13 printable characters before the null terminator, even though the array is 25 characters long.

The point is that the length of the string is less than the length of the character array in which the string is stored. There are times when knowing the length of the string is important. For example, suppose you want to center a string on the screen. If you know the length of the string, you can determine the number of blank spaces that must be printed before the string in order to center it.

Writing a function to find the length of a string is easy. Figure 13-1 shows a function that accepts a pointer to a character array as a parameter and returns the string's length as an integer. The parameter must be a pointer variable so that any character array may be passed to the function. The program uses a while loop to move from one character to the next in the character array and stops when the null terminator is reached. The position of the null terminator is returned as the length of the string.

```
int stringlength(char *string_in)
{
  int countlength = 0;

  while(string_in[countlength] != '\0')
    countlength++;

  return(countlength);
}
```

FIGURE 1 3 - 1
This short function returns the length of any string.

EXERCISE 13-1   FINDING A STRING'S LENGTH

1. Open *STRNLEN.CPP*. A program that includes the **stringlength** function in Figure 13-1 appears.

2. Compile and run the program to see the value returned by the **stringlength** function.

3. Leave the source file open for the next exercise.

Although the function to calculate string length is small, you do not have to write your own as was done in the previous exercise. There is a C++ library function named **strlen** which will return the length of a string. You can use **strlen** in the same way you used the **stringlength** function, with a call like the one below.

```
i = strlen(mystring);
```

Note

The **strlen** *function requires that the compiler directive* **#include <string.h>** *appear at the top of the program.*

EXERCISE 13-2   USING strlen

1. Modify the main function of the program on your screen to match the one below. Save the source code as *STRNLEN2.CPP*.

```
int main()
{
  char mystring[] = "This is my string";

  cout << "The length of the string is " << stringlength(mystring)
       << " characters long.\n";
  cout << "The strlen function returns a length of " << strlen(mystring)
       << " characters.\n";
  return 0;
}
```

2. Add the **#include<string.h>** compiler directive at the top of the program.

3. Run the program again to see that the **strlen** function returns the same value as the **stringlength** function.

4. Close the source code file.

COMPARING STRINGS

Comparing individual variables in C++ is easy. For example, the if structure below makes a decision based on whether two variables have the same value.

```
if (x == y)
 {
   cout << "x and y are equal.\n";
 }
```

Comparing strings, however, is not as straightforward. To determine whether two character arrays are storing the same string, each character of one array must be compared to each corresponding character in the other array. Therefore, a special function must be used to compare strings.

The **string.h** library, which you used in the previous exercise, also includes a function for comparing strings. The library function named **strcmp** performs a comparison of two strings and returns one of the following values:

➤ it returns a zero (0) if the strings are the same

➤ it returns a negative value if the first string comes before the second in alphabetical order

➤ it returns a positive value if the first string comes after the second in alphabetical order

Below is an example of how the **strcmp** function can be used within an if structure to determine if two strings are the same.

```
if (strcmp(string1, string2) == 0)
  {
   cout << "The strings are the same.\n";
  }
```

EXERCISE 13-3   USING strcmp

1. Open *STRCOMP.CPP.*

2. Compile and run the program to see how the **strcmp** function works.

3. After running the program a few times, using strings that are both the same and not the same, close the source code file.

ADDING ONE STRING ONTO THE END OF ANOTHER

Adding one string onto the end of another string is called *concatenation*. Suppose for example that you have one character array that is holding a person's first name, and another that is holding the same person's last name. To get both the first and last names together in one character array, you would need to concatenate the last name onto the first name. *Note:* A space must be concatenated first to insert a space between the first and last name.

The library function that concatenates strings is called **strcat**. The **strcat** function receives two strings as parameters, as shown in the example call below.

```
strcat(phone_number, extension);
```

After the call to **strcat**, the string stored in **phone_number** will still have all of the characters it had before the call, plus all of the characters that are in the string stored in **extension**. The string stored in **extension** remains the same.

WARNING

*The character array that is going to receive the additional characters must have enough memory allocated to it in order to hold the additional characters. The **strcat** function will continue to add characters even if it reaches the end of the destination character array. The result is that other memory is overwritten with the remaining string data.*

EXERCISE 13-4   USING strcat

1. Enter the following program and save it as *FULLNAME.CPP*.

```
#include<iostream.h>
#include<string.h>

int main()
{
 char firstname[15];
 char lastname[20];
 char fullname[35];

 // prompt user for first and last names
 cout << "Enter your first name: ";
 cin.get(firstname, 14);
 cin.ignore(80, '\n');
 cout << "Enter your last name: ";
 cin.get(lastname, 19);
 cin.ignore(80, '\n');

 strcpy(fullname, firstname); // copy first name into fullname
 strcat(fullname, " ");    // add a space between first and last names
 strcat(fullname, lastname); // concatenate last name onto the string

 cout << "Your full name is " << fullname << ".\n";
 return 0;
}
```

2. Compile and run the program to see how **strcat** is used to combine the strings.

3. Close the source code file.

PITFALLS

Remember that the **strcat** *function requires strings as arguments. Even when adding a single character to a string, as in the example below, double quotes must be used so that the blank space is interpreted as a string rather than a character.*

```
strcat(fullname, " ");
```

On the Net

See other C++ library string functions at http://www.ProgramCPP.com. See topic 13.1.1.

SECTION 13.1 QUESTIONS

1. What C++ library function is used to determine the length of a string?

2. What header file must be included in order to use the string functions?

3. Write a statement that assigns the length of the string named **title** to a variable named **title_length**.

4. Write a statement that adds the characters in the character array named **four_digit_extension** to the character array named **ZIP**.

5. What does the **strcat** function do with concatenated characters that do not fit in the character array?

PROBLEM 13.1.1

Write a program that asks the user for a string then prints the string centered on the screen. Use the **strlen** function to determine the length of the string and decide how many spaces must be printed to the left of the string in order to center the string on the screen. Save the source code as *CENTERIT.CPP*.

PROBLEM 13.1.2

Write a function that performs the same function as the **strcpy** function. Name your function **stringcopy** and write a main function that demonstrates the function. Name the source code file *STRCOPY.CPP*.

CHAPTER 13, SECTION 2
Using a String Class

As you have learned, C++ strings must be used very carefully in order to avoid problems. In addition, the functions that manipulate C++ strings are not as natural to use as they could be. For example, wouldn't it be nice if you could compare strings using the == operator instead of **strcmp**?

Using a string class can make strings in C++ much easier to use and less prone to have problems. A string class can encapsulate the string and the functions you want to perform with the string into a string object that is flexible and reliable. In this section, you will learn about the benefits of encapsulating a string inside a string class, and how to read and use a basic C++ string class.

BENEFITS OF USING A STRING CLASS

Using a string class rather than standard C++ strings offers many benefits. Two of the most important benefits of a string class are error checking and the ability to use standard operators when working with strings.

As you have learned, standard C++ strings do not have any error checking. A string class can implement error checking to prevent a string from overflowing the bounds of the array in which it is stored. This type of error checking is called *bounds checking*. Bounds checking guarantees that when you modify a string by changing it or adding to it, you do not accidentally write over some other data in memory. Recall the exercise in Chapter 6 that demonstrated how character arrays can overwrite one another.

Another benefit of a string class is the ability to use standard C++ operators like + and == to concatenate and compare strings rather than using the **strcat** and **strcmp** functions. The same operators used for mathematical purposes can be used with strings. This makes using strings much simpler, and makes reading source code easier. The ability to redefine how operators behave is called operator overloading and will be discussed later in this section.

A BASIC STRING CLASS

Figure 13-2 is the header file *OOSTRING.H* that contains the definition for a basic C++ string class. We have named our string class **OOSTRING.H** to prevent a conflict with the non-object-oriented **STRING.H** header file.

As you begin reading through the string class definition, it should look somewhat similar to the **circle** class definition that was examined in Chapter 12. There may, however, be some code that you are less familiar with. Let's take a look a some of the features of the string class that you have not used before.

A CONSTRUCTOR THAT INITIALIZES

The first change you should notice in the string class is the additional constructor shown below.

```
oostring(const char * s);
```

This constructor allows the value of a string object to be set when the object is created rather than at a later time. Therefore, to create an empty string the statement below could be used.

```
oostring MyString;
```

However, if you wanted **MyString** to be initialized with text at the time you instanciate it, you could use the statement below.

```
oostring MyString("This is my string.");
```

You may recall that with standard C++ strings, you are able to initialize the character array at the time it is declared. A constructor that initializes allows you to instanciate and initialize in one statement.

STRING ACCESSOR FUNCTIONS

The next section of the string class provides the accessor functions. *Accessor functions* are member functions that access the string in the object but do not change the data in the object. There are three accessor functions in this class, **length**, **find**, and **substr**.

The **length** function returns the length of the string and is just like the **strlen** function studied in the previous section. A statement like the one below would return the length of the string in the **MyString** object.

```
l = MyString.length();
```

```
#ifndef _OOSTRING_H
#define _OOSTRING_H

#include <iostream.h>
// uncomment line below if bool not built-in type
// #include "bool.h"


class oostring
{
  public:

  // constructors/destructor

    oostring( );                          // construct empty string ""
    oostring( const char * s );           // construct from string literal
    oostring( const oostring & str );     // copy constructor
    ~oostring( );                         // destructor

  // accessors

    int    length() const;                // length of string
    int    find(const oostring & str) const;// index of str in string
    int    find(char ch) const;           // index of ch in string
    oostring substr(int pos, int len) const; // substring starting at pos
                                          // with a length of len
    char * c_str() const;                 // returns pointer to C style str

  // assignment
    const oostring & operator = ( const oostring & str ); // assign str
    const oostring & operator = ( const char * s );     // assign s
    const oostring & operator = ( char ch );            // assign ch

  // indexing
    char & operator[]( int k );     // range-checked indexing

  // modifiers
    const oostring & operator += ( const oostring & str ); // append str
    const oostring & operator += ( const char * s );     // append s
    const oostring & operator += ( char ch );            // append ch


  private:
     int Capacity;                    // capacity of string
     char * CString;                  // storage for characters
};

// Non-member functions and operator overloads

ostream & operator << ( ostream & os, const oostring & str );
istream & operator >> ( istream & is, oostring & str );
istream & getline    ( istream & is, oostring & str );

// comparison operators

bool operator == ( const oostring & lhs, const oostring & rhs );
bool operator != ( const oostring & lhs, const oostring & rhs );
bool operator <  ( const oostring & lhs, const oostring & rhs );
bool operator <= ( const oostring & lhs, const oostring & rhs );
bool operator >  ( const oostring & lhs, const oostring & rhs );
bool operator >= ( const oostring & lhs, const oostring & rhs );

// concatenation operator +

oostring operator + ( const oostring & lhs, const oostring & rhs );
oostring operator + ( char ch, const oostring & str );
oostring operator + ( const oostring & str, char ch );

#endif
```

F I G U R E   1 3 - 2
A string class simplifies C++ string
operations.

The **find** function returns the index (position in the string) of the first occurrence of a character or another string. You will notice that there are two different definitions of the **find** function, one that accepts a string object as a parameter and one that accepts a character as a parameter. When a program is compiled, the compiler will select the correct function to use whenever **find** is called. The statement below is an example of the use of **find**.

```
position = MyString.find("Kevin");
```

The final function **substr** returns a substring of the string. A *substring* is a string that is contained inside of another string. Therefore, "This," "is," "This is my," and "my str" are all substrings of "This is my string." To use the **substr** function, pass it the starting position and the number of characters to return in the substring. For example, the statement below places the text "my" in **substring** if **MyString** is "This is my string."

```
substring = MyString.substr(8, 2);
```

OPERATOR OVERLOADING

The next three sections of the header file (assignment, indexing, and modifiers) are all accessor functions. What makes them different from the other accessor functions is that they all use operator overloading. *Operator overloading* is the process of creating a new procedure to execute whenever a standard C++ operator is used with a standard data type or a class.

Within the class definition the =, [], and += operators are overloaded. These operators are overloaded inside of the definition because they need access to all of the private data in the class. Because they are overloaded inside of the class definition, they are members of the string class.

To overload an operator, you create a statement similar to the function prototype. The prototype has a return type followed by the keyword **operator**. The operator being overloaded is next, then in parentheses come the parameters for the operator.

```
// assignment
   const oostring & operator = ( const oostring & str ); // assign str
   const oostring & operator = ( const char * s );       // assign s
   const oostring & operator = ( char ch );              // assign ch
```

Every possible way that the overloaded operator may be used must be prototyped, then defined. Because there are three statements overloading the assignment operator, the assignment operator can be used with string objects in three ways. You can assign one string object to another, you can assign a standard C++ string to a string object, and you can assign a character to a string object.

The index operator ([ ]) provides the same function as it does with standard C++ strings. However, by overloading the index operator, bounds checking and other error detection algorithms can be implemented.

The last operator overloaded inside of the class is the += operator. The += operator replaces the **strcat()** function that was discussed in the first section of this chapter. The statements below are all legal because of the overloading of the += operator.

```
MyString += "text to be added to the string";
MyString += MyChar;        // MyChar is a variable of type char.
MyString += YourString;    // YourString can be a standard C++ character array
                           // or another string object.
```

Recall from the first section of this chapter that before you could use the **strcat** function you had to verify that the original string was large enough to hold the characters that were going to be concatenated onto it. When using the string class, the memory allocation of the receiving string is checked and enlarged if necessary.

OTHER OVERLOADED OPERATORS

Outside of the class definition, several other C++ operators have been overloaded. These operators are overloaded outside of the class definition because they do not require access to the private data of the object. Operators overloaded outside of the class definition are not members of the string class, merely overloaded operators.

The insertion (>>) and extraction (<<) operators and **getline** are overloaded to allow the string object to be used with these operators. The **getline** function is a C++ library function which is similar to the **get** function you have been using in your programs. The string class overloads the **getline** function to allow you to accept input directly into the string object. For example, the statement below will prompt the user for string input and then store the string in the string object.

```
getline(cin, MyString);  // MyString is a string object
```

You can use the overloaded extraction operator just like you have used it with character arrays.

```
cout << MyString;
```

The equality and relational operators have been overloaded, and so has the plus sign (+) for concatenation. Rather than using **strcmp** to compare strings, you can use code like the segment below.

```
if(MyString == YourString)
  {
    cout << "The strings are equal.";
  }
```

On the Net

The string class is divided into a header file (OOSTRING.H) and an implementation file (OOSTRING.CPP). To successfully compile programs that use classes that are divided into two files, you may have to learn how to create groups of source code called projects. Your instructor and your compiler's documentation can help you take the required steps. For more information about working with projects on the major compilers, see http://www.ProgramCPP.com. See topic 13.2.1.

USING THE STRING CLASS

1. Open *OOSTRING.CPP* and *STRINGEX.CPP* into a project in your compiler. The file *OOSTRING.H* must also be available to the compiler.

2. Read through the *STRINGEX.CPP* program and see how the different accessor functions and operators are used in the program.

3. Compile and run the program. The file *OOSTRING.H* includes *BOOL.H* to provide the bool data type. If your compiler has the bool type built in, you may remove the `#include "bool.h"` statement from *OOSTRING.H*.

4. Close all source code files.

SECTION 13.2 QUESTIONS

1. What is one benefit of using a string class?

2. What is an advantage of having a constructor that initializes the string?

3. Define substring.

4. What is operator overloading?

5. Why are some operators overloaded inside the class definition?

PROBLEM 13.2.1

Modify your solution from Problem 13.1.1 so that it uses the string class instead of standard C++ strings. Save the source code file as *OOCENTER.CPP*.

PROBLEM 13.2.2

Write a program that uses the string class to instanciate two string objects: **FirstName** and **LastName**. Use **getline** to prompt the user for a name for each object. Then use the += operator to add LastName to FirstName. *Hint:* Use the += operator in two statements: first to add a space to appear between the names and second to add the last name. Save the source code file as *OONAMES.CPP*.

CHAPTER 13, SECTION 3

Converting Strings to Numeric Data Types

Because strings can store alphabetic or numeric symbols, character arrays sometimes store numbers. To perform math functions on a number stored in a string, the number must be converted to a numeric data type. In this section you will learn about the three most common C++ functions that allow you to convert strings to numbers. You will also learn how to modify the string class to support these numeric conversions.

CONVERTING A STRING TO AN INTEGER

The **atoi** function, which is short for alphabetic to integer, takes a string as a parameter and returns a value of type int. Consider the program in Figure 13-3. The number of feet in a mile and the number of miles are stored in character arrays. The **atoi** function is called twice to convert the strings to integer values.

```cpp
#include <iostream.h>
#include <stdlib.h>

int main()
{
  char feet_in_a_mile[] = "5280";
  char number_of_miles[] = "3";
  int feet_per_mile, miles;

  feet_per_mile = atoi(feet_in_a_mile);
  miles = atoi(number_of_miles);

  cout << "There are "  << feet_per_mile * miles << " feet in "
       << miles << " miles.\n";
  return 0;
}
```

FIGURE 13-3
Numbers stored in character arrays must be converted to numeric data types before they can be used in calculations.

Note

The functions that convert strings to numbers require that the compiler directive #include <stdlib.h> appear at the beginning of the program.

EXERCISE 13-6   **CONVERTING STRINGS TO INTEGERS**

1. Enter the program in Figure 13-3.

2. Compile and run the program.

3. Leave the source code file open for the next exercise.

When converting a string to an integer, the number in the string must be within the range allowed for the variable type to which you are converting. To convert a string to a long integer, use the **atol** function. Use it just like **atoi**. Assign the value returned by the function to a variable of type long.

ADDING INTEGER CONVERSION TO THE STRING CLASS

Modifying the string class to support different types of number conversions is very straightforward. First, the member function prototype below must be added to the class definition, before the **private** keyword.

```cpp
int converttoint() const;
```

```
int oostring::convertoint() const
{
  return(atoi(Cstring));
}
```

FIGURE 1 3 - 4
The definition of the accessor
function **converttoint()**.

Figure 13-4 shows the C++ source code that should be added to the *OOST-RING.CPP* file to implement an integer conversion function. Note that as in the earlier example, *stdlib.h* must be included in *OOSTRING.H*.

Note

Later in this chapter, you will learn why the **const** *keyword appears in the function prototype and definition.*

CONVERTING A STRING TO A FLOATING POINT NUMBER

Converting a string to a floating-point number is performed with the **atof** (alphabetic to floating-point) function. The function accepts a string as a parameter and returns a value of type double. The statement below is an example of how the **atof** function can be used.

```
price = atof(mystring);
```

Note

Like the functions that convert strings to integers, **atof** *requires that the compiler directive* **#include <stdlib.h>** *appear at the beginning of the program.*

EXERCISE 13-7   **CONVERTING STRINGS TO FLOATING-POINT NUMBERS**

1. Add the following statements to the variable declarations of the program on your screen.

```
char retail_price[] = "19.99";
float price;
```

2. Add a statement at the bottom of the program that converts the string stored in **retail_price** to the variable named **price**. *Note*: Even though the **atof** function returns a value of type double, the value can be assigned to a variable of type float.

3. Add a statement that prints the value of **price** to the screen.

4. Compile and run the program.

5. Save the source code file as *CONVSTR.CPP* and close.

If the string passed to the **atoi**, **atol**, or **atof** functions does not contain a number that the function can convert, the function returns the value 0.

ADDING FLOATING-POINT CONVERSION TO THE STRING CLASS

Adding a member function to convert a string to a floating-point number is similar to adding the integer conversion. Again, a new member function prototype must be added to the class definition. The function prototype below should be added below the **converttoint** prototype.

```
double converttofloat() const;
```

The source code for the **converttofloat** function is shown in Figure 13-5.

```
double oostring::convertofloat() const
{
   return(atof(Cstring));
}
```

FIGURE 13-5
The definition of the member function **converttofloat()**.

EXERCISE 13-8   MODIFYING THE STRING CLASS

1. Open the *OOSTRING.H* file and *OOSTRING.CPP* file.

2. Modify the files accordingly to support integer and floating-point conversion as specified in this section.

3. Open *STRINGEX.CPP*. Add the following lines after the **oostring** declarations at the beginning of the program.

```
oostring IntegerString("100");
oostring FloatString("99.99");
```

4. Add the following lines to the end of the program.

```
cout << "The numeric value of IntegerString is "
     << IntegerString.converttoint() << endl;
cout << "The numeric value of FloatString is "
     << FloatString.converttofloat() << endl;
```

5. Compile and run the *STRINGEX.CPP* program and look at the new output generated by the two statements that were added to the program.

6. Save and close the modified source code files.

SECTION 13.3 QUESTIONS

1. What C++ library function converts a string to a floating-point number?

2. What do the functions that convert strings to numbers return if the string contains no numbers that the function can convert?

3. Write a statement that converts the number in the character array named **A** to a long integer.

4. Write a statement that converts the number in the character array named **B** to a variable of type int.

5. Write a code segment that converts the numbers in the character arrays named **multiplicand** and **multiplier** to floating-point numbers and then multiplies them together. Print the result to the screen.

PROBLEM 13.3.1

Write a program that implements the code segment you wrote in question 5 above using standard C++ character arrays. Have the user input the **multiplicand** and **multiplier** strings. Save the source code file as *MULTSTR.CPP*.

PROBLEM 13.3.2

Write a program that implements the code segment you wrote in question 5 above using the string class which you modified to support numeric conversion. Have the user input the **multiplicand** and **multiplier** strings. Save the source code file as *OOMULT.CPP*.

CHAPTER 13, SECTION 4
Advanced Features of the String Class

As you have seen, the string class uses some features that were not used in the classes in Chapter 12. Many of these features are common in C++ classes. In this section, we will examine some of these features more closely.

MEMBER VARIABLES

All of the abilities and activities of the string class center around the two member variables: **CString** and **Capacity**. **CString** is a character pointer that points to a standard character array in memory. As you know, you must allocate space for a character array. The **Capacity** variable contains the current number of characters that can be stored in the array pointed to by **CString**.

Note

While reading this section, it is helpful to have hard copies of the OOSTRING.H *and* OOSTRING.CPP *files or have them open on the screen.*

MORE ABOUT const

You learned about constants in Chapter 4. The keyword **const**, however, can also be used in other ways. When you first saw **const**, it was used to make variables constant so that they could not be changed anywhere in a program. The **const** keyword can also be used in functions and member functions to guarantee that no changes are made to parameters that are being passed to the function. The syntax for using **const** in this way is shown below.

```
int multiply(const int , const int );

int multiply(const int x, const int y)
{
   return(x * y);
}
```

The **multiply** function receives two arguments (**x** and **y**) which both have the **const** keyword before them. This placement of **const** tells the compiler that **x** and **y** should remain constant and that the function should not attempt to make any changes to the **const** variables. Determining if arguments should be **const** is usually a design decision. Because the variables are passed by value, changes would not pass back to the calling function anyway. Using **const** parameters allows the data to be treated as a constant.

The **const** keyword can also be used with member functions to make sure that they do not change any member variables. For example, you can see in the string class definition that the **length** function is prototyped as **length() const;**. The **const** following the closing parenthesis but before the semicolon prevents the **length** function from changing any member variables. The **const** keyword is in the same place in the **length** function definition which is in the *OOSTRING.CPP* file (see Figure 13-6).

```
int oostring::length() const
{
   int countlength = 0;

   while(CString[countlength] != '\0')
     countlength++;

   return(countlength);
}
```

F I G U R E   1 3 - 6
The **const** keyword prevents the **length** function from changing any member variables.

CONSTRUCTORS AND DESTRUCTORS IN THE STRING CLASS

The class definition for the string class is in the *OOSTRING.H* header file. The constructor definitions are at the beginning of the class definition. The first constructor (shown in Figure 13-7) is the standard default constructor. When this constructor is called, the instanciated object does not contain a string so the capacity is set to zero and the **CString** pointer is set to NULL. The capacity of the string object is set to zero because no memory has been allocated to the object so that it can hold a string. The **CString** pointer is set to NULL because it does not yet point to a memory location.

```
oostring::oostring()
{
  Capacity = 0;                         // Set Capacity equal to zero
  CString = '\0';                       // Set CString Pointer to NULL
}
```

FIGURE 13-7
The default constructor sets the capacity to zero and the string pointer to NULL.

The second constructor allows the string object to be initialized with a string (see Figure 13-8). This is accomplished by having a single character pointer as an argument. The constructor verifies that the character pointer references some position in memory. Then it calculates the amount of memory that needs to be allocated for the character array by determining the length of **s** and adding one byte to make room for a NULL value which signifies the end of the string. Once the required amount of memory is calculated and stored in **Capacity**, the constructor requests that a character array with the length of **Capacity** be allocated. After the memory has been allocated, the string pointed to by **s** is copied to **CString**.

```
oostring::oostring(const char * s)
{
    Capacity = strlen(s) + 1;          // Make room for NULL char
    CString = new char[Capacity];
    strcpy(CString,s);
}
```

FIGURE 13-8
This constructor allows the object to be initialized with a passed string.

As you know, when you declare a variable or instantiate an object, memory is allocated for that data. To manually allocate memory for some purpose, you can use the **new** operator. In the constructor in Figure 13-8, the statement `CString = new char[Capacity];` requests that a character array with the size **Capacity** be allocated. The **new** operator returns a pointer to the character array and **CString** is set to this pointer.

Note

The **new** operator and dynamic memory allocation is discussed in detail in Chapter 16.

Because of this constructor, a string object can be initialized using a string literal or a standard C++ character array, as shown below.

```
oostring MyOtherStringObject("This is my other string");
oostring MyStringObject(MyString);   // MyString is a character array
```

The last constructor is the copy constructor. The copy constructor is used when an object is passed by value to another function. When a variable is passed by value, you want a copy to perform operations on. You do not want to modify the original. The copy constructor makes a copy of an object when it is passed by value.

If a programmer does not implement a copy constructor when he or she creates a class the compiler will create its own copy constructor. The copy constructor created by the compiler creates an exact duplicate of the original object. For classes like the **circle** class covered in Chapter 12, this would cause no problems. However, if an exact copy of a string object was created the **CString** member variable in both objects would point to the same character array in memory. So if the copy modified the string, the original string would be modified.

The string class copy constructor shown in Figure 13-9 creates a copy of a string object by determining the required capacity of the character array, allocating the memory with the **new** operator, and then copying the string from the original to the copy. Using this method, if the string contained in the copy is modified, the string contained in the original is not. Objects instanciated from the same class have access to one another's private data, which allows the copy constructor to access the data from the string object being copied.

```
oostring::oostring(const oostring & str)
{
   Capacity = str.length() + 1;
   CString = new char[Capacity];
   strcpy(CString,str.CString);
}
```

FIGURE 13-9
This copy constructor will safely copy the string object.

Immediately following the constructors is a member function called a *destructor*. The destructor looks like a constructor except that it has a tilde (**~**) before its name. A destructor is necessary when an object manually allocates memory. The memory allocated manually must be disposed of (deallocated) manually to free the memory up for other purposes.

When a string object has completed its work, the destructor for the class is called automatically to deallocate any memory used by the object. The **delete** operator performs the function of freeing the manually allocated memory. In the case of the string class, the destructor has a single statement that deallocates the array pointed to by **CString**.

```
oostring::~oostring()
{
   delete [] CString;                   // Free the memory allocated to CString
}
```

Only classes which dynamically allocate memory or have other special duties that must be performed before they are removed from memory need to have destructors.

On the Net

If you use a debugger to step or trace through a program that uses a class with a destructor, you can see how the compiler automatically calls the destructor when it is finished with an object. To learn more about destructors and when they are necessary, see http://www.ProgramCPP.com. See topic 13.4.1.

ASSIGNMENT OPERATOR OVERLOADS

The next part of the class definition contains the assignment operator overloads. You can see that these overloads have only one argument. Whenever operator overloads are declared inside of a class definition they have only one argument. This argument is always the operand on the right side of the operator. The current object is assumed to be the left operand.

Another important aspect of the assignment operator overload is that it has a return type of **oostring &**. Overloading operators with the correct return type allows for statements like the one below.

```
StringOne = StringTwo = StringThree;
```

OVERLOADING THE SUBSCRIPT OPERATOR

The next item in the class definition worth mentioning is the subscript operator overload.

```
// indexing
    char & operator[]( int k );      // range-checked indexing
```

Notice that the overload has the return type **char &**. You might think that the overload should have the return type **char**, since the subscript operator accesses a single character. The return type of **char &**, however, allows the subscript operator to be used more flexibly.

For example, suppose you have the two declarations below.

```
char c;
oostring MyString("Hello, World!");
```

Whether the operator is overloaded with the **char** or **char &** type, the statement below will work.

```
c = MyString[index];
```

The statement below, however, only works if the return type is **char &**.

```
MyString[index] = c;
```

The **&** in the return type performs the same operation that it performs in a pass by reference.

Also notice that the overload has one argument: the index value. Even though the argument comes between the brackets (**[]**) when you use subscript notation, the operator overload places the argument after the operator.

I/O OPERATOR OVERLOAD

Earlier in the chapter you learned that the I/O operators are overloaded to make it easy to use the object with the standard I/O operators. The I/O operators can be overloaded because streams can be passed as parameters to functions.

```
ostream & operator << ( ostream & os, const oostring & str );
istream & operator >> ( istream & is, oostring & str );
istream & getline    ( istream & is, oostring & str );
```

Notice that the overloads are expecting the left operand to be of the type **istream** or **ostream**. Therefore, since the **<<** operator is expecting an **ostream** variable, you can pass it **cout** or a file stream that you had previously declared and opened.

On the Net

*There are other **ostream** class objects that are used to alert the user when an error has occurred. These objects are **cerr** and **clog**. To learn more about these objects, see http://www.ProgramCPP.com. See topic 13.4.2.*

Also notice that the overloads have a return type of stream reference, either **ostream &** or **istream &**. Having this return type allows the multiple overloads to different data types used in the same statement. For example, the statement below is allowed because the stream handle is passed from one overload to the next.

```
cout << line_number << ": " << StringOne << endl;
```

You could also use the concept of stream passing in a program that did not utilize objects and operator overloading. For example, you might have a program that created a report that could be displayed to the screen or saved to a file. Instead of creating two different functions to output the report, you could create one function that had an **ostream &** parameter. Then you could pass the desired output stream to the function using function calls like the ones shown below.

```
output_results(cout);    // send output to the screen
output_results(outfile); // send output to a file
```

THE this KEYWORD

The keyword **this** is used throughout the **oostring** class implementation. The **this** keyword is a pointer to the current object. For example, if in a member function you need to refer to the object in which the member function is contained, use the **this** keyword. If you examine the source code of the **oostring** class, especially the assignment operator overloads, you notice that the statement **return *this;** is at the end of all of the overload functions. This statement dereferences the **this** pointer and returns the current object.

Returning ***this** is required for multiple assignments such as the one below to work in the same statement.

```
StringOne = StringTwo = StringThree;
```

SECTION 13.4 QUESTIONS

1. What member variables are used in the string class and what is the purpose of each?

2. Why is the **const** keyword sometimes in the parameters of functions?

3. What is the effect of placing the **const** keyword after the closing parenthesis of a member function?

4. Why is it necessary to create a copy constructor for the string class?

5. What operator allows you to manually allocate memory?

6. What is a destructor?

7. What syntax distinguishes a destructor from a constructor?

8. When is a destructor necessary?

9. How can a program benefit from the ability to pass streams?

10. What is the **this** keyword?

KEY TERMS

accessor function

bounds checking

concatenation

destructor

operator overloading

substring

SUMMARY

➤ There are library functions available to manipulate strings. You can find the length of a string, compare strings, and add one string onto the end of another. Adding one string onto the end of another is called concatenation.

➤ A string class can make C++ strings much easier to use. A string class can encapsulate the string and the functions you want to perform with the string into a string object that is flexible and reliable.

➤ A string class can provide bounds checking to avoid string errors. A string class can also allow the use of standard C++ operators like +, =, and == when working with strings.

➤ Operator overloading is the process of creating a new procedure to execute whenever a standard C++ operator is used with a standard data type or a class.

➤ There are C++ library functions that allow you to convert numbers stored in strings to integer and floating-point values.

➤ The string class uses some advanced OOP features such as **const** parameters and the **this** keyword.

➤ A destructor is called when an object is disposed of. The destructor deallocates memory allocated by the constructor or performs other necessary duties before the object is deleted.

PROJECT 13-1 • STRING FUNCTIONS

Write a function that performs concatenation of strings. Name your function **stringcat** and write a main function that demonstrates the function. Name the source code *STRNGCAT.CPP*.

PROJECT 13-2 • PALINDROMES

Write a program that uses the **reverse_string** function from Project 10-1 as part of a program that tests a word to determine if it is a palindrome. A palindrome is a word that reads the same backward as forward. The word *madam* is an example of a palindrome. Your program should copy the string you are testing into a temporary character array, then send the copied string to the **reverse_string** function. Compare the reversed string to the original string to see if the word is a palindrome.

PROJECT 13-3 • PALINDROMES

Modify the string class to include a **reverse_string** method. Then rewrite the program from Project 13-2 to use the string class rather than a character array.

PROJECT 13-4 • STRING MANIPULATION

Extend the program you wrote in Problem 13.2.2 to use the **find** function to find the space between the first and last names and the **length** function to find the string length. Given that information, use the **substr** function to copy the last name into a third string object.

PROJECT 13-5 • EXTENDING THE STRING CLASS

Modify the string class to include a method that converts the characters in the string to uppercase. You can write an algorithm for the conversion or use any C++ library function you can find that might help you. Then add a method to the string class that will convert the characters in the string to lowercase.

PROJECT 13-6 • EXTEND THE STRING CLASS

Modify the string class to include a method that will set a specified number of the characters in the string to the same character. For example, the call **MyString.setchars(20,'*');** will set the first 20 characters of the string to asterisks (*). You can use any name you wish for the member function.

STRING CLASS

Purpose: The string class provides easy-to-use, safe strings for your programs.

Required Header File

```
#include "oostring.h"
```

To Instanciate a String Object

```
oostring MyString1;                    // instanciate empty string object
oostring MyString2("Hello, World!");   // initialize while instanciating
```

To Obtain the Length of a String

```
length = MyString2.length();
```

To Find First Occurrence of One String within Another

The statement below returns the character position of the first occurrence of the string *Wor* in the **MyString2** object and stores it in the variable named **location**. If the string is not found, the function returns –1.

```
location = MyString2.find("Wor");
```

To Find First Occurrence of a Character within the String

The statement below returns the character position of the first occurrence of the character *W* in the **MyString2** object and stores it in the variable named **location**. If the string is not found, the function returns –1.

```
location = MyString2.find('W');
```

To Return a Substring of Characters from the String

The **substr** function allows you to specify a starting position and the number of characters you wish to copy from the string. The substring is returned as a string and can be assigned to another string object. In the example below, five characters are copied from **MyString2**, beginning at position zero. The new string of five characters is assigned to the **MyString1** object.

```
MyString1 = MyString2.substr(0, 5);
```

Assigning Values to Strings

You can assign the contents of one string to another.

```
MyString1 = MyString2;
```

You can assign a string literal to a string object.

```
MyString1 = "string literal";
```

You can assign a character literal to a string object.

```
MyString1 = 'A';
```

Indexing Characters in a String Object

You can set the characters of the string individually.

```
MyString1[0] = 'B';
```

You can retrieve the characters of the string individually.

```
ch = MyString1[0];
```

String Object I/O

You can display the contents of a string object using cout.

```
cout << MyString1 << endl;
```

You can prompt for a string using cin, but no spaces or tabs are allowed.

```
cout << "Please enter a string ( no spaces or tabs please ): ";
cin  >> MyString1;
```

You can prompt for a string using a function called **getline**. The **getline** function accepts spaces and tabs.

```
cout << "Please enter another string ( spaces and tabs are ok ): ";
getline(cin, MyString1);
```

Comparing Strings

You can use the standard relational operators to compare string objects.

```
YesNo = (MyString1 == MyString2);   // equal to
YesNo = (MyString1 != MyString2);   // not equal to
YesNo = (MyString1 <  MyString2);   // less than
YesNo = (MyString1 <= MyString2);   // less than or equal to
YesNo = (MyString1 >  MyString2);   // greater than
YesNo = (MyString1 >= MyString2);   // greater than or equal to
```

String Concatenation

String concatenation is most flexible when you use the compound operator. You can concatenate a string object, a character array, a string literal, a character variable, or a character literal to the string.

```
MyString1 += MyString2;
MyString1 += MyCharArray;
MyString1 += "string literal";
MyString1 += Ch;
MyString1 += 'A';
```

Using the + operator, you can add two string objects together, or add a character on either end of the string.

```
MyString3 = MyString1 + MyString2;
MyString1 = 'A' + MyString2;
MyString1 = MyString2 + 'Z';
```

14

Arrays, Templates, and Vectors

OBJECTIVES

➤ Use one-dimensional arrays.

➤ Understand templates, template classes, and template functions.

➤ Use a vector class.

Overview

From your use of character arrays, you have a basic understanding of the concept of an array. An *array* is like a list of variables or other data structures that are accessed using a single identifier. A character array is a list of variables of type char that are accessed using the identifier for the array, rather than a separate identifier for each character.

In this chapter, you will learn how to use arrays of data types other than char. You will learn about one-dimensional arrays, which are like the character arrays you have already worked with. In the next chapter, you will learn about multi-dimensional arrays.

You will also learn to use a vector class, which is an object-oriented representation of an array. The advantages of a vector class will also be covered. While studying the vector class, you will learn about another important OOP concept: templates. Templates allow a class to work with multiple data types.

One-Dimensional Arrays

You have already worked with *one-dimensional arrays* of characters. Arrays, however, may be of any data type and used for many purposes within your programs.

DECLARING ONE-DIMENSIONAL ARRAYS

Recall that when you declared a one-dimensional character array, you used statements like the one below.

```
char name[21];
```

The syntax for declaring arrays of types other than char is the same, except for the data type. Below is a declaration for an array of floats.

```
float x[20];
```

The number in the brackets instructs the compiler to set aside memory for a given number of floating-point numbers (in this case 20 numbers). The array is just like a list of variables that share the same name. Each variable in the array is called an *element.*

Most arrays of characters are used to store strings. When you intend to store a string in a character array, you declare one more element than the number of printable characters in your string. As you know, the extra element is for the null terminator. Arrays that store values other than strings are declared for the exact number of elements needed. For example, all 20 elements of array **x**, declared above, can be used for floating-point numbers.

WHEN ARE ARRAYS NEEDED?

Using an array of characters makes sense, but why would you want to store an array of integers or floating-point numbers? Actually, you will find lots of uses for arrays of data other than characters. Let's look at some examples.

Suppose you want to write a program that stores the high temperature for every day of the month and then calculates an average. You could use a 31-element array, like the one declared below, to store the high temperature for every day of any given month.

```
int daily_temp[31];
```

Let's look at another example. Suppose you have written a computer game and you want to display the ten highest scores between games. The array declaration below could hold the scores. The statement declares a ten-element array of unsigned long integers.

```
unsigned long score[10];
```

On the Net

Obviously, the contents of the score array above are lost when the user quits the game. Therefore, the ten highest scores would reset every time the game is loaded into memory. To see how the array of high scores could be saved to disk and reloaded the next time the game is run, see http://www.ProgramCPP.com. See topic 14.1.1.

More advanced data like structures and classes can also be declared in arrays. In the example below, a structure named **product** is declared. An array of 100 structures named toys is then declared using the same syntax as used when declaring other arrays.

```
struct product
  {
    char item_ID[11];
    char name[11];
    float price;
  };

product toys[100];
```

An array of circle objects like the one used in Chapter 12 can be declared with a statement like the one below.

```
circle ArrayOfCircles[100];
```

INITIALIZING AND ACCESSING THE ELEMENTS OF AN ARRAY

You can initialize arrays with values when you declare the array. The statement below declares and initializes an array.

```
unsigned int distance[5] = {458, 288, 506, 379, 490};
```

Recall that you have created character arrays without specifying the length of the array. You can do the same thing with any array when it is declared. The statement below creates the same array as the statement above.

```
unsigned int distance[] = {458, 288, 506, 379, 490};
```

WARNING

When you declare an array without providing a subscript, its size is initialized to the number of values contained in the braces. Be sure the number of values in the braces is sufficient to hold the maximum number of elements in your array.

Most arrays are initialized while the program is running. Once an array is declared, elements must be accessed individually to change their values.

Each element is accessed using subscript notation, which you used to access individual characters of a character array in Chapter 10. Recall that a 20-element array is accessed using the subscripts 0 through 19. For example, the first element in the array declared as **float x[20];** is accessed using **x[0]**. The final element in the array is **x[19]**.

Address

201248	458	distance[0]
201249		
201250	288	distance[1]
201251		
201252	506	distance[2]
201253		
201254	379	distance[3]
201255		
201256	490	distance[4]
201257		

F I G U R E   1 4 - 1
This one-dimensional array has five elements.

WARNING

*The compiler will not prevent you from assigning a value to **x[20]** or even **x[100]**. Those subscripts will access memory locations outside of your array. Assigning values to subscripts outside of your array will overwrite other data in memory.*

Figure 14-1 shows how the array related to distance declared earlier is stored in memory. The actual memory addresses are not important, and will vary. Because of the data type selected, each element takes two bytes of memory. (On some systems, unsigned ints may occupy four bytes.) The array is accessed using subscripts 0 through 4.

The code below uses an integer variable named **index** to access the elements of the distance array and initialize the elements with values from the user.

```
int index;

for(index = 0; index <= 4; index++)
   cin >> distance[index];
```

The same kind of loop can be used to print the values in the array to the screen, as shown below.

```
for(index = 0; index <= 4; index++)
   cout << distance[index] << '\n';
```

The program in Figure 14-2 illustrates a simple array. The array named **num** has three elements. The array is accessed using the subscripts 0, 1, and 2.

```
#include<iostream.h>

int main()
{
  int num[3];

  num[0] = 12;
  num[1] = 16;
  num[2] = 32;

  cout << num[0] << ' ' << num[1] << ' ' << num[2] << endl;
  return 0;
}
```

F I G U R E   1 4 - 2
This simple program uses a three-element array.

EXERCISE 14-1   SIMPLE ONE-DIMENSIONAL ARRAY

1.   Enter the program in Figure 14-2. Save the source code as *INTARRAY.CPP*.

2.   Compile and run the program, then close the source code file.

A ONE-DIMENSIONAL ARRAY EXAMPLE

The program in Figure 14-3 uses a one-dimensional array to store high temperatures for a series of days. At the end of the program, the temperatures are printed back to the screen and averaged. Let's examine the program.

The program first declares a constant and the variables it needs. The **array_size** constant is used to declare the array. Having the value in a constant makes the size of the array available later in the program. The constant will be used to make sure that the number of values the user wants to enter will fit in the array.

The prompt for **num_values** is in a do while loop so that the prompt can repeat until the user enters a valid number.

The first for loop (repeated below) prompts the user for each of the daily high temperatures. Even though the array subscripts range from 0 to 31, this program begins with subscript 1. Beginning with subscript 1 allows the array subscripts to correspond directly with the day number. The drawback to this approach is that one element of the array remains unused.

```
for(index = 1; index <= num_values; index++)
 {
  cout << "Enter the high temperature for day " << index << ": ";
  cin >> daily_temp[index];  // input value into array
 }
```

The program's second for loop (repeated below) prints the values in the array to the screen, and totals the values in the same loop. The total will be used after the loop to calculate the average temperature.

```
// HIGHTEMP
// This program averages the high temperatures over a user-defined
// number of days.

#include<iostream.h>
#include<iomanip.h>

int main()
{
  const int array_size = 32;  // constant to define size of array
  int daily_temp[array_size]; // array of daily high temperatures
  int num_values;             // number of days in a row to enter values
  int index;                  // index for loop counter and array access
  float average_high;         // calculated average high temperature
  int total = 0;              // used to total temps before averaging

  do  // loop to ask for number of days until valid input is received
  {
    cout << "Enter the number of days for which you have data: ";
    cin >> num_values;
    if ((num_values < 1) || (num_values > array_size - 1))
      {
        cout << "The number of days must be in the range 1 to "
             << array_size - 1 << endl;
      }
  } while ((num_values < 1) || (num_values > array_size - 1));

  // The following loop gets the high temperatures from the user for as
  // many days as the user specified in num_values. The subscript 0 is
  // not used so that the subscript will correspond with the day number.
  for(index = 1; index <= num_values; index++)
   {
     cout << "Enter the high temperature for day " << index << ": ";
     cin >> daily_temp[index];  // input value into array
   }

  // Print the values in the array to the screen.
  cout << "The array contains high temperatures for " << num_values
       << " days.\n";
  cout << "The values are as follows.\n";
  for(index = 1; index <= num_values; index++)
   {
     cout << "Day " << index << ": " << daily_temp[index] << endl;
     total = total + daily_temp[index]; // update total for averaging
   }

  // Calculate average by typecasting total and num_values to floats
  // before dividing and assigning the result to average_high.
  average_high = float(total) / float(num_values);

  // Print the results to the screen.
  cout << "The average high temperature during the " << num_values
       << "-day period was " << setprecision(2) << average_high
       << " degrees.\n";
  return 0;
}
```

F I G U R E   1 4 - 3

This program uses an array of integers to store high temperatures for a series of days.

```
for(index = 1; index <= num_values; index++)
{
  cout << "Day " << index << ": " << daily_temp[index] << endl;
  total = total + daily_temp[index]; // update total for averaging
}
```

When the temperatures are averaged, **total** and **num_values** (which are both ints) are typecasted to floats so that the average will be a floating-point number. In the exercise that follows, you will compile and run the program from Figure 14-3.

EXERCISE 14-2   ONE-DIMENSIONAL ARRAYS

1. Open *HIGHTEMP.CPP*. The program from Figure 14-3 appears on the screen.

2. Compile and run the program. Test the program by providing about five temperatures as input.

3. Run the program again. When prompted for the number of days for which you have data, enter a value less than 1 or greater than 31. The program should prompt you to enter a valid value. Enter a valid value and complete the session with the program.

4. Close the source code file.

SECTION 14.1 QUESTIONS

1. Write a statement that declares an array named **n** of type float with 10 elements .

2. Give an example of a situation where an array could be used in a program.

3. How many elements are declared by the statement below?

```
int group_size[] = {9, 12, 8, 16};
```

4. Write a loop that will print the values in a 20-element array named **quantity** to the screen.

5. Write a loop that will initialize the values in a 100-element floating-point array named **x** with the square root of the element number. For example, element 25 should be initialized with the square root of 25, which is 5.

PROBLEM 14.1.1

Modify the program from Exercise 14-1 (*INTARRAY.CPP*) so that it uses an array of five elements. Initialize the values of elements 3 and 4 to the values 38 and 44 respectively. Replace the output statement with a for loop that outputs all five elements on the same line, separated by a space. Save the new program as *INTARR2.CPP*.

PROBLEM 14.1.2

Modify the program from Exercise 14-2 (*HIGHTEMP.CPP*) so that it identifies the coolest and warmest days in the array by printing them to the screen. Save the new program as *HTEMP2.CPP*.

Templates

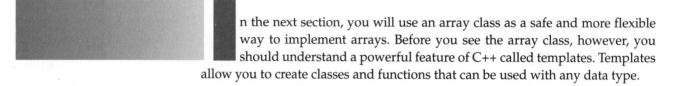

n the next section, you will use an array class as a safe and more flexible way to implement arrays. Before you see the array class, however, you should understand a powerful feature of C++ called templates. Templates allow you to create classes and functions that can be used with any data type.

UNDERSTANDING TEMPLATE CLASSES

As you know, you can create an array of any data type, structure, or class. If you began to plan an array class, you may come to the conclusion that a separate array class should be created for each data type. For example, you could write an array class for storing an array of variables of type int and another class for storing variables of type float. To create a different class for each data type would be time consuming and not very convenient.

Fortunately, C++ allows the creation of classes that can be used with any data type. For example, an array class can be created that will allow the programmer to choose the data type used to store the data in the array. The result is simplified code and a saving of time and energy. C++ allows you to perform that kind of operation through *templates*. The use of templates allows a programmer to construct a class that can be utilized by any data type.

The class definition in Figure 14-4 shows an extremely simple template class.

```
template <class DataType>
class TemplateExample
{
  public:
    TemplateExample();                   // default constructor
    void SetValue(DataType New Value);   // simple method to set value of data
    DataType Value();                    // simple method to return the
                                         // private variable data

  private:
    DataType data;                       // variable data of type DataType
};
```

FIGURE 14-4
A template class allows any data type to be utilized within the class.

The definition in Figure 14-4 begins with the keyword **template** followed by the expression **<class DataType>**. This statement tells the compiler that this is a template class and to replace all occurrences of **DataType** with the data type specified by the programmer. **DataType** is simply an identifier and can be replaced with any name the programmer would like to use. This technique is known as *parameterizing* the data type. In other words, the **DataType** identifier serves as a parameter for passing a data type such as int or float.

The same syntax is used for defining member functions. The syntax for defining a member function with a template class is shown in Figure 14-5.

A programmer using this class would use the statement below to create an integer object from the class definition **TemplateExample**.

```
TemplateExample <int> MyObject;
```

```
      template <class DataType>
      return_type class_name<DataType>::function_name(parameters)
      {
        // necessary code
      }
```

F I G U R E   1 4 - 5
Defining a member function in a template class.

The compiler would then replace the **DataType** variable in the **TemplateExample** class with the int data type to form the class definition shown in Figure 14-6.

```
      class TemplateExample
      {
        public:
             TemplateExample();            // default constructor
             void SetValue(int NewValue);  // simple method to set value of data
             int Value(){return data;}     // simple method to return the
                                           // private variable data

        private:
             int data;                     // variable data of type int
      };
```

F I G U R E   1 4 - 6
When the template class is compiled, the parameterized type is treated in the same way as a hard-coded type would be treated.

The compiler can replace the **DataType** parameter with any data type from a basic integer type to a class. The identifier **DataType** is not a keyword. You can use any desired identifier. One of the most popular identifiers to use is **T**.

Extra for Experts

Template classes can also have multiple parameterized data types. This is done by adding another data type between the angle brackets. For example, the statement below could be used to create a template class that requires more than one data type be variable.

```
      template <class DataType1, class DataType2>
```

You can see that the template feature in C++ can save a programmer a lot of time and hard work because only one class definition has to be designed, programmed, and debugged.

EXERCISE 14-3   TEMPLATE CLASSES

1. Open *TEMPEX.H* and *USETEMP.CPP*. The code for the simple template shown in Figure 14-4 example appears.

2. Compile and run the example to see how the same class is used to create an integer and a floating point object.

3. Close all open source code files.

USING TEMPLATE FUNCTIONS

Templates are not restricted to object-oriented programming. You can also use the template feature of C++ with functions. One of the most useful template functions is a swap function. A swap function takes two variables and swaps the values they hold. For example, suppose a variable **a** is equal to 2 and another variable **b** is equal to 3. After passing the two variables (by reference) to the swap function, the variable **a** would equal 3 and **b** would equal 2. Figure 14-7 shows how the swap function would be defined as a template function.

Note

Functions that swap data between two variables are often used in code that sorts data. You will see the concept of swapping again in Chapter 19.

```cpp
template <class DataType>
void swap(DataType &x, DataType &y)
{
  DataType temp = x;
  x = y;
  y = temp;
}
```

FIGURE 14-7
Templates can be used in non-object-oriented functions.

EXERCISE 14-4   TEMPLATE FUNCTIONS

1. Open *TEMPFUN.CPP*.

2. Compile and run the program to see how the same function can be used for multiple data types.

3. Close the source code file.

On the Net

To learn more about templates, see http://www.ProgramCPP.com. See topic 14.2.1.

SECTION 14.2 QUESTIONS

1. What added benefit does the template keyword provide to a class?

2. If templates or some similar feature were not available, what would a programmer be required to do when writing classes in which data types must vary?

3. What data types can be passed to a template class?

4. Rewrite the following statement to instantiate an object of type float named **FloatObject**.

        TemplateExample <int> MyObject;

5. How can templates be used in C++ outside of object-oriented programming?

PROBLEM 14.2.1

Modify the program from Exercise 14-4 (*TEMPFUN.CPP*) to declare two variables of type char. Initialize one of the variables to the first letter of your first name and the other to the first letter of your last name. Use the template function **swap** to swap the characters. Save the source code as *TEMPFUN2.CPP*.

CHAPTER 14, SECTION 3

Using a Vector Class

After studying standard C++ arrays, you can see from all of the rules and warnings that implementing an array as an object would have several benefits. For example, an array class could prevent you from accessing data outside the array. In this section, you will see and use an array class called a vector class.

VECTORS

The vocabulary of computer scientists often relates to the field of mathematics because much of what computer scientists do is mathematical. Vector is an example of a computer science term that comes from the field of mathematics. In math courses, you have probably used the type of vector that is specified by a magnitude and a direction. In the field of mathematics, the term vector also refers to a one-dimensional array.

For our purposes, a *vector* can be defined as a one-dimensional array of any data type. The terms array and vector can be used interchangeably. In this book, we will avoid confusion by using the term vector only when referring to the vector class you will use in this chapter.

A VECTOR CLASS

A vector class is especially useful because it can be reused in many programs, without rewriting the array functions for each program. And as mentioned before, a vector class can perform error-checking functions, including bounds checking.

When written as a template class, a vector class can be used to create a simple array of integers or an array of classes. A single program can use the vector class for as many different arrays as necessary, and the data types can differ among the vector objects.

Using a vector class also lets a programmer use operator overloading, thereby making the code easier to write and to read. For example, the assignment

```
        template <class itemType>
        class vector
        {
          public:

          // constructors/destructor
            vector( );                              // default constructor (size==0)
            vector( int size );                     // initial size of vector is size
            vector( int size, const itemType & fillValue ); // Set size and value
                                                            // with which to fill
                                                            // vector.
            vector( const vector & vec );           // copy constructor
            ~vector( );                             // destructor

          // operator overloads
            const vector & operator = ( const vector & vec );
            itemType & operator [ ] ( int index ); // indexing with range checking

          // member functions
            int  length( ) const;                   // capacity of vector
            void resize( int newSize );             // change size dynamically;
                                                    // can result in losing values
          private:
            int  mySize;                            // # elements in array
            itemType * myList;                      // array used for storage
        };
```

FIGURE 14 - 8
The vector class header file defines a template class for implementing an array object.

operator (=) can be used to assign one vector to another. Figure 14-8 is a basic vector class which utilizes bounds checking and operator overloading.

The vector class definition begins with the **template** keyword to indicate that a programmer can use any data type necessary with the vector class. The parameter **itemType** will be replaced with a valid data type through the definition whenever a programmer uses the class.

The vector class has four constructors and a destructor. The first constructor is the default constructor. The second constructor allows the programmer to specify the starting size of the vector, while the third constructor allows the programmer to specify a starting size and a default value for the array. The fourth and final constructor is the standard copy constructor. Because memory will be dynamically allocated for the vector, a destructor is also needed for this class.

The remainder of the **public** section of the class includes two operator overloads and two member functions. The vector class overloads the assignment operator and the subscript operator. The assignment operator allows one vector to be easily copied to another. Overloading the subscript operator allows bounds checking to be performed before elements of the vector are viewed or modified. Member functions allow the programmer to find the number of elements in the vector and to resize the vector to increase or decrease the number of elements. The **length** function is used to find the number of elements in the vector and the **resize** function is used to change the number of elements in the array.

The **private** section of the class definition contains only two variables, **my-Size** and **myList**. The variable **mySize** is the current size of the vector. A pointer to the array is held by the variable **myList**.

EXERCISE 14-5 USING THE VECTOR CLASS

1. Open the vector class header file *VECTOR.H*.

2. Open the *VECTOREX.CPP* file.

3. Read through the *VECTOREX.CPP* file and see how all of the functions of the vector class are used.

4. Compile and execute the *VECTOREX* program using a project file.

5. Close all the files used in this exercise.

On the Net

To learn more about how the vector class is implemented, see http://www. ProgramCPP.com. See topic 14.3.1.

SECTION 14.3 QUESTIONS

1. From what field of study does the term *vector* come?

2. Define vector.

3. Why is the vector class written as a template class?

4. How is the overloaded assignment operator (=) used?

5. Why does the vector class require a destructor?

PROBLEM 14.3.1

Rewrite the program from Exercise 14-1 to use a vector object rather than the standard C++ array. Save the source code file as *INTVECT.CPP*.

PROBLEM 14.3.2

Rewrite the program from Exercise 14-2 (*HIGHTEMP.CPP*) to use a vector object rather than the standard C++ array. Save the source code file as *HTEMPVEC.CPP*.

KEY TERMS

array

element

one-dimensional array

templates

vector

SUMMARY

➤ One-dimensional arrays are declared using the same syntax as character arrays.

➤ Each variable in an array is called an element.

➤ Arrays can be initialized when they are declared. Most arrays, however, are initialized by user input or by data that is calculated in the program.

➤ Templates allow classes and functions to be utilized by any data type.

➤ A vector is a one-dimensional array of any data type.

➤ A vector class is a class that is used to create array objects. A vector class supports bounds checking and allows for operator overloading. By implementing the vector class as a template class, any data type can be used with the vector class.

PROJECTS

PROJECT 14-1 • LIST PROCESSING

Write a program that declares an array of ten floating point values. Have the program prompt the user for each of the ten floating point values and store them into the array. The program should then report how many of the values entered are larger than the value in the first element of the array. For example, if the values entered are 5.2, 6.1, 2.8, 8.9, 3.3, 2.0, 9.7, 1.4, 7.3, and 5.5, the program should report that 5 of the values in the array are larger than the value in the first element.

PROJECT 14-2 • LIST PROCESSING

Write a program that is functionally identical to the program described in Project 14-1. In this version, however, use the vector class instead of a standard C++ array.

PROJECT 14-3 • TEMPLATE CLASSES

Think of a class other than a vector class that could benefit from templates. Write a short report describing the class and explaining why it would benefit from templates.

PROJECT 14-4 • TEMPLATE FUNCTIONS

Think of a non-object-oriented function that could benefit from templates. Write a short report describing the purpose of the function and why it would benefit from templates.

PROJECT 14-5 • CHEMISTRY

Write a program that uses an array of structures to hold information for the elements of the periodic table. Include fields for the symbol, name, atomic number, and atomic mass. Enter the elements of the periodic table into a data file that the program will load. Once loaded into the array, have the program allow the user to look up elements by symbol, name, or atomic number.

VECTOR CLASS

Purpose: The vector class provides easy-to-use, safe one-dimensional arrays for your programs.

Required Header File

```
#include "vector.h"
```

To Instanciate a Vector Object

Because the vector class is a template class, you must specify a data type when instanciating the vector object.

```
vector <int> MyVector;        // instanciate empty vector object
```

You can instanciate a vector and specify the number of elements the vector should contain.

```
vector <int> MyVector(100);    // a vector with 100 elements
```

You can instanciate a vector and specify the size and a value with which to initialize each element. In the example below, **MyVector** is initialized with 100 elements, each holding the value 1.

```
vector <int> MyVector (100,1); // vector with 100 elements initialized to 1
```

To Obtain the Length of a Vector

You can determine the number of elements in the vector using the **length** function.

```
length = MyVector.length();
```

To Resize a Vector

You can specify a new size for the vector using the **resize** function. Keep in mind that shortening the vector can result in lost data.

```
MyVector.resize(50);
```

Indexing Elements in a Vector

You can set the elements of the vector individually.

```
MyVector[5] = 3;
```

You can retrieve the elements of the vector individually.

```
value = MyVector[10];
```

Assigning One Vector to Another

You can assign the contents of one vector to another. The vector receiving the contents of the other is resized.

```
MyVector1 = MyVector2;
```

Multi-Dimensional Arrays and Matrices

- ➤ Use parallel arrays.
- ➤ Use multi-dimensional arrays.
- ➤ Use the **sizeof** operator.
- ➤ Use a matrix class.

Overview

lthough one-dimensional arrays are the most common type of array, multi-dimensional arrays are also widely used. In addition, groups of one-dimensional arrays are often used to store related data. In this chapter, you will learn how to use parallel arrays and multi-dimensional arrays. You will also learn about an operator that calculates the size of arrays and other data structures. Finally, you will use the object-oriented representation of a two-dimensional array: a matrix class.

CHAPTER 15, SECTION 1

Parallel and Multi-Dimensional Arrays

ften, a one-dimensional array is all you need to handle your program's data. Some programs, however, require the use of multiple arrays or multi-dimensional arrays. In this section, you will learn to use parallel arrays and multi-dimensional arrays. You will also learn to use the **sizeof** operator to calculate the size of arrays and other data structures.

PARALLEL ARRAYS

Suppose you need to store the data in Table 15-1 in a data structure. Because of the tabular organization of the data, you can use what are called *parallel arrays* to store the data.

GOLD RESERVES OF SELECTED COUNTRIES*
(in millions of fine troy ounces)

Year	United States	Japan	Germany	United Kingdom
1980	264.32	24.23	95.18	18.84
1981	264.11	24.23	95.18	19.03
1982	264.03	24.23	95.18	19.01
1983	263.39	24.23	95.18	19.01
1984	262.79	24.23	95.18	19.03
1985	262.65	24.33	95.18	19.03
1986	262.04	24.23	95.18	19.01
1987	262.38	24.23	95.18	19.01
1988	261.87	24.23	95.18	19.00
1989	261.93	24.23	95.18	18.99

TABLE 15-1

* Source: *The World Almanac and Book of Facts,* 1995.

Using parallel arrays, each country's data is stored in a separate array with subscripts 0-9. Figure 15-1 shows the code required to declare and initialize the arrays.

```
float United_States[10] =  {264.32, 264.11, 264.03, 263.39, 262.79,
                            262.65, 262.04, 262.38, 261.87, 261.93};

float Japan[10] =          { 24.23,  24.23,  24.23,  24.23,  24.23,
                             24.33,  24.23,  24.23,  24.23,  24.23};

float Germany[10] =        { 95.18,  95.18,  95.18,  95.18,  95.18,
                             95.18,  95.18,  95.18,  95.18,  95.18};

float United_Kingdom[10] = { 18.84,  19.03,  19.01,  19.01,  19.03,
                             19.03,  19.01,  19.01,  19.00,  18.99};
```

FIGURE 15-1
These are called parallel arrays.

The arrays are called parallel because the same subscript can access any country's data for a given year. For example, the subscript 0 accesses the first element of any of the arrays, which is the 1980 data. One index variable can index all of the arrays to give the data for the chosen year. The code in Figure 15-2 shows how a simple for loop can print the table to the screen using the same index variable for each array.

```
int index;
cout.setf(ios::showpoint);
cout.setf(ios::fixed);
for(index = 0; index <= 9; index++)
 {
  cout << "    " << 1980 + index
       << setw(10) << United_States[index]
       << setw(10) << Japan[index]
       << setw(10) << Germany[index]
       << setw(10) << United_Kingdom[index] << '\n';
 }
```

FIGURE 15-2
In this code segment, a loop increments the variable **index** and accesses data in the parallel arrays.

EXERCISE 15-1   PARALLEL ARRAYS

1. Write a program that combines the declarations from Figure 15-1 and the code from Figure 15-2 with the code necessary to have a complete program. Save the program as *GOLD.CPP*.

2. Compile and run the program to see the data printed from the parallel arrays.

3. Add headings over the columns the program outputs.

4. Save and run the program again. When you have your column headings working correctly, close the source code file.

Parallel arrays can consist of different data types. The data in Table 15-2, for example, shows the times attained by a runner in each of six events.

DISTANCE (in meters)	TIME (in seconds)
50	7.39
100	13.44
200	27.67
400	69.82
800	160.68
1000	230.13

TABLE 15-2

The data in Table 15-2 can be stored in two parallel arrays. The code segment below shows that the distance can be stored in an array of ints, and the time can be stored in a parallel array of floats.

```
int distance[6] = {50, 100, 200, 400, 800, 1000};
float time[6] = { 7.39, 13.44, 27.67, 69.82, 160.68, 230.13};
```

EXERCISE 15-2   MORE PARALLEL ARRAYS

1. Write a program that uses parallel arrays based on Table 15-2. Initialize the distance array to the values in the table, but have the program prompt the user for their times in each event.

2. After the user provides the six values for the time array, have the program print the distance and time arrays back to the screen in a table similar to Table 15-2.

3. Save the program as *RUNNING.CPP*. After testing the program, close the source code file.

Note

To implement parallel arrays using the vector class, instanciate a vector for each array.

MULTI-DIMENSIONAL ARRAYS

You have discovered by now that there is more than one way to represent the same data in a computer. Part of what makes a good programmer is the ability to choose an efficient method of storing and processing data. The multi-dimensional array is an alternative to parallel arrays. Using a *multi-dimensional array,* a single identifier (or variable name) can access values in a table or even more complex arrangement.

TWO-DIMENSIONAL ARRAYS

The *two-dimensional array* is the most common type of multi-dimensional array. A two-dimensional array can be visualized as a table or spreadsheet with rows and columns. The table of shipping rates shown in Figure 15-3 can be implemented using a two-dimensional array. What makes the table a good candidate for a two-dimensional array is the fact that all of the values can be easily managed from a single identifier, and all of the values can be stored with the same data type. All elements of a two-dimensional array must be the same data type.

Shipping Rates

Weight (up to)	Shipping Zones							
	1	2	3	4	5	6	7	8
5 lbs.	2.65	2.75	2.87	3.06	2.65	3.35	4.73	6.13
10 lbs.	3.05	3.18	3.35	3.84	4.60	5.58	7.68	9.33
15 lbs.	3.25	3.40	3.63	4.24	5.08	6.13	8.46	10.38
20 lbs.	4.10	4.28	4.59	5.34	6.20	7.39	9.93	11.85
25 lbs.	4.65	4.95	5.35	6.23	7.25	8.66	11.55	13.58
30 lbs.	5.25	5.49	5.99	6.90	8.03	9.69	12.69	15.49

F I G U R E   1 5 - 3
The rates in this table are a good candidate for a two-dimensional array.

When the table of shipping rates is placed in a two-dimensional array, the rows and columns of the table become subscripts of the array, as shown in Figure 15-4. For example, **ship_rate[2][3]** points to the value at the intersection of the third row and fourth column (4.24). Because array subscripts begin at zero, the third row is identified with subscript 2, and the fourth column is identified with subscript 3.

ship_rate	Shipping Zones							
	0	1	2	3	4	5	6	7
0	2.65	2.75	2.87	3.06	2.65	3.35	4.73	6.13
1	3.05	3.18	3.35	3.84	4.60	5.58	7.68	9.33
W 2	3.25	3.40	3.63	4.24	5.08	6.13	8.46	10.38
e i g h t 3	4.10	4.28	4.59	5.34	6.20	7.39	9.93	11.85
4	4.65	4.95	5.35	6.23	7.25	8.66	11.55	13.58
5	5.25	5.49	5.99	6.90	8.03	9.69	12.69	15.49

F I G U R E   1 5 - 4
In a two-dimensional array, the subscripts relate to rows and columns.

Declaring the **ship_rate** array is simple. The two dimensions, however, make initializing the array more difficult. The array is declared by providing two subscripts in the declaration, as in the code below. The first subscript declares the number of rows, and the second subscript declares the number of columns.

```
double ship_rate[6][8];
```

Note

A two-dimensional array can be thought of as an array of arrays.

To initialize the array when you declare it, you must make use of additional braces to group the values into rows. The declaration and initialization of the multi-dimensional array **ship_rate** is shown below. Notice how you can use the free-form style of C++ to arrange the initializing values into a readable format. Each row of data is enclosed in a set of braces and followed by a comma. Also, note that all six rows of data are enclosed by a set of outer braces and treated as a single statement followed by a semicolon.

```
double ship_rate[6][8] = {
        { 2.65,   2.75,   2.87,   3.06,   2.65,   3.35,   4.73,   6.13},
        { 3.05,   3.18,   3.35,   3.84,   4.60,   5.58,   7.68,   9.33},
        { 3.25,   3.40,   3.63,   4.24,   5.08,   6.13,   8.46,  10.38},
        { 4.10,   4.28,   4.59,   5.34,   6.20,   7.39,   9.93,  11.85},
        { 4.65,   4.95,   5.35,   6.23,   7.25,   8.66,  11.55,  13.58},
        { 5.25,   5.49,   5.99,   6.90,   8.03,   9.69,  12.69,  15.49}
                          };
```

The main function shown in Figure 15-5 looks up a shipping cost after asking the user for the package weight and zone number.

```
int main()
 {
  double weight;          // weight of package
  int weight_category;    // weight category in table
  int zone;               // zone of package's destination

  weight = get_weight();  // call function to get package weight
  zone = get_zone();      // call function to get shipping zone number

  zone--; // Subtract one from the zone number so the number will
          // correspond to the subscript of the array.

  weight_category = weight / 5.0; // Divide by 5 and truncate to get
                                  // subscript for the array.

  cout.setf(ios::showpoint);
  cout << "The cost of shipping the package is $" << setprecision(4)
       << ship_rate[weight_category][zone] << '\n';
  return 0;
 }
```

FIGURE 15-5
This main function looks up a shipping cost in the two-dimensional array.

The functions **get_weight** and **get_zone** return the weight in pounds and the zone number of the package's destination. Before looking up the shipping cost in the table, the zone must be decremented so that the zone numbers 1 through 8 will correspond with the array subscripts 0 through 7.

Because the shipping rate changes every five pounds, we are able to get the subscript for the table row by dividing the weight by 5 and allowing the fractional part to be truncated. Any weight under five pounds becomes 0; a weight over five pounds, but less than ten, becomes 1; and so on. Storing the result of the floating-point division in an integer variable automatically truncates the result, leaving an integer that can be used as a subscript to access the array.

Note

Recall that truncation means that digits to the right of the decimal point are removed.

EXERCISE 15-3   MULTI-DIMENSIONAL ARRAYS

1. Open *SHIPRATE.CPP*. A complete program that implements the shipping rate two-dimensional array appears on your screen.

2. Study the source code to see how the program is divided into functions. Notice the error checking performed in the functions that get the values from the user.

3. Compile and run the program. Give the program a weight that is 30 pounds or greater. Then enter a valid weight.

4. Give the program a zone number that is outside of the allowable range of 1 to 8. Then enter a valid zone number.

5. Check the shipping cost provided by the program against the table in Figure 15-3 to make sure the program provided the output you expected.

6. Close the source code file.

On the Net

See http://www. ProgramCPP.com for more information about arrays of more than two dimensions and examples of how they are used. See topic 15.1.1.

BEYOND THE TWO-DIMENSIONAL ARRAY

Your compiler will allow you to declare arrays of three, four, or even more dimensions. These kinds of arrays are less common than two-dimensional arrays, but can be declared by simply adding more subscripts to a declaration. You should keep the size of arrays in mind when declaring multi-dimensional arrays. The limit on array size will vary depending on your system, but there is a limit.

You can calculate the size of an array by multiplying the number of elements by the size of the data type used. For example, the declaration below declares a two-dimensional array that is 50 by 10, or 500 elements. Because the array is of type long double, each element occupies ten bytes. Therefore the array occupies a total of 5000 bytes of memory.

```
long double t[50][10];
```

Note

Using some compilers, variables of the type long double may occupy more or fewer bytes than in this example.

THE sizeof OPERATOR

C++ provides an operator for calculating the size of arrays and other data structures: the **sizeof** *operator*. For example, the statement below assigns the number of bytes occupied by the character array **address** to the variable **size_of_address**.

```
size_of_address = sizeof(address);
```

The **sizeof** operator will also return the size in bytes of any variable. For example, the program in Figure 15-6 is an example of how the **sizeof** operator can be used to determine the size of variables.

```
#include <iostream.h>

int main()
{
  float A = 5.46;
  double B = 2.342311;
  long double C = 3.46647483;

  cout << "The float variable A is occupying " << sizeof(A)
       << " bytes.\n";
  cout << "The double variable B is occupying " << sizeof(B)
       << " bytes.\n";
  cout << "The long double variable C is occupying " << sizeof(C)
       << " bytes.\n";
  cout << "The total number of bytes occupied by the variables of this "
       << "program is " << sizeof(A) + sizeof(B) + sizeof(C) << ".\n";
  return 0;
}
```

F I G U R E   1 5 - 6
The **sizeof** operator returns the
number of bytes that data occupies.

EXERCISE 15-4   THE sizeof OPERATOR

1. Enter the program in Figure 15-6. Save the source code as *SIZES.CPP*.

2. Compile and run the program to see if the number of bytes reported by the **sizeof** operator correspond to what you expect. Because the program outputs the size of the variables rather than the contents of the variables, you may get a warning from your compiler saying that some variables are never used. You may ignore this warning.

3. Add the following character array declaration to the program.

```
char microprocessor[] = "Intel Pentium";
```

4. Add a statement that prints the size of the **microprocessor** character array to the screen.

5. Run the program to see the size of the array as reported by the **sizeof** operator. Remember, the compiler adds an element for the null terminator.

6. Add the following array declaration to the program.

```
float D[10];
```

7. Add a statement that prints the size of the **D** array to the screen. Can you predict the size of the array in bytes?

8. Run the program.

9. Add the array declaration that we used as an example of calculating array size (**long double t[50][10];**) and a statement that prints the size of the array.

10. Run the program to see if our calculation of 5000 bytes is consistent with what the **sizeof** operator reports. If your program reports a size other than 5000, it could be that long double types occupy a different amount of memory on your system. After you run the program, save and close the source code file.

Note

*The fact that data types on some C++ compilers use slightly different amounts of memory than the examples in this book is one reason the **sizeof** operator is important. Using the **sizeof** operator ensures that you have an accurate representation of the memory occupied on your system.*

SECTION 15.1 QUESTIONS

1. What type of array allows multiple columns to be accessed with a single identifier?

2. In one statement, declare and initialize a two-dimensional array that stores the data below.

1.223	3.422	2.988
3.572	4.008	1.982

3. Describe some data that could be stored in parallel arrays and explain why parallel arrays are a good choice for the data.

4. How many bytes are occupied by the array declared below (assume doubles occupy eight bytes each).

   ```
   double look_up_table[5][10];
   ```

5. Write a statement that uses the **sizeof** operator to print to the screen the size of an array named **my_array**.

PROBLEM 15.1.1

Modify the *GOLD.CPP* program to include a loop that creates a table that shows the amount of change in the gold reserves in the years 1981 through 1989. For example, the 1981 values should show how much the gold reserves increased or decreased from 1980. Show decreased reserves with negative numbers. Save the new program as *GOLDCHNG.CPP*.

PROBLEM 15.1.2

Modify the *GOLD.CPP* program or *GOLDCHNG.CPP* to use the vector class rather than an array. Save the new program as *GOLDVECT.CPP*.

Using a Matrix Class

ow that you understand how multi-dimensional arrays are created and used in C++, you may realize that creating an object to support two-dimensional arrays would be very useful. Recall that we refer to the one-dimensional array class as a vector class. A two-dimensional array class is referred to as a matrix class. There are a lot of similarities between the classes, and the matrix class offers many of the same benefits as the vector and string classes, including bounds checking and improved readability.

MATRICES

Like the term *vector,* the term *matrix* comes from the field of mathematics. A **matrix** is a two-dimensional array of any data type. The plural form of the word is **matrices**. You may have seen or heard the term *matrix* in a math course.

Note

Before laser and ink-jet printers became available at affordable prices, most microcomputer users had a type of printer called a dot-matrix *printer. A dot-matrix printer creates characters on the page by using a matrix of pins that impact the paper through an ink-ribbon. The matrix used in a dot-matrix printer is a two-dimensional array of pins.*

MATRIX CLASS

When the object-oriented paradigm was first discussed, object reuse was listed as one of the primary benefits. The matrix class you will use in this chapter is a good example of reusability. Not only can the matrix class be reused in many programs, but the matrix class actually reuses the vector class.

If you analyze a matrix, you will realize that a matrix can be represented by a group of vectors. The main difference between a matrix and a vector is that a matrix is two dimensional while a vector is one dimensional. Therefore, we could say that a matrix is a vector of vectors. This containment relationship allows us to reuse the vector object, thereby reducing the amount of source code and debugging time.

On the Net

There are operations commonly performed on matrices that are not implemented in our matrix class. For more information on some of these other operations, see http://www.ProgramCPP.com. See topic 15.2.1.

The vector class and the matrix class have the same basic operations. Notice how similar the matrix class is to the vector class as you read through the matrix class definition in Figure 15-7.

```
#include "vector.h"

template <class itemType>
class matrix
{
  public:

  // constructors/destructor
    matrix();                                        // default size 0 x 0
    matrix(int rows, int cols);                      // size rows x cols
    matrix(int rows, int cols, const itemType & fillValue); // set fill
    matrix(const matrix & mat);                      // copy constructor
    ~matrix();                                       // destructor

  // operator overloads
    const matrix & operator = (const matrix & rhs);
    vector<itemType> & operator [ ] (int k);         // range-checked index

  // member functions
    int  numrows() const;                            // number of rows
    int  numcols() const;                            // number of columns
    void resize(int newRows, int newCols); // resizes matrix to Rows x Cols
                                           // (can result in losing values)

  private:

    int myRows;                            // # of rows (capacity)
    int myCols;                            // # of cols (capacity)
    vector <vector<itemType>> myMatrix;    // the matrix of items
};
```

FIGURE 15-7
The matrix class header file is similar to the vector class header file.

The beginning of the matrix class has the same constructors as the vector class: a default constructor, a constructor to set the number of rows and columns, a constructor to set the number of rows and columns and to set a fill value for the matrix, and finally, the standard copy constructor. A destructor is also required because memory is dynamically allocated to and from the class.

The same operators that were overloaded in the vector class are also overloaded in the matrix class. The assignment operator overload makes source code easier to write and to read. The subscript operator overload provides the benefit of bounds checking. The subscript operator overload definition looks the same as the subscript overload in the vector definition except that the return type in the matrix class is a vector.

The fact that the return type of a matrix is a vector may be confusing until you think about the relationship between the matrix class and the vector class. Indexing a position in a matrix uses two subscript operators:

```
MyMatrix [MyRow] [MyColumn]
```

The matrix class uses the value in the first subscript operator, **[MyRow]**, to return the appropriate row, a vector, from the matrix. The compiler then uses the assignment operator overload from the vector class to return the value indicated in the second subscript operator, **[MyColumn]**.

The matrix class also has three member functions (shown again below). The first two return the number of rows and the number of columns, respectively. The third member function allows the programmer to resize the matrix. When using the resize function, the programmer must be careful because the function can result in the loss of data if the new size is smaller than the original size.

```
// member functions
    int  numrows() const;                       // number of rows
    int  numcols() const;                       // number of columns
    void resize(int newRows, int newCols); // resizes matrix to Rows x Cols
                                            // (can result in losing values)
```

The private section (shown again below) of the class definition provides some insight into how the class holds, maintains, and checks for data integrity. The class holds the current number of rows and columns. The final variable **MyMatrix** is the vector of vectors.

```
private:

    int myRows;                          // # of rows (capacity)
    int myCols;                          // # of cols (capacity)
    vector <vector<itemType>> myMatrix;  // the matrix of items
```

EXERCISE 15-5   Using the Matrix Class

1. Open the files *MATRIXEX.CPP* and *MATRIX.H*. Put these source code files into a project file.

2. Read through the *MATRIXEX.CPP* file to see how the matrix class can be used.

3. Compile and run the program.

4. If you have a debugger, use it to step through the subscript operator usage. Depending on the compiler you are using, stepping through the matrix operation may produce strange results. If so, restart the program without the debugger.

5. Close all the files used in this exercise.

SECTION 15.2 QUESTIONS

1. What is the difference between a vector and a matrix?

2. Why does the matrix class need a destructor?

3. What does the member function **int numrows() const** do?

4. Why must the [] operator be overloaded in the matrix class?

5. How could the resize function cause data to be lost?

data structure   parallel arrays

element   primitive data structures

matrices   simple data structures

matrix   **sizeof** operator

multi-dimensional array   two-dimensional array

one-dimensional array

SUMMARY

➤ Parallel arrays separate arrays that are indexed with the same variable in order to create columns of data. Parallel arrays do not have to be of the same data type.

➤ Two-dimensional arrays are the most common multi-dimensional array. The subscripts in a two-dimensional array relate to rows and columns in a table.

➤ The **sizeof** operator returns the size in bytes of arrays and other data structures.

➤ A matrix is a two-dimensional array of any data type.

➤ A matrix class can be used anywhere a two-dimensional array is needed. A matrix is actually a vector of vectors.

PROJECTS

PROJECT 15-1

Write a program that asks the user for his or her name and stores it in a character array. The program should then print the user's name to the screen by dividing the characters between lines and presenting them diagonally as in the example below.

```
B
  r
    i
      a
        n

          D
            a
              v
                i
                  s
```

PROJECT 15-2

Write a program that declares a two-dimensional array of integers or instanciates a matrix with four rows and four columns and uses a loop to initialize the array in the pattern below. Name the program *TWODIM.CPP*. *Hint:* Study the pattern of the numbers in the array to discover a simple way to initialize the array.

0	0	0	0
0	1	2	3
0	2	4	6
0	3	6	9

PROJECT 15-3 • GAME PROGRAMMING

Write a program that pits the user against the computer in a game of tic-tac-toe. Use characters in the ASCII table to display the progress of the game.

PROJECT 15-4 • MATHEMATICS

Write a program that implements two mathematical matrices as two-dimensional arrays or using the matrix class. Use the rules of algebra to multiply one matrix by the other.

MATRIX CLASS

Purpose: The matrix class provides easy-to-use, safe two-dimensional arrays for your programs.

Required Header File

```
#include "matrix.h"
```

To Instanciate a Matrix Object

Because the matrix class is a template class, you must specify a data type when instanciating the matrix object.

```
matrix <float> MyFloatMatrix;  // instanciate a matrix with size 0 x 0
```

You can instanciate a matrix and specify the size in rows and columns. The example below instanciates a matrix with 3 rows and 2 columns.

```
matrix <char> CharMatrix(3,2);
```

You can instanciate a matrix and specify the size and a value with which to initialize each element. In the example below, **MyMatrix** is initialized with 4 rows and 3 columns, each holding the value 0.

```
matrix <int> CharMatrix(4,3,0);
```

To Obtain the Size of a Matrix

You can determine the number of rows in the matrix using the **numrows** function.

```
rows = MyMatrix.numrows();
```

You can determine the number of columns in the matrix using the **numcols** function.

```
columns = MyMatrix.numcols();
```

To Resize a Matrix

You can specify a new size for the matrix using the **resize** function. Keep in mind that resizing the matrix can result in lost data. The example below resizes the matrix to have 5 rows and 7 columns.

```
MyMatrix.resize(5,7);
```

Indexing Elements in a Matrix

You can set the elements of the matrix individually. The example below sets the element in the first row of the second column to 3.

```
MyMatrix[1][2] = 3;
```

You can retrieve the elements of the matrix individually. The example below retrieves the value of the element in the third row of the second column.

```
value = MyMatrix[3][2];
```

Assigning One Matrix to Another

You can assign the contents of one matrix to another. The matrix receiving the contents of the other is resized.

```
MyMatrix1 = MyMatrix2;
```

Overview

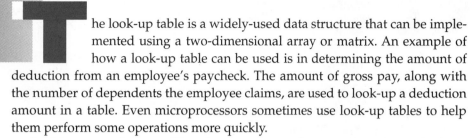

he look-up table is a widely-used data structure that can be implemented using a two-dimensional array or matrix. An example of how a look-up table can be used is in determining the amount of deduction from an employee's paycheck. The amount of gross pay, along with the number of dependents the employee claims, are used to look-up a deduction amount in a table. Even microprocessors sometimes use look-up tables to help them perform some operations more quickly.

In this case study, you will analyze a program that uses a matrix as a look-up table of mileage between major cities. The program will ask for two cities as input, and provide output in the number of miles between the cities.

Building the Look-Up Table

he look-up table is the heart of our program. Each possible output value will be stored in the matrix. Therefore, obtaining the distance between two cities can be done without calculation. Figure III-1 shows the look-up table required for our program.

To keep the problem manageable, ten cities have been selected for the look-up table. To find the mileage between two of the cities, locate the row of your originating city and the column of your destination. The intersection of that row and column gives the road mileage between the cities.

	Atlanta	Boston	Chicago	Cincinnati	Dallas	Denver	Detroit	Los Angeles	New York	Seattle
Atlanta	0	1037	674	440	795	1398	699	2182	841	2618
Boston	1037	0	963	840	1748	1949	695	2979	206	2976
Chicago	674	963	0	287	917	996	266	2054	802	2013
Cincinnati	440	840	287	0	920	1164	259	2179	647	2300
Dallas	795	1748	917	920	0	781	1143	1387	1552	2078
Denver	1398	1949	996	1164	781	0	1253	1059	1771	1307
Detroit	699	695	266	259	1143	1253	0	2311	637	2279
Los Angeles	2182	2979	2054	2179	1387	1059	2311	0	2786	1131
New York	841	206	802	647	1552	1771	637	2786	0	2815
Seattle	2618	2976	2013	2300	2078	1307	2279	1131	2815	0

F I G U R E   I I I - 1

Implementing the Look-Up Table

n our program, the look-up table must be implemented as a matrix. We will declare the matrix then initialize it later in the program with values from a data file.

```
matrix <int> cities(10,10,0);

input_file.open("mileage.dat", ios::in);  // open input
for(row_counter = 0 ; row_counter < 10 ; row_counter++)
{ // iterate through input file to get data for each row
  for(column_counter = 0 ; column_counter < 10 ; column_counter++)
  {  // iterate through input file to get data for each column
    input_file >> cities[row_counter][column_counter];
  }
}
input_file.close();  // close input file
```

The matrix **cities** is declared with a size of ten by ten. Then the input file, *MILEAGE.DAT*, is opened. Two nested for loops iterate through the data file and fill the matrix row by row with the values from the file. Finally, the data file is closed.

Now that we have the look-up table, all that is required is to get input from the user, look up the correct value, and output it to the screen.

The Completed Program

elow is a listing of the entire completed program. Let's run the program, then analyze it piece-by-piece.

```
// Road Mileage Finder

#include<iostream.h>    // necessary for input/output
#include<fstream.h>     // necessary for file input/output
#include"matrix.h"      // necessary for the matrix class

// function prototypes
void get_cities(int &originating_city, int &destination_city);

// main Function
int main()
{
  // Integer matrix declared for the look-up table
  matrix <int> cities(10,10,0);
  int originating_city; // Holds the choice of the starting point
  int destination_city; // Holds the choice of the ending point
  int row_counter;      // Used to count rows in loops
  int column_counter;   // Used to count columns in loops
```

```cpp
  char answer;          // Used for ending or not ending the loop
  ifstream input_file;  // Holds file pointer for input file

  input_file.open("mileage.dat", ios::in);  // open input
  for(row_counter = 0 ; row_counter < 10 ; row_counter++)
  { // iterate through input file to get data for each row
    for(column_counter = 0 ; column_counter < 10 ; column_counter++)
    { // iterate through input file to get data for each column
      input_file >> cities[row_counter][column_counter];
    }
  }
  input_file.close();   // close input file


  do
   { // iterate until user chooses not to continue

    // call get_cities function to get input from the user
    get_cities(originating_city, destination_city);

    originating_city--;   // Decrement the number of the originating and
    destination_city--;   // destination cities for use in the matrix

    // index matrix using the decremented city numbers and print mileage
    cout << "\nMileage = " << cities[originating_city][destination_city]
         << endl;

    // ask user if he/she wants to repeat look-up
    cout << "\nContinue? [Y]es [N]o: ";
    cin >> answer;
    // loop as long as user answers y or Y
   } while ((answer == 'y') || (answer == 'Y')); // end of do loop
   return 0;
} // end main function

// function that gets the input from the user
void get_cities(int & originating_city, int & destination_city)
 {
  cout << "\nOriginating City     Destination City\n";
  cout << "-----------          ----------------\n";
  cout << " 1 Atlanta            1 Atlanta\n";
  cout << " 2 Boston             2 Boston\n";          // Table of starting
  cout << " 3 Chicago            3 Chicago\n";         // and ending points
  cout << " 4 Cincinnati         4 Cincinnati\n";
  cout << " 5 Dallas             5 Dallas\n";
  cout << " 6 Denver             6 Denver\n";
  cout << " 7 Detroit            7 Detroit\n";
  cout << " 8 Los Angeles        8 Los Angeles\n";
  cout << " 9 New York           9 New York\n";
  cout << "10 Seattle           10 Seattle\n";

  cout << "\nOriginating City [1-10]: ";
  cin >> originating_city;

  cout << "\nDestination City [1-10]: ";
  cin >> destination_city;
 } // end of get_cities function
```

EXERCISE III-1 Compiling and Running the Program

1. Open *MILEAGE.CPP*. The program shown on the previous pages appears on your screen.

2. Compile and run the program so you will understand how it works. Try several combinations of cities.

3. Enter the same city number for both the originating and the destination city. The mileage should be reported as zero.

4. Exit the program and leave the source code file open.

The program begins with comments that identify the program, followed by the compiler directives necessary for console input and output, file input and output, and the matrix class definition. The program consists of only two functions (**main** and **get_cities**), so only the **get_cities** function requires a prototype.

Next, the main function begins. As usual, the main function begins with variable declarations, as shown again below. In addition to the matrix discussed earlier, two variables that hold the numbers of the originating and destination cities are declared. Two other variables are declared that are used as counters in the for loops that load the values from the data file into the matrix. Another variable is declared that is used to store the user's response to a question of whether to continue. Finally, a file pointer is declared so that a data file can be used.

```cpp
// Integer matrix declared for the look-up table
matrix <int> cities(10,10,0);
int originating_city; // Holds the choice of the starting point
int destination_city; // Holds the choice of the ending point
int row_counter;      // Used to count rows in loops
int column_counter;   // Used to count columns in loops
char answer;          // Used for ending or not ending the loop
ifstream input_file;  // Holds file pointer for input file
```

Following the variable declaration the program opens the data file *MILEAGE.DAT* which contains the data needed to initialize the matrix. Two nested for loops initialize the matrix. The first loop iterates through all of the rows in the matrix, while the second loop is responsible for initializing each column in the current row with a value from the data file. When each position in the matrix has been initialized, the data file is closed.

```cpp
input_file.open("mileage.dat", ios::in);  // open input
for(row_counter = 0 ; row_counter < 10 ; row_counter++)
{ // iterate through input file to get data for each row
  for(column_counter = 0 ; column_counter < 10 ; column_counter++)
  {  // iterate through input file to get data for each column
    input_file >> cities[row_counter][column_counter];
  }
}
input_file.close();  // close input file
```

After the matrix is initialized, the main function enters the loop shown below. The loop calls the **get_cities** function to get the originating and destination cities from the user. The variables **originating_city** and **destination_city** are passed by reference to allow the user's input to be passed back to the main function.

```
do
  { // iterate until user chooses not to continue

    // call get_cities function to get input from the user
    get_cities(originating_city, destination_city);

    originating_city--;    // Decrement the number of the originating and
    destination_city--;    // destination cities for use in the array

    // index array using the decremented city numbers and print mileage
    cout << "\nMileage = " << cities[originating_city][destination_city]
        << endl;

    // ask user if he/she wants to repeat look-up
    cout << "\nContinue? [Y]es [N]o: ";
    cin >> answer;
    // loop as long as user answers y or Y
  } while ((answer == 'y') || (answer == 'Y')); // end of do loop
```

The values returned for the cities are in the range of 1 to 10. Recall, however, that array and matrix subscripts in C++ begin with zero. Therefore the look-up table is indexed using the values 0 to 9. To adjust for the difference, the lines shown below subtract one from the values in the variables to prepare them to index the matrix.

```
originating_city--;    // Decrement the number of the originating and
destination_city--;    // destination cities for use in the array
```

Now that the city numbers have been adjusted to properly index the matrix, a single statement is used to look-up the value and output the result.

```
// index matrix using the decremented city numbers and print mileage
cout << "\nMileage = " << cities[originating_city][destination_city]
    << endl;
```

Finally, the main function asks the user if he or she wants to repeat the look-up process. The control expression of the do while loop, shown below, tests the user's response to determine whether the loop should repeat or exit.

```
} while ((answer == 'y') || (answer == 'Y')); // end of do loop
```

The **get_cities** function, shown below, is very straightforward. First, a table of cities is displayed to give the user the options. Next, the user is asked for the originating city, and finally, the destination city. The ampersands (&) in the function declaration causes the parameters to be passed by reference, so the values entered by the user can be returned to the main function.

```
// function that gets the input from the user
void get_cities(int & originating_city, int & destination_city)
{
  cout << "\nOriginating City      Destination City\n";
```

```
cout << "----------             --------------\n";
cout << " 1 Atlanta             1 Atlanta\n";
cout << " 2 Boston              2 Boston\n";       // Table of starting
cout << " 3 Chicago             3 Chicago\n";      // and ending points
cout << " 4 Cincinnati          4 Cincinnati\n";
cout << " 5 Dallas              5 Dallas\n";
cout << " 6 Denver              6 Denver\n";
cout << " 7 Detroit             7 Detroit\n";
cout << " 8 Los Angeles         8 Los Angeles\n";
cout << " 9 New York            9 New York\n";
cout << "10 Seattle            10 Seattle\n";

cout << "\nOriginating City [1-10]: ";
cin >> originating_city;

cout << "\nDestination City [1-10]: ";
cin >> destination_city;
} // end of get_cities function
```

Modifying the Program

As an additional exercise, modify the program to include Memphis, Tennessee. Below is the road mileage between Memphis and the other 10 cities.

Atlanta	371	Denver	1040
Boston	1296	Detroit	713
Chicago	530	Los Angeles	1817
Cincinnati	468	New York	1100
Dallas	452	Seattle	2290

Finally, modify the program to check the validity of the values entered by the user. *Hint:* Use a do while loop to continually call the **get_cities** function until valid input is received.

On the Net

To see this program implemented using a two-dimensional array, open the program named MILEARRY.CPP *from your template disk or see http://www.ProgramCPP.com. See the topic labeled Case Study III.*

16

Introduction to Linked Lists

Overview

magine you are participating in two scavenger hunts. The first scavenger hunt requires that you go to each house on a residential block to obtain a clue. Your search ends at the last house on the block when you discover the final clue.

The second scavenger hunt is different. You are given the address of a house that contains the first clue, but you have no other information. When you arrive at the first house and locate the clue, you are also given the address of the house that contains the second clue. At the second house you find a clue and another address. You are unaware of how many houses you must visit or their locations, but eventually you reach a house that has the last clue.

In C++ programming, arrays are like the first scavenger hunt. The data in an array is lined up in a row like houses on a city block. An array has a certain number of elements like a city block has a certain number of houses.

Like the first scavenger hunt, arrays have limitations and sometimes lack the flexibility needed for our data. If you were organizing the first scavenger hunt, what would you do if you didn't have enough clues for every house on the block? You would probably just use the houses you needed and leave the others unused. But what if you had more clues than houses on the block?

You probably agree that the second method makes for a better scavenger hunt. Using the second method, you involve only the number of houses you need.

In C++ programming, you can use a method like the second scavenger hunt to store data: the linked list. In a *linked list,* memory is assigned to your data as it is needed, rather than all at once like arrays. Like the houses in the second scavenger hunt, the data in a linked list may be at scattered addresses. Each piece of data in the linked list holds the address of the next piece of data.

In this chapter, you will learn how to use linked lists to store data in your programs. You will learn the difference between a static data structure and a dynamic data structure. You will also learn how linked lists are created using C++, and how to use data once it is in a linked list.

CHAPTER 16, SECTION 1

Linked List Basics

rogramming a linked list can be tricky. However, if you understand how a linked list works before you do the programming, you'll find the programming is not that difficult. In this section, you will learn how a linked list works. Also, you will learn more about the difference between static data structures (like variables and arrays) and dynamic data structures (like linked lists).

STATIC VS. DYNAMIC DATA STRUCTURES

In previous chapters, you have learned several different ways to store data. You have created variables, arrays, structures, and even arrays of structures. Although the data structures you have used up to this point serve different purposes, they have one common characteristic. They are static data structures.

A *static data structure* occupies the same amount of memory every time the program is run. For example, suppose you create a program that loads a list of your friends' names and telephone numbers into an array. Because you are such a likable person, you are confident that you will gain many new friendships. Therefore, your program declares an array of 500 structures, as shown below.

```
struct phone_record
 {
  char name[35];
  char phone_num[15];
 }

phone_record my_friends[500];
```

Note

The vector and matrix classes you used in the previous chapters are also dynamic data structures because they can be resized as the program executes.

The array named **my_friends** is occupying 25,000 bytes of memory because each structure in the array occupies 50 bytes regardless of whether you have stored data in the structure. This waste of memory may seem to be an insignificant problem, but what if the structure were expanded to include address, city, state, and ZIP code? The waste of memory would be even greater.

Another problem with the static array is that you can store only as much data as your array can hold. If you become surprisingly popular and need to expand your phone list beyond 500 friends, the program must be modified to allow more structures in the array.

Dynamic data structures are used when a more flexible way of storing data is needed. A *dynamic data structure* reserves memory as it is needed. The amount of memory used by a dynamic data structure changes while the program runs.

There are many types of dynamic data structures. In this chapter, you will be concerned only with the linked list. Many programs become more flexible when linked lists are used. On the other hand, linked lists add complexity to programs and are inappropriate for many programs. Let's consider an example of a program that can benefit from a linked list.

USING A LINKED LIST

Suppose you are developing a program that accepts the names and populations of the counties in a state and ranks them by population. Texas has 254 counties, California has 58, and Hawaii has only 4. Why reserve memory for 254 counties when only a few states have more than 100 counties? Using a linked list allows you to use only the amount of memory necessary for each state.

Recall the analogy of the second scavenger hunt at the beginning of this chapter. Each clue to the puzzle was contained in a house, and each house contained the address of the next house. In a linked list, the data is contained in a structure called a *node*, and each node has a memory address.

Figure 16-1 is an illustration that may help you visualize a node for our program. The node is made up of three parts: the name of the county, the population of the county, and the address of the next node.

Each node in the linked list has this same structure. To create a list, all we have to do

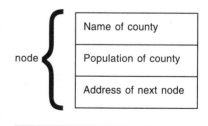

F I G U R E   1 6 - 1
A linked list is a collection of nodes like this one.

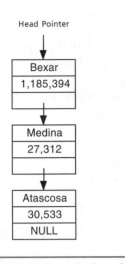

Head Pointer

Bexar
1,185,394

Medina
27,312

Atascosa
30,533
NULL

FIGURE 16-2
The nodes of a linked list are connected by pointers.

is link them together. Figure 16-2 shows a linked list with three counties entered. Let's examine the figure piece by piece.

At the top of Figure 16-2 you see an arrow pointing to the first node. This represents a pointer (called the head pointer) to the first node in the list. You must always have a pointer that points to the first node in the list. Without this pointer that gives the address of the first node, the whole list is lost, just like you need the address of the first house to begin the scavenger hunt.

The first node has data for the first county (name and population), and a pointer which provides the address of the next node. The second node also has data for a county and an address of a third node.

The third node has a null terminator to let your program know the end of the list has been reached. You are familiar with null terminators from your work with strings. In this case, the null terminator is a pointer variable with a value of zero, called a *null pointer.*

In the next section you will implement the program described above that uses a linked list to store the names and populations of counties.

HANDLING MEMORY WITH DYNAMIC DATA

When you declare a static array, you use a statement like the one below.

```
int my_array[100];
```

In one statement, you specify the size, type, and name of your array. The compiler reserves memory for the array and later frees that memory for use by other data.

When using dynamic data structures, you must use special operators to reserve and free memory manually. You must also keep track of the location of your dynamic data using pointers.

MEMORY AND DATA

Dynamic data structures are stored in a portion of memory called the *heap.* Exactly where and what the heap is varies among operating systems, but basically the heap is the memory left over after your operating system and programs are loaded.

Reserving memory on the heap is called *allocating.* Returning reserved memory to the heap for use by other data is called *deallocating* or *freeing.* When memory is allocated, the operating system returns the address of the memory location where the data is stored. That address is stored to a pointer variable that you will use to access the data. Let's look at how memory is allocated and deallocated in C++.

THE new AND delete OPERATORS

The **new** operator allocates memory on the heap and the **delete** operator frees memory. The program in Figure 16-3 demonstrates some features of C++ that you will use when creating linked lists. We'll analyze the program listed in Figure 16-3 in the pages to come.

Examine Figure 16-4. The **new** operator is used to allocate the memory for the data. The **new** operator returns the address of the allocated memory and the program assigns the address to the pointer variable named **my_ptr.**

```cpp
// ALLOCATE.CPP
#include<iostream.h>
#include<string.h>

struct chemical_element
  {
    char element_name[20];
    double atomic_weight;
  };

int main()
{
  chemical_element *my_ptr;   // Declare pointer to point to the
                              // dynamically-allocated structure.
  my_ptr = new chemical_element; // Allocate memory for structure.

  if(my_ptr != NULL)   // Check to make sure allocation was successful.
   {
     // Initialize members of the structure.
     strcpy(my_ptr->element_name, "Nitrogen");
     my_ptr->atomic_weight = 14.0067;

     // Display members of the dynamically-allocated structure.
     cout << "Element Name: " << my_ptr->element_name << endl;
     cout << "Atomic Weight: " << my_ptr->atomic_weight << endl;

     delete my_ptr;   // Free memory used by the data.
   }
  else
   {
     cout << "Memory allocation was unsuccessful.\n";
   }
  return 0;
}
```

F I G U R E   1 6 - 3
This program dynamically allocates and deallocates memory for a structure.

You should test the address returned by the **new** operator to make sure that the memory was successfully allocated. If an error occurs during allocation, the **new** operator returns a null pointer. The most common reason for unsuccessful allocation is insufficient free RAM to satisfy your request. The programs you will write in this course are unlikely to result in an allocation error, but you should get

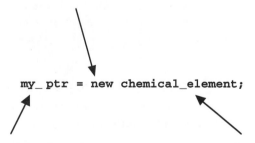

The **new** operator allocates memory for the structure.

my_ptr = new chemical_element;

F I G U R E   1 6 - 4
The new operator allocates memory on the heap.

The address of the allocated memory is assigned to **my_ptr**.

The memory allocated is of type **chemical_element**.

into the habit of checking the operation. In the program shown in Figure 16-3, the value of **my_ptr** is checked in an **if** statement, as shown below.

```
my_ptr = new chemical_element; // Allocate memory for structure.

if(my_ptr != NULL)  // Check to make sure allocation was successful.
 {
   // successful allocation
 }
else
 {
   cout << "Memory allocation was unsuccessful.\n";
 }
```

As you saw in Figure 16-4, memory allocated by the **new** operator is associated with a data type. The data type allows the compiler to allocate the correct amount of memory. In addition, the data type makes it easier to use the allocated memory.

Individual members of a dynamically-allocated structure are accessed using the *structure pointer operator* (->). Examine the statements below. Notice that the period normally used to access members of a structure has been replaced by the structure pointer operator.

```
// Initialize members of the structure.
strcpy(my_ptr->element_name, "Nitrogen");
my_ptr->atomic_weight = 14.0067;

// Display members of the dynamically-allocated structure.
cout << "Element Name: " << my_ptr->element_name << endl;
cout << "Atomic Weight: " << my_ptr->atomic_weight << endl;
```

Note

The structure pointer operator is actually two characters: the hyphen (-) and the greater-than symbol (>). Used together, they are interpreted as the structure pointer operator (->).

Extra for Experts

The structure pointer operator (->) is a shortcut provided to simplify the pointer syntax. The same result can be obtained by combining the dereferencing operator and dot operator. For example, **my_ptr->element_name** *could be replaced by* **(*my_ptr).element_name***.*

Finally, the program frees (deallocates) the memory it allocated. Memory is deallocated with the **delete** operator, as shown below. When deallocating, only the **delete** operator and the name of the pointer are necessary.

```
delete my_ptr;  // Free memory used by the data.
```

ALLOCATING AND DEALLOCATING MEMORY

1. Retrieve the source code file *ALLOCATE.CPP.*

2. Compile and run the program.

3. Add a member of type **int** to the **chemical_element** structure. Name the new member **atomic_number**.

4. Initialize the atomic number of the Nitrogen element to 7, and add a statement to output the value.

5. Save the source code, compile, and run the program again.

6. Close the source code file.

On the Net

See *http://www.ProgramCPP.com* for more information about memory usage in computers, the heap, and memory allocation. See topic 16.1.1.

SECTION 16.1 QUESTIONS

1. Define dynamic data structure.

2. Give an example of a static data structure.

3. What is the term for the structures that store data in a linked list?

4. What is the name of the portion of memory where dynamic data structures are stored?

5. What operators allow you to allocate and deallocate memory?

PROBLEM 16.1.1

Describe a data-storage problem that could be solved using a linked list. Draw a diagram like Figure 16-2 that illustrates your linked list.

PROBLEM 16.1.2

Modify *ALLOCATE.CPP* so that it allocates memory for two chemical elements. Name the pointer that points to the nitrogen data **N_ptr**. Name the pointer that points to the second chemical element **Pb_ptr** and initialize it with the data for lead given below. Print the data from both elements to the screen. Remember to delete both elements from memory at the end of the program. Save the new source code as *ELEMENTS.CPP*.

Element: Lead
Atomic Weight: 207.19
Atomic Number: 82

Linked Lists in C++

 ow that you have seen how linked lists work in general, let's look at how linked lists are implemented in C++.

DECLARING NODES AND NECESSARY POINTERS

The first step in implementing a linked list is declaring the structure that will serve as the nodes for the list. Let's continue working with the program that collects data about counties. The structure below declares a node that stores the county name, population, and the link to the next node.

```
const NAME_LENGTH = 20;

struct county_node          // node for linked list
  {
   char county_name[NAME_LENGTH];
   long population;
   county_node *next;       // link to next node
  };
```

The declaration above looks like other structures you have used, except for the link to the next node.

Recall that in Chapter 10 you used the asterisk when declaring pointers, as in the statement below.

```
int *i_ptr;      // declares a pointer to an integer
```

The asterisk causes the compiler to declare a pointer named **i_ptr** that can be used to point to any integer. In our **county_node** structure, the last member is a pointer named **next**. The **next** pointer can hold the address of any node that is created using the **county_node** structure. In our case, the pointer will hold the address of the next node in the linked list.

The program will need two pointers in addition to the pointer in the **county_node** structure. Recall from Figure 16-2 that a pointer is necessary to point to the first node in the list. We will also need a pointer to keep track of the current node as we use the list. The statements below will declare two pointers for those purposes.

```
county_node *head_ptr;       // pointer to first node of linked list
county_node *current_ptr;    // pointer to current node
```

Note

Remember, a pointer is a variable and can point to any data of the pointer's data type. The pointer named **current_ptr** *can point to any node in the linked list.*

The two pointers declared in the statements above must be initialized before they point to anything. The pointers will be initialized in the main function.

INITIALIZING THE LINKED LIST WITH THE FIRST NODE

The next step is to create a node, initialize it with data, and initialize your pointers. The **county_node** structure (shown again in Figure 16-5) creates a data type that will be used to create nodes. The actual nodes have yet to be created.

Consider the main function in Figure 16-6. First, a local character array and variable are declared to temporarily hold the name and population of a county. These local variables are used to hold the user's input before the node that will eventually hold the data is created.

Notice that most of the main function is in an if structure. Within the parentheses of the if statement is a call to a function named **get_county_data**, which prompts the user for the name and population of a county. The name is returned in the **name** character array and the population is returned in the **popul** variable. The data in the character array and variable will be used to create the first node of the list.

As you'll see later, the if structure is there because the **get_county_data** function returns a value that lets us know if the user entered valid data that needs to be added to the linked list. For now, let's assume the data is valid and focus on the first four lines within the if structure.

The statements below are all that is necessary to create the first node.

```
head_ptr = new county_node; // initialize list head
strcpy(head_ptr->county_name, name);
head_ptr->population = popul;
head_ptr->next = NULL;      // initialize next node pointer to NULL
```

As you learned earlier in the chapter, the first statement in the code segment above allocates memory for the node we are creating and assigns the address of the node to the pointer named **head_ptr**. We don't know or care exactly where the node is located in memory. We do, however, want the address of the new node to be placed in **head_ptr** so that we can find the first node in our list. The next three statements use the pointer (**head_ptr**) to initialize the node with data.

```
// global structure definitions, variables, and constants
  const NAME_LENGTH = 20;

  struct county_node            // node for linked list
    {
      char county_name[NAME_LENGTH];
      long population;
      county_node *next;        // link to next node
    };

  county_node *head_ptr;        // pointer to head of linked list
  county_node *current_ptr;     // pointer to current node
```

FIGURE 16-5
The **county_node** structure is a data type that will be used to create nodes for the linked list.

```
// beginning of main function
int main()
{
 char name[NAME_LENGTH];
 long popul;

 if(get_county_data(name, popul))   // prompt user for data for the node
   {
     head_ptr = new county_node; // initialize list head
     strcpy(head_ptr->county_name, name);
     head_ptr->population = popul;
     head_ptr->next = NULL;       // initialize next node pointer to NULL

     while(get_county_data(name, popul))
      {
        add_node(name, popul);
      }
     display_list();  // display the counties and populations
     delete_list();   // free the memory used by the linked list
   }
}
 return 0;
```

F I G U R E   1 6 - 6
The main function is where the first node is created.

The pointer named **next** is assigned the value **NULL** because at this point it is the last (and only) node in the list. Remember, the last node in the list must always have a **NULL** value in the **next** pointer to signify the end of the list. **NULL** is a constant defined in the **iostream.h** header file. Use **NULL** whenever you need to assign a **NULL** value to a pointer.

On the Net

As you learned in the previous section, programs should check the value of the pointer assigned to a new node. The linked list program in this chapter does not implement the error checking because the added complexity might get in the way of other important concepts. See http://www.ProgramCPP.com for an example of the proper way to check for allocation errors in a linked list program. See topic 16.2.2.

As a preview of what is coming, let's quickly look at the remaining statements in the main function (see below). A while loop is used to continually ask the user for additional counties for the list. The name and population of each of the counties will be added to the linked list by the **add_node** function, which we will study later. When the user has entered all of the counties, the **display_list** function will display all of the nodes in the linked list, and the **delete_list** function will free the memory used by the linked list. You'll see how this is done later in this chapter.

```
while(get_county_data(name, popul))
 {
   add_node(name, popul);
 }
display_list();  // display the counties and populations
delete_list();   // free the memory used by the linked list
```

We have covered a lot of material so far. To take a short break from the reading, let's enter the parts of the program we have covered so far.

EXERCISE 16-2   DECLARING AND INITIALIZING A LINKED LIST

1. Enter the code below into a blank editor screen. As you enter the source code, remind yourself of the purpose of each statement. If you come to a statement you don't yet understand, go back and read about it again. The function prototypes appear in the source code below, although the contents of each function have yet to be covered. Go ahead and enter their prototypes now. We'll add the actual functions in a later exercise.

```cpp
// COUNTIES.CPP
// Example of a dynamically-allocated linked list.

// include files
#include<iostream.h>
#include<iomanip.h>
#include<string.h>

// global structure definitions, variables, and constants
  const NAME_LENGTH = 20;

  struct county_node           // node for linked list
    {
      char county_name[NAME_LENGTH];
      long population;
      county_node *next;       // link to next node
    };

  county_node *head_ptr;       // pointer to head of linked list
  county_node *current_ptr;    // pointer to current node

// function prototypes
int get_county_data(char name[NAME_LENGTH], long &popul);
void add_node(char name[NAME_LENGTH], long popul);
void move_current_to_end();
void display_list();
void delete_list();

// beginning of main function
int main()
{
 char name[NAME_LENGTH];
 long popul;

 if(get_county_data(name, popul))    // prompt user for data for the node
   {
      head_ptr = new county_node; // initialize list head
      strcpy(head_ptr->county_name, name);
      head_ptr->population = popul;
      head_ptr->next = NULL;       // initialize next node pointer to NULL
```

```
      while(get_county_data(name, popul))
        {
         add_node(name, popul);
        }
      display_list();   // display the counties and populations
      delete_list();    // free the memory used by the linked list
     }
  return 0;
}
```

2. The program is incomplete, so it will not yet run. Save the source code on your screen as *COUNTIES.CPP* and leave the file open for the next exercise.

COMMUNICATING WITH THE USER

Let's take a break from pointers and nodes for a while and add the part of the program that interacts with the user.

Our county population program is designed to work regardless of how many counties a particular state may have. That's why we are using a linked list to store the data. We must also give the user the flexibility to enter however many counties he or she needs to enter. In our design for this program, the user is repeatedly asked for a county name and population until the county name is left blank.

Let's look at the **get_county_data** function (shown in Figure 16-7) to see how it works.

```
// Function that gets data from user.
int get_county_data(char name[NAME_LENGTH], long &popul)
 {
   int keep_data = 1;

   cout << "Enter county name (Press Enter alone to stop): ";
   cin.get(name,NAME_LENGTH);
   cin.ignore(80,'\n');
   if(name[0] != '\0')
     {
     cout << "Enter county population: ";
     cin >> popul;
     cin.ignore(80,'\n');
     }
   else
     {
     keep_data = 0;
     }
   return(keep_data);
 }
```

F I G U R E   1 6 - 7
This function asks the user for a county name and population. If the user leaves the county name blank, the function ends and returns a value that alerts the calling function that the data is to be ignored.

The function has a character array and a long integer as parameters. Because the long integer is passed by reference, the value will be passed back to the calling function. Because character arrays are always passed by address, the string assigned to **name** will also be passed back to the calling function.

The function returns the value of a local variable named **keep_data**. If, at the end of the function, the value in **keep_data** is 1, the data entered by the user is intended to be used. If the user presses the Enter key without entering a county name, **keep_data** becomes 0 and the calling function will ignore the data.

> ## Note
>
> *To detect a blank county name, the function checks to see if the first character in the character array is a null terminator. Therefore, if the user enters any character (including a space) before pressing Enter, the entry will be accepted as a valid county name. An alternative way to detect a blank county name would be to use the* **strlen** *function to check for a length of zero.*

EXERCISE 16-3   GETTING DATA FROM THE USER

1. Add the function shown in Figure 16-7 to the bottom of the program on your screen. The program still lacks the code necessary to run.

2. Save the source code and leave the file open for the next exercise.

ADDING A NODE TO THE END OF THE LIST

The purpose of our program is to rank the counties of a state by population. Therefore, we must have the ability to add counties to the linked list. Adding a node to the end of the linked list is similar to creating the first node. First, you must create the new node that you want to add on. After creating the node, you attach it to the list by changing the **next** pointer of the last node in the list to point to the newly created node. Figure 16-8 illustrates the process.

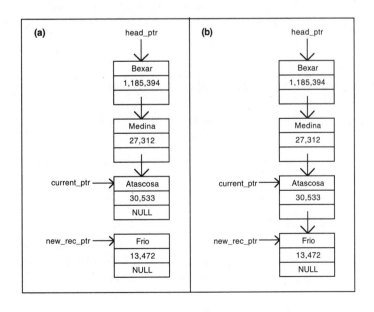

FIGURE 16-8
To add a node to the end of a linked list, first (a) create the new node and keep track of it using a temporary pointer. Next (b) attach the new node to the end of the list.

```
// Function that adds a node to the end of the linked list.
void add_node(char name[NAME_LENGTH], long popul)
{
  county_node *new_rec_ptr; // Declare local pointer for the new node.

  new_rec_ptr = new county_node; // Allocate memory for a new node and
                                 // initialize pointer to point to it.

  strcpy(new_rec_ptr->county_name, name);
  new_rec_ptr->population = popul;
  new_rec_ptr->next = NULL;   // Set next pointer of new node to NULL.

  move_current_to_end();      // Make sure current_ptr is at end of list.
  current_ptr->next = new_rec_ptr; // Place new node at end of the list.
}
```

FIGURE 16-9
The **add_node** function adds a node to the end of the linked list.

In the (a) portion of Figure 16-8, you see that a new node (Frio county) has been created. It has yet to become part of the list. The temporary pointer (**new_rec_ptr**) is keeping track of the address of the new node until it is safely attached to the list. In the (b) portion of the figure, the next pointer of the Atascosa county node has been changed from **NULL** to point to the new node.

Figure 16-9 shows the **add_node** function. Let's analyze the code to see how the new node is added.

First, a local pointer is declared (**new_rec_ptr**), which will be used to keep track of the new node until it is attached to the list. Next, memory is allocated for the new node, and its address is assigned to **new_rec_ptr**.

The next three statements are like the statements used to initialize the data in the first node. The data for the node is passed into the function as parameters. What happens next is what makes adding a node at the end of the list different from creating the first node.

The function **move_current_to_end** moves the pointer **current_ptr** to the end of the linked list. Later, you'll see how the **move_current_to_end** function works. For now, just understand that the function is called to make sure **current_ptr** is pointing to the last node in the list.

Finally, the next node pointer of the last node in the list is changed to point to the new node. At the end of the function, the new node is the last node in the list.

EXERCISE 16-4   ADDING A NODE TO THE END OF THE LIST

1. Add the function in Figure 16-9 to the end of the source code on your screen. The program is still not ready to run.

2. Save the source code and leave the source code file open for the next exercise.

ACCESSING THE NODES OF THE LIST

To be useful, the data in a linked list must be accessible. As you learned earlier in the chapter, the head pointer to the first node is the key to the linked list. The address of the second node in the list is contained in the first. The address of

```
// Function that moves current_ptr to end of the linked list.
void move_current_to_end()
{
 current_ptr = head_ptr;   // Move current_ptr to head of the list.

 while(current_ptr->next != NULL)
   {                           // Traverse list until NULL is reached.
    current_ptr = current_ptr->next;
   }
}
```

FIGURE 16-10
This function traverses the list to move current_ptr to the end of the list.

the third node is contained in the second, and so on. To get to a particular node in the list, start at the node pointed to by the head pointer and move through the list. The process of accessing (also called *visiting*) every node in the list is called *traversing* the list.

Let's look at the function that moves **current_ptr** to the end of the linked list. The function is executed before a new node is attached to make sure that the new node is being attached at the end of the list. The function simply moves through the list looking for the null pointer at the end of the list (see Figure 16-10). In other words, it traverses the list.

The function begins by setting **current_ptr** equal to **head_ptr**, which puts **current_ptr** at the beginning of the list. A while loop then moves **current_ptr** through the list until a node with the null pointer is reached, signaling the end of the list. Only one statement within the loop is necessary. In the statement, the address of the next node in the list is assigned to **current_ptr**.

Note

The statement current_ptr = current_ptr->next; *may seem strange to you. Remember, however, that the right side of the equal sign is evaluated and then assigned to the variable on the left side. Therefore, even though* current_ptr *is on both sides of the equal sign, the statement is valid.*

EXERCISE 16-5   TRAVERSING THE LIST

1. Add the function in Figure 16-10 to the end of the source code on your screen. The program is nearly ready to run.

2. Save the source code and leave the source code file open for the next exercise.

DISPLAYING THE LIST

To display the list, the same method of traversing the list is used (see Figure 16-11). This time, instead of just traversing the list to reach the end, the data in the list is displayed as **current_ptr** moves through the list.

```
// Function that displays entire linked list.
void display_list()
{
 current_ptr = head_ptr;    // Move current_ptr to head of list.
 cout << "County                     Population\n";
 cout << "-------------------         ----------\n";
 do
  {
    cout.setf(ios::left);
    cout << setw(25) << current_ptr->county_name;
    cout.setf(ios::right);
    cout << setw(12) << current_ptr->population << endl;
    current_ptr = current_ptr->next; // point current_ptr to next node
  } while(current_ptr != NULL); // loop until end of list
}
```

FIGURE 16-11
This function traverses the list, displaying the data from each node as it goes.

EXERCISE 16-6   DISPLAYING THE LIST

1. Add the function in Figure 16-11 to the end of the source code on your screen. There is only one more function to add before the program is ready to run.

2. Save the source code and leave the source code file open for the next exercise.

DISPOSING OF THE LIST

The final step in using a linked list is to dispose of it properly when you are finished with it. Just as the **new** keyword reserved memory for our list, the **delete** keyword releases that memory to be used for other purposes.

> **Note**
>
> When you declare variables, the compiler allocates and disposes of the variables at the appropriate time. In the case of a linked list, you must dispose of the memory manually because you allocated it manually.

To dispose of a linked list, you again must traverse the list (see Figure 16-12). This time, an additional pointer is necessary to prevent losing track of the list as nodes are being deleted.

On each iteration of the loop we set the temporary pointer (**temp_ptr**) to point to the node that follows the current node. It is then safe to delete the current node, because we have a pointer to the rest of the list. As soon as the current node is deleted, we copy the address in **temp_ptr** to **current_ptr** so that we can repeat the process to delete the next node. When the **NULL** at the end of the list is reached, the loop ends and the entire list has been deleted.

```
// Function that frees the memory used by the linked list.
void delete_list()
{
 county_node *temp_ptr;  // pointer used for temporary storage

 current_ptr = head_ptr;  // Move current_ptr to head of the list.

 do    // Traverse list
  {
   temp_ptr = current_ptr->next;   // Set temporary pointer to point
                                   // to the remainder of the list.
   delete current_ptr;   // Delete current
   current_ptr = temp_ptr;
  } while(temp_ptr != NULL);
}
```

FIGURE 16-12
This function disposes of the linked list by freeing the memory each node uses.

Dispose of a linked list only when you have completed the necessary processing of data in the list. The linked list exists only in RAM, and therefore is accessible only when your program is running. Depending on your operating system, however, the memory occupied by the list may not be automatically freed when your program terminates.

Note

In the next section, you will learn about saving the data in a linked list to disk before disposing of the list in RAM.

EXERCISE 16-7   FINISHING THE PROGRAM

1. Add the function shown in Figure 16-12 to the bottom of your program. Save the source code file.

2. Compile and run the program. If the program does not successfully compile and run, check the source code against the figures in this section for errors.

3. As input, let's enter the counties of New Hampshire. When entering the populations, enter the numbers without entering the commas.

County	Population
Belknap	49,216
Carroll	35,410
Cheshire	70,121
Coos	34,828
Grafton	74,929
Hillsborough	335,838
Merrimack	120,240
Rockingham	245,845
Strafford	104,233
Sullivan	38,592

4. After you have entered the last county, leave the next prompt for county name blank to signal the program that you have entered all the counties.

5. The program will print the counties back to the screen by traversing the linked list and delete the linked list.

6. Save any changes you have made to the source code file and close.

SECTION 16.2 QUESTIONS

1. What is the purpose of the head pointer?

2. What is purpose of the next pointer in a linked list node?

3. In the example in this section, what pointer moves through the linked list pointing to the current node?

4. What steps are involved when adding a node to the end of a linked list?

5. Why does disposing of a linked list require an additional pointer?

PROBLEM 16.2.1

Open the *COUNTIES.CPP* source code you saved in this chapter. Add a function named **sum_pop()** to the program that traverses the list, sums the populations of all of the counties in the linked list, and displays the result to the screen. Call the function at the end of the **display_list** function. Save the new program as *CNTYSUM.CPP*.

CHAPTER 16, SECTION 3

Advanced Linked List Operations

The linked lists with which you have worked up to this point allowed nodes to be added to the end of the list only. In this section, you will learn how to insert a node anywhere in the list. You will also learn how to delete individual nodes from the list and how a linked list can be saved to disk.

INSERTING LINKED LIST NODES

You may recall that the ultimate goal for the program that stores the names and populations of counties is to rank the counties by population. If the program were to insert the nodes in the proper position in the list as the information is entered, the final display would be ranked by population.

Let's consider what must occur for a node to be inserted in a linked list. Examine the linked list illustrated in Figure 16-13(a) which consists of four nodes. A new node, for Penobscot county, is to be inserted between Cumberland and Kennebec counties. For this to happen, the next pointer of the first node must be changed to point to the new node. In addition, the next pointer of the new node must be initialized to point to the remainder of the list, as shown in Figure 16-13(b).

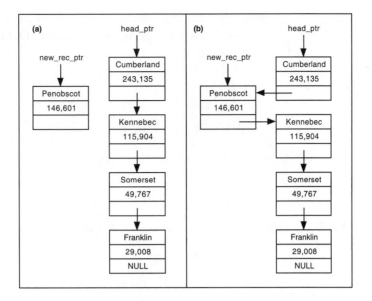

F I G U R E   1 6 - 1 3
Inserting a node in a linked list requires that pointers be redirected
to include the new node.

The process illustrated in Figure 16-13 is sufficient if the node is to be inserted in the middle of the list. There are times, however, when placing a new node in a proper sequence may mean adding it to the beginning or the end of the list. Figure 16-14 shows that a node may be inserted somewhere in the middle of a list, at the head of a list, or at the end of a list.

To insert at the head of the list, the new node's next pointer must point to the node that was first in the list. In addition, the head pointer must be changed to point to the new node.

You have experience with inserting at the end of the list. The next pointer of the node that used to be the end of the list is changed to point to the new node. When adding to the end of a linked list, remember to place a null pointer in the next pointer of the new node.

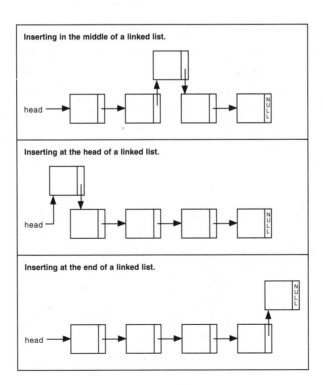

F I G U R E   1 6 - 1 4
A node may be inserted in one of
three ways.

In the exercise that follows, you will run a version of the county population program that ranks the counties by inserting them in the proper position as the counties are entered.

On the Net

You can analyze the code in the program from Exercise 16-8 to see how the insertion functions are programmed. For a detailed explanation, see http://www.ProgramCPP.com. See topic 16.3.1.

EXERCISE 16-8   INSERTING NODES IN A LINKED LIST

1. Retrieve the file *INSERT.CPP*.

2. Compile and run the program. The prompts are just like the program you ran in the previous chapter. Enter the following counties as input again. Remember to leave out the commas when entering the populations.

County	Population
Belknap	49,216
Carroll	35,410
Cheshire	70,121
Coos	34,828
Grafton	74,929
Hillsborough	335,838
Merrimack	120,240
Rockingham	245,845
Strafford	104,233
Sullivan	38,592

3. Leave the county prompt blank and press Enter to terminate input. The program will display the counties ranked from largest to smallest.

4. If you would like, run the program again using the counties of your own state. If your state has more counties than you wish to enter, enter only the counties in your area.

5. Close the source code file.

DELETING NODES INDIVIDUALLY

You already know how to traverse a linked list while deleting each node. Sometimes, however, you will want to delete a node from a linked list without disposing of the entire list. Deleting a node from a linked list involves re-routing a pointer and freeing the memory used by the node you are deleting. Figure 16-15 graphically illustrates the concept behind deleting a node from a linked list.

Figure 16-15(a) illustrates a linked list consisting of four nodes. In Figure 16-15(b), the node that holds the data for Stacy Finn is deleted, and the pointer that previously pointed to the deleted node is re-routed to skip the deleted node.

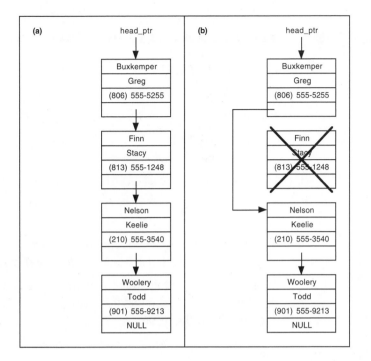

FIGURE 16-15
When a node is deleted from a linked list, the pointer from the previous node must be re-routed to skip to the node that follows the deleted one.

Like inserting a node, deleting a node from a linked list can occur in the middle of the list, at the head of the list, or at the end of the list (see Figure 16-16).

In the exercise that follows, you are going to run a program that manages a database of your friends and their phone numbers. The first time the program is run, there are no records in the database. Each time the user chooses to add a record, a node is inserted into a linked list in alphabetical order, by last name. The user can display the records, search for a specific record, or delete a specific record. When the exit option is selected, the data in the linked list is saved to disk. The next time the program runs, the data in the disk file is loaded into the linked list.

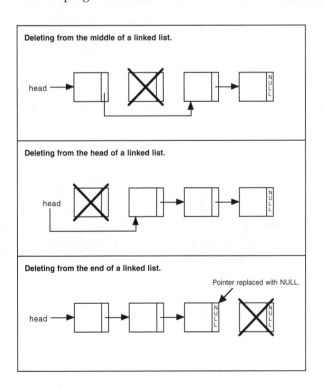

FIGURE 16-16
The position of the node to be deleted dictates the method used to perform the deletion.

EXERCISE 16-9   DELETING AND SAVING LINKED LIST NODES

1. Retrieve *PHONELST.CPP.*

2. Compile and run the program.

3. Add the following record to the linked list:

    Name: Mark Tittle
    Phone Number: (806) 555-8517

4. Choose the Display all records command to see the record.

5. Enter three more records using names and phone numbers of people you know.

6. Use the Display all records command again to view the records. Notice that the records were inserted in order according to last name.

7. Use the Search command to find one of the people in your list. You must enter the entire last name the way it appears in the list in order for the program to find the record.

8. Use the Delete record command to delete the Mark Tittle record.

9. Display the records again to see that it was deleted.

10. Exit the program.

11. Run the program again.

12. Display the records to see that the data you entered was reloaded from disk.

13. Add another record before exiting again.

14. Exit the program and close the source code file.

SAVING A LINKED LIST TO A FILE

A linked list is a flexible way to store data in RAM. To save the data beyond the execution of your program, however, you must save the data from the linked list to a file. The program you ran in the previous exercise does just that.

Saving data from a linked list to a file requires that you traverse the list and save the data from each node to the file. A sequential-access data file is all that is necessary because the list will be traversed sequentially.

When you save a linked list to a file, you are saving only the data stored in the linked list. The pointers are not saved. Because memory usage and availability changes each time a program executes, the linked list must be rebuilt when the data is reloaded.

When data from a disk file is reloaded into a linked list, each node must be created and added to the list individually. The data will occupy different memory, and therefore, the pointers linking the nodes will be different.

You can see the source code required to save and load linked list data in the next case study.

SECTION 16.3 QUESTIONS

1. Identify the three ways a node can be inserted.

2. When does inserting a node involve changing the head pointer?

3. Describe, with words only, the process of deleting a node from the middle of a linked list.

4. Describe, with words only, the process of deleting a node from the end of a linked list.

5. Why are pointers not saved to disk when saving the data from a linked list?

Doubly and Circularly Linked Lists

inked lists like the ones you have studied so far can be traversed in only one direction. Even if the node you need is only a few nodes back from the current node, you must start at the head of the list and traverse until you reach the desired node. This type of linked list is called a *singly-linked list.*

To improve the efficiency and usefulness of a linked list, you can link the nodes together in more elaborate ways: the doubly-linked list and the circularly-linked list.

DOUBLY-LINKED LIST

In a *doubly-linked list* each node has a pointer linking it to the next node *and* the previous node, as shown in Figure 16-17. A doubly-linked list allows you to traverse a list in both directions and reverse the direction of traversal at any time.

Each node has a pointer to the previous node, as well as a pointer to the next node. Because there are twice as many pointers, programming a doubly-linked list adds a new level of complexity. Each time a node is added or deleted, two pointers must be properly initialized to form links in both directions.

FIGURE 16-17
A doubly-linked list uses an extra pointer on each node to allow traversal in both directions.

Suppose you wanted to expand the friends database to include the ability to browse through the records by choosing to move to the next or previous record. Without the doubly-linked list, moving to the previous record would require traversing from the head of the list.

The structure used for the nodes of the friends database linked list must be expanded to include a pointer to the previous node in the list, as shown below.

```
struct friend_node
  {
  char last_name[20];
  char first_name[15];
  char phone_num[15];
  friend_node *next;
  friend_node *previous;
  };
```

As mentioned previously, the change to a doubly-linked list requires that functions which add and delete nodes be modified to work with both pointers. In the exercise that follows, you will compile the modified source code of the friends database program.

EXERCISE 16-10   DOUBLY-LINKED LIST

1. Retrieve *DOUBLE.CPP*. An extended version of the friends database appears on your screen.

2. Compile and run the program to see the new browsing capabilities. Use commands 5 and 6 to move to the next and previous records in the database. If you attempt to browse past the beginning or end of the list, the message FIRST RECORD or LAST RECORD will appear.

3. After you have experimented with the program, exit the program and close the source code file.

On the Net

See an analysis of the doubly-linked list program at http://www.Program CPP.com. See topic 16.4.1.

CIRCULARLY-LINKED LIST

A *circularly-linked list* is like a singly-linked list, with one exception. Instead of the last node's next pointer having a null pointer, the last node points back to the first node, as shown in Figure 16-18.

FIGURE   16-18
The only difference between a standard linked list and a circularly-linked list is that the null pointer is replaced with a pointer to the first node in the list.

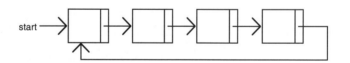

A circularly-linked list does not necessarily have a head pointer. Some circularly-linked lists have a pointer called "first" that points to one of the nodes as a starting point. Depending on your problem, however, you may keep a pointer that moves among the nodes rather than a stationary one.

Suppose you are representing a batting rotation for a baseball team. A circularly-linked list could be used to represent the batters in the rotation. As shown in Figure 16-19, a pointer could be maintained to point to the current batter.

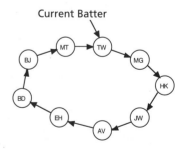

FIGURE   16-19
A circularly-linked list could be used to represent a batting rotation.

EXERCISE 16-11 CIRCULARLY-LINKED LIST

1. Retrieve the file *BATORDER.CPP*. A program that implements the batting rotation linked list described above appears on your screen.

2. Compile and run the program.

3. Enter nine players' names and then enter a blank player name to begin the rotation. You can enter players from a real team or make up names.

4. Press Enter until you have moved through the batting rotation at least twice.

5. When you have finished rotating through batters, press Q and Enter to quit the program.

6. Close the source code file.

On the Net

See an analysis of the circularly-linked list program at http://www.Program CPP.com. See topic 16.4.2.

SECTION 16.4 QUESTIONS

1. What is the term for the simple linked list that requires you to begin traversing at the head of the list and allows traversing in only one direction?

2. What type of linked list uses two pointers per node to allow traversal in two directions?

3. Of the two types of linked lists listed in questions 1 and 2 above, which uses more memory, assuming the data stored is identical?

4. Of the two types of linked lists listed in questions 1 and 2 above, which makes for more efficient use of the list?

5. What type of linked list does not necessarily have a head pointer?

PROBLEM 16.3.1

Some programming problems call for a circular doubly-linked list. Draw a diagram like the ones in this chapter that represents a circular doubly-linked list.

KEY TERMS

allocate	linked list
circularly-linked list	node
deallocate	null pointer
doubly-linked list	singly-linked list
dynamic data structure	static data structure
free	structure pointer operator
heap	traversing

➤ A static data structure occupies the same amount of memory every time the program is run. A dynamic data structure reserves memory as it is needed.

➤ In a linked list, data is contained in nodes. Each node contains a pointer to the next node in the list. The last node in the list has a null pointer.

➤ Dynamic data structures are stored in a portion of memory called the heap. Reserving memory is called allocating. Freeing memory is called deallocating. The **new** operator allocates memory and the **delete** operator frees memory.

➤ When accessing members of a structure with a pointer, the structure pointer operator (->) is used rather than the period (.).

➤ To add a node to the end of a linked list, a new node is first created. After creating the node, you attach it to the list by changing the **next** pointer of the last node to the newly created node.

➤ The process of moving through every node of a linked list is called *traversing*.

➤ Each node of a linked list must be deleted when no longer needed.

➤ Inserting a node in a linked list involves redirecting pointers to include the new node at the appropriate position in the list.

➤ A node may be inserted at the head of the list, the middle of the list, or the end of the list.

➤ Deleting an individual node from a linked list involves re-routing the pointers to bypass the removed node and deallocating the memory occupied by the node.

➤ A node may be deleted at the head of the list, the middle of the list, or the end of the list.

➤ A linked list may be saved to a file by traversing the list and saving the data to disk during the traversal. The pointers are not saved to disk because the linked list must be reallocated when the data is loaded again.

➤ A doubly-linked list has pointers pointing in each direction. Each node has a pointer to the next and previous nodes.

➤ In a circularly-linked list, the next pointer of the last node points back to the first node.

PROJECTS

PROJECT 16-1 • METEOROLOGY

Write a program based on *HIGHTEMP.CPP*. However, instead of using an array for the temperatures, implement the program using a linked list.

PROJECT 16-2 • HEALTH CARE

Write a program that extends the blood donor structure from *DONORS.CPP* to make a linked list of blood donors. The program should allow the user to add donors to the linked list and print the donors' names to the screen.

PROJECT 16-3 • LIST PROCESSING

Write a program that allows the user to enter a series of positive floating-point numbers. Store the numbers in a linked list. Allow the user to enter numbers until a negative number is entered. Do not include the negative number in the linked list. Next, traverse the list to total the numbers entered and count the number of nodes in the list. Use the count to average the numbers in the list. Report the total, number of nodes, and average to the screen.

PROJECT 16-4 • BATTING ROTATION

Extend *BATORDER.CPP* to maintain two linked lists. The first is the circularly linked list already in the program. Add a second linked list of all players not in the batting rotation. Expand the program to include a menu that allows the user to move a player to and from the batting rotation, and a command that substitutes players. Rather than copy the data from one list to another, move existing nodes between the lists.

PROJECT 16-5 • TIME LINE

Write a program that creates a linked list of historical events. The program should insert events in the proper order (by year) in the linked list as they are entered by the user. Provide a way to display the time line.

Overview

I n this case study, you will analyze the phone number database program you compiled and ran in Chapter 16. The program is a complete, working program that manages a database of names and phone numbers. The program allows you to add, delete, and search for records. Also, the program allows you to display a list of the records. The records are loaded from a file into a linked list each time the program is run, and they are saved back to a file when the program exits.

A Look at the Entire Program

A s C++ programs become more useful, they often become larger. It is not unusual for a C++ program to consist of thousands of lines of code. The program listed below is about 500 lines long. Familiarize yourself with the program. The comments throughout the program are designed to help you understand its operation.

```cpp
// PHONELST.CPP
// PHONE NUMBER DATABASE
// By Todd Knowlton
// Complete linked list database program.

// compiler directives
#include<fstream.h>
#include<iostream.h>
#include<iomanip.h>
#include<string.h>

// global structures and variables
  struct friend_node
    {
      char last_name[20];
      char first_name[15];
      char phone_num[15];
      friend_node *next;
    };

  friend_node *head_ptr;
  friend_node *current_ptr;

// function prototypes
void handle_choice(int choice);
void add_record();
void insert_node(friend_node *new_rec_ptr);
friend_node *position_insertion_point(char lastname[20]);
void make_node_new_head(friend_node *new_rec_ptr);
void add_node_to_end(friend_node *new_rec_ptr);
void move_current_to_end();
```

```cpp
void display_list();
void delete_record();
void delete_head_of_list();
void delete_end_of_list(friend_node *previous_ptr);
void delete_from_middle_of_list(friend_node *previous_ptr);
int verify_delete();
void delete_node(friend_node *previous_ptr);
void delete_list();
void search_by_lastname();
void write_list_to_file();
void load_list_from_file();

// main function
int main()
{
  int choice;

  head_ptr = NULL;        // Initialize head pointer to NULL.
  load_list_from_file(); // Load data from the disk file into linked list.
  do
   { // Display menu.
    cout << "\nFRIEND DATABASE\n";
    cout << "0 - Exit program\n";
    cout << "1 - Add record\n";
    cout << "2 - Display all records\n";
    cout << "3 - Search for friend by last name\n";
    cout << "4 - Delete record\n";
    cout << "Enter choice: ";
    cin >> choice;
    handle_choice(choice); // Call function to direct flow based on choice.
   } while(choice != 0);  // Repeat menu until user chooses to exit.
  return 0;
} // end of main function

// Function to direct program flow based on user's choice.
void handle_choice(int choice)
 {
  switch(choice) // choice is passed into the function by value.
   {
    case 0:  // If choice was to exit,
     write_list_to_file();  // save database to a file and
     if(head_ptr != NULL)   // delete the list from memory.
      {
       delete_list();
      }
     break;
    case 1:  // If choice was to add a record to the database,
     add_record();  // call function to add a record to the linked list.
     break;
    case 2:  // If choice was to display all records in the database,
     display_list(); // call function to display all records in
     break;          // the linked list.
    case 3:  // If choice was to search for a record in the database,
     search_by_lastname(); // call function to search for record by
     break;                // last name.
```

```
       case 4:  // If choice was to delete a record in the database,
         delete_record(); // call a function that searches for record
         break;          // by last name and deletes it.
       default : // If any other (invalid) choice was entered,
         cout << "Invalid choice\n"; // display error message.
         break;
     }
 } // end of function handle_choice

// Function to add record to the linked list.
void add_record()
 {
   friend_node *new_rec_ptr; // Declare temporary pointer for the new node.

   new_rec_ptr = new friend_node; // Allocate memory for a new node and
                                  // initialize pointer to point to it.
   if(new_rec_ptr != NULL) // If no error allocating memory, get data
     {                     // and insert node.
       // Get name and phone number from the user.
       cin.ignore(80,'\n');
       cout << "\nEnter a new record.\n";
       cout << "Last Name: ";
       cin.get(new_rec_ptr->last_name,20);
       cin.ignore(80,'\n');
       cout << "First Name: ";
       cin.get(new_rec_ptr->first_name,15);
       cin.ignore(80,'\n');
       cout << "Phone Number: ";
       cin.get(new_rec_ptr->phone_num,15);
       cin.ignore(80,'\n');

       insert_node(new_rec_ptr);
     }
   else  // If error occurred allocating memory, display warning
     {    // and do not create node.
       cout << "WARNING: Memory error. New record cannot be added.\n";
     }
 } // end of function add_record

// Function to insert new node into correct position in list.
void insert_node(friend_node *new_rec_ptr)
 {
   friend_node *before_ptr;
   friend_node *after_ptr;

   if(head_ptr == NULL)
     {                              // If no nodes exist, make the node
       new_rec_ptr->next = NULL;    // the head.
       head_ptr = new_rec_ptr;
     }
   else
     {
       if(strcmp(new_rec_ptr->last_name, head_ptr->last_name) < 0)
         {                              // If new record comes before head,
           make_node_new_head(new_rec_ptr);  // make it the new head.
```

```
            }
        else                                // Else, determine where the new node
            {                               // should be inserted.
            current_ptr = position_insertion_point(new_rec_ptr->last_name);
            before_ptr = current_ptr;        // Use pointers to keep track of nodes
            after_ptr = current_ptr->next;  // on each side of the insertion point.

            if(after_ptr == NULL) // If after_ptr is NULL, the node needs to be
                {                            // added to the end of the list.
                add_node_to_end(new_rec_ptr);
                }
            else                            // Else add the node between the nodes pointed to
                {                           // by before_ptr and after_ptr.
                before_ptr->next = new_rec_ptr;
                new_rec_ptr->next = after_ptr;
                }
            }
        }
    } // end of function insert_node

// Function that positions current_ptr at the node before the position
// where the new node should be inserted.
friend_node *position_insertion_point(char lastname[20])
    {
    char temp_name[20];
    friend_node *temp_ptr;
    int tempint;

    if(head_ptr->next != NULL) // If more than one node exists, search the
        {                             // list for the correct insertion point.
        current_ptr = head_ptr;
        temp_ptr = current_ptr->next;
        strcpy(temp_name, temp_ptr->last_name);
        // Loop until the proper insertion point is located.
        tempint = strcmp(lastname,temp_name);
        while((tempint > 0) && (current_ptr->next !=NULL))
            {
            current_ptr = temp_ptr;
            temp_ptr = current_ptr->next;
            strcpy(temp_name, temp_ptr->last_name);
            tempint = strcmp(lastname,temp_name);
            }
        }
    else  // If only one node exists in the list, current_ptr is the same
        {    // as head_ptr. New node will be added to the end of the list.
        current_ptr = head_ptr;
        }
    return(current_ptr);
    } // end of function position_insertion_point

// Function that makes the node pointed to by new_rec_ptr the new
// head of the linked list. It handles the special case of inserting at
// the front of the list.
void make_node_new_head(friend_node *new_rec_ptr)
    {
```

```
      friend_node *temp_ptr;   // temporary pointer to keep track of the head

    temp_ptr = head_ptr;   // Set temp_ptr to point at the current head.
    new_rec_ptr->next = temp_ptr; // Make new nodes next pointer point to
    head_ptr = new_rec_ptr;         // current head and make new node the head.
  } // end of function make_node_new_head

// Function that adds a node to the end of the linked list. It handles
// the special case of inserting at the end of the list.
void add_node_to_end(friend_node *new_rec_ptr)
  {
    new_rec_ptr->next = NULL;   // Set next node pointer of new node to NULL.

    move_current_to_end();        // Make sure current_ptr is at end of list.
    current_ptr->next = new_rec_ptr; // Place new node at the end of the list.
  } // end of function add_node_to_end

// Function that moves current_ptr to end of the linked list.
void move_current_to_end()
  {
    current_ptr = head_ptr;   // Move temp_ptr to head of the list.

    while(current_ptr->next != NULL)
      {                                 // Traverse list until NULL is reached.
        current_ptr = current_ptr->next;
      }
  } // end of function move_current_to_end

// Function that displays entire linked list.
void display_list()
  {
    char fullname[36];   // used to combine names into one array

    current_ptr = head_ptr;   // Move current_ptr to head of list.
    if(current_ptr != NULL)
      {
        cout << endl;
        cout << "Friend                              Phone Number\n";
        cout << "---------------------------------- ------------\n";
        do
          {
            strcpy(fullname,""); // Clear fullname.
            strcat(fullname, current_ptr->last_name);   // Put last name, then a
            strcat(fullname, ", ");                      // comma, then the
            strcat(fullname, current_ptr->first_name); // first name into fullname.
            cout.setf(ios::left);
            cout << setw(36) << fullname;
            cout.setf(ios::right);
            cout << setw(12) << current_ptr->phone_num << endl;
            current_ptr = current_ptr->next; // Set current_ptr to next node.
          } while(current_ptr != NULL); // Loop until end of list.
      }
    else  // If list is empty, display message.
      {
        cout << "\nNO RECORDS TO DISPLAY\n";
```

```
    }
  } // end of function display_list

// Function that searches linked list for the first occurrence of a given
// last name and displays the record to the screen.
void search_by_lastname()
  {
    char search_string[20];   // Character array for last name to search for.

    current_ptr = head_ptr;   // Move current_ptr to head of list
                              // to begin search.
    cin.ignore(80,'\n');
    cout << "\nEnter the last name for which you want to search: ";
    cin.get(search_string,20);
    cin.ignore(80,'\n');

    // Loop until search_string is found or end of list is reached.
    while((strcmp(current_ptr->last_name, search_string) != 0) &&
        (current_ptr != NULL))
      {
        current_ptr = current_ptr->next;
      }

    if(current_ptr != NULL) // If current_ptr is not NULL, then match was
      {                     // found.
        cout << "\nRECORD FOUND\n";
        cout << current_ptr->first_name << ' '
             << current_ptr->last_name << endl;
        cout << current_ptr->phone_num << endl;
      }
    else
      {
        cout << "NO MATCH FOUND\n";
      }
  } // end of function search_by_lastname

// Function that deletes individual nodes from the linked list.
void delete_record()
  {
    char search_string[20];
    friend_node *previous_ptr;

    previous_ptr = NULL;      // Initialize previous_ptr to NULL.
    current_ptr = head_ptr;   // Move current_ptr to head of list
                              // to begin search.
    cin.ignore(80,'\n');
    cout << "\nEnter the last name of the friend you want to delete: ";
    cin.get(search_string,20);
    cin.ignore(80,'\n');

    // Loop to find matching record.
    while((strcmp(current_ptr->last_name, search_string) != 0) &&
        (current_ptr != NULL))
      {
        previous_ptr = current_ptr;       // A pointer must be maintained that
```

```
      current_ptr = current_ptr->next; // points to the node before the node
    }                                  // to be deleted.

  if(current_ptr != NULL) // If current_ptr is not NULL, then match was
    {                     //   found.
    cout << "\nRECORD FOUND\n";
    cout << current_ptr->first_name << ' '
         << current_ptr->last_name << endl;
    cout << current_ptr->phone_num << endl;
    if(verify_delete()) // Ask user if he/she wants to delete the record.
      {                                 // If user wants to delete the record,
      delete_node(previous_ptr);        // delete the node that follows the
      cout << "\nRECORD DELETED\n";     // one pointed to by previous_ptr.
      }
    else                                // Otherwise, do nothing.
      {
      cout << "\nRECORD NOT DELETED\n";
      }
    }
  else // If no match for the record found, display message.
    {
    cout << "\nNO MATCH FOUND. NO RECORD DELETED.\n";
    }
} // end of function delete_record

// Function to ask user to verify intention to delete the node.
int verify_delete()
 {
 char YesNo;

 cout << "\nDo you wish to delete this record? (Y/N) ";
 cin >> YesNo;
 if((YesNo == 'Y') || (YesNo == 'y'))
   {
   return(1); // Return TRUE if user wants to delete.
   }
 else
   {
   return(0); // Return FALSE if user does not want to delete.
   }
 } // end of function verify_delete

// Function that deletes node pointed to by current_ptr.
void delete_node(friend_node *previous_ptr)
 {

 if(current_ptr == head_ptr)  // If node to be deleted is the head of the
   {                          // list, call a special function that
   delete_head_of_list();     // deletes the first node in the list.
   }
 else
   {                                 // Otherwise:
   if(current_ptr->next == NULL)     // If node to be deleted is at the
     {                               // end of the list, call a special
     delete_end_of_list(previous_ptr); // function to delete that node.
```

```
      }
   else                              // Otherwise:
    {                                                // Delete the node from the
     delete_from_middle_of_list(previous_ptr); // middle of the list using
    }                                                // a function that does that.
  }
 } // end of function delete_node

//Function that deletes the head of the list.
void delete_head_of_list()
 {
  current_ptr = head_ptr;  // Make current_ptr point to the head of the list.
  if(head_ptr->next != NULL)
   {                                  // If more than one node is in the list,
    head_ptr = current_ptr->next; // make second node in list the new head.
   }
  else                              // Otherwise, just set head_ptr to NULL
   {                                  // to signal that the list is empty.
    head_ptr = NULL;
   }
  delete current_ptr; // Deallocate memory used by the deleted node.
 } // end of function delete_head_of_list

// Function that deletes the last node of the linked list.
void delete_end_of_list(friend_node *previous_ptr)
 {
  delete current_ptr; // Deallocate memory used by the deleted node.
  previous_ptr->next = NULL; // Make node before deleted node the end of list.
  current_ptr = head_ptr; // Set current_ptr to head to give it a value.
 } // end of function delete_end_of_list

// Function that deletes a node from the middle of the list.
void delete_from_middle_of_list(friend_node *previous_ptr)
 {
  // Set pointers of the nodes before and after the node to be deleted to
  // skip the node that is to be deleted.
  previous_ptr->next = current_ptr->next;
  delete current_ptr; // Deallocate memory used by the deleted node.
  current_ptr = head_ptr; // Set current_ptr to head to give it a value.
 } // end of function delete_from_middle_of_list

// Function that frees the memory used by the linked list.
void delete_list()
 {
  friend_node *temp_ptr;  // pointer used for temporary storage

  current_ptr = head_ptr;  // Move current_ptr to head of the list.

  do     // Traverse list, deleting as we go.
   {
    temp_ptr = current_ptr->next;   // Set temporary pointer to point
                                    // to the remainder of the list.
    delete current_ptr;    // Delete current node.
    current_ptr = temp_ptr;    // Set current_ptr to next node after the
   } while(temp_ptr != NULL); // deleted one.
```

```
  } // end of function delete_list

// Function to write linked list data to the data file.
void write_list_to_file()
 {
  ofstream outfile;  // output file pointer

  outfile.open("FRIENDS.DAT",ios::out);  // Open file for output.

  if (outfile)  // If no error occurred while opening the file,
   {            // it is okay to write the data to the file.
    current_ptr = head_ptr;  // Set current_ptr to head of list.
    if(head_ptr != NULL)  // If the list is not empty, begin
     {                     // writing data to the file.
      do     // Traverse list until the end is reached.
       {
        // Write the nodes data to the file.
        outfile << current_ptr->last_name << endl;
        outfile << current_ptr->first_name << endl;
        outfile << current_ptr->phone_num << endl;
        current_ptr = current_ptr->next;  // Move current_ptr to next node.
       } while(current_ptr != NULL); // Loop until end of list is reached.
     }
    // The words END OF FILE are written to the end of the file to make it
    // easy to locate the end of the file when the data is read back in.
    outfile << "END OF FILE" << endl;
    outfile.close(); // Close the file.
   }
  else // If an error occurs while opening the file, display a message.
   {
    cout << "Error opening file.\n";
   }
 } // end of function write_list_to_file

// Function to load the linked list from the data file.
void load_list_from_file()
 {
  friend_node *new_rec_ptr;
  ifstream infile;  // input file pointer
  int end_loop = 0;

  infile.open("FRIENDS.DAT",ios::in);  // Open file for input.

  if (infile)  // If no error occurred while opening file
   {           // input the data from the file.
    do
     {
      new_rec_ptr = new friend_node; // Allocate memory for a node.
      if(new_rec_ptr != NULL) // Check for allocation error.
       {
        // Get the next last name from the file.
        infile.get(new_rec_ptr->last_name,20);
        infile.ignore(80,'\n');
        // If the end of the file has not yet been reached, get other data.
        if(strcmp(new_rec_ptr->last_name, "END OF FILE") != 0)
         {
```

```
        infile.get(new_rec_ptr->first_name, 15);
        infile.ignore(80,'\n');
        infile.get(new_rec_ptr->phone_num, 15);
        infile.ignore(80,'\n');
        insert_node(new_rec_ptr);
        }
      else // If end of file has been reached, delete the most recently
        {  // created node and set the flag that ends the loop.
        delete new_rec_ptr;
        end_loop = 1;
        }
      }
    else  // If a memory allocation error occurs, display a message and
      {     // set the flag that ends the loop.
      cout << "WARNING: Memory error. Load from disk was unsuccessful.\n";
      end_loop = 1;
      }
    } while(end_loop == 0); // Loop until the end_loop flag becomes TRUE.
    infile.close(); // Close the file.
  }
 else  // If error occurred opening file, display message.
  {
    cout << "No usable data file located. List is empty.\n";
  }
} // end of function load_list_from_file
```

We will analyze only selected portions of the program in this case study because of the program's large size. To refresh your memory as to the operation of the program, let's compile and run the program again.

EXERCISE IV-1   COMPILING AND RUNNING THE PROGRAM

1. Open *PHONELST.CPP*. Compile and run the program.

2. Choose the option to display all records. If a data file exists from the last time the program was run, there may already be records in the database.

3. Enter three new records into the database. Use your friends' names or make up fictitious names.

4. Display all records again.

5. Use the search function to find one specific record in the database.

6. Use the delete function to delete one of the records in the database.

7. Exit the program and leave the source code open for the next exercise.

Global Structures and Variables

As you learned in the previous chapters, nodes of a linked list are implemented as structures. The globally-defined structure below defines a node for the friends database. Two additional global variables are also necessary. The variable **head_ptr** keeps track of the head of the linked list, and **current_ptr** is used throughout the program to perform operations on the list. Any other variable you see used in a function is either declared locally or passed in as a parameter.

```
// global structures and variables
  struct friend_node
    {
      char last_name[20];
      char first_name[15];
      char phone_num[15];
      friend_node *next;
    };

  friend_node *head_ptr;
  friend_node *current_ptr;
```

The Main Function and Menu Processing

Refer back to the program listing at the **main** and **handle_choice** functions. The **main** function begins by initializing the head pointer (**head_ptr**) to null to indicate that the list is empty. Next, the disk file that holds the friends database is loaded into the linked list. Later in this case study, we will analyze the functions that load and save the linked list.

The **main** function displays the menu and gets the user's choice. The choice is passed to a function named **handle_choice** that directs the flow of the program based on the user's menu choice. The menu and call to **handle_choice** are in a loop that continues until the user chooses to exit.

Adding Records to the Database

A major part of the program's code is dedicated to adding records to the database. Because the database is maintained in a linked list in RAM, the data must be placed in linked list nodes and inserted into the linked list. As an added feature, the nodes are inserted in last name order.

Examine the **add_record** function (shown again below). First, a temporary pointer is declared to point to the new node until the node is properly inserted in the list.

Next, memory is allocated for the new node. Recall that in the previous chapters you learned that errors can occur when a program attempts to allocate memory. The **add_record** function uses an if statement to check for an error. If an error occurs, a message is displayed and the function ends without adding a record.

```
// Function to add record to the linked list.
void add_record()
  {
    friend_node *new_rec_ptr; // Declare temporary pointer for the new node.
```

```
        new_rec_ptr = new friend_node; // Allocate memory for a new node and
                                       // initialize pointer to point to it.
    if(new_rec_ptr != NULL) // If no error allocating memory, get data
     {                      // and insert node.
       // Get name and phone number from the user.
       cin.ignore(80,'\n');
       cout << "\nEnter a new record.\n";
       cout << "Last Name: ";
       cin.get(new_rec_ptr->last_name,20);
       cin.ignore(80,'\n');
       cout << "First Name: ";
       cin.get(new_rec_ptr->first_name,15);
       cin.ignore(80,'\n');
       cout << "Phone Number: ";
       cin.get(new_rec_ptr->phone_num,15);
       cin.ignore(80,'\n');

       insert_node(new_rec_ptr);
     }
    else  // If error occurred allocating memory, display warning
     {    // and do not create node.
       cout << "WARNING: Memory error. New record cannot be added.\n";
     }
  } // end of function add_record
```

If no errors occur during memory allocation, the user is prompted for data for the record, and the pointer to the new record is passed to the **insert_node** function (shown again below). The **insert_node** function determines where the node should be inserted. If the linked list is empty, then the new node becomes the head of the list. If the list is not empty, the function determines whether the node should be inserted before the current head, somewhere in the middle of the list, or at the end of the list.

```
// Function to insert new node into correct position in list.
void insert_node(friend_node *new_rec_ptr)
 {
  friend_node *before_ptr;
  friend_node *after_ptr;

  if(head_ptr == NULL)
   {                                  // If no nodes exist, make the node
    new_rec_ptr->next = NULL;    // the head.
    head_ptr = new_rec_ptr;
   }
  else
   {
    if(strcmp(new_rec_ptr->last_name, head_ptr->last_name) < 0)
     {                                      // If new record comes before head,
      make_node_new_head(new_rec_ptr);  // make it the new head.
     }
    else                                  // Else, determine where the new node
     {                                    // should be inserted.
      current_ptr = position_insertion_point(new_rec_ptr->last_name);
      before_ptr = current_ptr;        // Use pointers to keep track of nodes
```

```
        after_ptr = current_ptr->next; // on each side of the insertion point.

        if(after_ptr == NULL) // If after_ptr is NULL, the node needs to be
         {                    // added to the end of the list.
          add_node_to_end(new_rec_ptr);
         }
        else                 // Else add the node between the nodes pointed to
         {                    // by before_ptr and after_ptr.
          before_ptr->next = new_rec_ptr;
          new_rec_ptr->next = after_ptr;
         }
      }
    }
} // end of function insert_node
```

The **position_insertion_point** function (shown again below) returns a pointer to the node that precedes the insertion point for the new node. The syntax of a function that returns a pointer is slightly different than functions that return other data types. The data type is **friend_node**, and the dereferencing operator (*) precedes the name of the function. This syntax causes the compiler to return a pointer to a **friend_node** as a return value.

```
// Function that positions current_ptr at the node before the position
// where the new node should be inserted.
friend_node *position_insertion_point(char lastname[20])
 {
  char temp_name[20];
  friend_node *temp_ptr;
  int tempint;

  if(head_ptr->next != NULL) // If more than one node exists, search the
   {                          // list for the correct insertion point.
    current_ptr = head_ptr;
    temp_ptr = current_ptr->next;
    strcpy(temp_name, temp_ptr->last_name);
    // Loop until the proper insertion point is located.
    tempint = strcmp(lastname,temp_name);
    while((tempint > 0) && (current_ptr->next !=NULL))
     {
      current_ptr = temp_ptr;
      temp_ptr = current_ptr->next;
      strcpy(temp_name, temp_ptr->last_name);
      tempint = strcmp(lastname,temp_name);
     }
   }
  else  // If only one node exists in the list, current_ptr is the same
   {    // as head_ptr. New node will be added to the end of the list.
    current_ptr = head_ptr;
   }
  return(current_ptr);
} // end of function position_insertion_point
```

If the node is to be inserted in the middle of the list, the **insert_node** function handles the insertion itself. If the node must be inserted as the new head or at the end of the list, special functions (shown again below) are called to perform those insertions.

```
// Function that makes the node pointed to by new_rec_ptr the new
// head of the linked list. It handles the special case of inserting at
// the front of the list.
void make_node_new_head(friend_node *new_rec_ptr)
 {
  friend_node *temp_ptr;  // temporary pointer to keep track of the head

  temp_ptr = head_ptr;  // Set temp_ptr to point at the current head.
  new_rec_ptr->next = temp_ptr; // Make new nodes next pointer point to
  head_ptr = new_rec_ptr;       // current head and make new node the head.
 } // end of function make_node_new_head

// Function that adds a node to the end of the linked list. It handles
// the special case of inserting at the end of the list.
void add_node_to_end(friend_node *new_rec_ptr)
 {
  new_rec_ptr->next = NULL;  // Set next node pointer of new node to NULL.

  move_current_to_end();      // Make sure current_ptr is at end of list.
  current_ptr->next = new_rec_ptr; // Place new node at the end of the list.
 } // end of function add_node_to_end

// Function that moves current_ptr to end of the linked list.
void move_current_to_end()
 {
  current_ptr = head_ptr;  // Move temp_ptr to head of the list.

  while(current_ptr->next != NULL)
   {                                // Traverse list until NULL is reached.
    current_ptr = current_ptr->next;
   }
 } // end of function move_current_to_end
```

Displaying a List of Records

Displaying a list of the records in this database is accomplished using a function similar to the one you studied in Chapter 15. The **display_list** function in this program uses **strcat** to build a string made up of the friend's last name, a comma, and first name. This string is used to output the names in a consistently formatted fashion.

Searching the Database

The ability to search the database is provided by a straightforward function named **search_by_lastname**. The function prompts the user for a last name and searches the database for an exact match. The program could be extended to be more flexible. For example, the search might be more useful if it were not case sensitive.

Another limitation of the current program is that the search will not locate the second record of two records with the same last name.

Deleting Individual Records

Deleting individual records from a linked list requires a set of functions similar in complexity to the function that add records. The **delete_record** function (shown again below) prompts the user for a last name and searches for the record. This function has the same limitations as the search function.

```
// Function that deletes individual nodes from the linked list.
void delete_record()
 {
  char search_string[20];
  friend_node *previous_ptr;

  previous_ptr = NULL;      // Initialize previous_ptr to NULL.
  current_ptr = head_ptr;  // Move current_ptr to head of list
                           // to begin search.
  cin.ignore(80,'\n');
  cout << "\nEnter the last name of the friend you want to delete: ";
  cin.get(search_string,20);
  cin.ignore(80,'\n');

  // Loop to find matching record.
  while((strcmp(current_ptr->last_name, search_string) != 0) &&
      (current_ptr != NULL))
   {
    previous_ptr = current_ptr;       // A pointer must be maintained that
    current_ptr = current_ptr->next; // points to the node before the node
   }                                 // to be deleted.

  if(current_ptr != NULL) // If current_ptr is not NULL, then match was
   {                      // found.
    cout << "\nRECORD FOUND\n";
    cout << current_ptr->first_name << ' '
         << current_ptr->last_name << endl;
    cout << current_ptr->phone_num << endl;
    if(verify_delete()) // Ask user if he/she wants to delete the record.
     {                                 // If user wants to delete the record,
      delete_node(previous_ptr);       // delete the node that follows the
      cout << "\nRECORD DELETED\n";   // one pointed to by previous_ptr.
     }
    else                               // Otherwise, do nothing.
     {
      cout << "\nRECORD NOT DELETED\n";
     }
   }
  else // If no match for the record found, display message.
   {
```

```
        cout << "\nNO MATCH FOUND. NO RECORD DELETED.\n";
    }
} // end of function delete_record
```

While searching for the record to be deleted, the **delete_record** function maintains a pointer to two nodes: the node being compared and the previous node. The reason is because when the node to be deleted is located, the program must have a pointer to the nodes on both sides so that the pointers can be properly redirected around the deleted node.

If the search is successful, the user gets an opportunity to verify that the correct record was located before the actual deletion takes place. The **verify_delete** function (shown below) is called to ask the user for verification.

```
// Function to ask user to verify intention to delete the node.
int verify_delete()
{
  char YesNo;

  cout << "\nDo you wish to delete this record? (Y/N) ";
  cin >> YesNo;
  if((YesNo == 'Y') || (YesNo == 'y'))
    {
      return(1); // Return TRUE if user want to delete.
    }
  else
    {
      return(0); // Return FALSE if user does not want to delete.
    }
} // end of function verify_delete
```

If the user verifies that the node is to be deleted, the **delete_node** function (below) is called to decide the method required to delete the node. Like adding nodes, deleting nodes requires that different methods be applied depending on whether the node is at the head, in the middle, or at the end of the list.

```
// Function that deletes node pointed to by current_ptr.
void delete_node(friend_node *previous_ptr)
{

  if(current_ptr == head_ptr)   // If node to be deleted is the head of the
    {                            // list, call a special function that
      delete_head_of_list();     // deletes the first node in the list.
    }
  else
    {                                    // Otherwise:
      if(current_ptr->next == NULL)      // If node to be deleted is at the
        {                                // end of the list, call a special
          delete_end_of_list(previous_ptr); // function to delete that node.
        }
      else                       // Otherwise:
        {                                      // Delete the node from the
          delete_from_middle_of_list(previous_ptr); // middle of the list using
        }                                      // a function that does that.
    }
} // end of function delete_node
```

If the node to be deleted is at the head of the list, the **delete_head_of_list** function (shown below) makes the second node in the list the new head. If the list only contains the one node, **head_ptr** is simply set to null to signal that the list is now empty. Either way, the memory allocated for the node is released by the **delete** operator.

```
//Function that deletes the head of the list.
void delete_head_of_list()
  {
  current_ptr = head_ptr;   // Make current_ptr point to the head of the list.
  if(head_ptr->next != NULL)
      {                                 // If more than one node is in the list,
      head_ptr = current_ptr->next; // make second node in list the new head.
      }
  else                         // Otherwise, just set head_ptr to NULL
      {                                 // to signal that the list is empty.
      head_ptr = NULL;
      }
  delete current_ptr; // Deallocate memory used by the deleted node.
  } // end of function delete_head_of_list
```

If the node to be deleted is at the end of the list, the **delete_end_of_list** function (shown below) frees the memory allocated to the node. Then it makes the **next** pointer of the second node from the end of the list null, which makes the list end there. Because **current_ptr** is a global variable, it should not be left pointing to a deleted node. To give it something to point to, **current_ptr** is set to point to the head of the list.

```
// Function that deletes the last node of the linked list.
void delete_end_of_list(friend_node *previous_ptr)
  {
  delete current_ptr; // Deallocate memory used by the deleted node.
  previous_ptr->next = NULL; // Make node before deleted node the end of list.
  current_ptr = head_ptr; // Set current_ptr to head to give it a value.
  } // end of function delete_end_of_list
```

Deleting from the middle of the list is also a simple task (see the function below). The **next** pointer of the node before the one being deleted is set to point to the node that follows the one being deleted. In other words, the pointers of the list are arranged to bypass the node being deleted. Then the memory is freed, and **current_ptr** is made to point to the head of the list so it will not point to a deleted node.

```
// Function that deletes a node from the middle of the list.
void delete_from_middle_of_list(friend_node *previous_ptr)
  {
  // Set pointers of the nodes before and after the node to be deleted to
  // skip the node that is to be deleted.
  previous_ptr->next = current_ptr->next;
  delete current_ptr; // Deallocate memory used by the deleted node.
  current_ptr = head_ptr; // Set current_ptr to head to give it a value.
  } // end of function delete_from_middle_of_list
```

Saving and Retrieving the Data

The functions at the end of the program allow the data in the linked list to be saved to a disk file and reloaded the next time the program runs. Let's first look at the function that writes the data in the linked list to a file.

The function (shown below) opens a file for output. If no errors occur, a do loop is used to traverse the list. As each node is visited, the data in the node is written to the data file, separated by end-of-line characters. When the last node's data has been written to disk, the string *END OF FILE* is written to the file. This string will be used to make detecting the end of the file easier when the data is read back in.

```
// Function to write linked list data to the data file.
void write_list_to_file()
 {
  ofstream outfile;  // output file pointer

  outfile.open("FRIENDS.DAT",ios::out);  // Open file for output.

  if (outfile)  // If no error occurred while opening the file,
   {             // it is okay to write the data to the file.
    current_ptr = head_ptr;  // Set current_ptr to head of list.
    if(head_ptr != NULL)  // If the list is not empty, begin
     {                     // writing data to the file.
      do    // Traverse list until the end is reached.
       {
        // Write the nodes data to the file.
        outfile << current_ptr->last_name << endl;
        outfile << current_ptr->first_name << endl;
        outfile << current_ptr->phone_num << endl;
        current_ptr = current_ptr->next;  // Move current_ptr to next node.
       } while(current_ptr != NULL); // Loop until end of list is reached.
     }
    // The words END OF FILE are written to the end of the file to make it
    // easy to locate the end of the file when the data is read back in.
    outfile << "END OF FILE" << endl;
    outfile.close(); // Close the file.
   }
  else // If an error occurs while opening the file, display a message.
   {
    cout << "Error opening file.\n";
   }
 } // end of function write_list_to_file
```

EXERCISE IV-2   ANALYZING THE OUTPUT FILE

1. Run the program again. Enter two or three additional names into the database. Use names of your friends, celebrities, or make up fictitious names.

2. Exit the program to cause the data file to be written.

3. Open the *FRIENDS.DAT* data file. Notice that the format is a straightforward text format.

4. Leave the *FRIENDS.DAT* data file and the program's source code open for the next exercise.

The function that reads the data from the file back into the linked list (shown below) is slightly more complicated than the function that writes the data to the file. The reason is because the function that loads the data from disk must rebuild the linked list from scratch. The task is simplified, however, by reusing the functions that allow records to be added from user input.

```cpp
// Function to load the linked list from the data file.
void load_list_from_file()
 {
  friend_node *new_rec_ptr;
  ifstream infile;  // input file pointer
  int end_loop = 0;

  infile.open("FRIENDS.DAT",ios::in);  // Open file for input.

  if (infile)  // If no error occurred while opening file
   {            // input the data from the file.
    do
     {
      new_rec_ptr = new friend_node; // Allocate memory for a node.
      if(new_rec_ptr != NULL) // Check for allocation error.
       {
        // Get the next last name from the file.
        infile.get(new_rec_ptr->last_name,20);
        infile.ignore(80,'\n');
        // If the end of the file has not yet been reached, get other data.
        if(strcmp(new_rec_ptr->last_name, "END OF FILE") != 0)
         {
          infile.get(new_rec_ptr->first_name, 15);
          infile.ignore(80,'\n');
          infile.get(new_rec_ptr->phone_num, 15);
          infile.ignore(80,'\n');
          insert_node(new_rec_ptr);
         }
        else // If end of file has been reached, delete the most recently
         {   // created node and set the flag that ends the loop.
          delete new_rec_ptr;
          end_loop = 1;
         }
       }
      else  // If a memory allocation error occurs, display a message and
       {    // set the flag that ends the loop.
        cout << "WARNING: Memory error. Load from disk was unsuccessful.\n";
        end_loop = 1;
       }
     } while(end_loop == 0); // Loop until the end_loop flag becomes TRUE.
    infile.close(); // Close the file.
   }
  else  // If error occurred opening file, display message.
   {
    cout << "No usable data file located. List is empty.\n";
```

```
        }
    } // end of function load_list_from_file
```

First, the input file is opened. An if statement performs a check after the attempt to open to make sure the file was located and no errors occurred. Next, a loop allocates memory for each node and assigns data from the file to the nodes. The **insert_node** function is called to actually build the linked list. The loop ends when the *END OF FILE* string is encountered.

EXERCISE IV-3   MODIFYING THE INPUT FILE

1. In your text editor, position the cursor at the bottom of the *FRIENDS.DAT* file, before the *END OF FILE* string.

2. To demonstrate the flexibility of the data file, insert another name and phone number before the *END OF FILE* string. Enter *Adams* on one line, *John* on the next line, and *555-1234* on the next line. Be sure to leave the other records unchanged. Also be sure to leave the *END OF FILE* string on a line by itself at the bottom of the file.

3. Save and close *FRIENDS.DAT* and run the program again. Although the John Adams record was not entered into the file in proper order, the linked list will be created in order because the **insert_node** function is used to place the nodes in the list.

4. Direct the program to display records to verify that the John Adams record appears in the list.

5. Exit the program. Exiting the program will cause the data file to be rewritten with the data from RAM.

6. Open *FRIENDS.DAT* again to see that the John Adams record is now in its proper place in the file, sorted alphabetically.

7. Close *FRIENDS.DAT* and *PHONELST.CPP*.

Modifying the Program

ere are some suggestions of ways you might modify the program.

1. Replace the character arrays in the program with string objects.

2. Modify the program to allow the birthday of each friend to be included in addition to the other data. Use a character array or string object to store dates of birth in the form MM/DD/YY. For example, someone born on July 10, 1980 would have his or her birthday entered as 07/10/80. Before you begin, analyze the code to determine all of the places the program will be affected by the added field. Also, delete the FRIENDS.DAT file the first time you run the modified program because it will not contain birthday information for the friends who are already in the database.

3. Rewrite the program to use the vector class rather than a linked list.

Stacks, Queues, and Trees

OBJECTIVES

➤ *Understand stacks.*

➤ *Understand the way stacks can be implemented.*

➤ *Use a stack class.*

➤ *Understand queues.*

➤ *Understand how a queue can be implemented with a linked list.*

➤ *Use a queue class.*

➤ *Understand binary trees.*

Overview

The linked lists you have been studying are an important and useful data structure. In this chapter, you will learn three more data structures that are also important in computer science: the stack, the queue, and the binary tree.

Stacks

A *stack* is a data structure that allows items to be added and deleted from only one end. Imagine a stack of books on a table. It is impractical to add a book to the bottom of the stack. The easiest way to add a book to the stack or take a book away from the stack is to work only with the top of the stack. A stack in a computer works the same way.

Special terms are used to describe putting items on a stack and taking items off a stack. Adding an item to the stack is called *pushing.* Removing an item from the stack is called *popping.*

Figure 17-1 shows a stack of books to illustrate the stack operations push and pop. Figure 17-1(a) shows a math book being pushed onto the stack. In (b), the book is part of the stack. In (c), the book is popped off the stack. A stack is a *last-in first-out (LIFO)* structure, meaning the last item pushed on the stack is the first item popped off the stack.

USES FOR A STACK

So what good is a stack? There are several good uses for a stack in programming. A stack is a good way to reverse the order of a list of items. A stack is also useful when evaluating expressions and when implementing many other algorithms. In the case study that follows this chapter, you will see an example of how expressions are evaluated with the assistance of stacks.

Every time you run a C++ program, a stack is created. This stack is used to store local variables used by your functions. The stack also stores addresses that the program needs for proper execution. Figure 17-2 illustrates how a program's stack changes as the flow of logic (represented by the arrow) progresses.

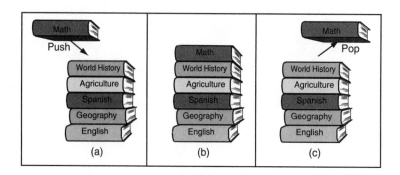

FIGURE 17-1
Items are "pushed" onto a stack and "popped" off a stack.

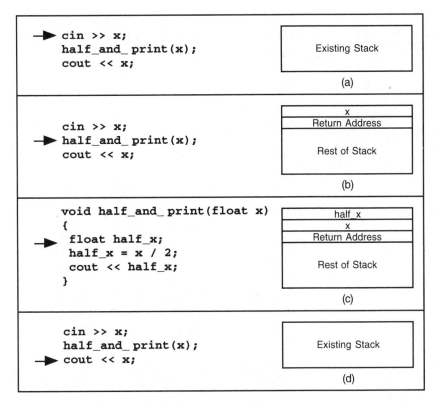

FIGURE 17-2
A stack is used to aid in the execution of programs and store local variables.

The (a) portion of Figure 17-2 shows a segment of code just prior to a call to a function. There are already items on the stack, but we are not concerned with what those items are. In (b), the program prepares to make the jump to the code of the **half_and_print** function. First, an address is pushed onto the stack. Execution returns to this address when the function terminates. Next, the value of the argument **x** is pushed onto the stack to make it available to the **half_and_print** function.

The (c) portion of Figure 17-2 shows the stack during execution of the function. The local variable **half_x** is created on the stack, as are all local variables. In (d), the function has terminated. The local variable and the parameter **x** were popped off the stack at the end of the function. The return address was also popped off and used to direct the flow of logic back to the function that made the call. Therefore, the stack is back to the state it was in before the call to **half_and_print**.

PROGRAMMING A STACK

A stack can be implemented in C++ using an array or a linked list. Let's look at both methods of programming a stack.

USING AN ARRAY AS A STACK

An array may be used to implement a stack. For example, assume you need a stack of floating point numbers. The declaration below creates the array for a stack of up to 100 numbers.

```
float my_stack[100];
```

When using an array as a stack, the stack starts at the top of the array and works its way down the array, as shown in Figure 17-3. You could build the stack from the bottom of the array, but starting at the top is easier.

To use the array as a stack, you must keep an integer variable (we will name it **top**) that holds the sub-script of the top of the stack. When the stack is created, **top** = 0 because the stack is empty. When an item is pushed onto the stack, **top** is incre-mented and the value being added to the stack is placed in the element indexed by the variable **top**. When an item is popped off the stack, the value in the element indexed by **top** is copied out of the array and top is decremented. Decrementing **top** gives an index to the new top of the stack.

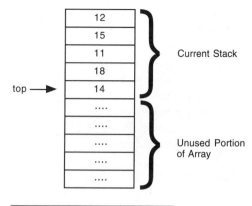

F I G U R E   1 7 - 3
When implementing a stack using an array, the stack begins at the top of the array.

Note

*Using an array as a stack requires that the maximum size of the stack be pre-determined. Reserving the space in advance makes an array less efficient than other methods of implementing a stack. Programs that use an array as a stack should check for a condition called **stack overflow** where the size of the array is too small to hold all the items being pushed on the stack.*

USING A LINKED LIST AS A STACK

Because you have already worked with linked lists, you will easily under-stand how to use a linked list to implement a stack. A stack is simply a linked list that allows nodes to be added and deleted at only one end of the list. Figure 17-4 shows how the head pointer is called the top when using a linked list as a stack.

Rather than adding nodes to the end of the list, or allowing nodes to be in-serted in the middle of the list, new nodes are attached to the head (or top) of the list. When an item is popped off the stack, the top pointer is moved to the second node in the list and the node that is being popped off the stack is deleted.

top

```
14
18
11
15
12
NULL
```

F I G U R E   1 7 - 4
A stack can be implemented using a linked list.

EXERCISE 17-1

USING A STACK

1. Retrieve *NAMESTAK.CPP*. A program that implements a stack using a linked list appears.

2. Compile and run the program.

3. Choose option 1 from the menu of choices. Enter any name at the prompt.

4. Repeatedly select option 1 until you have entered four names onto the stack.

5. Choose option 3 from the menu of choices to display the names in the stack. Notice the last person's name entered appears at the top of the stack.

6. Choose option 2 to pop the top name off the stack and then display the stack again.

7. Push another name onto the stack and display the stack again.

8. Repeatedly pop the names off the stack until the stack is empty.

9. Quit the program.

10. Close the source code file.

USING A STACK CLASS

After running the program in Exercise 17-1, you can see that the stack is a very useful data structure. However, programming a stack into a program can be very time consuming. To make using a stack easier, a template class could be programmed. Using a stack class that supports templates allows a programmer to create and use a stack of any data type anywhere in a program by simply declaring an instance of the stack class.

In Exercise 17-2, you will run a program that uses a simple stack class. You have seen how a stack can be implemented using an array or a linked list. If you open the header file for the stack class used in Exercise 17-2, you can see that this class is based on the vector class you used in Chapter 14. If you read further through the class definition you can see that there are methods for returning the object on the top of the stack, checking the status of the stack, and checking the length of the stack. Most importantly, the stack class has the standard stack operations, push and pop. The class also has a method for flushing the stack so that it contains no objects.

EXERCISE 17-2   USING A STACK CLASS

1. Open *STACKEX.CPP.* The program uses the stack class defined in *STACK.H.*

2. Read through the source code and examine the way the stack class is used in the program.

3. Compile and run the program.

4. Run the program multiple times, if desired.

5. Close all open source code files.

On the Net

To learn more about stacks and to see examples of how stacks can be used, see http://www.ProgramCPP.com. See topic 17.1.1.

SECTION 17.1 QUESTIONS

1. LIFO is an acronym for what kind of structure?

2. What term refers to adding an item to a stack?

3. What term refers to removing an item from a stack?

4. Identify two common uses for a stack.

5. Where are new nodes inserted when a linked list is used as a stack?

6. What is an advantage of using a stack class?

Queues

A *queue* (pronounced "Q") is another form of list. A queue allows additions at only one end (called the rear of the queue) and deletions at the opposite end (called the front of the queue). The best way to visualize a queue is to think of a line of people waiting for their turn; for example, a line waiting to get on a roller coaster. People are added to the back of the line, and people at the front of the line get on the roller coaster.

A queue is a *first-in first-out (FIFO)* structure. The first person in line is the first person who gets on the roller coaster.

USES FOR A QUEUE

Queues are very common in computer software, including the operating system. The **cin** stream you have been using to get data from the keyboard is an example of a queue. As you press keys on the keyboard, the characters are placed in the queue. Your program pulls the characters out of the queue.

Computer networks use queues to line up processes to be performed. For example, five people on a computer network may need the printer at the same time. Since that is not possible, the operating system "queues" the documents to be printed and feeds them to the printer one at a time.

IMPLEMENTING A QUEUE

A queue can be implemented using a linked list like the one in Figure 17-5. Instead of keeping a pointer to the head only, we keep a pointer to the head and the tail. Two pointers are used so that we can add new nodes at the tail and remove nodes from the head.

Note

*The terminology used to describe adding and removing items from a queue differs from stack terminology. Rather than push and pop, you **enqueue** to add an item to a queue and **dequeue** to remove an item from a queue.*

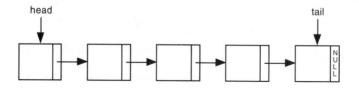

F I G U R E   1 7 - 5
A queue allows insertions at one end and deletions at the other.

Let's assume we have a queue of characters. The statements below declare a node structure and the two necessary pointers.

```
struct queue_node
  {
    char ch;
    queue_node *next;
  };


queue_node *head_ptr;
queue_node *tail_ptr;
```

Inserting a node at the tail of the queue is accomplished with the statements below. The statements assume that the new node already exists, and that it is pointed to by a pointer named **new_node**.

```
tail_ptr->next = new_node; // attach new node to the end of the list
new_node->next = NULL;     // make the new node's next pointer NULL
tail_ptr = new_node;       // move the tail pointer to the new node
```

Removing a node from the queue involves the other end of the list. As the statements below illustrate, the second item in the list becomes the new head as the first node is deleted. The statements below use a pointer named **temp_ptr** to keep track of the node being removed until the memory is deallocated.

```
temp_ptr = head_ptr;        // set temporary pointer to point to head
head_ptr = head_ptr->next;  // move head to the next node
delete temp_ptr;            // delete the old head of the list
```

The statements above show how to remove the node from the queue. Before removing the node, you will use the data stored in the node or copy the data to another data structure. For example, the queue discussed earlier that feeds documents to the printer would make sure the document had printed without error before removing the document from the queue.

EXERCISE 17-3   USING A QUEUE

1. Retrieve *NAMQUEUE.CPP*. A program appears that forms a queue of customers.

2. Compile and run the program.

3. Enter four customers in the queue.

4. Display the queue.

5. Take the next customer and redisplay the queue. Notice the first customer has been removed from the queue.

6. Take the next customer and redisplay the queue.

7. Add another customer to the queue and redisplay the queue.

8. Take customers from the queue until the queue is empty.

9. Quit the program.

10. Close the source code file.

USING A QUEUE CLASS

The header file *QUEUE.H* contains a queue class definition that supports templates. Using a simple queue class like the one defined in *QUEUE.H* allows a programmer to have all the benefits of using a queue without having to worry about how long it will take to program and test a new queue data structure for every program that could use a queue. After reading the *QUEUE.H* header file you can see that this queue is also based on the vector object you used in Chapter 14.

The queue class has member functions to return the object at the front of the queue, to check the status of the queue, and to check the total number of items in the queue. The methods that enqueue and dequeue items from the queue are the most important. Finally, the class has a method to empty the queue.

EXERCISE 17-4   USING A QUEUE CLASS

1. Retrieve *QUEUEEX.CPP*. The program utilizes the queue class defined in *QUEUE.H*.

2. Read through the file and see how the queue class is used.

3. Notice how easy it is to use the queue class and how you do not have to understand how the class is programmed in order to use it.

4. Compile and run the program.

5. Close all open source code files.

On the Net

To learn more about queue theory and the different kinds of queues, see http://www.ProgramCPP.com. See topic 17.2.1.

SECTION 17.2 QUESTIONS

1. A queue allows additions to the _____ of the queue.

2. A queue allows deletions from the _____ of the queue.

3. FIFO is an acronym for what kind of structure?

4. Identify a way your computer's operating system uses a queue.

5. Give a real-world example of a queue.

CHAPTER 17, SECTION 3

Binary Trees

The data structures you have been using are called ***linear data structures,*** meaning the elements or nodes are arranged in a line. In this section, you will learn about a ***nonlinear data structure*** called a tree.

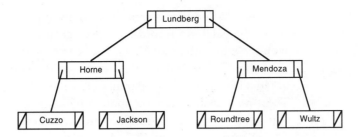

F I G U R E   1 7 - 6
Each node of a binary tree contains a maximum of two branches.

A *tree* is a data structure in which the nodes are in an arrangement that re-
sembles branches of a tree. There are many kinds of trees and even more variations of those kinds. In this chapter, you will learn about a special kind of tree
called a binary tree. A *binary tree*, like the one shown in Figure 17-6, can have
only two branches from each node.

WHY TREES?

The reason data is arranged in a binary tree is to allow it to be more easily
and quickly searched. The data in the tree is ordered by a *key* value. The key
might be a name or a number. In the example in Figure 17-6, the data is keyed by
last names. At the top is the name Lundberg. All the names on the half of the tree
to the left of Lundberg come before Lundberg alphabetically. All the names on
the right half come after Lundberg. The same is true of any node on the tree. For
example, Horne comes before Lundberg, so Horne is attached to the left of Lundberg. Jackson comes before Lundberg, but after Horne, so Jackson is attached to
the right of Horne.

Because of this arrangement, any name on the tree can be reached with only
a few comparisons. In the next chapter, you will learn more about searching.
Let's examine the characteristics of the tree itself.

TREE TERMINOLOGY

The way trees are represented in diagrams is actually more of an upside-
down tree, as shown in Figure 17-7. The top of the diagram is called the *root*.
Every element in the tree is a *node,* just like every element of a linked list is a
node. But a node can be classified in several different ways. A node has two
links. A link may be NULL, or may have a *branch* to another node. Nodes that
have branches are called *branch nodes* or *nonterminal nodes*. Nodes that do not
have branches are called *leaf nodes* or *terminal nodes*.

Trees are described as having *levels*. The root is the only node at Level 0. The
number of levels in a binary tree indicates the maximum number of comparisons

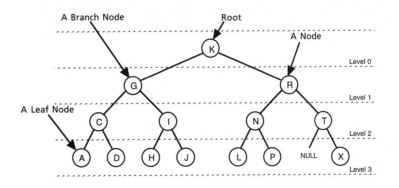

F I G U R E   1 7 - 7
A tree and its nodes are described
using special terminology.

necessary to find the desired data. For example, suppose the nodes in Figure 17-7 represent database records. In a search for the record labeled "P," the search would begin at the root ("K"). The search would progress to "R," then "N," and finally to "P." The worst case search would go only to level 3.

In a tree, nodes have parents, children, siblings, ancestors, and descendants. These relationships among nodes are like those in a family tree. A node's *parent* is the node above it to which it is linked. Every node except the root has a parent. For example, in Figure 17-7, the parent of node A is node C. The one or two nodes below a given node are its *children* (sometimes called *offspring*). Nodes H and J are children of node I. The children of a node are often referred to as the *left child* or *right child*. Node H is the left child of I, and J is the right child of I. Two nodes with the same parent (like H and J) are *siblings*.

Following all the links from a node back to the root give you the node's *ancestors*. All the nodes linked below a node are the node's *descendants*.

For purposes of discussion, trees are sometimes divided into *subtrees*. A subtree can be any node with branches extending below it. For example, the two nodes directly below the root form left and right subtrees.

TREE SHAPE AND EFFICIENCY

A tree is built by attaching nodes to the tree one at a time. Let's look at how a sorted binary tree of integer values grows. Assume that the tree is to be built using the values below in the order that the values appear.

7, 12, 9, 4, 15, 3, 11

Figure 17-8 illustrates the development of the tree by the first three nodes. The first value (7) becomes the root. The next value (12) is attached as the right child of the root, because 12 is greater than 7. The value 9 is also greater than 7, but it less than 12. Therefore it becomes the left child of the node containing 12.

FIGURE 17-8
A tree is built by attaching nodes one at a time. (a) The first node becomes the root. (b) The second node is greater than the root, so it is attached to the right of the root. (c) The third node is greater than the root (7), but less than 12, so it becomes the left child of the node containing 12.

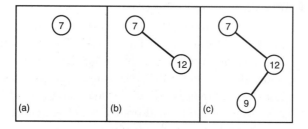

At this point, the tree looks more like a stick. But as Figure 17-9 shows, the addition of the next two nodes help the tree take shape. Because 4 is less than 7, a node is added to the left side of the root. Because 15 is the largest value yet, it attaches to the right of 12.

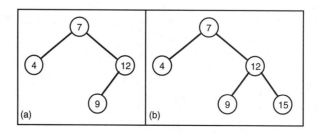

FIGURE 17-9
The two nodes added in this figure help the tree take shape.

Figure 17-10 shows the addition of the last two values. The node containing the value 3 becomes the left child of 4. The value 11 is greater than 7, less than 12, and greater than 9. Therefore it gets attached as the right child of 9.

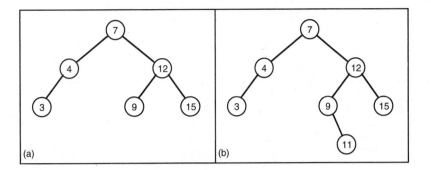

FIGURE 17-10
The last value added to the tree requires the addition of a new level.

The tree in the figures above has only two nodes to the left of the root and twice that many on the right. The shape of the tree depends on the order the nodes are attached. In tree terminology, the arrangement of nodes is referred to as the *balance* of the tree.

A balanced tree allows more efficient access to the data in the tree. Figure 17-11 shows the same values that built the tree above arranged in a perfectly balanced tree. The balanced tree has fewer levels, and therefore requires fewer comparisons to find any given node in the tree.

If the values being inserted into a tree structure are either in ascending or descending order, the result is just a list, as shown in Figure 17-12.

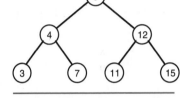

FIGURE 17-11
If the nodes had been inserted in the order 9, 12, 4, 7, 15, 3, 11, the tree would be perfectly balanced.

Having a balanced tree is important. An unbalanced tree lacks some of the efficiency that makes a tree desirable. Advanced programmers of trees use algorithms that detect an unbalanced tree and rearrange nodes to create a more balanced tree. Selecting a root that falls near the midpoint of the data is an important step in creating a balanced tree. For our purposes, understanding why a balanced tree is important is sufficient.

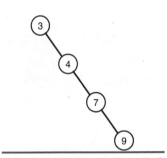

FIGURE 17-12
If the nodes attached to a tree are in ascending or descending order, the result is a linked list rather than a tree.

DELETING NODES FROM A TREE

You have seen how nodes are attached to a tree. But how is the removal of a node accomplished? Actually, deleting from a binary tree can be complicated, depending on whether the node has children and how many children it has.

If the node to be deleted has no children (in other words, a leaf node), then the node can simply be removed, as shown in Figure 17-13.

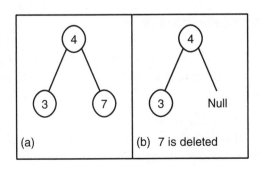

FIGURE 17-13
Deleting a node that has no children requires no rearranging of the tree's nodes.

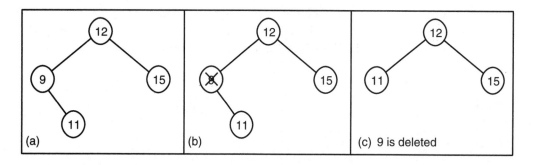

(a)　(b)　(c) 9 is deleted

FIGURE 17-14
Deleting a node that has one child requires that the child of the deleted node be attached to the deleted node's parent.

If the node to be deleted has one child, the parent of the node to be deleted is connected to the child of the node to be deleted, as shown in Figure 17-14.

If the node to be deleted has two children, the process can become very complicated. Some implementations simply mark the node as deleted without physically removing it. This can be done by adding a boolean data member to each node that indicates whether it is active or deleted.

Another method involves finding the node below which has the value closest to that of the deleted node and moving that value to the location of the node to be deleted. However, unless the node you move is a leaf, you must repeat the process to properly delete the node you moved.

On the Net

You will learn more about trees and how they are searched in the next chapter. To learn more about other types of tree structures, see http://www.ProgramCPP.com. See topic 17.3.1.

SECTION 17.3 QUESTIONS

1. What is the term used to describe the node at the top of a tree?

2. What level number contains the node at the top of the tree?

3. What is the maximum number of nodes that can appear in level 2 of a binary tree?

4. What happens if nodes that are inserted in a tree are in ascending or descending order?

5. What is the disadvantage of an unbalanced tree?

PROBLEM 17.3.1

Draw a tree built by inserting the numbers 29, 44, 17, 32, 11, 25, 50 in that order. Label the branch nodes and the leaf nodes, and answer the following questions about the tree.

1. Is the tree balanced?
2. What is the left child of the node containing the value 44?
3. List the ancestors of the node containing the value 25.

4. List the descendants of the node containing the value 17.
5. What values are in the root's right subtree?
6. What node is the sibling of the node containing the value 11?

KEY TERMS

ancestors	node
balance	nonlinear data structure
binary tree	nonterminal nodes
branches	offspring
branch nodes	parent
children	pop
dequeue	push
descendants	queue
enqueue	right child
first-in first-out (FIFO)	root
key	siblings
last-in first-out (LIFO)	stack
leaf nodes	stack overflow
left child	subtree
levels	terminal nodes
linear data structure	tree

SUMMARY

➤ A stack is a data structure that allows items to be added and deleted from only one end. Adding an item to a stack is called pushing, and removing an item is called popping.

➤ A stack is a last-in first-out (LIFO) data structure.

➤ A stack can be implemented using an array or a linked list.

➤ A stack class that supports templates allows you to use the same class to implement a stack anytime you need one.

➤ A queue is a data structure that allows additions at one end and deletions at the other.

➤ A queue is a first-in first-out (FIFO) structure.

➤ A queue can be implemented using a linked list or a queue class.

➤ A tree is a nonlinear data structure in which nodes are arranged like branches of a tree.

- A binary tree has a maximum of two branches from each node. Special terms are used to describe the nodes of trees.

- The shape of a tree affects the tree's efficiency. A tree with unevenly distributed nodes is called unbalanced.

- Deleting nodes from a tree can be complicated depending on whether the node has children.

PROJECTS

PROJECT 17-1

Write a program that uses the stack class to reverse a string. The program should use subscript notation to individually access each character of the string, pushing them onto a stack of characters. When the null terminator at the end of the string is reached, do not push it on the stack. Instead, begin to build a new string with the characters as they are popped off the stack. The result will be a reversed string.

PROJECT 17-2

Write a program that queues jobs for a desktop publishing company. Implement the queue using the queue class. For each job, store the customer's name and a description of the job. The program should have a menu similar to the one below.

```
0 - Exit
1 - Add incoming job to the queue
2 - Display the queue
3 - Remove job from the queue
```

STACK CLASS

Purpose: The stack class provides an easy-to-use, last-in first-out data structure for your programs.

Required Header File

```
#include "stack.h"
```

To Instanciate a Stack Object

Because the stack class is a template class, you must specify a data type when instanciating the stack object.

```
stack <float> MyStack;  // instanciate a stack of floating-point values
```

To Push an Item on the Stack

You can push an item on the stack using the **push** function.

```
MyStack.push(Value);
```

To Pop an Item Off the Stack

You can pop an item off the stack using the **pop** function.

```
Value = MyStack.pop();
```

To Get the Value of the Top Element without Popping

You can get a copy of the item at the top of the stack without removing it from the stack using the **top** function.

```
Value = MyStack.top();
```

To Determine If the Stack Is Empty

You can determine whether the stack is currently empty using the **isEmpty** function.

```
Empty = MyStack.isEmpty();
```

To Obtain the Size of the Stack

You can determine the number of elements in the stack using the **length** function.

```
size = MyStack.length();
```

To Empty the Stack

You can empty the stack using the **flush** function.

```
MyStack.flush();
```

Assigning One Stack to Another

You can assign the contents of one stack to another. The overloaded operator can be used to copy a stack.

```
MyStack1 = MyStack2;
```

Purpose: The queue class provides an easy-to-use, first-in first-out data structure for your programs.

Required Header File

```
#include "queue.h"
```

To Instanciate a Queue Object

Because the queue class is a template class, you must specify a data type when instanciating the queue object.

```
queue <float> MyQueue;   // instanciate a queue of floating-point values
```

To Place an Item in the Queue

You can place an item in the queue using the **enqueue** function.

```
MyQueue.enqueue(Value);
```

To Remove an Item from the Queue

You can remove an item from the queue using the **dequeue** function.

```
Value = MyQueue.dequeue();
```

To Get the Value at the Front of the Queue without Removing It

You can get a copy of the item at the front of the queue without removing it from the queue using the **front** function.

```
Value = MyQueue.front();
```

To Determine Whether the Queue Is Empty

You can determine whether the queue is currently empty using the **isEmpty** function. The **isEmpty** function returns a value of type bool.

```
Empty = MyQueue.isEmpty();
```

To Obtain the Size of the Queue

You can determine the number of elements in the queue using the **length** function.

```
size = MyQueue.length();
```

To Empty the Queue

You can empty the queue using the **flush** function.

```
MyQueue.flush();
```

Assigning One Queue to Another

You can assign the contents of one queue to another. The overloaded operator can be used to copy a queue.

```
MyQueue1 = MyQueue2;
```

Overview

n this case study, you will analyze a program that uses a stack as part of a calculator. First, you will learn about how a stack-based calculator works. Then you will study the source code of the program.

What Is a Stack-Based Calculator?

ost calculators require that numerical expressions be entered in the order in which they would be written. For example, to add 3 + 4, you press 3, press +, press 4, and press =. Although this form is more natural, it becomes complicated when more complex expressions must be evaluated. For example, evaluating (4 + 2) / (9 - 6) requires that you enter parentheses to control the order of operations.

Another method, called Reverse Polish Notation (RPN), is a way of representing expressions without parentheses. RPN takes some getting used to. When you are accustomed to how RPN works, however, complex expressions are much easier to calculate.

Calculators by Hewlett-Packard use RPN. To calculate 3 + 4, you press 3, press Enter, press 4, press Enter, and press +. The reason for the strange operation is that the calculator is using a stack to simplify operations.

Each time a number is entered, it is pushed on the stack. When an operator (such as +,-,*, or /) is entered, two values are popped off the stack and the operation is performed. The result is pushed back on the stack. Figure V-1 shows how adding 3 + 4 is accomplished using a stack-based RPN calculator.

Stack:		3	4 3	7
Keystrokes:		3 Enter	4 Enter	+

F I G U R E   V - 1
Using a stack makes performing calculations easier.

A Look at the Entire Program

he program you will analyze in this case study performs the operations of a stack-based calculator. The program repeatedly presents a prompt. At that prompt, you may enter an integer or an operator. You may also enter D to display the entire stack and Q to quit the program.

EXERCISE V-1   COMPILING AND RUNNING THE PROGRAM

1. Open *EVALSTAK.CPP*. Compile and run the program.

2. Enter 3 at the prompt. The prompt appears again.

3. Enter 4 at the prompt. The prompt appears again.

4. Enter D at the prompt. The stack is displayed, showing that both values entered are on the stack.

5. Enter + at the prompt. The values 3 and 4 are popped off the stack, added together, and the result (7) is pushed back on the stack.

6. Enter Q to quit the program.

7. Let's try a more complex expression: (4 + 2) / (9 - 6).
   a. Run the program again.
   b. Enter 4, then 2, then +. The result (6) is pushed on the stack.
   c. Enter 9, then 6, then -. The result (3) is pushed on the stack.
   d. Enter /. The 6 and 3 are popped off the stack, divided, and the result (2) is pushed back on the stack.

8. Quit the program and leave the source code open.

The listing below is the entire *EVALSTAK.CPP* program. Familiarize yourself with the source code before we analyze it function by function.

```
// EVALSTAK.CPP
// A stack-based calculator
// By Todd Knowlton

// compiler directives
#include <iostream.h>
#include <stdlib.h>
#include "stack.h"

// global structures and variables
stack <int> NumericStack;
const int OPERATOR = 2;
const int NUMERIC  = 1;
const int QUIT     = 0;

// function prototypes
int process_input(char ch);
int do_operation(char ch, int v1, int v2);
void display_stack();

// main function
int main()
{
  char user_input[10];    // character array for user input
  int value;              // int to hold value if user enters an integer
  int entry_status = NUMERIC;  // Flag to indicate whether the user's
                          // was a number, an operator, or quit.

  cout << "Enter an integer or operator (+,-,*,/) at the prompts below.\n";
  cout << "Enter D to display stack.\n";
```

```
      cout << "Enter Q to quit.\n";

    do
     {
        cout << ": ";              // display prompt
        cin.get(user_input,10); // get user input
        cin.ignore(80,'\n');
        // Pass the first character of the user's input to the process_input
        // function. The function will perform the appropriate operation
        // if the user entered an operator or if the user issued a command.
        // If the user entered an integer, entry_status will be NUMERIC.
        entry_status = process_input(user_input[0]);

        if(entry_status == NUMERIC)    // If entry_status is numeric,
         {                             // convert the number in the string
          value = atoi(user_input);    // to an actual integer and
          NumericStack.push(value);    // push the value on the stack.
         }
     } while (entry_status != QUIT); // Loop until user enters Quit command.
      return 0;
} // end of main function

// Function that processes the user's input. Only the first character of
// the user's input is passed to this function.
int process_input(char ch)
 {
   int v1, v2; // Variables to hold values while operation is taking place.
   int result; // Used to hold the result of an operation.
   int status; // Holds the status value returned by the function.

   switch(ch)
    {
      case '+':  // If user entered a +
      case '-':  // a -
      case '*':  // a *
      case '/':  // or a /, do the lines below.
        status = OPERATOR; // Set status to indicate user entered an operator.
        v1 = NumericStack.pop();   // Because all of the operators require two
        v2 = NumericStack.pop();   // operands, pop two values off the stack.
        result = do_operation(ch, v1, v2); // Call function to do operation.
        cout << result << endl;    // Output result of operation.
        NumericStack.push(result); // Push result on the stack.
        break;
      case 'D':
      case 'd':
        status = OPERATOR;
        display_stack();
        break;
      case 'Q':  // If user entered a Q
      case 'q':  // or a q, do the lines below.
        NumericStack.flush(); // Empty the stack
        status = QUIT;    // Set status to indicate user wants to quit.
        break;
      default :  // If anything not covered above is entered, assume
        status = NUMERIC; // the user entered an integer.
        break;
    }
```

```
    return(status); // Return the status to the calling function.
  } // end of function process_input


// Function that performs the mathematical operations.
int do_operation(char op, int v1, int v2)
  {
  int result;
  switch(op)
    {
    case '+':  // If operator is +, add the values.
      result = v1 + v2;
      break;
    case '-':  // If operator is -, subtract the values.
      result = v2 - v1;
      break;
    case '*':  // If operator is *, multiply the values.
      result = v2 * v1;
      break;
    case '/':  // If operator is /, divide the values.
      result = v2 / v1;
      break;
    }
  return(result); // Return the result of the operation.
  } // end of function do_operation


// Function that displays the contents of the stack.
void display_stack()
  {
  stack <int> TempStack;  // temporary stack
  int TempObject;         // temporary variable for holding stack items

  while(!NumericStack.isEmpty())
    {                                    // While the numeric stack is not
      TempObject = NumericStack.pop();   // empty, pop a value off, display
      cout << TempObject << endl;        // the value, and push the value
      TempStack.push(TempObject);        // on to the temporary stack.
    }

  cout << "BOTTOM OF STACK" << endl;

  while(!TempStack.isEmpty())
    {                                    // While the temporary stack is not
      TempObject = TempStack.pop();      // empty, pop a value off and push it
      NumericStack.push(TempObject);     // back on to the numeric stack.
    }
  } // end of function display_stack
```

Global Structures and Variables

n this program, the stack class that was studied in Chapter 17 is used. The first statement below declares a global integer stack named **Numeric-Stack**. The three constants (**OPERATOR**, **NUMERIC**, and **QUIT**) are used in the processing of input to identify the type of data the user entered.

```
// global structures and variables
stack <int> NumericStack;
const int OPERATOR = 2;
const int NUMERIC  = 1;
const int QUIT     = 0;
```

The Main Function and Menu Processing

The main function (shown again below) begins by declaring three local variables. The first (**user_input**) is the character array used to accept input from the user. Because the user may enter a value, an operator, or a command, the input must be received into a character array. If the user enters an integer value, the program will convert it to an integer and store it in the local variable named **value**. The integer variable **entry_status** is a flag that directs program flow based on the type of data entered by the user.

```
// main function
int main()
{
  char user_input[10];      // character array for user input
  int value;                // int to hold value if user enters an integer
  int entry_status = NUMERIC;  // Flag to indicate whether the user's
                               // was a number, an operator, or quit.

  cout << "Enter an integer or operator (+,-,*,/) at the prompts below.\n";
  cout << "Enter D to display stack.\n";
  cout << "Enter Q to quit.\n";

  do
   {
     cout << ": ";              // display prompt
     cin.get(user_input,10); // get user input
     cin.ignore(80,'\n');
     // Pass the first character of the user's input to the process_input
     // function. The function will perform the appropriate operation
     // if the user entered an operator or if the user issued a command.
     // If the user entered an integer, entry_status will be NUMERIC.
     entry_status = process_input(user_input[0]);

     if(entry_status == NUMERIC)    // If entry_status is numeric,
      {                             // convert the number in the string
        value = atoi(user_input);   // to an actual integer and
        NumericStack.push(value);   // push the value on the stack.
      }
   } while (entry_status != QUIT); // Loop until user enters Quit command.
   return 0;
} // end of main function
```

Before beginning the main loop, a three-line message is displayed to remind the user of the acceptable entries. The remainder of the main function is a do loop which is repeated until the user chooses to quit.

In the loop, the prompt is repeatedly presented and the program accepts a string from the user. The first character of whatever the user inputs is passed to the **process_input** function. The **process_input** function returns a status flag (**entry_status**) that provides important information to the main function. If **entry_status** is **NUMERIC**, the main function converts the value in the string to an integer and pushes the value on the stack. If the user chooses to quit, **entry_status** indicates so and the loop terminates.

If the input is an operator or other command, the **process_input** function handles the operation. Let's look at how the **process_input** function does its job.

Controlling the Flow of Logic

The **process_input** function (shown again below) accepts only the first character of the user's input. Only the first character is necessary because the operators and commands consist of only a single character. Local variables are used to hold the values as the stack is manipulated, and a local integer is used to store the status flag that will be returned to the main function.

The function is primarily a switch structure that controls the flow of logic based on the user's input. Notice how the first four case keywords appear together, followed by several lines of code. When case keywords are grouped in this way, the code between the last one and the break statement will be executed if any of the case expressions are true. In this case, the character +, -, *, or / will cause the same code to be executed.

```cpp
// Function that processes the user's input. Only the first character of
// the user's input is passed to this function.
int process_input(char ch)
 {
   int v1, v2; // Variables to hold values while operation is taking place.
   int result; // Used to hold the result of an operation.
   int status; // Holds the status value returned by the function.

   switch(ch)
    {
     case '+':  // If user entered a +
     case '-':  // a -
     case '*':  // a *
     case '/':  // or a /, do the lines below.
       status = OPERATOR; // Set status to indicate user entered an operator.
       v1 = NumericStack.pop();   // Because all of the operators require two
       v2 = NumericStack.pop();   // operands, pop two values off the stack.
       result = do_operation(ch, v1, v2); // Call function to do operation.
       cout << result << endl;    // Output result of operation.
       NumericStack.push(result); // Push result on the stack.
       break;
     case 'D':
     case 'd':
       status = OPERATOR;
       display_stack();
       break;
```

```
         case 'Q':  // If user entered a Q
         case 'q':  // or a q, do the lines below.
            NumericStack.flush(); // Empty the stack
            status = QUIT;    // Set status to indicate user wants to quit.
            break;
         default :  // If anything not covered above is entered, assume
            status = NUMERIC; // the user entered an integer.
            break;
      }
   return(status); // Return the status to the calling function.
} // end of function process_input
```

If the user enters an operator, two values are popped off the stack and the **do_operation** function is called to calculate the result. The result is then pushed on the stack.

If the user chooses to display the stack, the **display_stack** function is called, and if the user chooses to quit, the stack is emptied before exiting the program. We will look at the **display_stack** function in detail later.

If the user's input is not one of the operators or commands, it is assumed that the user entered a numeric value and the status flag is set accordingly. As you saw in the main function, if the status flag is returned as **NUMERIC**, the value will be converted to an integer and pushed on the stack.

Now let's examine how the **do_operation** function works.

Performing Operations

Each of the operators requires two values, which were popped off the stack and passed to this function, along with the character that indicates the function to be performed. A switch structure performs the appropriate operation, and the result is returned to the calling function.

```
// Function that performs the mathematical operations.
int do_operation(char op, int v1, int v2)
 {
  int result;
  switch(op)
   {
    case '+':  // If operator is +, add the values.
       result = v1 + v2;
       break;
    case '-':  // If operator is -, subtract the values.
       result = v2 - v1;
       break;
    case '*':  // If operator is *, multiply the values.
       result = v2 * v1;
       break;
    case '/':  // If operator is /, divide the values.
       result = v2 / v1;
       break;
   }
  return(result); // Return the result of the operation.
 } // end of function do_operation
```

Displaying the Stack

Because the stack class only lets us view the item on the top of the stack, the best way to display the entire stack is to create a temporary stack to hold the items from the numerical stack. The first loop in the function pops integers off the numerical stack until the stack is empty. As the integers are being popped off the numerical stack, they are displayed, then pushed onto the temporary stack. After the function displays a message indicating the bottom of the stack, the second loop pops integers off the temporary stack and pushes them back on to the numerical stack.

```
// Function that displays the contents of the stack.
void display_stack()
{
  stack <int> TempStack;   // temporary stack
  int TempObject;          // temporary variable for holding stack items

  while(!NumericStack.isEmpty())
    {                                 // While the numeric stack is not
      TempObject = NumericStack.pop();  // empty, pop a value off, display
      cout << TempObject << endl;       // the value, and push the value
      TempStack.push(TempObject);       // on to the temporary stack.
    }

  cout << "BOTTOM OF STACK" << endl;

  while(!TempStack.isEmpty())
    {                                 // While the temporary stack is not
      TempObject = TempStack.pop();     // empty, pop a value off and push it
      NumericStack.push(TempObject);    // back on to the numeric stack.
    }
} // end of function display_stack
```

EXERCISE V-2

RUNNING THE PROGRAM AGAIN

1. Now that you have analyzed the source code, run the program again.

2. Use the stack-based calculator to calculate the result of the expression below.

   (2 * 9) / (4 + 3 - 1)

3. If desired, try additional expressions.

4. Close the source code file.

On the Net

See this same program implemented without the stack class at http://www.ProgramCPP.com. Without the stack class, all of the stack operations must be handled in the calculator program. You can see how the program is simplified by the stack class. See topic V.1.

Modifying the Program

s additional exercises, try some of the modifications below.

1. Modify the program to use long integers rather than standard length integers. *Note:* Depending on your compiler, the length of an int may be equivalent to that of a long int. In any case, be sure you are using the longest integer type available.

2. Modify the program to use floating-point values rather than integers.

3. Add an operation that allows the user to enter S to change the sign of the value at the top of the stack. For example, if the value 6 is at the top of the stack, entering S would pop off the value, change it to -6, and push it back on the stack. Likewise, the same operation would change a negative value to a positive value.

4. Add an operation that allows the user to enter C to clear the stack without exiting the program. *Hint:* call the **flush** member function of the stack class.

18

Recursion and Searching

OBJECTIVES

➤ *Understand recursion.*

➤ *Understand sequential searching.*

➤ *Understand binary searching.*

➤ *Search binary trees.*

➤ *Traverse binary trees.*

➤ *Understand hashing.*

Overview

n this chapter, you will learn several important concepts, beginning with recursion. Recursion is a technique that allows functions to call themselves. Recursion can greatly simplify certain programming problems.

You will also learn about four methods of searching for data. Each method of searching has its advantages and disadvantages. You will first look at a simple sequential search. Then you will see how an ordered array can be searched more efficiently using a binary search. You will also see how binary trees are searched, and learn about a search method called hashing.

Recursion

ecursion is a programming technique used to simplify many programming problems, such as searching, sorting, and solving mathematical problems. A function is said to be recursive if the function calls itself, either directly or indirectly.

At first, recursion may seem impossible. In this section, however, we will cover the concept of recursion step by step and show you that it is possible for a function to call itself. In fact, recursion is often the best way to solve a problem.

WHY RECURSION?

There are some problems that are greatly simplified by using recursion. However, anything that can be programmed using recursive functions can be programmed without recursion.

Think of recursion as another type of loop. A for loop, while loop, or do while loop repeats a block of code until a specified condition is met. A recursive function repeats a block of code by calling itself until a specified condition is met.

A SIMPLE EXAMPLE OF RECURSION

Let's look at a simple example of recursion. The program in Figure 18-1 shows how something normally done with a loop can be accomplished with recursion. This program prints the word *Hello* on the screen a specified number of times. In most cases, including this one, a loop is faster and more efficient than using recursion.

The program in Figure 18-1 calls the function **PrintHello** repeatedly, each time reducing the integer it passes as an argument by one. Eventually, the number passed reaches the value zero, and the recursion ends.

```
// RECURSIV.CPP
// A simple example of recursion.
// By Macneil Shonle

#include<iostream.h>  // necessary for stream I/O

// function prototype
void PrintHello(int How_Many_Times);

// main function
int main()
{
 int n;

 cout << "How many times do you want to print the message? ";
 cin >> n;
 PrintHello(n);
 return 0;
}

// recursive function
void PrintHello(int How_Many_Times)
{
 if(How_Many_Times > 0)     // If How_Many_Times is greater than zero,
  {                         // make another recursive call.
    cout << "Hello\n";
    PrintHello(How_Many_Times - 1); // Reduce How_Many_Times by one.
  }
}
```

FIGURE 18-1
This simple program uses recursion to print the word "Hello" a specified number of times.

EXERCISE 18-1   SIMPLE RECURSION EXAMPLE

1. Retrieve the source code file named *RECURSIV.CPP*. A program similar to the one in Figure 18-1 appears. The version on your screen has added output statements to help you trace the path of the recursion.

2. Compile and run the program. If you have access to a debugger, step through the program to see the flow of logic as the recursive calls are made.

3. Provide the integer 5 as input.

4. Analyze the output to understand the flow of logic.

5. Close the source code file.

In the example that follows, you'll see how recursion can be used to calculate the factorial of a positive integer.

USING RECURSION TO SOLVE

Calculating the factorial of a positive integer can be accomplished with a simple recursive function. To calculate the factorial of a positive integer, the

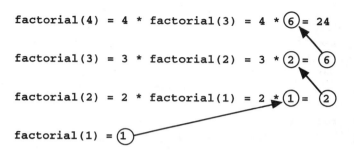

$$factorial(4) = 4 * factorial(3) = 4 * 6 = 24$$

$$factorial(3) = 3 * factorial(2) = 3 * 2 = 6$$

$$factorial(2) = 2 * factorial(1) = 2 * 1 = 2$$

$$factorial(1) = 1$$

FIGURE 18-2
Calculating a factorial is a problem that can be solved recursively.

integer is multiplied by each integer less than the original integer until the integer 1 is reached. For example, the factorial of 4 is calculated below.

factorial of four = 4 * 3 * 2 * 1 = 24

Calculating the factorial of an integer can be done recursively. Consider the factorial of four. As shown in the Figure 18-2, the factorial of four can be expressed as 4 times the factorial of three, the factorial of three can be expressed as 3 times the factorial of 2, and so on.

WRITING A RECURSIVE FUNCTION

Figure 18-3 shows a complete program for calculating a factorial recursively. The user is asked for a non-negative integer, and the program returns the factorial of the integer.

Let's look at the factorial function. When the function is originally called, the number the user enters is passed in through the parameter **n**. If the value in **n** is not equal to 1, the statement below is executed.

```
fact = n * factorial(n - 1);
```

Let's analyze the statement above piece by piece because it is the heart of the function. The variable named **fact** is local to the factorial function. The statement assigns the value of **n * factorial(n - 1)** to **fact**. The function is recursive because this statement includes a call to the function that is already being executed.

Each recursive call passes an integer that is one less than the previous call. Eventually, the integer 1 will be passed, which will end the recursion.

WHAT HAPPENS IN A RECURSIVE CALL?

To understand recursion, you must understand what happens when a recursive call takes place. Recall what you learned in Chapter 17 about the way a stack is used during the execution of a program. When a function is called, the address needed to return from the function is pushed on the stack, along with local variables and the values being passed to the function.

When a function "calls itself," the instructions of the function are used again. To the compiler, however, the function call is treated like any other function. Even though the same function's instructions are being used again, new values are pushed on the stack as if an entirely different function was called.

Eventually, a recursive function stops calling itself. When the flow of logic reaches the end of the last recursive call, the stack begins to shrink as each recursive call is exited in last-in first-out order.

Note

Because each recursive call adds to the stack, too many recursive calls can result in a stack overflow, which often crashes your program. Most compilers allow you to increase the size of the stack for programs that rely heavily on the stack.

```cpp
// FACTFIND.CPP
// A program that calculates the factorial of an integer recursively.

#include<iostream.h>   // necessary for stream I/O

// function prototype
long factorial(long n);

int main()
{
 long n;         // number entered by user
 long result;    // result returned by factorial function

 cout << "Enter a non-negative integer: ";
 cin >> n;
 if(n == 0) // If the integer is 0, print message and do no calc.
  {
   cout << "By definition, the factorial of 0 is 1.\n";
  }
 else
  {
   if(n > 0) // If the integer is greater than zero, calculate
    {         // the factorial.
     result = factorial(n);  // Call the recursive function.
     cout << "The factorial of " << n << " is " << result << ".\n";
    }
   else    // If the integer is less than zero, entry is not valid.
    {
     cout << "Not a valid integer.\n";
    }
  }
 return 0;
}


// Recursive function that calculates factorial.
long factorial(long n)
{
 long fact;   // Local variable returned by function.

 if(n > 1)
  {            // If n is not one, make another recursive call.
   fact = n * factorial(n - 1);
  }
 else
  {            // Exit condition
   fact = 1; // If n is one, recursion stops and flow of logic
  }            // begins "backing out" of recursive calls.
 return(fact); // Return fact to the next level of recursion.
}
```

F I G U R E   1 8 - 3
The factorial function calls itself
until the exit condition is met.

A recursive algorithm must have an *exit condition,* sometimes called a base case or base clause. Each time the recursive function is called, the exit condition is tested. If the exit condition has yet to be met, statements are executed that result in another recursive call. In the factorial function below, the value passed in as **n** is checked to determine if it is 1. As long as **n** is not 1, the recursion continues. When the number passed in is 1, the exit condition is met. Instead of making another recursive call, the value 1 is returned.

```
// Recursive function that calculates factorial.
long factorial(long n)
{
 long fact;    // Local variable returned by function.

 if(n > 1)
   {             // If n is not one, make another recursive call.
    fact = n * factorial(n - 1);
   }
 else
   {             // Exit condition
    fact = 1; // If n is one, recursion stops and flow of logic
   }             // begins "backing out" of recursive calls.
  return(fact);  // Return fact to the next level of recursion.
}
```

As each of the separate occurrences of the factorial functions exit, the statement that made the recursive call is completed. In other words, **n** is multiplied by the value returned from the function that just exited. The local variable **fact** is assigned the result of the multiplication, and then the value of **fact** is returned to the previous recursive call. Figure 18-4 illustrates how the value returned by each recursive call completes the function that made the call.

```
(a)
fact = 4 * factorial (3)

              3 * factorial (2)

                   2 * factorial (1)

                        1   <- Exit condition
```
```
(b)
fact = 4 * factorial (3)

              3 * factorial (2)

                   2 * 1 = 2
```
```
(c)
fact = 4 * factorial (3)

              3 * 2 = 6
```
```
(d)
fact = 4 * 6 = 24
```

FIGURE 18-4
As the recursive calls are exited, the value returned by each call is used to complete the calculation of the call that precedes it.

EXERCISE 18-2   USING RECURSION TO SOLVE

1. Retrieve *FACTFIND.CPP*. The program shown in Figure 18-3 appears.

2. Compile and run the program. Enter 4 as input.

3. Run the program again and enter 12 as input. Twelve is the largest number that the program can calculate due to the limits of the long integer.

4. Close the source code file.

On the Net

As you read earlier, any problem that can be solved recursively can also be solved with an iterative approach (loops). Many problems are best solved with loops, but some are obviously more efficient when solved using recursion. Sometimes the recursive solution is more difficult to visualize and program. The more you use recursion, however, the more natural it becomes.

Recursion should not be used unless there is a benefit to doing so. See http://www.ProgramCPP.com for a side-by-side comparison of a problem solved first by using loops and then with recursion. See topic 18.1.1.

SECTION 18.1 QUESTIONS

1. What makes a program recursive?

2. What is the reason that recursive algorithms are used in programming?

3. What can happen if too many recursive calls occur?

4. What is the purpose of the exit condition?

5. At what point in a program that uses recursion does the stack have the most values on it?

PROBLEM 18.1.1

Write a program that uses a recursive function to sum the even integers less than a given even integer. For example, if the integer 12 is provided as input, the program should calculate $10 + 8 + 6 + 4 + 2 = 30$.

Test the user's input to make sure he or she has entered an even number using a statement like the one below.

```
if(n % 2 == 0)   // if n modulo 2 is zero, then the number is even.
```

Save the source code as *EVENSUM.CPP*.

Sequential and Binary Searching

When working with large data structures such as arrays, linked lists, and trees, it is often important to search for specific data. For example, a database of library books may need to be searched by subject or author. The item upon which the search is based is called the *key,* and the field being searched is the *key field.*

Computers are uniquely suited for searching large databases because computers can compare data very quickly. Even though a computer can search much more quickly than a human, searching a large database can require special techniques.

Two common methods of searching are the sequential search and the binary search.

SEQUENTIAL SEARCH

The simplest search is the sequential search. In a *sequential search,* each record in the database is compared in the order it appears until the desired record is found. The array of characters shown below could be searched with a sequential search.

N H V E J Y C X S F P L

If you are searching for the character H or another character near the front of the array, a sequential search finds the character quickly. To find the character L, however, requires that every character in the array be compared. The more data that must be searched, the longer it may take to find the data that matches the key.

As you will see later in this section, there are methods of searching that are more efficient than sequential searches. When the amount of data to be searched is small, the simplicity of a sequential search sometimes makes it a good choice. The function in Figure 18-5 searches an array for a given value (**search_num**) and returns the position of the value in the array.

As you can see from Figure 18-5, a sequential search can be accomplished with a while loop. The loop continues until a match is found or the array is completely searched.

```
// Sequential search function.
int sequential_search(int x[100], int search_num)
{
 int index = 0;

 while((index < 100) && (search_num != x[index]))
  {  // Loop while not found and while more elements remain.
   if(x[index] != search_num)
    {         // If current element is not the one for which we are
     index++; // searching, increment subscript index.
    }
  }
 return(index);
}
```

F I G U R E   1 8 - 5
If this function returns a value less than 100, the value was found.

BINARY SEARCH

If the array that contains your data is in order based on the key field, you can use what you know about the list to locate the data more quickly. For example, suppose you are searching in the phone book for a friend whose last name is Stence. You would not begin on page 1 and turn pages until you reach the page that lists the Stences. You would probably open the phone book about in the middle. You would judge from the page to which you have turned the direction you need to move from there and the number of pages you should skip. Eventually, you will narrow the search to the exact page.

You can search an ordered array in a way similar to the way you search a phone book, using a *binary search.* To see how such a search is performed, consider the array of characters below. (*Note:* The numbers below the characters represent subscripts of the array.)

C	E	F	H	J	L	N	P	S	V	X	Y
0	1	2	3	4	5	6	7	8	9	10	11

Suppose we are searching the array above for the character N. First the middle is located by adding the array subscript of the first character to the subscript of the last character and dividing by two: (0 + 11) / 2 = 5. The actual middle would be between elements 5 and 6. Integer division is used to arrive at element 5 as the middle.

Element 5 holds the character L, which comes before N. Therefore, we know that N exists in that portion of the array to the right of L and we need to find the middle of that portion of the array by using the formula (6 + 11) / 2 = 8.

Element 8 holds the character S, which comes after N, so we next find the middle of the portion of the array to the right of L, but to the left of S using the formula (6 + 7) / 2 = 6.

Element 6 holds the character N, which is the character for which we are searching.

The function in Figure 18-6 performs a binary search on an array of 100 integers.

The **binary_search** function in Figure 18-6 uses the **lowerbound** and **upperbound** parameters in its search of the ordered array. The variables **lowerbound** and **upperbound** are passed in as parameters so that the calling function can specify the range of the search. For example, if only 70 of the 100 elements in the array are in use, there is no need to search the entire array. In such a case, **lowerbound** would be 0 and **upperbound** 69.

With each iteration of the loop, **lowerbound** and **upperbound** close in on the value for which we are searching. If **lowerbound** ever becomes greater than **upperbound**, we know the value is not in the array.

EXERCISE 18-3   SEQUENTIAL AND BINARY SEARCHES

1. Retrieve *SEARCH.CPP*. A program that performs a sequential and binary search appears. The program will need access to the data file named *NUMBERS.DAT*.

2. Compile and run the program. An ordered array of 100 integers are loaded. The numbers are positive integers less than or equal to 350.

3. When prompted for the number for which you want to search, enter 350. The program will perform both a binary and sequential search, and report the number of comparisons required to locate the number. Because 350 is the last

integer in the array, the sequential search required 100 comparisons to locate the number. The binary search, however, required only 6 comparisons.

4. Run the program again. Enter 9, which is the first integer in the array. The binary search requires 6 comparisons. The sequential search located the number in one comparison, because it was the first number in the array.

5. Run the program again. Enter 21. None of the elements in the array contain the integer 21. It takes the binary search 8 comparisons to determine that 21 is not in the array. The sequential search searches the entire array before determining that the value is not in the array. *Note:* In the case of an ordered array, a sequential search could be programmed to stop searching once a value larger than the key is encountered.

6. Run the program additional times trying search values like 39, 161, 252, and 260.

7. Close the source code file.

```cpp
// Binary search function
// Function accepts an array, a range of elements for the search,
// and the number for which we are searching.
void binary_search(int x[100], int lowerbound, int upperbound,
                   int search_num)
{
 int search_pos;
 int compare_count = 1; // Variable used to count the comparisons.

 // Calculate initial search position.
 search_pos = (lowerbound + upperbound) / 2;

 while((x[search_pos] != search_num) && (lowerbound <= upperbound))
  {
    compare_count++;
    if(x[search_pos] > search_num) // If the value in the search
     {                             // position is greater than the number
      upperbound = search_pos - 1; // for which we are searching, change
     }                             // upperbound to the search position
    else                           // minus one.
     {                             // Else, change lowerbound to search
      lowerbound = search_pos + 1; // position plus one.
     }
    search_pos = (lowerbound + upperbound) / 2;
  }
 if(lowerbound <= upperbound)
  {
    cout << "A binary search found the number in "
      << compare_count << " comparisons.\n";
  }
 else
  {
    cout << "Number not found by binary search after "
      << compare_count << " comparisons.\n";
  }
}
```

F I G U R E   1 8 - 6
This function performs a binary search, and counts the number of comparisons required to find the data.

On the Net

For an example of how the sequential and binary searches can be implemented when using a vector class, see http://www.ProgramCPP.com topic 18.2.1.

SECTION 18.2 QUESTIONS

1. When searching a data structure, what is the term for the item upon which the search is based?

2. Describe how a sequential search works.

3. In what case is a sequential search more efficient than a binary search?

4. In a binary search, what formula is used to locate the middle of a 100-element array?

5. Which type of search (sequential or binary) may be conducted without the array being ordered?

PROBLEM 18.2.1

In a paragraph or two, describe how a binary search algorithm functions.

CHAPTER 18, SECTION 3

Searching Binary Trees and Hashing

There are many methods of searching more advanced than the sequential and binary searches of the previous section. In this section you will learn about two advanced search techniques: searching a binary tree and hashing.

SEARCHING BINARY TREES

Searching a binary tree is similar to the binary search of an array. Using a tree, however, gives added flexibility because the data is ordered as the tree is created. Binary trees also have the added benefits of a dynamic data structure, meaning the amount of data can vary each time the program is run, as opposed to arrays that always have to stay the same size.

In the previous chapter, you learned that the search of a binary tree begins at the root. The data stored at the root of the tree is compared to the key. If a match is not found, the search moves down the tree. If the key comes before the value in the root, the left subtree is searched. If the key comes after the value in the root, the right subtree is searched.

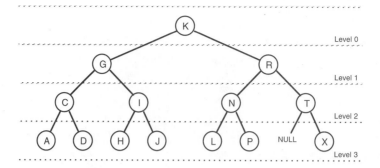

For example, consider the tree in Figure 18-7. To locate node H, the search would begin at the root. Because H comes before K, the node to the left of K (G) is compared next. H comes after G, so the search moves to the node to the right of G (I). Because H comes before I, the node to the left of I is compared. That is where H is found.

Each comparison of data ordered in a binary tree eliminates half of the remaining nodes. There are 14 nodes in the tree. After the first comparison, 7 of the nodes have been eliminated from the search. The second comparison eliminates 4 more, leaving only 3 more possibilities.

The efficiency of a binary tree becomes evident as the number of nodes increases. A four-level tree like the one in Figure 18-7 can have a maximum of 15 nodes. Each added level, however, can accommodate twice the nodes of the level above it. Table 18-1 shows how the maximum number of nodes increases geometrically.

NUMBER OF LEVELS	MAXIMUM NUMBER OF NODES	NUMBER OF LEVELS	MAXIMUM NUMBER OF NODES
1	1	11	2,047
2	3	12	4,095
3	7	13	8,191
4	15	14	16,383
5	31	15	32,767
6	63	16	65,535
7	127	17	131,071
8	255	18	262,143
9	511	19	524,287
10	1,023	20	1,048,575

What is so great about the way the number of nodes increases so quickly with each level of a binary tree? It means that a binary tree is a very efficient way to search a large amount of data. As the table shows, a twenty-level tree could have more than one million nodes. That means that any one of more than a million items in the tree could be located in 20 comparisons or less.

TREE TRAVERSALS

Traversing a tree involves "visiting" every node in the tree. You have experience traversing a linked list. Traversing a tree is a bit more complicated because the nodes are not linear. Let's look at three ways to traverse trees: the in-order

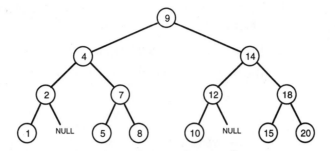

F I G U R E   1 8 - 8
Traversing a tree involves visiting every node in the tree.

traversal, the preorder traversal, and the postorder traversal. For the discussion of these traversal methods, let's use the tree in Figure 18-8.

IN-ORDER TRAVERSALS

An *in-order traversal* visits all the nodes of a tree in its sorted order. The first node visited is the lower-left node of the tree, because that's where the smallest value is found. The traversal works its way back up to the root, and then down the right subtree until the lower-right node is reached. The result of an in-order traversal on the tree in Figure 18-8 results in the nodes being visited in the order below.

1, 2, 4, 5, 7, 8, 9, 10, 12, 14, 15, 18, 20

PREORDER TRAVERSALS

A *preorder traversal* visits the root first, then always goes as far left as it can before traversing to the right. Preorder traversals are useful when working with trees used to aid in evaluating mathematical expressions. The nodes of the tree in Figure 18-8 would be visited in the order below by a preorder traversal.

9, 4, 2, 1, 7, 5, 8, 14, 12, 10, 18, 15, 20

POSTORDER TRAVERSALS

A *postorder traversal* always visits the left node first, then the right node, and then the root. To visualize a postorder traversal, understand that the traversal begins at the node at the lower-left node of the tree, like an in-order traversal. The difference is that before a node is visited, every node below it has been visited from left to right. The last node to be visited is the root. Postorder traversals are also used with trees that aid in evaluating mathematical expressions. The nodes of the tree in Figure 18-8 would be visited in the order below by a postorder traversal.

1, 2, 5, 8, 7, 4, 10, 12, 15, 20, 18, 14, 9

EXERCISE 18-4   TRAVERSING TREES

1. Retrieve *TREE.CPP*. The program that loads allows you to enter a list of names or other strings. The strings are placed in an ordered binary tree.

2. Compile and run the program. Enter at least 10 (but not more than 20) last names as input. Do not enter the names in alphabetical order. The tree will order the data as the tree is created. Enter a blank string to stop the input.

3. The program displays the last names in alphabetical order by doing an in-order traversal. Press Enter to continue.

4. The program displays the last names in preorder. Press Enter to continue.

5. The program displays the last names in postorder. Press Enter to continue.

6. Close the source code file.

On the Net

See an object-oriented version of TREE.CPP *at http://www.ProgramCPP.com. See topic 18.3.1.*

HASHING

Suppose you are assigning seats to people as they enter an auditorium. The goal is to have the youngest people seated at the front of the auditorium, and the oldest people in the back. Your challenge is that you have no control over the order in which people will enter the auditorium. When the first people arrive, you must estimate the proper seating position for each person. When all of the people are seated, you can find people of a given age by looking in a particular section of the auditorium.

Hashing is a method similar to that described above that is sometimes used to arrange records in a data file. When using hashing, a specified field in the record is used as the key for the hash-coding. Computer hashing differs from the example of seating people in an auditorium because the key used in computer hashing must be unique to each record. In other words, no two records can have the same key. In a customer database, a customer number could be used as the key, since no two customers will share a customer number.

Hashing requires that a *hashing algorithm* be used to convert the key to a number that corresponds to the position of the record. Several different hashing algorithms are commonly used. Possibly the most common method is the *division-remainder method,* which involves dividing the key value by a prime or odd number and using the remainder of the division as the relative address for the record.

No hashing algorithm is perfect. You will almost certainly have situations where two key values produce the same result, called a *collision.* Collisions can be solved in a variety of ways. One way is to move forward in the file from the location of the collision until an available location is found. Another popular method involves applying a second hashing algorithm in the event of a collision.

Searching a file ordered by hashing follows a process similar to that which stored the data. The key for which you are searching is converted to a location in the file using the same hashing algorithm that stored the data.

SECTION 18.3 QUESTIONS

1. The search of a binary tree begins at what node?

2. What is the maximum number of nodes in a four-level tree?

3. What type of traversal visits the nodes in sorted order?

4. What type of traversal visits the root last?

5. What is the term that describes the situation in which a hashing algorithm places two records at the same position?

PROBLEM 18.3.1

Draw a binary tree created by adding the following nodes in the order that they appear below.

45, 12, 15, 67, 8, 90, 53

Write the order in which the nodes of the tree would be visited by:

1) an in-order traversal
2) a pre-order traversal
3) a post-order traversal

KEY TERMS

binary search	key
collision	key field
division-remainder method	postorder traversal
exit condition	preorder traversal
hashing	recursion
hashing algorithm	sequential search
in-order traversal	

SUMMARY

➤ Recursion is a programming technique in which a function calls itself. Recursion is used to simplify many programming problems.

➤ A recursive function must have an exit condition that ends the recursive calls.

➤ When searching for specific data in a data structure, the data for which you are searching is called the key. The field being searched is called the key field.

➤ In a sequential search, each record in the database is compared in the order it appears until the desired record is found.

➤ In a binary search, a sorted array is searched by starting in the middle and narrowing the search in a way similar to the way you search for a name in a phone book.

➤ Searching a binary tree is very efficient and has the added flexibility of a dynamic data structure.

> Traversing a tree involves visiting every node in the tree. An in-order traversal visits the nodes in sorted order. A preorder traversal visits the root first, then the left node, then the right node. A postorder traversal visits the left node first, then the right node, then the root.

> Hashing is a search method that processes the key through a hashing algorithm to find the position of the data in a file.

PROJECTS

PROJECT 18-1 • SEARCHING STRINGS SEQUENTIALLY

Write a program that loads an array of strings with names of movies from a data file. The program should allow you to enter a name of a movie, and then perform a sequential search to find the movie you entered.

PROJECT 18-2 • TREE OF INTEGERS

Modify *TREE.CPP* to accept integers, rather than strings.

PROJECT 18-3 • BUILDING A TREE FROM A FILE

Modify the program from Project 18-2 to accept integers from a data file, rather than from the keyboard.

Sorting

Overview

Many computer programs require that data be arranged in a certain order. Rearranging data in alphabetical or numerical order is called *sorting.* One use for sorting is alphabetizing a list of names. Most database programs can sort records by date, state, ZIP code, area code, or other fields that are contained in a record.

Sorting is sometimes necessary to prepare data for a search algorithm. Recall from Chapter 18 that the binary search of an array requires that the array be sorted. A sorting algorithm must be used if the array is unsorted.

As you might guess, there is more than one algorithm you can use to sort data. In this chapter, you will learn about six different sorting algorithms. As you will see, each of the algorithms has advantages and disadvantages.

CHAPTER 19, SECTION 1

Introduction to Sorting Algorithms

Some sorting algorithms described in this chapter are best for sorting linked lists or data files, but most are designed for sorting arrays. In most of our examples we will be sorting arrays of integers, but it is possible to sort virtually any other data type. Before a sorting procedure can begin, the key field and input size must be defined. The *key field* is the field by which the data is sorted. In a simple integer array, every element is a key field. But if we were sorting an array of structures (like the one below) by last name, then **last_name** would be the key field.

```
struct friend_data
  {
  char last_name[20];        // <- key field
  char first_name[15];
  char phone_num[15];
  };
```

The value of the key field is known as the *key value.* The key value of **friend_data** is the string stored in **last_name**. If we were sorting an array such as the one below, the numbers assigned to the array **nums** are all key values.

```
int nums[5] = {20, 31, 17, 47, 14};
```

The number of elements in a list to be sorted is known as the *input size,* because the list itself is input to the sorting procedure. If we were sorting the array **nums**, the input size would be five, because there are five elements in the array.

Each sorting algorithm explained in this chapter was designed with one of two approaches in mind: either an incremental or divide and conquer approach. A sorting algorithm designed with an *incremental approach* is usually characterized by loops that pass through the list, one element at a time. The number of passes through the list varies by algorithm and input size. A sorting algorithm that uses a *divide and conquer approach* splits the original unsorted list into smaller sublists. The sublists are then repeatedly split into even smaller sublists. The smallest sublists are then sorted and combined with other small sorted lists. After all sublists are combined the result is a fully sorted list. Divide and conquer approaches often use recursion.

Linked lists, a file, and other data structures may be sorted as well. In this chapter, the term *list* will apply to the data structure we are sorting, regardless of its type. Generally, it is possible to sort a list only if all elements are of the same type.

SELECTION SORT

The *selection sort* uses an incremental approach to sort a list. The number of times the sort passes through the list depends on the size of the list. The algorithm makes one less pass than the number of items in the list (**input_size - 1**). During each pass, the unsorted element with the smallest or largest key value is moved to its proper position in the list. If the list is to be sorted in *ascending order*, meaning from smallest to largest, the largest key value is moved. If the list is to be sorted in *descending order*, meaning from largest to smallest, the smallest key value is moved.

If we are given the array {54, 39, 90, 18, 27, 63} to sort in descending order with a selection sort, the first thing we know is the input size will be 6. The sort itself begins by passing through the list and sending the element with the smallest value to the end of the array. Figure 19-1 shows the result of the first pass, step-by-step. Notice that a variable named **small** holds the smaller of the two numbers each time a comparison is made.

Each successive pass through the list is similar to the first pass, as the next smallest value is sorted, as shown in Figure 19-2.

(a)
{ 54, 39, 90, 18, 27, 63 }
small = 54

(b)
{54, 39, 90, 18, 27, 63}
small = 39

(c)
{54, 39, 90, 18, 27, 63}
small = 39

(d)
{54, 39, 90, 18, 27, 63}
small = 18

(e)
{54, 39, 90, 18, 27, 63}
small = 18

(f)
{54, 39, 90, 18, 27, 63,}
small = 18

(g)
{54, 39, 90, 63, 27, 18}
18 is switched with 63

F I G U R E   1 9 - 1
The smallest element of the list is found by looking at each item in the list. The smallest element is then exchanged with the last item.

Initial list:	{ 54, 39, 90, 18, 27, 63 }
After Pass 1:	{ 54, 39, 90, *63*, 27, *18* }
After Pass 2:	{ 54, 39, 90, 63, *27*, *18* }
After Pass 3:	{ 54, *63*, 90, *39*, *27*, *18* }
After Pass 4:	{ *90*, 63, *54*, *39*, *27*, *18* }
After Pass 5:	{ 90, *63*, *54*, *39*, *27*, *18* }
After Pass 6:	{ *90*, 63, 54, 39, 27, 18 }

F I G U R E   1 9 - 2
After each pass, the next smallest element is placed into its proper place in the list.

```
// Selection sort procedure. Sorts an array of ints in descending order.
void selection_sort(int input_array[], int input_size)
{
  int i, j;
  int small, temp;

  for (i = input_size - 1; i > 0; i--)
   {
    small = 0;  // Initialize small to first element.

    // Find the smallest element between the positions 1 and i.
    for (j = 1; j <= i; j++)
     {
       if (input_array[j] < input_array[small])
        {
          small = j;
        }
     }
    // Swap the smallest element found with element in position i.
    temp = input_array[small];
    input_array[small] = input_array[i];
    input_array[i] = temp;
   }
}
```

F I G U R E   1 9 - 3
This selection sort function sorts an array of integers in descending order.

A selection sort function is shown in Figure 19-3. Notice that the function **selection_sort** is composed of two loops. There is an inner loop that passes through the list and finds the next smallest value, and an outer loop that places that value into its proper position.

The selection sort is one of the easiest sorts to implement, but is among the least efficient. Selection sort provides no way to end a sort early even if it begins with an already sorted list.

EXERCISE 19-1

SELECTION SORT

1.   Retrieve the file *SELSORT.CPP*.

2.   Compile and run the program.

3.   Change the initial values of the elements of the **nums** array to **{0, -31, 19, 104, 19}**.

4.   Compile and run the program again.

5.   Append the elements {73, -4} to **nums**. To do so, you must change **nums_length** to 7, and the **nums** array declaration length from 5 to 7.

6.   Compile and run the program again.

7.   Save the modified version of the source code as *SELSORT2.CPP* and close.

INSERTION SORT

Like the selection sort, the *insertion sort* uses an incremental approach for sorting lists. Unlike the selection sort, however, the insertion sort passes through the list only once. The insertion sort works similar to the way you might organize a hand of cards. The unsorted cards begin face down on the table and are picked up one by one. As each new unsorted card is picked up, it is inserted into the correct place in your organized hand of cards. The insertion sort works by splitting the list into two sublists. The first sublist, which is always fully sorted, gets larger as the sort progresses. It can be thought of as the hand that holds the organized cards. The second sublist is unsorted and contains all the elements not yet inserted into the first sublist. The second sublist gets smaller as the first sublist gets larger. The second sublist is like the table from where cards are picked up.

Sorting the list {54, 39, 90, 18, 27, 63} in descending order with an insertion sort begins by separating it into the two sublists, as shown below.

First sublist: {*54*}
Second sublist: {39, 90, 18, 27, 63}

Note that the first sublist is sorted, even though it contains only one element, which is the first element of the original list. The algorithm then begins stepping through the second sublist.

For the first step, the first element of the second sublist (39) is placed into its proper position (descending order) into the first sublist and is removed from the second sublist, as shown below.

First sublist: {**54, 39**}
Second sublist: {90, 18, 27, 63}

Next, the first element of the second sublist, 90, is once again inserted into its proper position in the first sublist and removed from the second sublist.

First sublist: {**90, 54, 39**}
Second sublist: {18, 27, 63}

The insertion continues until the second sublist is empty, as shown in the three insertions below.

First sublist: {**90, 54, 39, *18***}
Second sublist: {27, 63}

First sublist: {**90, 54, 39, 27, 18**}
Second sublist: {63}

First sublist: {**90, *63*, 54, 39, 27, 18**}
Second sublist: {}

Figure 19-4 shows an insertion sort function that sorts an array of integers into descending order. The function maintains the two sublists within the same array. Initially, the first element in the array is considered a sorted list, although only one element exists in that list. With each iteration of the loop, the next value in the unsorted portion of the array is placed in the proper position in the sorted portion of the array.

Although insertion sort would not be a very efficient sorting algorithm when used with large lists, it can be a very efficient way to sort small lists. If a list is partially or fully sorted to begin with, then the insertion sort can be very quick.

EXERCISE 19-2 INSERTION SORT

1. Retrieve the file *INSSORT.CPP*.

2. Compile and run the program.

3. Append the elements {35, -10, 35} to the array **nums** and change **nums_length** to 8. Also change the length of the array to 8 to accommodate the three new elements.

4. Compile and run the program again.

5. Save the modified version of the source code as *INSSORT2.CPP* and close.

```
// Insertion sort function. Sorts an array of ints in descending order.
void insertion_sort(int array[], int array_length)
{
  int j, i, key;

  for (j = 1; j < array_length; j++)
   {
     key = array[j];

     // Move all values smaller than key up one position.
     for (i = j - 1; (i >= 0) && (array[i] < key); i--)
       {
         array[i + 1] = array[i];
       }
     array[i + 1] = key;  // insert key into proper position
   }
}
```

FIGURE 19-4
Insertion sort function which sorts an array of ints in descending order.

On the Net

A sort function can be built into a class such as the vector class in order to allow a vector to sort itself when it receives the appropriate message. See an example of this at http://www.ProgramCPP.com. See topic 19.1.1.

SECTION 19.1 QUESTIONS

1. What are the two approaches algorithms use when sorting?

2. Which of the two approaches you identified in question 1 is used by a selection sort?

3. Which of the two approaches you identified in question 1 is most likely to be implemented using recursion?

4. What kind of sort (ascending or descending) would rank salaries from lowest to highest?

5. Suppose the two sublists below are part of a descending insertion sort. After the next item in the second sublist is processed, how will the first sublist appear?

First sublist: { 45 }
Second sublist: { 33, 88, 23, 67 }

6. What sort (selection or insertion) is most efficient when sorting a list which is partially sorted?

PROBLEM 19.1.1

On paper, step through a selection sort of the following list: {2, 4, 9}

Sort the elements in descending order, and write out each step.

PROBLEM 19.1.2

Improve *SELSORT.CPP* by allowing the user to enter any five values they want for **nums**. Save the improved source code file as *SELSORT3.CPP*.

PROBLEM 19.1.3

Rewrite the selection sort procedure (*SELSORT.CPP* or *SELSORT3.CPP*) to sort the array of ints in ascending order. (*Hint:* Change the name of **small** to **large**. Besides that, you will only need to change a single operator.) Save the new source code file as *ASCEND.CPP*.

PROBLEM 19.1.4

Rewrite the selection sort procedure (*SELSORT.CPP* or *SELSORT3.CPP*) to sort an array of floats in ascending order. Save the new source code file as *SORTFLOT.CPP*.

CHAPTER 19, SECTION 2
More Incremental Sorting Algorithms

The selection and insertion sorts you learned in the previous section are examples of incremental sorting algorithms. In this section, you will learn about two more incremental sorting algorithms: the bubble sort and the Shell sort.

BUBBLE SORT

The *bubble sort* gets its name because as elements are sorted they gradually rise to their proper positions, like bubbles rising in water. A bubble sort works by repeatedly comparing adjacent elements of a list, starting with the first and second elements, and swapping them if they are out of order. After the first and second items are compared, the second and third items are compared, and swapped if they are out of order. This continues until the end of the list is reached. When the end is reached, items one and two are compared again, and the process continues until all elements are in their proper positions.

Let's examine how an ascending order bubble sort of the list of integers shown below would occur, step-by-step.

```
{54, 39, 76, 56, 90, 46}
```

The bubble sort begins by comparing the first two elements, 54 and 39. Because the sort is to be done in ascending order, 54 and 39 are exchanged, because 54 is greater.

```
{39, 54, 76, 56, 90, 46} <- 39 exchanged with 54
```

Next, 54 is compared with 76. Since 54 is less than 76, it remains in the same position.

```
{39, 54, 76, 56, 90, 46} <- no exchange (54 < 76)
```

The steps below show what happens as the algorithm continues down the list until the first pass is complete.

```
{39, 54, 56, 76, 90, 46} <- 56 exchanged with 76

{39, 54, 56, 76, 90, 46} <- no exchange (76 < 90)

{39, 54, 56, 76, 46, 90} <- 46 exchanged with 90
```

The number 90 is now in its proper position, at the end of the list (because it is the greatest number).

During the second pass, the process starts again from the beginning of the list. This time, however, we do not need to go all the way down to the very end, because the last item is already correctly sorted. The steps below make up the second pass.

```
{39, 54, 56, 76, 46, 90}  <- no exchange (39 < 54)

{39, 54, 56, 76, 46, 90}  <- no exchange (54 < 56)

{39, 54, 56, 76, 46, 90}  <- no exchange (56 < 76)

{39, 54, 56, 46, 76, 90}  <- 46 exchanged with 76
```

For this next pass, we do not need to do any comparisons with the last tw
ements, because they are both correctly sorted.

```
{39, 54, 56, 46, 76, 90}  <- no exchange (39 < 54)

{39, 54, 56, 46, 76, 90}  <- no exchange (54 < 56)

{39, 54, 46, 56, 76, 90}  <- 46 exchanged with 56
```

In the next pass, the last *three* elements are skipped.

```
{39, 54, 46, 56, 76, 90}  <- no exchange (39 < 54)

{39, 46, 54, 56, 76, 90}  <- 46 exchanged with 54
```

In the final pass, the elements are finally sorted from lowest to highest.

```
{39, 46, 54, 56, 76, 90} <- no exchange (39 < 46)
```

The bubble sort provides a way to end a sort early, if the list is completely partially sorted to begin with. Consider the array below.

```
{17, 75, 67, 54, 37, 29}
```

If we are to sort in descending order, notice that the first element, 17, is out place but all other elements are already in the right order. The lines below illu trate the steps of the first pass.

```
{75, 17, 67, 54, 37, 29}  <- 75 exchanged with 17

{75, 67, 17, 54, 37, 29}  <- 67 exchanged with 17

{75, 67, 54, 17, 37, 29}  <- 54 exchanged with 17

{75, 67, 54, 37, 17, 29}  <- 37 exchanged with 17

{75, 67, 54, 37, 29, 17}  <- 29 exchanged with 17
```

We can see that the whole list is now completely sorted. The bubble sor function, however, is not yet finished. In the next pass, no exchanges take place, indicating that the list is sorted. A bubble sort algorithm should include provisions to terminate the bubble sort early when a pass is made without exchanges occurring.

The function in Figure 19-5 performs a bubble sort on an array of integers. The variable named **flag** is set to zero before each pass. If an exchange occurs during the pass, **flag** is set to one, indicating that another pass is necessary. If **flag** remains zero, indicating to the algorithm that the list is completely sorted, the bubble sort ends.

Although the bubble sort's level of performance is often below that of other sorts, it does provide a way to end early, which can speed up the sort in some instances.

```
// Bubble sort function. Sorts an array of ints in descending order.
void bubble_sort(int array[], int arrayLength)
{
  int i, j, flag = 1;
  int temp;

  for(i = 1; (i <= arrayLength) && flag; i++)
   {
     flag = 0;
     for(j = 0; j < (arrayLength - i); j++)
      {
        if (array[j + 1] > array[j])
         {
            // swap items at
            // positions j + 1 and j:

            temp = array[j + 1];
            array[j + 1] = array[j];
            array[j] = temp;
            flag = 1; // indicate that a swap has occurred
         }
      }
   }
}
```

FIGURE 19-5
A bubble sort function which sorts an array of ints in descending order.

EXERCISE 19-3   BUBBLE SORT

1. Retrieve the file *BUBSORT.CPP*.

2. Compile and run the program.

3. Change the line: **if (array[j + 1] > array[j])** to
   if (array[j + 1] < array[j])

   What is the effect of the change above?

4. Compile and run the program again.

5. Save the modified version of the source code as *BUBSORT2.CPP* and close.

SHELL SORT

The *Shell sort* (named after its inventor D. L. Shell) is similar to the bubble sort, but instead of adjacent elements repeatedly being compared, elements that are a certain distance away from each other (**d** positions away) are repeatedly compared. The value of **d** is initially half the input size and is halved after each pass through the list. Elements are compared and swapped, if necessary, like in a bubble sort.

In a Shell sort in descending order with the list below, **d** would initially equal $(6 + 1) / 2 = 3$.

```
{54, 39, 76, 56, 90, 46}
```

We use the equation $d = (N + 1) / 2$ so d is rounded up and never drops below 1. The value of d is 3 and not 3.5 because numbers after the decimal place in integer calculations are truncated.

The first pass would begin by comparing the first and fourth items (with values 54 and 56) because they are three positions away from each other:

```
{56, 39, 76, 54, 90, 46}   <- 56 exchanged with 54
```

Next, the second and fifth items are compared:

```
{56, 90, 76, 54, 39, 46}   <- 90 exchanged with 39
```

And the pass concludes with comparing the third and sixth items.

```
{56, 90, 76, 54, 39, 46}   <- no exchange (76 > 46)
```

After each pass the value of d is halved (and rounded up), so for the second pass d equals $(3 + 1) / 2 = 2$. Because d now equals 2, during the second pass items two places away from each other are compared:

```
{76, 90, 56, 54, 39, 46}   <- 76 exchanged with 56

{76, 90, 56, 54, 39, 46}   <- no exchange (90 > 54)

{76, 90, 56, 54, 39, 46}   <- no exchange (56 > 39)

{76, 90, 56, 54, 39, 46}   <- no exchange (54 > 46)
```

For the next pass d is halved again, so it now equals 1.

```
{90, 76, 56, 54, 39, 46}   <- 90 exchanged with 76

{90, 76, 56, 54, 39, 46}   <- no exchange (76 > 56)

{90, 76, 56, 54, 39, 46}   <- no exchange (56 > 54)

{90, 76, 56, 54, 39, 46}   <- no exchange (54 > 39)

{90, 76, 56, 54, 46, 39}   <- 46 exchanged with 39
```

We can clearly see that the list is now fully sorted. However, the Shell sort continues until d equals 1 *and* the pass occurs without an exchange.

The value of d cannot drop below 1, so it remains at 1 for the final pass.

```
{90, 76, 56, 54, 46, 39}   <- no exchange (90 > 76)

{90, 76, 56, 54, 46, 39}   <- no exchange (76 > 56)

{90, 76, 56, 54, 46, 39}   <- no exchange (56 > 54)
```

```
{90, 76, 56, 54, 46, 39}   <- no exchange (54 > 46)

{90, 76, 56, 54, 46, 39}   <- no exchange (46 > 39)
```

The Shell sort is now done because **d** equals 1 and the last pass occurred without an exchange.

Although similar to bubble sort in some ways, Shell sort is generally more efficient than the bubble sort. Comparing values that are non-adjacent results in a more efficient algorithm than comparing adjacent values. The function in Figure 19-6 performs a Shell sort on an array of integers.

```cpp
// Shell sort function. Sorts an array of ints in descending order.
void shell_sort(int array[], int arrayLength)
{
  int flag = 1, d = arrayLength, i;
  int temp;

  while (flag || (d > 1))
    {
      flag = 0;
      d = (d + 1) / 2;
      for (i = 0; i < (arrayLength - d); i++)
        {
          if (array[i + d] > array[i])
            {
              // swap items at
              // positions i + d and i:

              temp = array[i + d];
              array[i + d] = array[i];
              array[i] = temp;
              flag = 1; // indicate that a swap has occurred
            }
        }
    }
}
```

FIGURE 19-6
This Shell sort function sorts an array of ints in descending order.

On the Net

Sorting is an important feature of much of the software in use today. There are many types of sorts and variations of the types you have seen. For more about the types of sorts, and to see other sorting algorithms, see http://www.ProgramCPP.com. See topic 19.2.1.

SECTION 19.2 QUESTIONS

1. What type of sort compares adjacent elements in an array?

2. Where does the bubble sort get its name?

3. In the bubble sort function, what is the purpose of the **flag** variable?

4. Is the Shell sort an incremental or divide and conquer sort?

5. How does a Shell sort differ from a bubble sort?

PROBLEM 19.2.1

On paper, step through a bubble sort of {4, 19, 8}. Sort in descending order, and write out each step.

PROBLEM 19.2.2

Modify the bubble sort program from Exercise 19-3 to use a Shell sort function instead of a bubble sort. Save the new source code as *SHELLSRT.CPP*.

CHAPTER 19, SECTION 3
Divide and Conquer Sorting Algorithms

n this section, you will learn about two divide and conquer sorting algorithms: the quicksort and the merge sort.

QUICKSORT

The *quicksort* uses a divide and conquer algorithm and is known to be very efficient. It starts by breaking down the original list into two *partitions* (sections) based on the value of the first item in the list. Because the example below will sort in descending order, the first partition will contain all the elements with values greater than the first item. The second partition will contain elements with values less than or equal to the first element. The first element itself can end up in either partition.

The array below will be partitioned into two partitions.

```
{54, 39, 76, 56, 90, 46}
```

The first of the two partitions will contain all the elements greater than the first element (greater than 54), as shown below.

```
1: {90, 56, 76}
```

The second partition will contain the remaining elements less than or equal to the first element (it happens to contain the first element also).

```
2: {39, 54, 46}
```

If the two partitions are concatenated into one new list we have:

```
{{90, 56, 76}, {39, 54, 46}}
```

Now the lists **{90, 56, 76}** and **{39, 54, 46}** must be sorted, and this is accomplished in exactly the same way as with the original list.

We now partition **{90, 56, 76}** into two new lists:

```
1: {90}

2: {56, 76}
```

The first new list contains the first element, 90. The second list contains 76 and 56 because they are both less than or equal to 90.

Concatenating those two new lists we get:

```
{{90}, {56, 76}}
```

When and only when an element is placed in a partition by itself is it considered to be correctly sorted. Putting all partitions back into the big list we get the following list.

```
{{{90}, {56, 76}}, {39, 54, 46}}
```

In the same manner as above, partitioning **{56, 76}** creates the lists below.

```
1: {76}

2: {56}
```

Placing those partitions back into the full list gives us the list below.

```
{{{90}, {{76}, {56}}}, {39, 54, 46}}
```

Partitioning **{39, 54, 46}** gives the lists below.

```
1: {46, 54}

2: {39}
```

Placing those partitions back into the full list give us the list below.

```
{{{90}, {{76}, {56}}}, {{46, 54}, {39}}}
```

Finally, partitioning **{46, 54}** gives the lists below.

```
1: {54}

2: {46}
```

The full list is shown below. Note that each element is in its own partition. That means the entire list is completely sorted.

```
{{{90}, {{76}, {56}}}, {{{54}, {46}}, {39}}}
```

The quicksort is recognized as being one of the most efficient sorting algorithms. Although with some data it is not always the most efficient, the average quicksort requires very few steps.

A quicksort can be implemented using recursion or a stack. In the exercise that follows, you will run a program that uses a recursive quicksort algorithm.

EXERCISE 19-4   QUICKSORT

1. Retrieve the file *QUIKSORT.CPP*.

2. Compile and run the program.

3. Examine the functions **quicksort** and **partition** carefully.

4. Reverse the positions of the following two lines:

```
quicksort(input_array, top, middle);
quicksort(input_array, middle + 1, bottom);
```

5. Compile and run the program again. Did exchanging the two lines make a difference?

6. Save the modified version of the source code as *QUIKSRT.CPP* and close it.

MERGE SORT

Like quicksort, the *merge sort* is a divide and conquer algorithm. As shown in Figure 19-7, the merge sort begins by placing each element into its own individual list, thus dividing the original list into equal sized parts. The merge sort then combines every two small lists into one list. The lists are merged in a way so that the newly created lists are all sorted. Every two new lists are then merged into a new sorted list. This continues until all smaller lists have been merged into a single list, which is completely sorted.

There are many different ways to implement the merge sort. The example we will present is to use it as an external sort. An *external sort* is designed specifically to sort data in a file. External sorts usually only read a portion of files into memory at one time. An external sort is helpful when sufficient internal memory is a concern and huge amounts of data must be sorted. Because an external sort

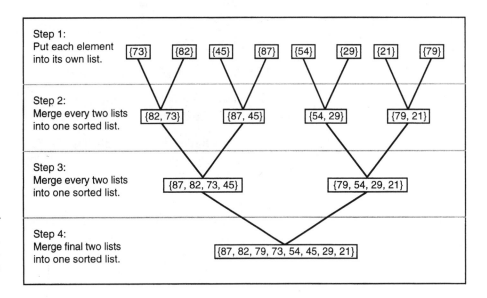

F I G U R E   1 9 - 7
This merge sort example successively combines groups of elements until a single sorted list is achieved.

loads only some data from a file into memory at once it is capable of sorting very large quantities of data while using very little memory. The external merge sort in the example below only loads two elements into memory at once.

The merge sort function uses two files during the intermediate stages of sorting which may be discarded after the sorting process. Our merge sort function begins its multiple passes, ultimately resulting in a list sorted in ascending order by distributing elements of the original file into the two scratch files. The initial file contains:

{38, 93, 48, 84, 79, 77, 28, 80}

Because the data being manipulated is in files, the number of items in the list may be unknown. To create two scratch files, alternate items are placed in each of the two files. In this case, the first, third, fifth, and seventh elements are placed in the first scratch file, and the second, fourth, sixth, and eighth elements are placed into the second scratch file.

First scratch file:	{38}, {48}, {79}, {28}
Second scratch file:	{93}, {84}, {77}, {80}

At this point, each element can be thought of as being in a different sublist.

Next, the sublists are copied back to the original file, beginning with the first elements of each scratch file ({38} and {93}). The elements are merged into the original file.

Merge {38} and {93} yielding the list {38, 93}

This new sublist {38, 93} is copied back to the original file. Because 38 is smaller, and we are sorting in ascending order, 38 is copied from the first scratch file to the original file first. Then 93 is copied from the second scratch file to the original file. Then the next two sublists are merged:

Merge {48} and {84} yielding the list {48, 84}

Here 48 is copied to the original file, then 84.

Merge {79} and {77} yielding the list {77, 79}

In this case 77 is copied before 79.

Merge {28} and {80} yielding the list {28, 80}

Now, at the end of the first pass, the original file contains all of the elements and looks like the list below.

{{38, 93}, {48, 84}, {77, 79}, {28, 80}}

During the next pass, elements are again placed in the scratch files. This time, each newly created sublist from above is copied to the scratch files.

First scratch file:	{38, 93}, {77, 79}
Second scratch file:	{48, 84}, {28, 80}

The first sublists in each scratch file are now merged and copied back to the original file.

First, the sublists {38, 93} and {48, 84} are merged to form {38, 48, 84, 93}. Then {77, 79} and {28, 80} are merged to form {28, 77, 79, 80}. At this point, the merged file contains {38, 48, 84, 93, 28, 77, 79, 80}.

Next, the two new sublists are copied to the scratch files to form the sublists below.

First scratch file: {38, 48, 84, 93}
Second scratch file: {28, 77, 79, 80}

This time through, there is only one merge. The sublists {38, 48, 84, 93} and {28, 77, 79, 80} are merged to form {28, 38, 48, 77, 79, 80, 84, 93}, which is a sorted file.

On the Net

There are several factors to consider when choosing an appropriate sorting algorithm:

1. *Will the data be sorted in RAM or on disk (internal or external sort)? Larger sets of data may have to be sorted on disk, in which case your algorithm options are limited to those designed to sort externally.*
2. *How much data is involved? If the amount of data to be sorted will always be fairly small, any convenient and easy to implement algorithm may be acceptable. It is not worth spending too much time choosing just the right algorithm if there is not much to gain in speed or performance.*
3. *How often will the sort be called? A small amount of data may sort so quickly that the algorithm you use seems unimportant. If the sort occurs regularly in the program, however, a more efficient algorithm may pay off.*
4. *In what condition is the data generally presented to the sorting algorithm? Some algorithms perform well on data which is highly "out of sorts," while others perform better on data that is partially or almost completely sorted.*

Appendix E discusses how algorithms (including sorting algorithms) are analyzed. To learn more about analyzing sorts and choosing the best sorting algorithm for the job, see http://www.ProgramCPP.com. See topic 19.3.1.

SECTION 19.3 QUESTIONS

1. Which of the divide and conquer sort algorithms mentioned in this section is often used to sort data in a file?

2. What are two ways the quicksort can be implemented?

3. What type of sort breaks down the original list into two partitions as a first step?

4. What type of sort puts each element of the list into its own sublist as a first step?

5. What distinguishes an external sort from an internal sort?

PROBLEM 19.3.1

On paper, draw a diagram similar to Figure 19-7 that illustrates an ascending merge sort of the list {64, 79, 43, 85, 51, 27, 19, 77}.

ascending order	key field
bubble sort	key value
descending order	merge sort
divide and conquer approach	partition
external sort	quicksort
incremental approach	selection sort
input size	Shell sort
insertion sort	sorting

SUMMARY

➤ Arrays, linked lists, binary trees, or any other collection of homogeneous objects may be sorted.

➤ Before sorting a list, you must first choose the key field. Records or elements are sorted based upon the values contained in the key field.

➤ An incremental approach to sorting generally iterates through the elements of a list slowly putting elements in their proper positions.

➤ A divide and conquer approach to sorting repeatedly breaks the unsorted list down into smaller lists until each small list is sorted. Divide and conquer algorithms often use recursion.

➤ A selection sort uses an incremental approach to sort lists. After the first pass through the list, the element with the largest key value is sorted. After each successive pass, the next largest element is put in its proper position until all elements are sorted.

➤ An insertion sort uses an incremental approach and sorts elements the same way one might sort a hand of cards. The list is passed through only once and as each element is reached it is placed in its proper position in a sorted list.

➤ A bubble sort works incrementally by repeatedly comparing adjacent elements of an array, starting with the first and second elements, and swapping them if they are out of order.

➤ A Shell sort is similar to bubble sort but instead of comparing adjacent elements it compares elements d positions away from each other. d initially is equal to half the length of the list and is halved after each iteration.

➤ A quicksort uses a divide and conquer approach and works by repeatedly breaking the list into partitions until each partition contains a single element.

➤ A merge sort merges small sorted lists into larger sorted lists. New lists are repeatedly merged until there is one large list.

➤ An external sort usually sorts files. External sorts load only a limited number of elements into memory at a time.

PROJECTS

PROJECT 19-1 • SORTING STRUCTURES

Rewrite the selection sort procedure to sort an array of **friend_data** by last name. Don't worry if more than one friend has the same last name.

```
struct friend_data
  {
  char last_name[20];// key field
  char first_name[15];
  char phone_num[15];
  };
```

PROJECT 19-2 • SORTING STRINGS

Write a program that asks the user to enter eight strings. Begin by using a bubble sort to alphabetize the strings. Insert a counter variable into the bubble sort routine itself to see how many iterations are needed to sort the strings. Rewrite the program using an insertion sort, and later try a selection sort. In each instance use a counter variable to see how many iterations took place.

PROJECT 19-3 • SORTING INTEGERS

Write a program that reads 50 integers from a data file and stores them in memory. Use a quicksort to sort the integers in descending order. After sorting is complete, write the integers back to the file.

PROJECT 19-4 • COMBINING SORTING WITH SEARCHING

Extend Project 19-3 to ask the user to enter an integer. After the sort is complete, try to find the number using a binary search, reporting the position of the integer if it is found. If the integer is not found then report that the search was unsuccessful.

PROJECT 19-5 • SORTING LINKED LISTS

Modify the program *COUNTIES.CPP* from Chapter 16 to sort the county data after the user is finished entering data. Use your own merge sort implementation to sort the county data, which is a linked list data structure. Instead of two scratch files, use two scratch linked lists.

PROJECT 19-6 • SECURITY

Suppose you are writing a program that verifies user IDs for a computer system. Your part of the project involves sorting an array of user IDs so that a binary search can be performed on the array when a user enters his or her ID.

Write a program that sorts an array of user IDs. Each element of the array should allow up to eight characters and the null terminator. Use any of the sorting algorithms to which you have access.

When you have completed and tested the sorting algorithm, extend the program to perform a binary search for a user ID provided at a prompt. The program should report whether the user ID is found or not. If desired, you may extend the program further to associate a password with each user ID.

Computer Programming Careers

By Annabelle Benin

Many job opportunities exist today in computer-related fields; choosing one that suits your interests may become a difficult task. One area that might be considered may be computer programming. Computer programmers are in high demand and are needed to keep up with the fast-paced developing world of computer technology. Computer programming with a technical or engineering emphasis is becoming more popular. Having the proper education and training will allow you to fully experience this fascinating profession and enjoy what its future has to offer.

Obtaining a proper education is a good base in any computer-related field, especially those in professional-level positions. As these professions mature, an undergraduate degree in computer science is becoming the standard certification for acceptance into many positions, particularly those with a technical or systems emphasis. As more students enter this growing field with formal computer science degrees, competition will be expected. Employers are looking for individuals who have outstanding grades or possess applicable work experience. Emphasis in mathematics and learning as much as possible about computers and computing in high school will prove extremely helpful in future years.

English courses that emphasize writing will be extremely important, as good communication skills will be needed in college and future jobs. Developing good study habits and planning early for college will also provide an edge. Starting early and getting ahead is very beneficial in entering the highly competitive and challenging field of computer technology.

Many opportunities are open to those who are willing to work hard and strive to succeed. One area that might be considered is software engineering. Software engineers provide efficient methods of approaching design, development, and maintenance of large software systems. They use various methods to control the high cost of software, and create programs that account for the continuous change in real-world situations.

Another occupation that may be considered is engineering and/or scientific applications programming. These programmers work in scientific or engineering environment design, coding, testing, and debugging programs to solve specific technical problems. They also help to develop hardware, software, and input/output specifications for computer systems applied to science and engineering.

Still another field to explore may be in systems software programming. Systems programmers specify, design, and develop operating systems, compilers, assemblers, debuggers, utility and database management programs, and other software that directs entire computer systems and enables applications programs to be processed. They also install, debug, and maintain systems software in use. No matter which area of study you choose to pursue, computer programming in technical and engineering fields remains highly challenging and competitive.

The future outlook for these programmers is very promising. The field has a steady growth of employment for all sections of the computer industry, and is ranked among the top twenty fastest-growing occupations of today. Employers are becoming more selective and competition is becoming intense. A sizable salary accompanies this growing interest as computer programmers are generally seen as the most highly paid individuals in the U.S. today. The profession virtually has no limitations and the rate at which discoveries and developments are being made is mind-boggling.

Starting early and obtaining the proper education will provide good preparation in order to fully experience all that computer-related professions have to offer. The future of technical and engineering areas looks promising, although acquisition of actual jobs may be competitive. Many diverse and equally satisfying careers are available in this fast-paced, growing profession, and many people find their work very rewarding.

Annabelle Benin is a Junior at Oak Forest High School, Oak Forest, Illinois.

Overview

This case study will guide you through the development of an object-oriented program. The program we will analyze in this case study is a simulated FM radio. The program consists of multiple objects comparable to the objects that compose a real radio. Our simulated radio will consist of a power switch, a volume knob, a tuning knob, an amplifier, a tuner, and a display. Each of these components will be implemented as objects in our program. The switches and knobs are simple objects. The amplifier, tuner, and display are more complicated objects, but their responsibilities are easily described and implemented.

Designing the Objects

To design each of the objects that make up the radio, you must decide what data and functions each object will contain. Next, you will determine what messages will be exchanged among the objects in order to make the objects function together.

Because the radio consists of several small objects, the bottom up design method will be used. Each of the objects will be created and tested before they are combined to make the radio. This approach is much like how you would work on objects in the real world. Each part must be completed before the parts can come together to form a final product.

We will begin by designing the basic objects of the radio: the toggle switch, knobs, amplifier, tuner, and display.

TOGGLE SWITCH

The radio has one switch to turn the power on and off. A switch's responsibility is to open or close a circuit. Therefore, the toggle switch object needs a member to store its current state and methods to toggle and report the current state of the switch.

KNOBS

The radio object has two knobs, one for the volume and one for tuning in the desired station. A knob is a device that has a position between an upper and a lower bound. Because the bounds will change depending on how the object is being used, the upper and lower bounds will be set by the programmer who instantiates a knob object from the knob class.

For a knob object to perform its responsibilities, it needs a member that stores the knob's current position, its upper bound, and its lower bound. A knob object needs methods to turn it clockwise, turn it counterclockwise, and check its current position.

AMPLIFIER

In an actual radio, the job of the amplifier is to power the speakers with the proper volume level. In our simulator, the amplifier has two properties. The amplifier can be on or off and it has an amplification level. The power switch will turn the amplifier on or off and the volume knob will set the amplifier's volume level.

The amplifier needs members that indicate whether it is on and what its amplification level is. The amplifier's methods will turn the device on and off, change the amplification level, and check the current amplification level.

TUNER

Much like the amplifier, the tuner has two properties: the state of being turned on or off and the frequency to which it is currently tuned. Therefore, it needs members that have the current power status and the current frequency. The tuner requires methods to turn the device on and off, set the frequency, and check the current frequency.

DISPLAY

Although the display on a typical radio is a complicated electronic object, its responsibility is very simple: displaying information. But, like the amplifier and tuner, it can be on or off, so it needs members that indicate its current power status and the current message being displayed. In addition to methods needed to turn the device on and off, the object needs methods to set the current message and display the current message.

THE RADIO OBJECT

The radio object will contain each of the objects discussed above. All of the objects which are normally accessible by the user of a radio will be in the public section of the object. The amplifier, tuner, and display will be in the private section of the object. The radio object should not have any other members. However, it does need a method to display the status of all the components in the radio and a method to tell the radio to update all the components when a change has been made.

THE INTERFACE

The interface to the radio will be provided through a small program that displays a menu and allows the user to change a property of the radio or display the current status of the radio.

Coding and Testing the Objects

Now that all the objects have been designed, they must be coded and tested. Because the coding has been done for you in this case study, we will compile and run the program and then analyze it piece by piece.

EXERCISE VI-1

1. Create a new project with your compiler and add the following files:

OORADIO.CPP	TUNER.H
RADIO.H	TUNER.CPP
RADIO.CPP	KNOB.H
AMP.H	KNOB.CPP
AMP.CPP	TSWITCH.H
DISPLAY.H	TSWITCH.CPP
DISPLAY.CPP	ON_OFF.H

2. Compile and run *OORADIO.CPP*. Notice the change in the display when the power is on versus when it is off.

3. Set the tuner and volume, then turn the power off. Without exiting the program, turn the power back on and check the tuner and volume settings.

4. Turn the power off and exit the program.

TOGGLE SWITCH

When designing the switch we determined that it needed a member to indicate its current state and methods to toggle its current state and to report its current state. The header file containing the class definition for a toggle switch object is shown in Figure VI-1.

```
// TSWITCH.H
// Toggle switch class definition

#ifndef _TOGGLE_SWITCH_H
#define _TOGGLE_SWITCH_H

#include "on_off.h" // defines the constants ON and OFF

class ToggleSwitch
{
  public:
    ToggleSwitch(); // constructor
    ToggleSwitch(int StartingState); // constructor with init
    ToggleSwitch(ToggleSwitch & ts); // copy constructor

    void ChangeState();  // toggle the switch
    int  CurrentState(); // return current switch position

  private:
    int SwitchState; // stores the current switch position
};

#endif
```

F I G U R E   V I - 1
The toggle switch class holds a value of on or off and allows itself to be toggled.

The header file *ON_OFF.H* is included so that the constants **ON** and **OFF** will be defined. This header file is included in several of the classes in this case study. The source code for *ON_OFF.H* is shown in Figure VI-2.

```
#ifndef _ON_OFF_H
#define _ON_OFF_H

const int OFF = 0;
const int ON  = 1;

#endif
```

F I G U R E   V I - 2
This header file allows the classes to use the constants ON and OFF to represent 1 and 0.

The implementation of the toggle switch class (shown in Figure VI-3) is also straightforward. It includes a standard constructor that initializes the switch to off. It also includes a constructor that allows you to set the original switch position.

The method that toggles the position of the switch (shown again below) uses the logical **not** operator to efficiently change the state of the switch. If the switch

```
// TSWITCH.CPP
// Toggle switch class implementation

#include "TSWITCH.H"

// Constructor
ToggleSwitch::ToggleSwitch()
:SwitchState(OFF)
{
}

// Constructor that allows you to specify the original
// state of the switch
ToggleSwitch::ToggleSwitch(int StartingState)
:SwitchState(StartingState)
{
}

// Copy constructor
ToggleSwitch::ToggleSwitch(ToggleSwitch & ts)
:SwitchState(ts.SwitchState)
{
}

// Method that toggles the position of the switch
void ToggleSwitch::ChangeState()
{
  SwitchState = !SwitchState;
}

// Method that returns the current state of the switch
int ToggleSwitch::CurrentState()
{
  return(SwitchState);
}
```

F I G U R E   V I - 3
The implementation of the toggle switch class reveals the simplicity of the object.

is on, the **not** operation will change the state of the switch to off. If the switch is off, the **not** operation will change the state of the switch to on.

```
// Method that toggles the position of the switch
void ToggleSwitch::ChangeState()
{
   SwitchState = !SwitchState;
}
```

KNOBS

The knob object has three members: one to hold the current position, one to hold the minimum position, and one to hold the maximum position. Following the design, the class has three methods: one to turn the knob clockwise, one to turn the knob counterclockwise, and one that returns the current position. The definition of the knob class is shown in Figure VI-4.

```
// KNOB.H
// Knob class definition

#ifndef _KNOB_H
#define _KNOB_H

class Knob
{
  public:
    Knob(int UpperBound, int LowerBound); // constructor
    Knob(Knob & k);  // copy constructor

    void TurnClockwise();        // turn knob to the right
    void TurnCounterClockwise(); // turn knob to the left
    int  CurrentPosition();      // return current knob position

  private:
    int Current,  // current knob position
    Minimum,      // minimum allowed knob position
    Maximum;      // maximum allowed knob position
};

#endif
```

FIGURE VI-4
Allowing the range of the knob to be set for each object helps make the knob class reusable.

The constructor in the knob class requires that the minimum and maximum values be provided. The same knob class will be used to create knobs for the radio's volume control and the tuner (station selector). The implementation of the knob class is shown in Figure VI-5.

```
// KNOB.CPP
// Knob class implementation

#include "knob.h"
```

FIGURE VI-5
The knob class will be used to instantiate two different knobs.

(continues)

```
// Constructor
Knob::Knob(int LowerBound, int UpperBound)
:Minimum(LowerBound), Maximum(UpperBound), Current(LowerBound)
{
}


// Copy constructor
Knob::Knob(Knob & k)
:Minimum(k.Minimum), Maximum(k.Maximum), Current(k.Current)
{
}


// Method that turns the knob clockwise by one notch unless
// the upper bound has been reached
void Knob::TurnClockwise()
{
  if(Current < Maximum)
    Current++;
}


// Method that turns the knob counterclockwise by one notch
// unless the lower bound has been reached
void Knob::TurnCounterClockwise()
{
  if(Current > Minimum)
    Current--;
}


// Method that returns the current knob position
int Knob::CurrentPosition()
{
  return(Current);
}
```

FIGURE VI-5
Continued.

If an attempt is made to turn the knob beyond the minimum or maximum settings, the value does not change. Before the current setting is incremented or decremented in the object, the current position is checked against the bounds to make sure the knob has not reached the upper or lower bound.

AMPLIFIER

The class definition for the amplifier is shown in Figure VI-6.

```
// AMP.H
// Amplifier class definition

#ifndef _AMPLIFIER_H
#define _AMPLIFIER_H
```

FIGURE VI-6
The amplifier class can be on or off and holds an amplifier volume setting.

(continues)

```
#include "on_off.h" // defines the constants ON and OFF

class Amplifier
{
  public:
    Amplifier(); // constructor

    void On();                  // turn amplifier on
    void Off();                 // turn amplifier off
    void Volume(int NewVolume); // set amplifier volume
    int  CurrentVolume();       // return current volume

  private:
    int power, // power status (on or off)
    volume;    // volume level
};

#endif
```

F I G U R E   V I - 6
Continued.

The class uses separate methods for turning the amplifier on and off. The third method sets the amplifier volume, and the **CurrentVolume** method returns the current volume of the amplifier. The implementation is shown in Figure VI-7.

```
// AMP.CPP
// Amplifier class implementation

#include "amp.h"

// Constructor
Amplifier::Amplifier()
:power(OFF), volume(0)
{
}

// Method that turns on the amplifier
void Amplifier::On()
{
  power = ON;
}

// Method that turns off the amplifier
void Amplifier::Off()
{
  power = OFF;
}

// Method that sets a new amplifier volume
void Amplifier::Volume(int NewVolume)
{
  if(power == ON)
```

F I G U R E   V I - 7
The implementation of the amplifier simulator is also straightforward.

(continues)

```
      volume = NewVolume;
}


// Method that returns the current volume setting
int Amplifier::CurrentVolume()
{
  return(volume);
}
```

F I G U R E   V I - 7
Continued.

The amplifier's constructor (shown again below) accepts no arguments. When instantiated, the amplifier is initialized as being off and having a volume setting of zero.

```
// Constructor
Amplifier::Amplifier()
:power(OFF), volume(0)
{
}
```

TUNER

The tuner class is similar to the amplifier class. The amplifier can be on or off and can have a frequency (station dial position) passed to it. The class definition is shown in Figure VI-8.

```
// TUNER.H
// Tuner class definition

#ifndef _TUNER_H
#define _TUNER_H

#include "on_off.h"  // defines the constants ON and OFF

class Tuner
{
  public:
    Tuner();  // constructor

    void  On();  // turn tuner on
    void  Off(); // turn tuner off
    void  Frequency(float NewFrequency); // set tuner frequency
    float CurrentFrequency(); // return current tuner frequency

  private:
    int power;          // power status (on or off)
    float frequency; // stores tuner frequency
};

#endif
```

F I G U R E   V I - 8
Our simulated tuner needs only to store the status of its power and the frequency of the current radio station.

The implementation of the class is shown in Figure VI-9.

```cpp
// TUNER.CPP
// Tuner class implementation

#include "tuner.h"

// Constructor
Tuner::Tuner()
:power(OFF), frequency(0.0)
{
}

// Method to turn the tuner on
void Tuner::On()
{
  power = ON;
}

// Method to turn the tuner off
void Tuner::Off()
{
  power = OFF;
}

// Method to set the tuner to a new frequency
void Tuner::Frequency(float NewFrequency)
{
  if(power == ON)
    frequency = NewFrequency;
}

// Method to return the current frequency
float Tuner::CurrentFrequency()
{
  return(frequency);
}
```

FIGURE VI-9
The tuner class is similar to the amplifier class.

DISPLAY

The display on an actual radio constantly displays the station and other information as long as the radio is on. Because our radio is a simple simulation, the display class will display only the current frequency. The radio class will display the status of the other components of the radio. The class definition is shown in Figure VI-10.

```
// DISPLAY.H
// Radio display class definition

#ifndef _DISPLAY_H
#define _DISPLAY_H

#include <iostream.h>
#include <iomanip.h>
#include <string.h>
#include "on_off.h"   // defines the constants ON and OFF

class Display
{
  public:
    Display();  // constructor

    void On();  // turn display on
    void Off(); // turn display off
    void FrequencyToDisplay(float value); // set message
    void DisplayMessage(ostream &); // display message

  private:
    int    power;      // power status (on or off)
    float  MyValue;    // frequency value for display
};

#endif
```

FIGURE VI-10
The display class displays the radio's tuner setting.

The display class demonstrates how output streams can be passed to an object. Look at the implementation in Figure VI-11. Notice how the **DisplayMessage** method allows you to pass an output stream, such as **cout**, to the function. The function outputs the frequency setting to whatever output stream is passed to the function. By making it possible to pass the output stream, the same object can be used to print to the screen or to an output file or other output device.

```
// DISPLAY.CPP
// Display class implementation

#include "display.h"

// Constructor
Display::Display()
:power(OFF), MyValue(0.0)
{
}

// Method that turns on the radio's display
```

(continues)

FIGURE VI-11
The display class allows the message to be sent to any output stream.

```
void Display::On()
{
  power = ON;
}


// Method that turns off the radio's display
void Display::Off()
{
  power = OFF;
}


// Method that creates the message for displaying the
// tuner frequency
void Display::FrequencyToDisplay(float value)
{
  MyValue = value;
}


// Method that displays the tuner frequency
void Display::DisplayMessage(ostream & out)
{
  out.setf(ios::fixed); // prevent E-notation
  out << setprecision(1) << MyValue << " MHz";
  out.unsetf(ios::fixed);
}
```

FIGURE VI-11
Continued.

RADIO OBJECT

The radio object includes instances of all of the other classes we have analyzed in this case study. Therefore, the radio object is an example of containment. The radio object does not inherit the properties of the other objects. It does, however, contain instances of the other objects. For example, you cannot say that the radio *is a* knob, but the radio *has a* knob. The radio class definition is shown in Figure VI-12.

```
// RADIO.H
// Radio class definition

#ifndef _RADIO_H
#define _RADIO_H

#include <iostream.h>
#include "on_off.h"   // defines the constants ON and OFF
#include "tswitch.h"  // toggle switch class
#include "knob.h"     // knob class
#include "amp.h"      // amplifier class
```

FIGURE VI-12
The radio object is an example of
containment.

(continues)

```
#include "tuner.h"    // tuner class
#include "display.h" // display class

class Radio
{
  public:
    Radio(); // constructor

    void Update();  // updates the status of components
    void DisplayStatus(ostream &);  // displays radio status

    ToggleSwitch Power;  // power switch
    Knob Volume,         // volume knob
         Frequency;      // tuner knob

  private:
    Amplifier    MyAmp;     // amplifier
    Tuner        MyTuner;   // tuner
    Display      MyDisplay; // radio display
};


    #endif
```

F I G U R E   V I - 1 2
Continued.

Because the radio object contains all of the previously created objects, it needs to know what members and methods they have and how they work. Therefore, the header files for all of the objects used in the radio object must be included in the definition.

The radio object instantiates one toggle switch object to be the power switch, two knobs (one for volume and one for the channel), an amplifier object, a tuner object, and a display object. To keep the object simple, there are only two methods and one constructor. One method updates the components of the radio to match the knob and switch settings. The other method displays the status of the radio's components. The implementation of the radio class is shown in Figure VI-13.

```
// RADIO.CPP
// Radio class implementation

#include "radio.h"

// Constructor for radio object
Radio::Radio()
:Power(OFF), Volume(1,10), Frequency(1,103)
{
}

// Method to update the status of the radio object
void Radio::Update()
{
```

F I G U R E   V I - 1 3
The radio class is responsible for making the components of the radio work together.

(continues)

```
      if(Power.CurrentState() == OFF)
      { // If power is off, make sure each component is off
        MyAmp.Off();
        MyTuner.Off();
        MyDisplay.Off();
      }
      else
      { // If power is on, make sure each component is on
        MyAmp.On();
        MyTuner.On();
        MyDisplay.On();

        // Set volume to the current volume knob position
        MyAmp.Volume(Volume.CurrentPosition());
        // Set frequency to the current tuner knob position
        MyTuner.Frequency( (Frequency.CurrentPosition() * 0.2) + 87.3 );
        // Set display message to reflect current frequency
        MyDisplay.FrequencyToDisplay( MyTuner.CurrentFrequency());
      }
    }


    // Method to display the current status of the radio
    void Radio::DisplayStatus(ostream & out)
    {
      Update(); // Execute Update method to ensure that all
                // components are operating at current knob settings.
      if(Power.CurrentState() == OFF)
      {                             // If power is off,
        out << "Radio:" << endl     // display message indicating
          << "------"  << endl     // that the power is off.
          << "Power: OFF" << endl
          << endl;
      }
      else
      {
        out.setf(ios::fixed);       // If power is on,
        out << "Radio:" << endl     // display current settings.
          << "------" << endl
          << "Power: ON" << endl
          << "Volume: " << MyAmp.CurrentVolume() << endl
          << "Frequency: " << setprecision(1) << MyTuner.CurrentFrequency()
          << endl << "Display: [ ";
        out.unsetf(ios::fixed);

        MyDisplay.DisplayMessage(cout);  // Activate the radio's display

        out    << " ]" << endl << endl;
      }
    }
```

FIGURE VI-13
Continued.

The constructor for the radio class (shown again below) initializes the radio's power to off and sets the ranges for the volume and tuner knobs. The volume is a straightforward range of 1 to 10. The tuner knob allows a range of 1 to 103. These values do not directly relate to the frequency of FM radio stations. The FM stations range from approximately 87.5 to 107.9. A formula will be used to convert the knob position to a station in the acceptable range of stations.

```
// Constructor for radio object
Radio::Radio()
:Power(OFF), Volume(1,10), Frequency(1,103)
{
}
```

The **Update** method reacts based on the position of the power switch. If the power is off, the function makes sure that all of the radio's components are off. If the power is on, the code shown again below is executed.

```
{ // If power is on, make sure each component is on
  MyAmp.On();
  MyTuner.On();
  MyDisplay.On();

  // Set volume to the current volume knob position
  MyAmp.Volume(Volume.CurrentPosition());
  // Set frequency to the current tuner knob position
  MyTuner.Frequency( (Frequency.CurrentPosition() * 0.2) + 87.3 );
  // Set display message to reflect current frequency
  MyDisplay.FrequencyToDisplay( MyTuner.CurrentFrequency());
}
```

First, the program makes sure that the amplifier, tuner, and display are turned on. Then statements are executed to set the amplifier, tuner, and display to the appropriate values. To set the tuner frequency, the knob setting is multiplied by 0.2 and added to 87.3. Because the knob ranges from 1 to 103, the resulting frequency range is 87.5 to 107.9, and the stations increment in steps of 0.2.

The **DisplayStatus** method also reacts based on the power switch position. If the power is off, a message to that effect is displayed. If the power is on, the status of each device is reported and the display object is activated to display the station.

THE OORADIO PROGRAM

The *OORADIO.CPP* program (see Figure VI-14) is a procedural program that makes use of the radio object. Recall that C++ is considered to be a hybrid language rather than a strictly object-oriented language. The *OORADIO.CPP* program instantiates a radio object, but defines no class itself. Notice also that *OORADIO.CPP* includes only **iostream.h** and **radio.h**. We do not have to include the classes that the radio object uses.

```
// OORADIO.CPP
// Object-Oriented Radio Case Study
// Written by Greg Buxkemper
//

#include <iostream.h>
```

F I G U R E   V I - 1 4
The *OORADIO.CPP* program instantiates a radio object and communicates with it through messages.

(continues)

```
#include "radio.h"

void DisplayMenu();

int main()
{
  int    MenuChoice;
  Radio MyRadio;      // instantiate radio object

  do{
      DisplayMenu();
      cout << "Choice: ";
      cin >> MenuChoice;
      cout << endl;

      switch(MenuChoice)
      {
         case 0 :  break;
         case 1 :  MyRadio.Power.ChangeState();
            break;
         case 2 :  MyRadio.Volume.TurnClockwise();
            break;
         case 3 :  MyRadio.Volume.TurnCounterClockwise();
            break;
         case 4 :  MyRadio.Frequency.TurnClockwise();
            break;
         case 5 :  MyRadio.Frequency.TurnCounterClockwise();
            break;
         case 6 :  MyRadio.DisplayStatus(cout);
            cout << endl;
            break;
         default:  cout << "Choice is not valid." << endl;
            break;
      }
   }while(MenuChoice != 0);

  return 0;
}

void DisplayMenu()
{
  cout << " 0 - Quit" << endl
       << " 1 - Toggle Power Switch" << endl
       << " 2 - Turn Volume Knob Up" << endl
       << " 3 - Turn Volume Knob Down" << endl
       << " 4 - Turn Frequency Knob Up" << endl
       << " 5 - Turn Frequency Knob Down" << endl
       << " 6 - View Radio Information" << endl;
}
```

FIGURE VI-14
Continued.

The program iterates until the user chooses to quit the program. A simple menu gives the user the options for operating the radio, and then appropriate messages are sent to the radio object to handle the user's requests.

Modifying the Program

ere are some suggestions for modifying or extending the program.

1. Add error checking to the amplifier and tuner. Currently, the knobs and the radio object set the limits as to what the amplifier and tuner will accept as values. A better approach may be to allow the amplifier and tuner to set their own limits to ensure that the user of the amplifier and tuner objects does not misuse the objects.

2. Add the ability to have preset stations. You may want to allow the user to program the letters A, B, and C to change frequency to preset stations. You may even want to save the preset station information to a file to preserve it for the next time the program is run.

3. Add a graphical user interface. If the system on which you are programming allows you to create graphical user interfaces, you may want to put a "pretty face" on the program. You could also change the program to automatically update the display each time a control is accessed.

ASCII CHARACTER	DECIMAL	HEXADECIMAL	BINARY
NUL	0	00	000 0000
SOH	1	01	000 0001
STX	2	02	000 0010
ETX	3	03	000 0011
EOT	4	04	000 0100
ENQ	5	05	000 0101
ACK	6	06	000 0110
BEL	7	07	000 0111
BS	8	08	000 1000
HT	9	09	000 1001
LF	10	0A	000 1010
VT	11	0B	000 1011
FF	12	0C	000 1100
CR	13	0D	000 1101
SO	14	0E	000 1110
SI	15	0F	000 1111
DLE	16	10	001 0000
DC1	17	11	001 0001
DC2	18	12	001 0010
DC3	19	13	001 0011
DC4	20	14	001 0100
NAK	21	15	001 0101
SYN	22	16	001 0110
ETB	23	17	001 0111
CAN	24	18	001 1000
EM	25	19	001 1001
SUB	26	1A	001 1010
ESC	27	1B	001 1011
FS	28	1C	001 1100
GS	29	1D	001 1101
RS	30	1E	001 1110
US	31	1F	001 1111
space	32	20	010 0000
!	33	21	010 0001
"	34	22	010 0010
#	35	23	010 0011
$	36	24	010 0100
%	37	25	010 0101
&	38	26	010 0110
'	39	27	010 0111
(	40	28	010 1000
)	41	29	010 1001
*	42	2A	010 1010
+	43	2B	010 1011
,	44	2C	010 1100

ASCII CHARACTER	DECIMAL	HEXADECIMAL	BINARY
-	45	2D	010 1101
.	46	2E	010 1110
/	47	2F	010 1111
0	48	30	011 0000
1	49	31	011 0001
2	50	32	011 0010
3	51	33	011 0011
4	52	34	011 0100
5	53	35	011 0101
6	54	36	011 0110
7	55	37	011 0111
8	56	38	011 1000
9	57	39	011 1001
:	58	3A	011 1010
;	59	3B	011 1011
<	60	3C	011 1100
=	61	3D	011 1101
>	62	3E	011 1110
?	63	3F	011 1111
@	64	40	100 0000
A	65	41	100 0001
B	66	42	100 0010
C	67	43	100 0011
D	68	44	100 0100
E	69	45	100 0101
F	70	46	100 0110
G	71	47	100 0111
H	72	48	100 1000
I	73	49	100 1001
J	74	4A	100 1010
K	75	4B	100 1011
L	76	4C	100 1100
M	77	4D	100 1101
N	78	4E	100 1110
O	79	4F	100 1111
P	80	50	101 0000
Q	81	51	101 0001
R	82	52	101 0010
S	83	53	101 0011
T	84	54	101 0100
U	85	55	101 0101
V	86	56	101 0110
W	87	57	101 0111
X	88	58	101 1000
Y	89	59	101 1001
Z	90	5A	101 1010

ASCII CHARACTER	DECIMAL	HEXADECIMAL	BINARY
[	91	5B	101 1011
\	92	5C	101 1100
]	93	5D	101 1101
^	94	5E	101 1110
_	95	5F	101 1111
`	96	60	110 0000
a	97	61	110 0001
b	98	62	110 0010
c	99	63	110 0011
d	100	64	110 0100
e	101	65	110 0101
f	102	66	110 0110
g	103	67	110 0111
h	104	68	110 1000
i	105	69	110 1001
j	106	6A	110 1010
k	107	6B	110 1011
l	108	6C	110 1100
m	109	6D	110 1101
n	110	6E	110 1110
o	111	6F	110 1111
p	112	70	111 0000
q	113	71	111 0001
r	114	72	111 0010
s	115	73	111 0011
t	116	74	111 0100
u	117	75	111 0101
v	118	76	111 0110
w	119	77	111 0111
x	120	78	111 1000
y	121	79	111 1001
z	122	7A	111 1010
{	123	7B	111 1011
l	124	7C	111 1100
}	125	7D	111 1101
~	126	7E	111 1110
DEL	127	7F	111 1111

n Chapter 5, you learned about the order of operations for the math operators. The chart below is a more complete table of the order of operators of all types. The operators shown in each group (divided by a line) have the same precedence level. The group with the highest precedence appears at the top of the table. Under the *Associativity* heading, you can see whether the operators are evaluated from right to left or left to right. If the operator you are looking for does not appear in the table below, check your compiler's documentation for a complete list.

GROUP	SYMBOL	DESCRIPTION	ASSOCIATIVITY
Scope Resolution	::	scope-resolution operator	Left to right
Structure Operators	-> .	structure pointer operator dot operator	Left to right
Unary Operators	! + - & * ++ -- ( ) sizeof new delete	logical negation unary plus unary minus address of dereferencing increment operator decrement operator typecasting sizeof operator memory allocation memory deallocation	Right to left
Multiplicative Operators	* / %	multiplication divide modulus	Left to right
Additive Operators	+ -	addition minus	Left to right
Relational Operators	< <= > >=	less than less than or equal to greater than greater than or equal to	Left to right
Equality	== !=	equal to not equal to	Left to right
Logical AND	&&	logical AND	Left to right
Logical OR	||	logical OR	Left to right
Assignment	= *= /= %= += -=	assignment operator compound assign product compound assign quotient compound assign remainder compound assign sum compound assign difference	Right to left

Introduction to Exceptions and Error Handling

When something goes wrong while a program is running, the error is known as a *run-time error* or *exception*. The term *exception* comes from the idea that a program usually performs in the expected fashion, but there is always the possibility of an exception to the usual behavior occurring. For example, when allocating memory on the heap, the operation normally results in successful allocation. The exception is when something goes wrong and the memory is not successfully allocated.

There are many things that can cause run-time errors. The exception may be the result of something your program is doing. The exception may also be caused by factors outside of your program. It is possible that another program has created a problem in memory or with operating system resources. Whatever the cause, it is up to you to write programs that handle exceptions of any kind and recover from the error or at least shut down gracefully.

Let's look at two ways of handing errors: assert and the C++ exception handling facility.

Using assert

Many libraries and operating systems have functions that return what are known as *error codes* to let the caller know if the function succeeded. An example of this is found with **new**; when it cannot allocate the memory desired, it returns the value of zero. This value should always be checked so as not to corrupt the program by accessing memory through the null-pointer.

Unfortunately, programmers are sometimes lazy and do not make such crucial checks (risking the integrity of the program), often because checking all error codes becomes tedious. To help alleviate this problem, there is an **assert** function (found in the header **assert.h**) that can be used as an "easy" way to check error codes. The **assert** function has one parameter: a condition that the programmer is *asserting* to be true. An example of such a condition is found in the code sample below, where the program is asserting that the pointer is not null.

```
// UsingAssert.cp, an example of using assert in a C++ program

#include <assert.h>

int main()
{
    // try to allocate an array of 1,000,000,000 longs
    long *big = new long[1000000000];

    // assert that the allocation succeeded
    assert(big != NULL);

    // ... use big ...
```

```
        delete big;

        return 0;
    }
```

In the above example, one billion long integers are being allocated on the heap via the **new** operator. For all current practical purposes, this allocation will certainly fail and the pointer **big** will be null. When the assertion **big != NULL** is made, **assert** will see that the condition is false and will terminate the program, printing the name of the file and which line the error occurred on.

On the Net

For more information on using assert, see http://www.ProgramCPP.com. See topic C.1.

Extra for Experts

The **assert** *function is actually what is known as a macro, a feature of the preprocessor that is similar to a function. Because* **assert** *is a macro, it is able to determine information such as the line and file from which it was called. This is something normal functions cannot know.*

Exception Handling

As one can see, using **assert** has limited capabilities. Instead of doing something about the error, the program terminates. For this reason, **assert** is normally used only when debugging a program. It is not fit for a final program. C++'s *exception handling* capabilities are more suited for the task when it comes to writing real programs. Exception handling allows all errors to be checked, without the tediousness of checking them by hand.

On the Net

Learn more about exception handling and see examples of using try, throw, and catch at http://www.ProgramCPP.com. See topic C.2.

Often programmers write exception handling routines that are called when an error occurs. These routines do their best to recover from the error and present some kind of error message that makes sense to the user. C++ provides a facility for implementing exception handling routines in a standard way. C++ exception handling introduces three new keywords: try, throw, and catch.

Code that may cause an exception is placed in a special block of code called a try block. In the code within the try block, the throw keyword can be used to *throw* an exception. Following the try block are a series of exception handlers with the keyword catch. If an error occurs in the try block, the exception will be thrown by the throw keyword and caught by one of the exception handlers.

KEY TERMS

error code

exception

exception handling

run-time error

ome mathematical problems require that an approximation be made because an exact answer cannot be found. Sometimes a result which is close to being correct is close enough. There are many methods of solving by approximation. In this appendix, we will look at two such methods: the bisection method of finding zeros of a function, and the Monte Carlo technique of using random data to find a nonrandom result.

Bisection Method

f using a computer, the bisection method is probably the fastest and most exact approach for finding where a continuous function $f(x)$ is equal to zero. The technique relies on the fact that an interval $x_1 \leq x < x_2$ has been found such that:

$$f(x_1) \leq 0 \leq f(x_2)$$

The method finds the root by continuously cutting the size of the interval in half. (See Figure D-1). This is accomplished by evaluating the function:

$$f\left(\frac{x_1 + x_2}{2}\right)$$

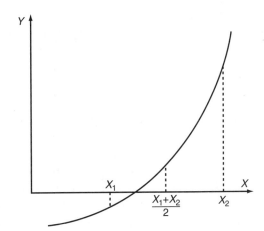

FIGURE D-1
The bisection method of finding the zeros of functions.

The above function is evaluated, and if it does not equal zero, the signs are compared. If the sign of $f(x_1)$ is different from that of the midpoint formula, the midpoint becomes the second endpoint. Meaning, $0.5(x_1 + x_2)$ takes the place of x_2. This method effectively cuts the interval in half. This process is repeated until the root is found. The more times the interval is split in half, the more exact the root will be.

On the Net

See a C++ function that will determine the root of a function using the bisection method at http://www.ProgramCPP.com. See topic D.1.

Monte Carlo Technique

he Monte Carlo technique relies on the generation of completely random numbers with a wide distribution. The best example as to how this technique works is finding the area of an oddly-shaped object. For example, suppose the area of the object in Figure D-2 needs to be found. We know the area of the square which contains the object. We can use the Monte Carlo technique to find the area of the oddly-shaped object.

The Monte Carlo technique begins by choosing n random points within the square that contains the oddly-shaped object. These points are to be evenly dis-

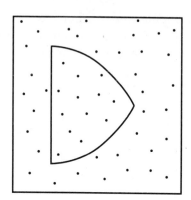

F I G U R E   D - 2
The Monte Carlo technique.

tributed, and completely random. Therefore, some of the points will fall inside the oddly-shaped object, and some will fall outside the object.

Let M represent the object for which you want to find the area. Let N be the number of points that are randomly distributed within the square and F be the number of points that fall in M. If the points are well distributed and completely random, the area of M can be found by taking the ratio F/N. In Figure D-2, 50 points were generated. Of those 50, 13 are inside M. This ratio is 13/50 or 26%. Therefore, the area of M is approximately 26% of the total area of the square.

Until the invention of the computer, this technique was not widely used because determining many random numbers is very time consuming. With the aid of a computer, however, determining random numbers is simplified. The more points that are used to determine the ratio, the more accurate the approximation.

On the Net

To learn more about how random numbers are generated on a computer, see http://www.ProgramCPP.com. See topic D.2.

How Algorithms Are Analyzed

The efficiency and speed of algorithms can be mathematically analyzed to help programmers design and implement programs. Analysis can show which algorithms are best for particular applications. For example, a programmer may want to know which sorting algorithm is best to use before writing a sorting function for a database program.

Algorithms can be analyzed for both execution time and memory space. When computer memory was very expensive, it was more important to find algorithms that used little memory space. Today, computer memory is relatively inexpensive, so programmers usually focus on finding the fastest algorithms.

The standard method of algorithm time analysis involves finding out how many steps an algorithm needs to complete. The more steps needed, the more time the algorithm takes to execute. Analysis is not always easy because many algorithms use different numbers of steps each time they are executed. Some sorting algorithms require fewer steps if the list being sorting is fully or partially sorted to begin with. The size of the input usually affects execution time more than any other factor. In fact, in algorithm time analysis, the primary concern is finding out how changes in input size affect performance.

For the purposes of our analysis, only the worst case will be taken into consideration. The worst case is when the input data for an algorithm is in the worst possible state. For example, the worst case for many ascending sorting functions is when data starts out in descending order. We focus on the worst case because it is often fairly close to the average case.

At times, it is interesting to discover the average case and the best case. However, the average case and best case do not guarantee anything about performance. By knowing the worst case, you have a guarantee that the algorithm cannot get any slower than the worst case.

Big-O Notation

A common way to refer to the running time of an algorithm is with *big-O notation*. A big-O equation shows how the input size effects an algorithm's running time in the worst case. For example, the big-O running time for the bubble sort is $O(n^2)$. This equation tells us that the running time grows quadratically relative to the input size. This means that when the input size for a bubble sort function doubles, the running time will quadruple (be about four times as long). If an algorithm's big-O running time is $O(1)$, then the running time is the same regardless of the input size. Some very slow algorithms have a big-O running time of $O(2^n)$, which means the running time grows exponentially relative to the input size.

ANALYZING THE SEQUENTIAL SEARCH

Consider the sequential search function shown in Figure E-1. If the value in **key** is found in the array, then 1 is returned, otherwise 0 is returned. To the right of each line of code is a comment giving the number of times the statement is

```
int sequential_search(int array[], int array_length, int key)
{
    int i;
    for ( i = 0;                    // 1 time
          i < array_length;         // array_length + 1 times
          i++)                      // array_length times
    {
        if (array[i] == key)        // array_length times
            return 1;               // 0 times
    }
    return 0;                       // 1 time
}
```

FIGURE E - 1
This sequential search function can be analyzed easily.

executed in the worst case (the worst case for the sequential search is when key is not found at all).

If the array length is represented by the variable n, the total number of steps in the worst case is $(1) + (n + 1) + (n) + (n) + (0) + (1)$. Simplified, the number of steps is $3n + 3$. Because we are analyzing the sequential search algorithm in general and not any particular implementation, we can ignore the specific constants and rewrite the equation as $k_1 n + k_2$. The constants referred to as k_1 and k_2 can change depending on how the sequential search algorithm is coded, so we are not concerned with their values.

The big-O notation for the sequential search running time is $O(n)$. The constants k_1 and k_2 do not need to be written because they are implicitly part of big-O notation. The particular value $O(n)$ indicates that the running time grows linearly relative to the input size. If the input size for the sequential search doubles, the running time will also double.

ANALYZING THE BINARY SEARCH

The binary search function shown in Figure E-2 is longer than the sequential search function, but it can search much more quickly through sorted arrays. The sequential search is more versatile because it can search through any array, regardless of the order of the elements. The binary search requires the input array to be sorted, but can operate much quicker because of its divide and conquer strategy.

The total number of steps in the worst case of the binary search function is $(1) + (\log_2 n + 1) + (\log_2 n) + (\log_2 n) / 2 + (\log_2 n) / 2 + (\log_2 n) + (1) + (0) + (1)$. Simplified, the number of steps is $4 (\log_2 n) + 4$. Ignoring the specific values of the constants, this can be rewritten as $k_1(\log_2 n) + k_2$.

In big-O notation, the running time for the binary search is $O(\log_2 n)$. The term $\log_2 n$ is used because the number of steps grows logarithmically. The binary search works by repeatedly halving the list until the element is found or the entire list is eliminated. If we were to search through an array with 16 elements, then the search would cut the list to 8, 4, 2, then finally 1 element. That means that there are 4 iterations total (the list is cut in half during each iteration). When n is 16, $\log_2 n$ equals 4 (and $2^4 = 16$), which shows that the number of iterations grows logarithmically relative to the input size. If we had 64 elements to search through, the list would be cut to 32, 16, 8, 4, 2, and 1 element after each of 6 iterations. This is shown by the equations: $\log_2 64 = 6$ and $2^6 = 64$.

It is easy to see the efficiency difference between sequential and binary searches for different input sizes. When the input size n is 4, the binary search is only twice as fast as the sequential search. When n is 256, the binary search is

```
    int binary_search(int array[], int lowerbound, intupperbound, int key)
    {
        int search_pos;

        search_pos = (lowerbound + upperbound) / 2;        // 1 time

        while((array[search_pos] != key)
              && (lowerbound <= upperbound)                // log₂n + 1 times
        {
            if (array[search_pos] > key)                   // log₂n times
                upperbound = search_pos - 1;               // (log₂n) / 2times
            else
                lowerbound = search_pos + 1;               // (log₂n) / 2times

            search_pos = (lowerbound + upperbound) / 2;    // log₂n times
        }
        if (lowerbound <= upperbound)                      // 1 time
            return 1;                                      // 0 times
        else
            return 0;                                      // 1 time

    }
```

F I G U R E   E - 2
The binary search algorithm is efficient when searching a sorted array.

32 times faster. Remember that this only applies to sorted lists, because the binary search is unable to search through unsorted lists.

SEARCH ALGORITHM	BIG-O	$n = 4$	$n = 16$	$n = 256$
Sequential	$O(n)$	4	16	256
Binary	$O(\log_2 n)$	2	4	8

ANALYZING SORTING ALGORITHMS

The table below summarizes the big-O running times of some common sorting algorithms. Incremental comparison-based sorting algorithms usually run in $O(n^2)$ time, while divide-and-conquer sorting algorithms usually have an $O(n \log_2 n)$ running time. Different implementations of these algorithms may yield different big-O running times.

On the Net

For more information about algorithm analysis and big-O notation, see http://www.Program-CPP.com. See topic E.1.

SORTING ALGORITHM	BIG-O	$n = 4$	$n = 128$
Selection	$O(n^2)$	16	16,384
Insertion	$O(n^2)$	16	16,384
Bubble	$O(n^2)$	16	16,384
Shell	$O(n^2)$	16	16,384
Quick	$O(n \log_2 n)$	8	896
Merge	$O(n \log_2 n)$	8	896

KEY TERM

big-O notation

What Is a Debugger?

A debugger is a program that helps programmers find errors in their programs. In many cases, a debugger is integrated into the compiler's programming environment to make it easy to use.

Debuggers offer many features that allow a programmer to see what is going on inside a running program. In this appendix, we'll concentrate on three of the most useful features: stepping through instructions, setting breakpoints, and watching variables.

Stepping Through Instructions

One of the most useful features of a debugger, especially for beginning programmers, is the ability to step through the lines of a program individually and see the effect each line has on the operation of the program. With this feature, the programmer can see the actual source code and control when the program executes the next line of code.

Stepping through instructions lets a programmer see things that otherwise would be difficult to verify, such as verifying that code within if structures is getting executed or watching the flow of logic through loops and function calls.

Setting Breakpoints

Another useful feature of a debugger is the ability to set a breakpoint. Setting a breakpoint is like putting a stop sign somewhere in your program. For example, if you are having trouble debugging a certain function, you can set a breakpoint that stops the program from executing at the point where the function is called. Once the program is stopped by the breakpoint, you can step through the instructions within that function to get a closer look at the problem area.

Watching Variables

Watching variables is particularly useful. While stepping through a program, you can select variables for which you would like to display their value as the program runs. The displayed values are updated each time you step through an instruction. As a result, you can see the value of a variable at any point in the program's execution.

Glossary

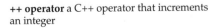

++ operator a C++ operator that increments an integer

-- operator a C++ operator that decrements an integer

A

accessor function member functions that access data in an object, but do not change it

address-of operator an operator that returns the "address of" the variable rather than the variable's contents

algorithm a set of sequential instructions that are followed to solve a problem

allocate to reserve computer memory

American Standard Code for Information Interchange (ASCII) a code most computers use to assign a number to each character. The numbers are used to represent the character internally.

analog quantities that are variable or exist in a range

ancestors a node's ancestors are the nodes that link it to the root

appending the process of adding data to the end of an existing file

argument data passed to a function

arithmetic and logic unit the calculator and decision maker in the microprocessor

arithmetic operators operators that perform math operations such as addition, subtraction, multiplication, and division

array a group of variables of the same data type that appear together in the computer's memory

ascending order arranged from A to Z or smallest to largest

assembler a program that reads assembly language code and converts it into a machine language

assembly language a programming language that uses letters and numbers to represent machine language instructions

assignment operator an operator (=) that changes the value of the variable to the left of the operator

automatic variable a variable declared within a function that is accessible only within that function (a local variable)

B

balance the arrangement of nodes in a tree

base class a class upon which other classes are built

basic input/output system (BIOS) the set of programs in the ROM of IBM-compatible computers used to interact with the screen, keyboard, and disks

binary number system a number system that uses a base (or radix) of 2, rather than the base of 10 that the decimal number system uses

binary search a search that works by starting in the middle and narrowing the search in a way similar to the way you search for a name in a phone book

binary tree a tree structure that allows only two branches from each node

bit a single binary digit

bitwise operators a set of operators that allow you to work with the actual bits within a number or character

boolean variable a variable which can have only two possible values: true or false

bottom-up design a program design method that involves beginning at the bottom of the VTOC (Visual Table of Contents) and working up

bounds checking error checking which prevents a string from overflowing the bounds or the array in which it is to be stored

braces special characters used to mark the beginning and ending of blocks of code

branches a link from one node in a tree to another

branch nodes nodes on a tree that have branches (also called nonterminal nodes)

bubble sort an incremental sort which repeatedly compares adjacent elements of an array, starting with the first and second ele-

ments, and swapping them if they are out of order

bugs logic errors and other problems which prevent a computer program from functioning as intended

bus a system of wires that connects the devices in a computer

bus interface unit the part of a microprocessor that links the microprocessor to the bus

byte a group of eight binary digits (bits)

C

C++ a high-level, compiled language that provides the programmer with much of the power and flexibility of a low-level language

case-sensitive a characteristic of the C++ language which provides for the interpretation of uppercase and lowercase letters differently

central processing unit (CPU) the part of a computer where the processing takes place

character literal a single character that appears in single quotes (') in a program

characters the letters and symbols available for use by a computer

children the one or two nodes below a given node (also called offspring)

circularly-linked list a linked list in which the last node's next pointer points back to the first node

class the definition of an object

class-member operator the period between the object identifier and the message

clock the device inside a computer that produces a signal that controls the speed of the microprocessor and other system components

close the final step of using a data file

collision in hashing, the condition where two key values produce the same result

comments remarks in a program that are ignored by the compiler

compiler a program that translates a high-level language into machine language, then saves the machine language so that the instructions do not have to be translated each time the program is run

compiler directive commands for the compiler, which are needed to effectively compile your program

complex instruction set computer (CISC) a microprocessor that accepts a comparatively large number of instructions, some of which perform complex operations. The Intel 80486 and Pentium processors are examples of CISC processors.

composition see containment

compound operators special operators that provide a shorthand notation for statements that change a variable

computer architecture a term used to describe the way the many devices in a computer are put together

concatenation adding one string onto the end of another string

console I/O using the screen and keyboard for input and output (I/O is an abbreviation of input/output)

constructor tells the compiler how to create an object in memory and what the initial values of its data will be

constant stores data that remains the same throughout a program's execution

containment the term used to describe a has-a relationship among classes

control expression an expression that provides for a decision to be made in an if statement or to end a loop

control unit the part of a microprocessor that coordinates the activity of the execution unit

copy constructor a constructor that receives a reference to another object as an argument, and is used when objects are passed to functions by value

crash when a program stops running or "locks up" due to an error

D

data a computer representation of something that exists in the real world

data structure a programming structure that holds data for a program

data type a specification that defines the type of data that can be stored in a variable or constant

deallocate to return memory to the heap for use by other data

decimal number system a number system that uses a base (or radix) of 10

declaring indicating to the compiler what type of variable you want and its name or identifier

decrementing subtracting 1 from a variable

default constructor a constructor used when the object is instanciated with no arguments

delimiter a character that signals the computer that one piece of data is ending and another one is beginning

dereferencing operator an operator for declaring pointers and returning the value in a variable pointed to by a pointer

derived class the class which inherits the properties of another class

descendants the nodes linked below a node in a tree

descending order arranged from Z to A or largest to smallest

destructor necessary when an object manually allocates memory. The destructor manually disposes of this memory.

digital a form of representation that uses distinct digits to represent data

divide and conquer approach a sorting method that repeatedly breaks the unsorted list down into smaller lists until each small list is sorted

division-remainder method a hashing algorithm which involves dividing the key value by a prime or odd number and using the remainder of the division as the relative address for the record

dot operator the operator used to access the members of a structure

doubly-linked list a linked list in which each node has a pointer linking it to the next node *and* the previous node

do while loop an iteration structure that repeats a statement or group of statements as long as a control expression is true at the end of the loop

dynamic data structure a data structure that reserves memory as it is needed

E

element a variable in an array

e-mail electronic mail sent from one computer user to another over a computer network

encapsulation the "hiding" of data and code inside a class

"E" notation exponential notation

enum a keyword that allows the creation of enumerated data types

event driven a program in which events such as the click of a mouse or a menu selection drives the flow of the program

event loop a loop in an event driven program which constantly iterates waiting for an event to occur

executable file the output of a linker that can be executed without the need for an interpreter

execution unit the part of the microprocessor that carries out instructions. The execution unit is made up of the control unit, the arithmetic and logic unit, and the registers.

exit condition the condition which must be met to end recursive calls

exponential notation a method of representing very large and very small numbers (also called scientific notation)

expression a math statement made up of terms, operators, and functions

external sort a sort that sorts data in a file, rather than in RAM

external variable a variable declared before the main function which is accessible by any function (global variable)

extraction operator the operator that outputs data to a stream

F

fields data items that make up a record

file pointer a special type of pointer used for working with files

first-in first-out (FIFO) a data structure in which the first data put into the structure is the first data to be taken out

floating-point unit a processor that works with floating-point numbers (also called a math coprocessor)

floppy disk a type of secondary storage media made of a thin, flexible, magnetic disk

flowchart a diagram made up of symbols used to illustrate an algorithm

for loop an iteration structure that repeats one or more statements a specified number of times

free to return memory to the heap for use by other data

function a block of code that carries out a specific task

fuzzy logic a logic system that allows for true, false, and variations in between

G

global variable a variable declared before the main function and accessible by any function

graphical user interface (GUI) a system for interacting with the computer user through pictures or icons

H

hard coded data that appears as part of the program's source code and therefore cannot be changed as the program runs

hard disk a form of secondary storage media made up of hard, magnetic platters. Hard disks are usually installed inside a computer.

hardware the equipment that makes up a computer system

has-a relationship the relationship between classes where one class contains another class

hashing a search method that processes the key through a hashing algorithm to find the position of the data in a file

hashing algorithm an algorithm used when hashing to convert the key to a number that corresponds to the position of the record

header file a file that serves as a link between your program code and standard C++ code that is needed to make your program run

heap the portion of memory in which dynamic data structures are stored

high-level language a programming language in which instructions do not necessarily correspond with the instruction set of the microprocessor

I

identifier names given to variables and constants

if/else structure a programming structure that executes one block of code if certain conditions are met and another block of code if the same conditions are not met

if structure a programming structure that executes code if certain conditions are met

incremental approach a sorting algorithm characterized by loops that pass through a list, one element at a time

incrementing adding 1 to a variable

infinite loop an iteration structure in which iterations continue indefinitely

information hiding data protection that is an important benefit of encapsulation

inheritance the ability of one object to inherit the properties of another object

initialize to assign a value to a variable

initializing expression an expression that initializes the counter variable of a for loop

in-order traversal a tree traversal that visits all the nodes of a tree in its sorted order

input data put into a computer for processing

input size the number of elements in a list to be sorted

insertion operator the operator that gets data from a stream and puts it into a variable

insertion sort an incremental sort in which the elements are arranged in a similar manner to a hand of cards

instance the data for one object which has been created in memory that has the behaviors defined by the class

instanciate to declare an object

instruction decode unit the part of a microprocessor that determines what must be done to get an instruction processed

instruction fetch unit the part of a microprocessor that gets instructions from RAM or ROM

instruction set the set of commands a microprocessor is designed to understand

integrated circuit a thin slice of photo-sensitive silicon, usually smaller than a dime, upon which microscopic circuits have been inscribed

interact getting input and giving a response

Internet a world-wide network of com-puter systems that allows for the exchange of electronic mail, public messages, data, and files.

interpreter a program that translates the source code of a high-level language into machine language

I/O manipulators a set of format options available in C++ that may be placed directly in the output statement

is-a relationship the relationship where one object inherits characteristics from another class

iteration a single loop or pass through a group of statements

iteration structures programming structures that repeat a group of statements one or more times (loops)

K

key the value by which the data in a tree is sorted or searched or data in a data structure is searched

key field the field upon which a search algorithm or the sorting of data is based

key value the value in a key field

keyword words that cannot be used as identifiers because they are part of the C++ language

L

last-in first-out (LIFO) a data structure in which the last data in is the first data out

leaf nodes nodes of a tree that do not have branches (also called terminal nodes)

left child the node attached to the left of the node above

levels a way of identifying the depth of a tree

library functions functions that come with your compiler

linear data structure a data structure in which the elements or nodes are arranged in a line

linked list a data structure that allows data to be stored in a list in which memory is assigned to your data as it is needed

linker a program that links object files created by a compiler into an executable program

local variable a variable declared within a function which is accessible only within that function

logical operators operators that allow *and*, *or*, and *not* to be implemented as part of logical expressions

loop a programming structure that repeats a group of statements one or more times

lowercase the non-capital (small) letters of the alphabet

low-level language a programming language in which each instruction corresponds to one or only a few microprocessor instructions

M

machine language the programming language (made up of ones and zeros) that a microprocessor understands

main function the function where every C++ program begins

math coprocessor a processor that works with floating-point numbers (also called a floating-point unit)

megahertz the units (which means millions per second) used to measure clock speeds of computers

members when refering to structures, a member is a variable in the structure. When referring to classes, a member is a function or variables in a class definition.

member functions allow programmers using an object to send information to an object and receive information from an object

member selection operator the dot operator that selects a member of a structure or class

menu a set of options presented to the user of a program

merge sort an algorithm which repeatedly merges smaller sorted lists into larger ones

message in object-oriented programming, the method used to transfer data

method code inside an object that is necessary to perform the operations on the object

microprocessor an integrated circuit that includes all of the main functions of a computer on a single chip

modem a device that allows interaction to occur between computers over the telephone

modulus operator the operator that provides integer division

motherboard a computer's main circuit board

multi-dimensional array an array that allows a single identifier to access data in a table or more complex arrangement

multilevel inheritance inheriting properties from the parent class' parent class

multiple inheritance inheriting properties from more than one parent class

N

nested a programming structure within a programming structure

nested loop a loop within a loop

nested structure a structure within a structure

network a group of computers that are connected by a communications link that allows them to share data or hardware resources

node the structure that contains the data in a linked list or tree

nonlinear data structure a data structure in which the elements or nodes do not appear in a line (a tree)

nonterminal nodes nodes on a tree that have branches (also called branch nodes)

null pointer a pointer variable with a value of zero

null terminator an invisible character, represented by the ASCII value zero, that marks the end of a C++ string

O

object an instance of a class. An entity that encapsulates both data and the functions that manipulate that data.

object code the machine language code produced by a compiler

object file the file produced by a compiler which contains machine language code

object-oriented paradigm a way of programming where data and operations are seen as existing together in objects that are similar to objects in the real world

object-oriented program a program that incorporates the object-oriented paradigm

object-oriented programming (OOP) building programs using the object-oriented paradigm

offspring the one or two nodes below a given node (also called children)

one-dimensional array an array that is essentially a list

one-way selection structure a selection structure in which the decision is whether to go "one way" or just bypass the code in the if structure

open the operation that associates a physical disk file with a file pointer so that data in the file may be accessed

operating system the program in charge of the fundamental system operations

operator overloading the process of creating a new procedure to execute whenever a standard C++ operator is used with a standard type or a class

order of operations the rules related to the order in which operations (such as math operations) are performed

output data or information provided by a computer to a user

overflow the condition where an integer becomes too large for its data type

P

paradigm a model or a set of rules that define a way of programming

parallel arrays two or more arrays that are indexed with the same variable

parameter the variable that receives the value or any other identifier in the parentheses of the function declaration

parent the node above a given node to which the given node is linked

parent class when one class inherits the properties of another, the class from which the properties come is the parent class

partition sections used in some sorting algorithms

pass to send an argument to a function

passing by address a method of passing the memory address of a variable rather than its value

passing by reference a method of passing variables in which any changes you make to the variables are passed back to the calling function

passing by value a method of passing variables in which a copy of the value in the variable is given to the function for it to use

pointer a variable or constant that holds a memory address

pointer constant a pointer that does not allow the memory address in the pointer to be changed

pointer variable a pointer that allows the memory address in the pointer to be changed

pop to remove an item from a stack

postorder traversal a tree traversal that visits the left node first, then the right node, then the root

preorder traversal a tree traversal that visits the root first, then the left node, then the right node

primary storage a computer's random-access memory (RAM)

primitive data structures the basic data types

private the keyword that indicates the parts of an object which are not accessible from outside the object

procedural paradigm a way of programming that focuses on the idea that all algorithms in a program are performed with functions and data that a programmer can see, understand, and change

programming language a language that provides a way to program computers using instructions that can be understood by computers and people

promotion the condition in which the data type of one variable is temporarily converted to match the data type of another variable so that a math operation can be performed using the mixed data type

prototype a statement that defines the function for the compiler

pseudocode a way to express an algorithm in everyday English, rather than in a programming language

public the keyword that indicates the parts of an object which are accessible from outside the object

push to add an item to a stack

Q

queue a data structure that allows additions at only one end (called the rear of the queue) and deletions at the opposite end (called the front of the queue)

quicksort a sorting algorithm that uses a divide and conquer approach and works by repeatedly breaking the list into partitions until each partition contains a single element

R

random-access file a data file that allows you to move directly to any data in the file

random-access memory (RAM) a computer's primary storage. RAM is where currently running programs and active data are stored.

reading getting data from a file

read-only memory (ROM) a set of memory chips that have instructions and data permanently stored upon them

records complete groups of database fields

recursion a programming technique in which a function calls itself

reduced instruction set computer (RISC) a microprocessor that accepts a relatively small number of instructions, each of which perform simple operations. The PowerPC processor is an example of a RISC processor.

registers a memory circuit that holds data that is being manipulated by the execution unit of a microprocessor

relational database systems a database program that uses multiple databases that use key fields to relate the data among the databases

relational operators operators used to make comparisons

reusability using an object again after it has been coded and tested

right child the node attached to the right of the node above

root the node at the top of a tree from which all nodes in the tree descend

run-time error occurs when a program gives a computer an instruction that it is incapable of executing, which may lead to a program crash

S

scope the availability of a variable to functions

scope-resolution operator the operator that separates the class name and the function name in a member function

secondary storage a form of data storage more permanent than RAM, usually magnetic disk media

selection sort a sorting algorithm that uses an incremental approach. After the first pass through the list, the element with the largest key value is sorted. After each successive pass, the next largest element is put in its proper position until all elements are sorted.

selection structures structures that allow for logical decisions in C++ programs

sequence structures execute statements one after another without changing the flow of a program

sequential-access file a file with which you must start at the beginning and search each record to find the one you want

sequential search a search technique in which each record in the database is compared in the order it appears until the desired record is found

Shell sort a sorting algorithm that compares elements **d** positions away from each other. **d** initially is equal to half the length of the list and is halved after each iteration.

short circuit evaluation a feature of C++ that allows the program to stop evaluating an expression as soon as the outcome of the expression is known

siblings two nodes with the same parent

simple data structures a category of data structures that includes arrays

singly-linked list a linked list in which the pointers link the nodes in only one direction

sizeof operator an operator that returns the number of bytes used by a data structure

sorting the process of arranging the items in a data structure in a certain order

source code a program in the form of a high-level language

stack a data structure that allows items to be added and deleted from only one end

stack overflow when the size of a stack is too small to hold all the items being pushed on the stack

standard input device the keyboard

standard output device the screen

statements lines of C++ code. Statements end with a semicolon.

states conditions

static data structure a data structure that occupies the same amount of memory every time the program is run

step expression the expression in a for loop that changes the counter variable

stream data flowing from one place to another

stream operation modes a mode that specifies the way you want to access the file

string a group of characters put together to make one or more words

string literal a string hard coded into a program

structure pointer operator the operator (->) used to access individual members of a dynamically-allocated structure

structures C++ data structures that allow variables to be grouped to form a new data type

subscript notation a method that allows you to access any character in a character array individually

substring a string that is contained in another string

subtree any node with branches extending below it

switch structure a selection structure capable of handling multiple options

syntax error occurs when a command or other part of a program is keyed incorrectly

T

template a class that can be used with any data type

terminal nodes nodes of a tree that do not have branches (also called leaf nodes)

text editor a program that allows source code to be entered and edited

text file a file saved in ASCII format without the font and formatting codes word processors use

Toolbox a set of programs in the ROM of Macintosh computers

top-down design a program design method in which the general organization and flow of the program is decided before the details are coded

traversing the process of accessing (also called *visiting*) every node in a list or tree

tree a nonlinear data structure in which nodes are arranged like branches of a tree

truncate to drop the digits to the right of the decimal point, without rounding the value

truth tables diagrams that show the result of logical operations

two-dimensional array an array that consists of columns and rows in a tabular arrangement

two-way selection structure a selection structure in which one block of code is executed if the control expression is true and another block is executed if the control expression is false

typecasting changing the data type of a variable using a typecast operator

typecast operators operators that force the data type of a variable to change

U

underflow when a value becomes too small for a variable to hold accurately

unsigned capable of storing only positive values

uppercase the capital letters of the alphabet

V

variable holds data that can change while the program is running

vector a one-dimensional array of any data type

Visual Table of Contents (VTOC) a diagram that shows the functions of a program

volatile in terms of memory, RAM is called volatile because it can be lost if power to the computer is interrupted

W

while loop an iteration structure that repeats a statement or group of statements as long as a control expression is true

whitespace blank space created by characters, such as spaces, tabs, and carriage returns

writing storing data to a file

Index

Boole, George, 59
Boolean algebra, 59
boolean data types, 195
Boolean variables, 59
bottom-up design, for computer programs, 158
bounds checking, 250
B programming language, 30
braces
    in C++ programs, 44, 47
    in if structures, 124, 129
    in loops, 141
    in structures, 197
brackets, in character arrays, 94
branch, of tree, 363
branch nodes, of tree, 363
break, as keyword, 131, 146
breakpoints, setting, 449
break statement, 146
bubble sort, 403-406, 447
buffer, flushing, 105
bugs, defined, 36
bus, 9, 10, 13-14
Business Software Alliance (BSA), 203
bus interface unit, 11, 12
byte, defined, 23

C

C++ computer programs. *See* computer programs
C++ programming language, 30, 227
    list of keywords used in, 61
C++ program structure, 44-48
calculating tools, 2-4
calculator, stack-based, 371-379
case keywords, 131
case sensitive, defined, 48
case statements, order of, 132
catch, as keyword, 442
cathode-ray tube (CRT), 89
ceil function, 171
central processing unit (CPU), 12
changing, computer programs, 49
character arrays, 92, 184, 189
    creating a pointer for, 184-185
    declaring, 93-94
    initializing with strings, 94
    vs. numeric data types, 94
    and pointers, 190
    vs. strings, 94
character literals, 92, 93
characters, 57
    ASCII, table of, 435-437
    inputting, 104
    special, 99-100

child class, 240
children, of node, 364
chips
    computer, 4
    ROM, 11
cin command, 98-99
cin operator. *See* input operator
circuits, computer, 22-23
circularly-linked list, 330-331
CISC, vs. RISC, 13
class, 229-232
    base, 241
    child, 240
    creating instance of, 230
    vs. data type, 238
    derived, 240
    designing, 233-234
    implementing, 234-238
    matrix, 286, 294-296, 299
    and object, 230
    parent, 240
    stack, 359, 369
    string, 250-255, 267
    template, 276-278
    vector, 279-280, 283, 288, 294
class definition, 236-237
class-member operator (.), 231
clearing screen, 106
clock speeds, 12-13
closing, data files, 208, 210
coding, computer program, 35-36
    standards for, 158
collision, in hashing, 394
color plotter, 89
commas, prohibited to separate data in
    C++ programs, 103
comments, in C++ programs, 44-46
compiler directives
    in C++ programs, 44, 46
    for class implementation, 234-236
compilers, 51
    defined, 29
    legal use of, 154
    library functions provided with, 170-172
    programming languages using, 30
    short-circuit disable option, 122
compiling, computer programs, 49, 50
Complex Instruction Set Computer. *See*
    CISC
compositional relationship, 240
compound assign difference operator (-=), 439
compound assign product operator (*=), 439

compound assign quotient operator (/=), 439
compound assign remainder operator (%=), 439
compound assign sum operator (+=), 253, 258, 439
compound operators, 75-76, 253, 258, 439
computer-aided design (CAD) systems, 89
computer ethics, 154
computer graphics, 89-90
computer language, 22-26. *See also* programming languages
computer programming
    careers in, 416-417
    object-oriented (OOP), 225-242, 278, 394, 418-433
    procedural, 226-227
    process of, 33-38
computer programs
    accountability for, 154
    algorithms in, 33-35
    autonomy of, 158
    bottom-up design, 158
    building with functions, 156-161
    to calculate compound interest, 176-182
    changing, 49
    coding, 35-36
    compiling, 49, 50
    cost analysis, 109-113
    database, 334-353, 388
    debugging, 36-37, 449
    decision making in, 115-132
    design of, 158
    documenting, 37
    encapsulation of, 158
    event driven, 146
    flow of, and functions, 160
    flowchart symbols in, 34
    linked lists in, 308
    linking, 49
    loading existing source files in, 50
    look-up table in, 301-306
    maintenance of, 37-38
    multi-function, 169
    organization of, 158
    and responsibilities of programmer, 51, 154
    reusability of, 158
    running, 49
    setting breakpoints in, 449
    single-function, 156
    stack-based calculator, 371-379
    standalone, 50
    stepping through instructions in, 449
    testing, 36-37

eof function, 218
equality operators, 439
equal to operator (==), 118, 124, 250, 251, 439
error codes, 441
errors
    allocation, in linked lists, 311
    caused by division by zero, 74
    finding with debugger, 449
    floating-point rounding, 85
    handling, 441-442
    opening file, 210
    programming, 36
    run-time, 36, 441
    string, 96
    syntax, 36
escape sequences, 100
event driven programs, 146
event loop, 146
exception, 441
    handling, 442
executable file, 30
execution unit, 11, 12
exit condition, in recursive algorithm, 386
exp function, 172
exponential notation, 63
expressions, 72
external sort, 411, 413
external variables, 163. *See also* global variables
extraction operator (<<), 98, 210, 254, 264. *See also* output operator

F

fabs function, 171
factorial function, 384, 385
false, representing in C++ programs, 117-118, 126, 128
fields, in database programs, 196
file handling functions, in operating systems, 207
file managers, 207
filenames, 209
    hard-coded, 222
    prompting for, 221
file pointer
    declaring, 208-209
    defined, 208
files
    appending data to end of, 216-218
    closing, 208, 210
    data, 205-222
    naming, 209
    opening, 208-210
    reading from, 209, 212-214

    storing to, 208
    working with multiple, 208, 219-221
    writing to, 208, 210-212
file streams, 209
File Transfer Protocol (FTP), 18-19
Finder, Macintosh operating system, 31
find function, 251, 253
first-in first-out structure, 360
fixed format option, 100, 101
float data type, 58, 59
floating-point data types, 58-59
    converting strings to, 257
floating-point rounding errors, 85
floating-point unit (FPU) processor, 58
floor function, 171
floppy disks, 14
    as secondary storage, 206
flowchart symbols, used in computer programming, 34
flushing, input stream, 105, 213
for loops, 138-142
format options, 100, 228
formatting output, 99-102
FORTRAN programming language, 227
forward declaration, 161
four-dimensional arrays, 291
freeing memory, 310
functional paradigm, 227
function prototypes, 160-161, 169, 237
functions, 44, 156-172
    abs, 171
    acos, 172
    asin, 172
    assert, 441-442
    atan, 172
    atan2, 172
    atof, 257
    atoi, 213, 256, 257
    atol, 256, 257
    building computer programs with, 156-161
    ceil, 171
    converttofloat, 258
    converttoint, 257, 258
    cos, 172
    cosh, 172
    data and, 163-172
    data types in, 168
    defined, 47
    eof, 218
    exp, 172
    fabs, 171
    factorial, 384, 385
    find, 251, 253
    floor, 171

    get, 104-105, 213, 254
    getline, 254, 268
    getting data to and from, 164-167
    hypot, 171
    ignore, 105
    isalpha, 172
    isdigit, 172
    islower, 172
    isupper, 172
    labs, 171
    length, 251, 260, 280, 283
    library, 170-172, 231, 249, 254
    log, 172
    log10, 172
    logarithmic, 172
    main, 44, 46-47, 156, 157, 158, 161
        in linked list, 315-316
    math, 171
    multiply, 260
    numrows, 299
    passing data into, 164-167
    pow, 170, 171
    pow10, 171
    and program flow, 160
    recursive, 383-384
    resize, 280, 283, 299
    sin, 172
    sinh, 172
    sort, 402
    sqrt, 171
    strcat, 248-249, 251, 253
    strcmp, 248, 250, 251, 254
    strcpy, 95, 190
    string, 246-250
    string accessor, 251-253, 257
    strlen, 247, 319
    substr, 251, 253, 267
    swap, 278
    syntax of, 158-159
    tan, 172
    tanh, 172
    template, 278
    tolower, 172
    toupper, 172
    trigonometric, 172
    variables in, 163
    void, 159
fundamental operators, 70-76
fuzzy logic, 118
fuzzy sets, 89

G

get function, 104-105, 213, 254
getline function, 254, 268
global variables, 163, 164

Photo Credits

Figure 1-3 © Courtesy of International Business Machines Corporation.
Figure 1-4 © Intel Corporation.
Figure 1-6 © Apple Computers, Inc.